"And the Word

Was Made Flesh

And Dwelt Among Us.

. . . We Beheld God's Glory."

QUANTUM SPIRITUALITY
A Postmodern Apologetic

QUANTUM SPIRITUALITY

A POSTMODERN APOLOGETIC

LEONARD I. SWEET

Published by
WHALEPRINTS
for
SpiritVenture Ministries, Inc.
Dayton, Ohio

Scripture quotations, unless otherwise noted, from the Revised Standard Version of the Bible are copyrighted 1946, 1952, 1971, 1973, and 1990 (NRSV) by the Division of Christian Education of the National Council of the Churches of Christ in the U.S.A. and are used by permission.

Book design by Karen Ingle

Second Printing

Whaleprints   SpiritVenture Ministries, Inc.
1405 Cornell Drive   1737 Ravenwood Avenue
Dayton, OH 45406-4727   Dayton, OH 45406

Printed in the United States of America

Library of Congress Catalog Card Number: 91-065420

ISBN: 1-882122-01-1

**To
Marie Aull
my best friend**

Saint Brendan's Cross

Brendan's fame as a sea-faring saint is legendary. On his voyages he allegedly encountered fire-slinging demons, floating crystal columns, and sea monsters. In sharp contrast to other tales of the deep, whales proved to be St. Brendan's guardian angels -- "helpers in our journeys" he called them. On special holidays, the ocean's greatest whales were said to raise up their backs upon which Brendan and his monks would climb to sing praises and conduct masses.

In commemoration of the many times whales saved St. Brendan and his crew from drowning, there evolved the little-known "St. Brendan's Cross" -- a cross formed out of four whales.

ACKNOWLEDGMENTS

The author's perennial plight when sitting down to write a book was first announced in Hebrews 11:8: "and he [Abraham] went out, not knowing whither he went." Even though I had no idea where I was headed when setting out on my quest of the quantum, I did have some notion of who to take with me. Certain extraordinary people, some of whom know me only as an admiring face in a vast auditorium or a signature on some unsolicited letter, crossed the hurdles before me, and lowered them. As with all great leaders, their lives are opening doors rather than closing them. Their fresh angles of vision are inspiring the church to expand its gravebound horizons and/or beyond-the-grave hopes.

I have followed these "New Light leaders," as I am calling them, from varying distances. But it is largely because of their writings and lives that I have been compelled to join Abraham on the journey. They are my personal role models (in an earlier day one could get away with "heroes") of the true nature of the postmodern apologetic. More than anyone else, they have been my teachers on how to translate, without compromising content, the gospel into the indigenous context of the postmodern vernacular.

There is nothing, of course, more dangerous than "naming names." All I can do is apologize in advance to the many more names which should be here but escape my memory at this time of writing. Many names listed here sit uneasily side-by-side other names (we in the academy are especially susceptible to what Sigmund Freud called "the narcissism of small differences").

But some of those who led this ungainly right-handed historian and left-handed theologian into new light are theologians Rubem Alves, Kenneth Cauthen, Rebecca Chopp, John Cobb, Edward Farley, Matthew Fox, Robert Michael Franklin, David Ray Griffin, Peter Hodgson, Joseph Hough, Catherine Keller, Kosuke Koyama, Belden C. Lane, Sallie McFague, David Miller, Richard J. Mouw, Sharon Parks, C. S. Song, Max Stackhouse, Marjorie Suchocki, Mark Kline Taylor, David Tracy, Sharon Welch, Cornel West, Rowan Williams.

Professors of preaching making good things happen again in the pulpit include Charles Booth, David Buttrick, Ernest Trice Campbell, Fred Craddock, Thomas Long, Eugene Lowry, Barbara Brown Taylor, Thomas Troeger. Pastors fashioning fresh scenarios of postmodern ministry include Philip Amerson, Amos Brown, John M. Buchanan, Gabe Campbell, Rebecca Dolch, Michael Dowd, Maxie Dunnam, Howard Edington, James Forbes, William Hinson, H. Beecher Hicks, Jr., Barry Johnson, Gene and Joyce Marshall, Blair R. Morie, James Parks Morton, Elizabeth O'Connor, Jaime Potter-Miller, William K. Quick, Melanie Robertson-Cole, Caswell Shaw, Donald Shelby, J. Barrie Shepherd, Michael Slaughter, Edward L. Wheeler, David Wilkinson, Jeremiah Wright.

Those who have taught me how to stump around postmodern environs are psychologists James Ashbrook, Carolyn Bohler, Harmon Bro, James Hillman, Morton Kelsey, M. Scott Peck, Anne Wilson Schaef, Frances Vaughan, Roger Walsh, Ken Wilber; historians Mary Farrell Bednarowski, Thomas Berry, William Dean, Martin E. Marty, David Mathews, James Nelson, David Noble, Mark Noll, Howard Snyder, William Irwin Thompson; sociologists Robert Bellah, Os Guinness, Parker Palmer, Tex Sample, Robert Wuthnow.

Biblical scholars who have teased out new connections for me include Thomas Boomershine, Walter Bruggemann, Joanna Dewey, Thomas Dozeman, James D. G. Dunn, Robert W. Funk, Beverly Roberts Gaventa, Michael D. Goulder, Robert Jewett, Luke T. Johnson, David Rhoads, Bernard Brandon Scott, Mary Ann Tolliver, Marion T. Soards, Walter Wink. Story teller and novelist Walter Wangerin, Jr., stands in a category all by himself.

Those who have taught me how to catch the tail winds of energies whooshing from new spiritual jet streams are entrepreneurs and business leaders Wynton ("Red") Blount, Curtis Carlson, George Gilder, Robert K. Greenleaf, Richard Zimmerman; scientists David Bohm, Willis Harman, Rustum Roy, Charles Townes; media pioneers Dennis Benson, Roger Burgess, Bruno Caliandro, Bill Moyers, Jeff Smith; missionary theologians and journalists William J. Abraham, J. Edward Carothers, Jim Forest, Sean McDonagh, Norman Thomas; retreat leaders Fritz and Vivian Hull, Sister Miriam T. MacGillis, June and Taylor McConnell, Robert Raines, Tom Skinner, McGregor Smith.

I have looked to artists and art historians Doug Adams, Diane Apostolos-Cappadonna, John Cooke, John and Jane Dillenberger, Gregor Goethals, Peter Hawkins, Catherine A. Kapikian, Margaret Miles to lay bare the spiritual roots of the postmodern condition. Even though I have never met Theodore Peters, Philip Hefner, Harold P. Nebelsick and Robert John Russell, I feel as if I know them intimately, for I have been an ardent follower of their pioneering studies on the relationship of religion and science.

I believe these are among the most creative religious leaders in America today. These are the ones carving out channels for new ideas to flow. In a way this book was written to guide myself through their channels and chart their progress. The book's best ideas come from them.

Literature, like New Light leadership, is a communal event. It entails a close working relationship between author, publisher, editors, and readers. For me it also involves a close seminary community working together to educate an upcoming generation of New Light leaders. Since books are bloodsuckers--draining of energy, happiness, humor, contentment--this book has taken its pound of flesh from a lot of undeserving colleagues. I cannot thank all of these wonderful people, but those whom I cannot **not** thank are the seminary library staff (Elmer J. O'Brien, Paul Schrodt, Shelometh Eichenauer), my secretarial staff (Carole Wood and Ruth Wert), the academic administrative staff (Newell Wert, Daryl Ward, Mary Olson, Timothy Forbess). Karen Ingle and Thelma Monbarren combined the forces of art and computer age technology to give this book its distinctive character, and to help bring book publishing into a mediatized world.

Without Betty O'Brien, I would have bungled more lines than I have. She deserves your gratitude as well as mine, for she prevented you many frustrations (not the least of which is getting even more of a fill of footnotes), and me innumerable embarrassments. William Faulkner's dictum that writing a novel is like nailing a hen-house together in a hurricane describes all too accurately my writing of this book while fulfilling executive duties for an institution I love dearly. A lot of detailed scholarship has been painlessly tucked away out of sight, but only Betty's painstaking research assistance made this possible. G. K. Chesterton, called the craziest sane man that ever lived, held that a writer ought not to look up quotations because literature should be a part of a writer. Too many times my quotations (or more precisely, misquotations) were by memory and needed to have major detective work done on them. Thankfully, Betty is not on friendly terms with the impossible. Her superb nose for hunting down lost citations and illegible notations, her balanced editorial judgments, good humor, good sense, and incredible limpa bread, nourished this book into existence.

The "Great Books Seminar," a group of peers from north Indiana who meet regularly with me in my home, has become an almost shamanic presence in my life. It was this group, the brainchild of Elvin Miller and Harold Oechsle, who first encouraged me to act as a guinea pig and pilot fish. It was their feedback to many of my ideas that challenged me to be clear without condescension, that convinced me that the book would be weakened by a need to explain too much. It was their communal example of equilibrium, the shamanic poise that keeps one's balance even when tipsy, that gave me the key clue to the secret of an "in-but-not-of" model.

Callimachus, the Hellenistic poet, was prejudiced against big books for artistic reasons: "A big book is equal to a big evil." I have as yet not inflicted the whole "big evil" on anyone. Those who were kind enough to read portions of what I "whelmed" down on paper include James B. Nelson (United Theological Seminary), William Willimon (Duke University), Mary Olson (United Theological Seminary), Ruth Daugherty (Board of Global Ministries), Eddie Fox (Board of Discipleship), Howard Snyder (United Theological Seminary), John Tyson (Houghton College), and Charles Walcott (Cornell Laboratory of Ornithology).

Peter Florey of Haddonfield, New Jersey, warned me to stay away from "re" words, advice which shall forever haunt me. John Young, campus minister at the University of Indianapolis, first turned me on to Ilya Prigogine, whose work has done so much to shape the contours of this study.

Carmen Wooster suggested the definition of "energy connectors" for New Light leadership.

Susan Ruach, whose name is becoming a commonplace in the acknowledgments section of postmodern theological texts, dared me to live my preachments in the book's design. She is the inspiration for the book's experiential, performative elements. Peter M. Jehrio, Director of Education for the American Philatelic Society, graciously provided me with a copy of the 1933 "Energy-Fire" Brazilian stamp that begins the *Logos* theme. Donald F. Smith, who knows the scientific literature cold while at the same time pastoring a New Light congregation, kept my central vision in balance with my peripheral vision. The best that can be hoped for a new book of this sort is that it will nourish rich thinking, like that being done by the Don Smiths of the world, in the same way as manure nourishes old soil.

No one has had a bigger role in my learning to dance to a new rhythm than conservationist/gardener Marie Aull. She found me five years ago, hating to dance, always squaring the circle. Now I know how to do both the square dance and the ring shout. She opened my eyes to nature, sensitized my ears to the "world of night," placed my feet on what the Amish call "the path that has heart" or what native Americans call the "Beauty Way," set before my nose some of the best smells this palate (and planet, for that matter) has ever sniffed, and opened my hands to receive bounties from the earth I never dreamed existed.

Carlyle Marney dedicated one of his books with this simple line: "To Victor, who agrees with me in nothing but is my friend in everything." Differentness is the essence of friendship. Marie will not agree with everything in this book. But her presence can be felt throughout its pages, most of which were written hiding upstairs in her "prophet's chamber." To her I dedicate this book.

Finally, I trust that the Spirit that led the author of *The Cloud of Unknowing* to write that "in all truth I know that I still have a very long way to go myself. So please help me as well as yourself" is present in this book's dancing, everywhere and always.

> I mean to sing to Yahweh all my life,
> I mean to play for my God as long as I live.
> May these reflections of mine give God pleasure,
> As much as Yahweh gives me!
> Psalm 104:31,34

TABLE OF CONTENTS

T A B L E O F C O N T E N T S
(in schematic form)

PREFACE

Does God
Have a Big TOE?

We are called to be in the world. Not of it. But not out of it, either.[1] This book holds the mirror to a single paradox: We must live the historical moment we are in without letting that moment explain us. Christianity must bring to every culture an indigenous faith that is true to its heritage without Christianity's becoming a culture faith. If every book has one idea, this is it for the one you are reading.

The cardinal sin for modernity has been antiintellectualism, a dissenting spirit against celebrating the powers of the mind that has gripped large segments of the Christian church. The sin governing much of the church today may be ahistoricalism or antihistoricalism. Large segments of the Christian community, finding the intellectual and social company of modernism more congenial than that of postmodernism, are in retreat, having disconnected from the unprecedented, restructuring changes taking place all around them.

The Christian mind is failing to comprehend the times, our times. The New Light apologetic chronicled in this book is devoted to enfranchising and energizing Christians to connect their faith with the indigenous historical place in which God has chosen them to live. It aims to jolt Christians into a sense of their own time, out of their fashionable out-of-itness. For the God who exists beyond time is the God who lives, moves, and has being in this time.

―――――――――――― 66 ――――――――――――

The ultimate hospitality is, then,
an entertainment of divine mystery in human life.
Benedictine/biblical scholar Demetrius R. Dumm[a]

―――――――――――― 99 ――――――――――――

This book also hopes to provide a prefacing sketch of what a sixth alternative to ethicist/theologian H. Richard Niebuhr's fivefold typology of what the relationship of Christian faith to human culture would look like: a Johannine paradoxical model of **Christ in-but-not-of culture.**[2] Missiologists have become quite sophisticated in the task of Paul's missionary mandate to "be all things to all people" (1 Cor. 9:22). The gospel has been inculturated into the thousands of indigenous cultures around the world through the latest in Bible translation, theological analogy and homology,

1

and spiritual disciplines respectful of the local traditions and customs of the native inhabitants. But missiology must also be defined to extend ethnographically in time as well as in space. It will not do to have a multicultural but monochronological church.

The missionary expansion of the gospel today is as much generational and chronological as it is geographical. In the same way Jesus entered into the culture of his day in complex ways; in the same way Paul in front of Areopagus presented the gospel to the Athenians by quoting two of their own poets (Epimenides and Aratus of Crete): so the church is to be a dialoguing fellow traveler with culture, exhibiting a critical but not unfriendly relationship to history.[3] The body of Christ must be in conversation with the body of knowledge of every day. Out of context, divorced from indigenous space and time, spirituality is but another word for a sauna.

This radical opening to God in trust; this constant process of historical incontextualization; this acceptance of the strange, the new, even the unwanted: these are the essences of the Gospel of John's interactive, paradoxical in-but-not-of model. The New Light apologetic, like Abraham in Genesis 18, greets all historical guests, even the unwanted ones, cheerfully and expansively, open to the God who is already at work in the world, the God who will not be without a witness. From this position of hospitality, faith addresses the wider public culture, the world beyond the church. In fact, our world of historical and intellectual experience becomes a primary arena for the church's own search for truth and faithfulness.[4] The church must be able to exist in both temporal and eternal time, to function at once historically and transcendentally.

The challenge of an in-but-not-of faith is knowing when to stand, timeless and transcendent as a rock, and when to surrender and let go, releasing oneself to be swept along by the relevant currents. A believer can become postmodern, or modern, or anything else because in one's innermost core of being a believer is neither postmodern, nor modern, nor anything else. The deep sense of being in the world is matched only by an even deeper sense of not being at one with the world.

That the title may not deceive: this book is rife with science, but science it most definitely is not. Neither "quantum" nor "spirituality" are words I use easily or comfortably. Biochemist/information theorist Jeffrey S. Wicken, in calling for theology and science to enter into dialogue, admits that "I feel diffident about commenting on theological treatises. I know little about theology, and much of my commentary will reflect that fact. This disdainer having been made, I put aside the diffidence."[5] Switch the words "theology" and "science," and Wicken's statement expresses my uneasiness exactly. My presentation of scientific ideas is sketchy, often willfully so. If your interest is in extended treatments of particular scientific fields and discoveries, or if you are naysayers to the quest for integration and synthesis, you should be warned to please look elsewhere. This book will be found in breach of contract. Similarly, if you are looking for a conventional, calculated treatment of topics related to spirituality, please pick up any number of good books racked together with this one on library stacks. "If you are going to understand anything as strange as quantum mechanics," looking-glass physicist/philosopher David Bohm has remarked, "you have to be ready to consider some strange ideas."[6] The late physicist/mountain climber Heinz R. Pagels calls the current state of reality "quantum weirdness."[7] The modern mind will find in this book some weird notions and nervy possibilities. Even the logic is sometimes less linear than cousinly.

―――――――――――――― 66 ――――――――――――――

If our senses were fine enough, we would experience the slumbering cliff as a dancing chaos.

Moralist/philosopher Friedrich Wilhelm Nietzsche

―――――――――――――― 99 ――――――――――――――

Nor is this a historian's accounting of scientific trends and developments as they impinge on theological and ethical issues. While I can discriminate between good and bad theology, or good and bad history, I confess to being virtually defenseless against scientific books, and one of the most defenseless against studies in math and physics. More a wide-eyed admirer than a squinting scholar of science, the reader will soon discover that I enjoy the company of the mathematicians and scientists insofar as I can follow them . . . which too many times is not very far. My learning curve gets left far behind far too quickly and far too often.

Besides, whole South American rain forests have been felled in pursuit of the religious and philosophical implications of quantum physics. True, this fat bibliography has almost all been produced by physicists or students of physics: Nathan Aviezer, Ian G. Barbour, David Bohm, Fritjof Capra, Freeman J. Dyson, Arthur Stanley Eddington, John L. Hitchcock, Henry Margenau, Denis Postle, Robert John Russell, Rustum Roy, Brian Swimme, Stephen Toulmin, Danah Zohar, Gary Zukav. Unfortunately, little of this literature is known or celebrated in the religious community, although British theologians are more and more bringing together the new queen of the sciences, biophysics, and the queen mother, theology, as symbolized in the physicist-turned-Anglican-priest John C. Polkinghorne, the physicist/mathematician-turned-Methodist-lay preacher Charles A. Coulron, the nuclear physicist-turned-Episcopal priest William G. Pollard, and the physical biochemist-turned-Anglican-priest Arthur R. Peacocke.

Designed to be read and appreciated on many levels, *Quantum Spirituality* is a hybrid work. After the fashion of that "deconstructive angel of contemporary thought,"[8] Jacques Derrida, it is written in a genre that is oddly mixed. Part intellectual curiosity, part synthetic bridging, part guided tour through a vast bibliography, part theological rumination, part "preaching it round," it is fundamentally a roundabout apologetic exercise in standing inside history and "getting looped"--upping the ante of theology to enter wholesale worlds like that of the quantum, the realm most scientists believe to be the most fundamental level of reality. I risk the criticisms that come to all who combine genres, who mix metaphors, who cross disciplines, who refuse to be confined to the questions addressed by a single metaphor of mind or discipline of inquiry because I have been inspired by historian/ literary critic Richard E. Brantley. His key insight into the secret of the theology that fueled the eighteenth-century New Light movement known as the Evangelical Revival is this: It brought together into shared space the Enlightenment project (the scientific method and rational empiricism) with natural and revealed religion.[9]

---------------- **66** ----------------

I think scientists and theologians have a lot more to say
to each other in talking about the sources
of the religious drive and the hunger for religious thought.
Sociobiologist/sometime Southern Baptist Edward O. Wilson

---------------- **99** ----------------

Unfortunately, the church is still under the scientific spell of old teachings that science itself has long since repudiated. By its own modernist standards, the church is not intellectually respectable. Too many theologians and pastors seem almost proud that they can't address the religious significance of $t = 0$ and have never heard of thermodynamics. I am not so much sticking my head into the wisps and vapors of postmodern science as I am reaching in and pulling out conceptual metaphors, especially those released by nonmechanistic physics, and joining them to interdisciplinary dilations on divinity.

It may be that I have, as Wicken accused one theologian, "put too many metaphysical eggs in the basket of physics." But I hope that I have not played fast and loose with hard-won scientific concepts in the interest of communication, or engaged in the dubious practices research biologist/humanistic psychologist/feminist Maureen O'Hara dubs "recombinant information."[10] Of particular appeal are, first, the ways in which postmodern scientific thought is now performing some rather dazzling loop-the-loops, offering us, in the words of German/theologian Wolfhart Pannenberg, the means whereby science "might lead us back towards a religious conception of mind . . . and away from the positivistic outlook of the nineteenth century." Second, the ways in which the Christian tradition can itself contribute to our knowledge and understanding of the physical and spiritual world.[11]

We easily forget that more than a few scientists were deeply religious (this is not a test, but instance Galileo, Bacon, Boyle, Kepler, and Faraday).[12] My first reading of materials scientist/technologist/marriage theorist/lay theologian Rustum Roy's *Experimenting with Truth* (1981) marked an early watershed in my thinking. Roy counseled theologians to stop chasing the neighbor next door (the social sciences) and take out the one across town ("the natural sciences, the 'harder' the better").[13] Physicists have been among the first to stop hiding behind the deceptive cloak of objectivity and murmur the word "God" out of the corner of their mouths. They have also been the leaders in showing theologians how to become more spiritually minded without losing their scientific minds--in carrying both a head and a heart.

The ethical and philosophical implications of postmodern science are not more Christian than ever before. But the climate of thought in physics is more qualitative, even spiritual, than it has been in centuries.[14] This is especially true when scientists venture beyond the dominant modern mentality rather than acquiescing in its limitations. The modernist disrobing of theology by science, as symbolized by the windowless chapel at Massachusetts Institute of Technology, has ended. Physicists are now as much scientists of the invisible as theologians used to be. In the new world of science and religion, it is difficult to tell which is which.

———————————— **66** ————————————

The future is an uncharted sea full of potholes.

Quoted by University of Chicago provost/law professor/
opening convocation speaker Gerhard Casper[b]

———————————— **99** ————————————

Physicists are also breaking one rule of scientism after another, including the unspoken law against teleological ruminations about a purposive cosmos.[15] If biographer/nature and science writer John Stewart Collis is correct in his decade-old impression that "for every one person who is interested in physics or physiology, a hundred, a thousand, are interested in metaphysics,"[16] then for hundreds of thousands the path to the latter has come to lead through the former. Ilya Prigogine, the Russian-born Belgian scientist who won the Nobel Prize in 1977 for his work on thermodynamics, even goes so far as to say that "it is now science that appears to lend credibility to mystical affirmation."[17] Economist/educator Karl Pribram was heard to joke publically over "why did the ancient mystics plagiarize what we modern scientists are discovering today?"[18]

One must never ground a religious apologetic on the shifting sands of physical science or on isolated scientific discoveries, no matter how important. Today's physics is tomorrow's folklore. What is more, today's physicists themselves have trouble agreeing about what is today's physics. In a deeply spiritual sense, mere science matters little in our relationship with God. But in a deeply theological sense, it matters very much. Science provides constant symbols and meta-fors for change. Without the universal

5

images and metaphoric meanings that emerge from the cosmological framework of the day, theology is unable to shape history's future. This may perhaps be why Jewish philosopher/physician/rabbi Maimonides in his *Moreh Nevukhim (Guide to the Perplexed, 1200)*, to the utter outrage of halakhists, Talmudists, and other students of the Torah, placed scientists and all those engaged in the study of physics and metaphysics on a higher plane of perfection and closeness to God than those engaged in religion.[19] The church's historical desecration of this moment's aboriginal culture, as it expresses itself in both the arts and the sciences, is an offense against the capacities of the human imagination and the Holy Spirit.

"

Do not confine your children to your own learning,
for they were born in another time.

Hebrew proverb

"

I am a personal devotee of historian/philosopher Huston Smith's scholarship. He enlivens every subject where he puts down his marker, and nowhere is his marker more acute than in his rebuking of those who preen the intellectual plumage of postmodernism. The brightness of Smith's insights on postmodernism and science usually puts others' thoughts into the shade. His stubborn emphasis on the differences between science and religion, and his insistent warnings about the dangers of their becoming bedfellows--"any credibility rub off from science onto religion that may derive from associating the two will be outweighed by the pull to conform religious truth to scientific"--have haunted the writing of every page of this book.

My audacity in entering this ground where angels fear to tread stems partly from an early theological training by interactionists like physicist/philosopher Ian G. Barbour and theologian/ethicist Kenneth Cauthen.[20] I am also in fundamental philosophical disagreement with Smith over whether science should relax its high modernistic standards for "objectivity, prediction and control" or whether it should be allowed to enter the more qualitative domains the modern world assigned to religion and art, thereby jeopardizing science's "power-to-control."[21] Smith would keep science as unbendingly linear as the lines drawn by L'Enfant's straightedge.[22] He believes science and religion constitute different ways of knowing.

A quantum spirituality remains open to science's turning in new, non-classical, even spiritual paths--"de-reductionist" directions that sometimes make it an ally and accomplice of religious truth. There are pursuits in which the organizing patterns and ambitions of "objectivity," "replicability," "quantifiability," and "predictibility" should remain central and not converge with religion. But with every advance in science, it seems that the views of postmodernist/theologian David Ray Griffin, one of our most sophisticated theologians of postmodernism, become more and more prophetic. The founder of the Center for a Postmodern World wonders whether the emerging science "can be clearly demarcated from metaphysics and theology."[23]

Scientists are criss-crossing disciplines like never before, their common meeting place the computer. As postmodern science reorients itself toward wholeness, the possibility opens for a fresh synthesis in which religion, science, philosophy, and aesthetics can synergize a hermeneutical vision of spirituality. The nascence of this hermeneutical consciousness, or what Max L. Stackhouse would call a "metaphysical-moral vision,"[24] I am calling the New Light apologetic. It is already present in bits and pieces, here and there in this discipline and that discipline, in this denomination and that denomination, in this thinker and that thinker. The New Light apologetic represents a Christian alternative to the largely Old Light "New Age" movement.

The emergence of this New Light apologetic is a harbinger and hope that a new, age-old world is aborning in the church, even that the church may now be on the edge of another awakening. Amidst all the cliffhanging circumstances and conditions of the church, the Spirit is at work. All around there is evidence that the church is learning to dance to a new rhythm, to adapt the metaphor of Harvard Business School professor/economist Rosabeth Moss Kanter. The New Light movement is characterized by bizarre, sometimes anxious alliances of a ragbag assortment of preachers, theologians, pastors, professors, artists, scientists, business leaders, and scholars. What ties their creative piracy together is a radical faith commitment that is willing to dance to a new rhythm.[25]

To be sure, the dance of multidisciplinary studies and holistic methodologies requires some of the trickiest steps going. It was one thing for theologian/metaphysician/pastor/university president Jonathan Edwards, for example, to draw on eighteenth-century physics to illustrate the infinitude of sin in his sermon "The Justice of God in the Damnation of Sinners."[26] It is another to survey the vast range of contemporary scientific research, from quantum physics to chaos and set theory, from astronomy to agronomy. Philosopher's philosopher/theologian's theologian Bernard Lonergan's pioneering models of multidisciplinary travel through science's "over-lapping neighborhoods" (Polanyi), "discourse communities" (Geertz), and "disciplinary matrices" (Kuhn) have demonstrated just how difficult it is to put into practice the simplest of rules: There is no hearing without listening, there is no seeing without looking.[27]

I have devoted my life to the ideal of disciplined scholarship. But disciplined thought is not the same thing as disciplinary thought or the disciplinary organization of knowledge. Furthermore, the barbed-wire boundaries between disciplines put up by the modern era's disciplinary chauvinism must be crossed for theological reasons.[28] Everything that exists is an integrated component of an indivisible whole. The unity of Truth resident in the oneness of the Trinity requires the restoration to this planet of an integrated, unified interpretation of reality.[29] To move from timid specialization and separation to dare wholeness and unity will entail many falls, will require much healing.

66

A poem always runs the risk of being meaningless, and would be nothing without this risk.
French philosopher/deconstruction strategist Jacques Derrida[c]

99

Quantum spirituality may not be news to those in university and multiversity academispheres struggling with the babelian confusion of a complete breakdown in agreements about holistic, sacramental visions of the **uni**-verse. What follow are my uncertain attempts at blowing a trumpet for a New Light apologetic, which plays some new notes from an ancient theological score of cosmic holism, which harmonizes the theological and historical *basso continuo* with the biological and social sciences. *Quantum Spirituality* is offered in the prayer that it might have some liberating effects on the church's own coming to terms with the emerging cosmology that is now as revolutionary as once were the Copernican and the Aristotelian-Ptolemaic cosmologies. Perhaps even others may find something of value in these boundary-crossing sallies and introductory postures of an imposter (I can't shake off the comparison by England's King James I [of King James Version fame] of the preaching of the learned Anglican Bishop Lancelot Andrewes, to a monkey playing with a diamond: "Here's a pretty thing, there's a pretty thing").

66

I do not know what I may appear to the world, but to myself, I seem to have been only like a boy playing on the seashore, and diverting myself in now and then finding a smoother pebble or a prettier shell than ordinary, whilst the great ocean of truth lay all undiscovered before me.
Mathematician/philosopher/botanist/biblical commentator Sir Isaac Newton[d]

99

I find dimensional language preferable to hierarchical language or stratification theory. For this reason I have been drawn since graduate school days to philosopher/zoologist/botanist/aestheticist/political scientist Aristotle's classic text entitled **Rhetoric**, in which he presents a model for persuasion which is dependent on the *Logos* of the message, the *Pathos* of the audience, and the *Ethos* of the speaker.[30] The invitation to write a study document for a November 1989 consultation on spirituality for the twenty-first century, sponsored by the Board of Higher Education and Ministry of The United Methodist Church and entitled "Toward a New Heaven and Earth," seemed the perfect opportunity to put together some long-standing convictions about the peculiar terrain, climate, and culture of my own spiritual neighborhood and township, the Wesleyan tradition, and the wider relevance of this "sub-system" to the whole of religion in America.

To encounter God in a particular place opens us to encounters with the God of all places. The ecological movement called bioregionalism is based on the principle that the only way to save the whole is to save its parts, even one small piece at a time, because every part, however minute, participates in the whole cosmic "holomovement" (David Bohm).[31] The "part" nearest home for me is The United Methodist Church. This relatively small tribal subsystem of the global village (twenty-five million out of five billion) is where I live.

―――――――――――――――― **66** ――――――――――――――――

A cartoon I once saw . . . showed an astronomer's wife ushering a visitor into the observatory, where the astronomer sat crouched at the end of a huge telescope, and remarking kindly, "My husband lives in a little world of his own."

Civil servant/classicist/ethologist Mary Midgley[e]

―――――――――――――――― **99** ――――――――――――――――

In the social sciences, anthropologist/researcher/professor Clifford Geertz has taught how "small facts speak to large issues." Similarly, the Annales School of historiography has demonstrated how the history of anything can reveal everything. At the same time, in the physical sciences we have been learning from Archimedes' bathtub, Newton's apple, Watt's teapot, perhaps even Bohm's hologram and Mandelbrot's coastline that the more mundane, the more metaphysical--that smaller and simpler are in inverse proportion. The **minute** of particle physics, with all its "bifurcations," "time horizons," "strange attractions," "solitons," "vacuum bubble instantons" (perhaps the universe's most bizarre and lethal object)[32] and "Lyapunov exponents," raises the **magnificence** of cosmology. Even mathematician/historian/philosopher Alfred North Whitehead, who is too widely quoted for defining religion as "what one does with one's solitariness," develops and deepens this definition until it leads him to this: "Religion is world-loyalty."[33]

This dynamic of the large and the little, of cosmic importance to postmodernist thought, led poet/critic/Nobel laureate T.S. Eliot to the conclusion that "a local speech on a local issue is likely to be more intelligible than one addressed to a whole nation, and we observe that the greatest muster of ambiguities and obscure generalities is usually to be found in speeches which are addressed to the whole world."[34] Hankerings for abstractions and generalities have little effect. Perspectives rooted in time and place carry large effect. The interplay of the unique and the universal, locality and generality, permits the minuteness of the Wesleyan movement, especially a treatment that resists straining Church of England evangelical preacher/hymn writer/editor John Wesley through Methodist muslin, to reveal some things of significance about the whole of oldline religion in America.

The structural skeleton remains. But the heart that once beat within oldline religion is dangerously silent. It will take defibrillation by a four-dimensional faith to jolt the church back to life and to end its standing apart from the world of history. The religious faith of the New Light movement seeks neither an embodiment nor an eminence outside of history. Hence this book's recasting of traditional spiritual resources in a postmodern idiom and its conversation with the great intellectual currents of our time.

——————————————— 66 ———————————————

What shall I do my God to love,
My loving God to praise!
The length, the breadth, and height to prove,
And depth of sovereign grace?

Hymn writer/evangelical preacher Charles Wesley

——————————————— 99 ———————————————

The shape of our physical universe is dependent partly on our means of perceiving it. The true "Quadrilateral" believer is not one who subscribes simply to a SERT methodology (Scripture, experience, reason and tradition).[35] Rather, the New Light apologetic's essence is its embodiment of an integrated, holistic, planetary spirituality (*Logos, Pathos, Ethos, Theos*), a four-dimensional faith for what theory of relativity formulator/Nobel laureate Albert Einstein by the 1920s postulated was a four-dimensional universe. When one or more dimensions are developed to the deprivation or exclusion of the others, there is spiritual entropy and bodily disease. When a multidimensional faith is lived synergistically and holistically, a biodance takes place between the heavens and the earth, the Creator and the creation.

The twentieth-century successor to Isaac Newton in the Lucasian chair of mathematics at Cambridge, mathematician/physicist Stephen Hawking has been called the greatest mind alive today. He certainly may be the smartest person in physics since that last of the great Newtonian scientists/the first of the great quantum theorists Albert Einstein. In his "best selling"/least read book, *A Brief History of Time* (1988), he recounts the story of his hunting down that singular law or at least set of fundamental laws that will relate everything to everything else--the law that unifies gravity, electromagnetism, and other forces that rule micro- and macrocosmic events.[36] The unity at the heart of the universe is now such an established part of the scientific quest that GUTs (grand unification theories, or grand-unified-field theories) and TOEs (theories of everything) have become "the Holy Grail of today's physicists."[37] Hawking believes that without that missing mathematical formula of a Theory of Everything, the "design" of the universe cannot be said to be "divine."

——————————————— 66 ———————————————

Arianna asked: "Mommy, I have a big toe, and you have a big toe, and Daddy has a big toe. Does God have a big toe too?"

Story-teller/humorist/rabbi Marc Gellman[f]

——————————————— 99 ———————————————

God has already given to the church, in all its diversity, a complete Theory of Everything, a unifying principle that binds things together. The church's big TOE was formulated in the Bible's smallest encapsulation of What It All Means: John 1:14. The Fourth Gospel elaborates the exchange as it extends an invitation to the quest and quandary of the quantum explored in this book.

The Word [the depth dimension of *Logos* which physicists call energy, ancients called fire and theologians call *metanoia*] . . .

became Flesh [the height dimension of *Pathos* which physicists call matter, ancients called land and theologians call *koinonia*] . . .

and dwelt among us [the breadth dimension of *Ethos* which physicists call space, ancients called wind and theologians call *diakonia*] . . .

and we beheld his [God's] glory [the fourth dimension of *Theos* which physicists call space-time, ancients called sea and theologians call *basileia*].

This tetrad is the church's big TOE, the closest the Bible ever comes to formulating a simple, compact description of how the universe works (i.e., a Grand Unified Theory). John 1:14 presents four eddies of experiencing God, comprising a single stream. All four dimensions--the experience of God in Christ and self, the experience of God in community and creation, the experience of God in social justice and compassion, the experience of God in the transpersonal and transcendent--while distinct, are interacting states rather than chronological or sequential stages. They demonstrate a remarkable unity, interpenetrating and mutually reinforcing one another

11

... as in life, so in the rather artificial partitions of this book.[38]

Since I am a firm believer that subject ought to dictate style, this book has been purposefully written with a postmodernist bent--kinematic, kaleidoscopic, kinesthetic, allusive, sometimes elusive, with greater density than normal (density produces energy), in field fashion without rigid chapter development, full of a diversity of sources and constructs, from folk, fantasy, fractals, irony, and paradox to simultaneity, chanting, reflectaphors, associative thinking, and visual effects. This book would have to go a long way yet to even catch up to any sentence by Jacques Derrida, whose writing moves less by logic and argumentation than by free association, motifs strung together, and word play.

----------------- **66** -----------------

Religion is danced out before it is thought out.

Anthropologist/cultural critic R.R. Marrett[g]

----------------- **99** -----------------

Nevertheless, the spirit of play is everywhere evident in the book's sometimes apparent, ofttimes hidden, language games--in alliteration, acronyms, and acrostics. My hope is that anyone, even backdoor readers like myself, could pick up this book, turn almost anywhere, and begin having fun. The book was not designed to be read in one sitting. The four brief "Image Intermezzos," for example, can serve either as playful bridges between sections or, when read back-to-back, as a sinuous synthesis of the book. If your interests lean more in the direction of spirituality than quantum, you may wish to begin *Quantum Spirituality* at the end, backtracking your way forward to the more explicitly quantum sections. And vice versa.[39]

----------------- **66** -----------------

Trust in God and you need not fear.

Last words of Jonathan Edwards

The best of all is, God is with us.

"Last" words of John Wesley[h]

----------------- **99** -----------------

If eighteenth-century Deism can be seen as "the doctrine of divine carpentry," as historian/naturist/theologian Charles E. Raven called it, twenty-first century energism, as postmodern theology is subject to being called, may someday be seen as the doctrine of divine dancing. The modern church, the child of one of the greatest scientists that ever lived, Isaac Newton and the Enlightenment Project, took as its patron saint Thomas of Didymus, who taught the "art of doubt" and trusted nothing that could not be examined with one's own hands.[40] This book is written with the hope and prayer that the postmodern church, the child of one of the greatest physicists of all time, Albert Einstein, will take as its patron saint Peter of Bethsaida, whose dancing demeanor even on water teaches the "art of belief" and trusts faith **in** Christ until it incarnates the faith **of** Christ.

If the church is to dance, however, it must first get its flabby self back into shape. A good place to begin is the stretching exercise of touching its TOEs. Not the lungs, not the hands, not the eyes, not even the heart, but the toes may be the most important organ of the body of Christ today. So far the church has refused to dip its toe into postmodern culture. A quantum spirituality challenges the church to bear its past and to dare its future by sticking its big TOE into the time and place of the present.

Then, and only then, will a flattened out, "one-dimensional," and at times dimensionless world have discovered the power and vitality of a four-dimensional faith. Then, and only then, will believers have discovered that "impossible" is a human, not a divine, category. Then, and only then, will the church not appear to be in a timecapsule, sealed against new developments. Then, and only then, will a New Light movement of "world-making" faith have helped to create the world that is to, and may yet, be. Then, and only then, will earthlings have uncovered the meaning of these words, some of the last words poet/activist/contemplative/bridge between East and West Thomas Merton uttered:

> We are already one. But we imagine that we are not. And what we have to recover is our original unity.[41]

**The First
Commandment**

And this will be a sign for you:

The most bankable name in best-selling fiction is Stephen King,
the world's number one brand-name horror novelist.

And this will be a sign for you:

David Duke, the former Ku Klux Klan Grand Wizard,
now sits in the Louisiana legislature, attends Sierra Club fundraisers
and runs for the U.S. Senate.

And this will be a sign for you:

The years 1990, 1987, 1983, 1981, and 1980 stand
on the meteorologists' books as the five hottest years in weather history.

And this will be a sign for you:

More heart attacks occur on Monday than any other day,
and they cluster around nine o'clock in the morning.

And this will be a sign for you:

Conservative direct-mail wizard Richard Viguerie
has sold his Virginia office building
to Sun Myung Moon's Unification Church.

And this will be a sign for you:

A dozen Australian children from the Kowanyama community
on Cape York peninsula, aged between four and eight,
were treated in 1990 in a Cairns hospital
for sexually transmitted diseases.

And this will be a sign for you:

After the Revolution of 1989, once-persecuted Christian ministers
are now serving as government ministers
in what used to be communist East Germany.

And this will be a sign for you:

Asthma mortality among children and young adults rose dramatically
in the United States during much of the last decade,
continuing a trend that began in the late 1970s.

And this will be a sign for you:

Credence Cassettes of Kansas City, Missouri, offers both "subliminal"
and "paraliminal" audiotapes designed to "correct and heal . . .
concepts of God that are negative, distorted or even hostile."

And this will be a sign for you:

Personality disorders replaced classical neuroses in the 1980s
as the most prominent type of psychiatric pathology.
The most common of all personality disorders,
and one of the major mental health problems in America today?
Borderline personality disorder.

And this will be a sign for you:

When one generation hears the name "Madonna,"
the last person they think about is the Mother of Jesus.
When that same generation hears the name "God," the first person
that comes to their mind is the guitarist/rock singer Eric Clapton.
In 1987 three of the most popular rock songs and albums in America
were George Michael's *Faith*, Madonna's *Like a Prayer*, and Prince's
musical rendition of what a relationship to God is like, entitled *Lovesexy.*

And this will be a sign for you:

The cultural wave of "oldieism" has brought with it "oldies radio,"
the fastest growing type of radio programing in the country.
It plays back the musical "golden oldies" of our youth--
no matter whether of the fifties, sixties, seventies, or eighties.

And this will be a sign for you:

The name "Smoky Mountain" is now world famous,
not for some Tennessee mountains "etched in smoke
through the leaded panes of the oak trees,"
as one *New Yorker* poet put it, but for the city of Manila's garbage dump,
on top of which live hundreds of people.

And this will be a sign for you:

Between ten to thirty million species of land life exist on the planet
today. One of those species, humanity, now arrogates to itself
almost forty percent of the energy available to all--
and it will double its numbers in the next century.

And this will be a sign for you:

It took a million years to produce the first billion people. Today's world
produces a billion people in thirteen years--two people per second.
In the next forty years more people will be added to the earth
than have been added in all history up to now.

And this will be a sign for you:

The religiously unaffiliated are the fastest growing religious group
in America. Islam is the fastest growing formal religion in America,
especially among blacks. There are now as many Muslims
in the United States as there are in all of Western Europe (six million).
There are more Muslims in the United States
than there are Episcopalians, Presbyterians, Lutherans,
or members of the United Church of Christ.

And this will be a sign for you.

Are You Living in the New World?

During the intense days of fighting in the 1967 Six-Day War, General Avraham Yoffe held up the shelling of Egyptian encampments on the Sinai to let the eight-foot-wingspanned/long-legged great bustards (*Otis tarda*) pass by safely on their migratory passage through the Gulf of Akkaba. At the same time a devotee of the traditional "First Commandment"--"Thou shalt have no other gods before me"--Yoffe was also a disciple of the true "first commandments," the first instructions God gave to Adam and Eve according to the second creation account in Genesis 2: "Be fruitful" and "Tend the garden" (Gen. 2:15).

Vast numbers of species became extinct sixty-six million years ago after a celestial body collided with this planet. A meteor crashed through the atmosphere, then as now an atmosphere as thin as apple skin, and struck the earth, kicking up dust and destruction that left only a few million species extant. The Day of the Dinosaurs ended with only one species of dinosaur saved to perpetuate the memory of what took place. All around us there are miniature dinosaurs carrying the story of that fateful impact. We call these modern dinosaurs "birds," birds such as that flock of bustards saved from annihilation by General Yoffe.

---------------------------------- **66** ----------------------------------

And I brought you into a plentiful land
to enjoy its fruits and its good things.
But when you came in you defiled my land.
. . . .
How long will the land mourn,
and the grass of every field wither?

Creator/sustainer God through priest/prophet Jeremiah[a]

---------------------------------- **99** ----------------------------------

We are living today in an ecological era comparable only to the Mesozoic era's Day of the Dinosaurs sixty million years ago. Ecologists, our new eschatologists, have yet to produce their Dante of the hell of environmental collapse. But they have done enough research to convince us that the major biological reality today is one of extinction on the way to Big Bang or Big Burnout.[1] Humans are pulling the plug on the planet's life-systems at an unprecedented pace. We now live in the phenomenon and phase of "drawdown," whereby humans are consuming the planet's resources faster than they are being replenished. Tropical forests are shriveling by twenty-five acres per minute, cumulating to an area the size of the state of West Virginia each year. Twenty-six billion tons of cropland topsoil are eroding annually. Every minute four football fields of forest disappear from the face of the earth; every minute two hundred football fields of arable land disappear under concrete.

A fifth of the world's plant and animal species are expected to be extinct by the year 2000, 25 percent of all Earth's lifeforms extinguished by the end of the first decade of the next century.[2] Before the year 2000, in the United States alone, the life-lights of 680 unique native plants will be snuffed out forever, "clearly the most catastrophic loss of [plant] species in evolutionary time," says Donald Falk, director of the nonprofit Center for Plant Conservation, which conducted the poll of botanists.[3] A Soviet newspaper admitted that one Siberian lake is so polluted that stray dogs are routinely tossed into it to disintegrate. The environment of the Soviet Union has been so destroyed, particularly in the Central Asian region, that scientists claim it is beyond the point of recovery.

What has brought about this second Day of the Dinosaurs? The same event that brought about the first Day of the Dinosaurs--a violent impact on this planet by a colliding body. This time, however, the impact came from within rather than from without. Humans have impacted Planet Earth to the point of extinction, humans who are subsidizing, on a grand and criminal scale around the globe, pollution and the depletion and extinction of species.

We have forgotten and broken God's first commandments given to Adam and Eve. God's "first commandments" were not what Jewish commentaries list as numbers twenty-five to thirty-nine of the 613 biblical commandments found in the Torah (or what the Hebrews came eventually to call the Ten Words [Exod. 34:28; Deut. 4:13; 10:4] and Christians the Ten Commandments). Rather, the God who creates first commanded Eden's gardeners to be partners in the divine creativeness: "Be fruitful" and "tend the garden." In the words of literary naturist/farmer/scientist Wes Jackson, the Hebrews who "received the revelation . . . that our **first charge** is to care for the garden, had a revealed truth of more importance and lasting significance than the combined discoveries of Darwin, Einstein, Galileo, Copernicus, Newton, and all the rest of the scientific community."[4] If it is in and through human activity that God's creativity reveals itself, then we humans are showing ourselves more agents of hell than agents of heaven, more participants in evil's creativity than in God's. We stand in violation of the very first commandment: We are not doing God's work in the world.

————————————— 66 —————————————

Live with your century, but do not be its creature;
render to your contemporaries what they need,
not what they praise.

German poet/dramatist/historian Friedrich Schiller

————————————— 99 —————————————

It is not simply species and ecosystems that are going extinct. It is also the sensibilities of our global *Gemeinschaft* that are becoming extinct, our ability to register the significance of such cautions as "universes are not as plentiful as blackberries," in the famous words of sociologist/philosopher Charles Sanders Peirce. American Christians have a long history of being very aware of their "chosen people," "redeemer nation" status among the countries of the world. But we seem virtually comatose to the privileged planet status Earth enjoys in the universe. As far as anyone has been able to tell to date, this planet is the only place in the universe that sustains life and consciousness. Earth is the garden planet of the galaxy. Human sensitivities are deadening to what is taking place all around us.

Over two hundred years ago, goldsmith/copper smelter/engraver Paul Revere sat on his horse in the darkness on the outskirts of Boston and watched for a signal from the Old North Church tower. The country was in a state of red alert. The signals were set for a revolution:

One if by land, two if by sea;
And I on the opposite shore will be,
Ready to ride and spread the alarm
Through every Middlesex village and farm.[5]

Today we have no lanterns; people use lasers instead. Today church towers no longer are looked to as the centering, ordering symbols of community life. They have been replaced for industrial humanity, first by steel cathedrals called skyscrapers,[6] then by the horizontal skyscraper popularly known as the shopping mall.

Only the warning signals are still with us. But few there are who bother to read them. Fewer still pick up Planet Earth's distress signals. In the same way as the Nazis placed lovely landscapes on the windows of the gas trucks so that the Jews would have something nice to look at as they were being asphyxiated, so we have devised all sorts of cover-ups to conceal the social facts and awesome truths that unprecedented things are taking place all around us.[7] The reality of revolution--the fact that we are living, in English historian/cultural critic Eric J. Hobsbawm's words, in "the most revolutionary era in the recorded history of the globe"[8]--must be faced if we are to avoid extinction. The world is now, as then, in a state of red-alert.

"Red sky at morning/sailor take warning;/red sky at night/sailor's delight" is a relatively recent rendition of an ancient proverb quoted by Jesus in Caesarea Philippi:

When it is evening, you say, "It will be fair weather; for the sky is red." And in the morning, "It will be stormy today, for the sky is red and threatening." You know how to interpret the appearance of the sky, but you cannot interpret the signs of the times. (Matt. 16:2 RSV)

Postmodern theology must speak to the signs of the times, many of which are prodigal, many of which are perverse. Keeping the "first commandments" of creativity and trusteeship entails learning how to read the signs of the times as much as the signs of the sky. Keeping the "first command-

ments" entails an honest answer to the question the Chinese used as a social greeting after the Revolution of 1911: "Are you living in the new world?"[9]
Are you living in the new world?

Blind spots and Blindsight

Are we living in this new world? Or have we missed, in art critic/social reformer John Ruskin's phrase, "the sign sternly given"? How badly have we violated the "first commandments" with our biocentric blindness? How dare we criticize those obsessed with biblical portents, especially conflicts along the historic borders of the three Abrahamic religions (Judaism, Christianity, and Islam), while we ourselves prove unable to read even the billboard signs of the times?

As with that proverbial frog in the pot on the stove[10]--when tossed into boiling water, he jumped immediately out, but when put in cold water, so that the temperature rose gradually, he cooked to death--the church has failed to register what management theorists have come to call the LNDs of life--least noted differences. Conditioned to react to sudden changes, we have trouble responding to slow changes intimately connected with us-- swelling world populations, steady environmental degradation, decrepit educational systems.[11] That is why subtle changes that are introduced with a minimum of disruption often become the most profound and out of control. People are transformed the most by the changes that they accept without even knowing it. For the church to negotiate change and prepare for a future full of unprecedented challenges, it must not only pick up the obvious messages, fraught with meta-messages. Deep lessons must and can easily be learned from the LNDs of our age.

In 2 Samuel 18:29, Ahimaaz answers David's request for "tidings" or news in this fashion: "I saw a great tumult, but I did not know what it was about" (NKJV). We are living in the midst of a great tumult. Pastor/ theologian John H. Snow defines ministry today in the title of his book: *The Impossible Vocation: Ministry in the Mean Time* (1988), with "mean time" meaning both "in between" and "nasty."[12] We sense we are living, in Paul's phrase, "in the overlap of the ages," in a transitional time. But can we tell from whence we come, or where we go? Do we know what is going on? Do we know where the danger is coming from? What "tidings" will we be able to give when God asks for an accounting?

Historian/futurist William Irwin Thompson compares us to flies crawl-ing on the ceiling of the Sistine Chapel. We do not perceive the meaning of where we are; we are blind to the beauties and wonders that surround us. Ophthalmologists are excitedly researching two "awareness" defects re-cently isolated and identified. The first is Anton's syndrome, a condition in which patients are blind to their own blindness. They think they can see, but they can't. It is the most extensive sort of blind spot, that spot on the retina

21

that cannot be stimulated by light, thus preventing one from seeing how things are in a certain portion of one's visual field.

Everyone has a unique and distinctive blind spot. Philosopher/parahistorian/researcher Roy A. Sorensen points this out graphically in his fascinating book *Blindspots* (1988). It begins by inviting readers to locate their blind spot:

O   X

Hold this page about twelve inches from your eyes. Close your left eye. Now look steadily at the left-hand dot while moving the page first slowly away from you and then slowly back toward your face. The right-hand dot will disappear from your field of vision when its image falls on your blind spot.[13]

The second awareness defect is called "blindsight"--a condition in which patients are blind to their own sight. They actually have visual experience, but their visual consciousness is divorced from their visual receptivity. The church today veers wildly between the awareness defects of its blind spot and blindsight. It is in dire straits because of its lack of see-ers and seers. "I come to you because I want to see" is what Native Americans would say to a medicine man or shaman. This is where we get our word for wise man, "seer," literally, "one who sees."

Where the church should be cooperating with the transformative processes of creation, it systematically screens out of consciousness the changes of which it is a part. What is more, it finds itself continually blindsided by the changes taking place all around it. "To the blind," the saying goes, "all things are sudden." Where is the evidence for our having donned blinders on the brain? A sign of the times for me came during Holy Week 1989, which was dominated by two announcements. The first one came on Maundy Thursday (23 March) from Utah, where two chemists upstaged physicists and unveiled their then hotly contested hypotheses for harnessing nuclear fusion, the energy-releasing process that makes stars shine. The secret to an unlimited supply of cheap and clean energy, they precipitously announced to the media, might be in a process called "cold fusion," which squeezes hydrogen nuclei together in electrolytic cells, using something as plentiful and common as sea water.

The next day, on Good Friday morning (24 March), came news from Alaska that the *Exxon Valdez* had run aground on Bligh Reef in Prince William Sound and spilled 10.8 million gallons of toxic North Slope crude oil into the sea. Belief blind spots prevent us from knowing what is known to be true by everyone else around us. Belief blindsight prevents us from knowing what we already know to be true. As a Native American shaman would say, we have a problem of seeing, the seeing that involves much more than the eye. We are only beginning to "see."

Coming to terms with our blind-spotting and blindsighting behavior means coming to terms with Jesus' ecology of the mind, as it expressed itself in the requirement that his followers learn to read the signs of the times. There are two kinds of reading. The first and most normative is the Enlightenment way of referential reading: reading that distances the reader from what is being read through analytical, objective, clinical thinking. Much of the "new" thinking that goes by the name of "systems thinking" or "cybernetical thinking" is really a "cleaner," more efficient version of referential thinking's critical detachment.

The second and most natural (i.e., nature's way of thinking) is what philosopher/University of Michigan professor Henryk Skolimowski calls "reverential" reading: reading that connects the reader to what is being read through more empathetic, celebrative, creative levels of knowledge.[14] Reverential reading entails first **naming** the dangers and powers that this present age is facing. It then involves **claiming** these problems and powers as spiritual and moral issues--or, if you will, claiming them for God. Finally, it involves **framing** an alternative vision, a new picture, of how the world ought to be. Reading the signs of the times means moving beyond and leaving behind our life in the "Country of the Blind."[15]

Today's Problems and Yesterday's Analysis

The church is becoming increasingly tense and alarmed, confused and cynical. More and more clergy and laity are breaking down, burning out, cracking up, dropping out. Ministry seems to be an increasingly unrewarding and unrewarded profession. Why? Because leadership has been consumed with asking the wrong diagnostic questions for America's churches and synagogues. Or worse, leadership has defined the problem in such a way that solutions are not possible. Or worst, leadership has become nothing more than fashionable slogans and cliched retreads. Prisoners of our own definitions, liberation begins when we turn around and recognize ourselves.

Granted, it is extremely difficult to recognize who we are and to face consciously the awesome truth of the transformations taking place all around us. This is why so many people are choosing death, disease, addictions, or insanity as techniques for avoiding transformation and evading fear. In fact, why more minds don't take the various paths of insanity is sometimes beyond imagining, a testimony perhaps to the dynamic elasticity of the human mind and spirit. The immense stress that religious leaders are under is only partly revealed in the number one ranking of psychosis as the leading diagnosis in the total hospital claims count for Southern Baptist church workers.[16] Our pews are filled with people suffering from borderline personality disorders--ten to twenty million in America alone exhibit borderline syndrome--partly because we are living in a borderline society.[17]

It is not easy to understand the changes taking place in the world, especially when conclusions are more interim than postmortem. But two things are clear, even to anyone half-alert.

First, within the lifetimes of persons not yet fifty, human culture and consciousness have been more radically transformed than at any other known period of history. Second, the next ten years will bring with them more radical changes than we have experienced in the past three decades.

Our paralyzing problem, therefore, has been above all else a "failure of attention," which philosopher/psychologist Jacob Needleman suggests may be our original sin.[18] We have been trying to be church on intellectual capital and theological brainpower that is not only inadequate and incomplete but also fatally flawed in its basic assumptions. We are about as prescient and plugged in to what is happening around us as the managers of Chernobyl. Hence our failure of **naming**, naming this displaced period in which we are living as a hinge period of history. Philosopher/historian Michel Foucault has called our historical epoch an "epistemic break" in the structure of time--a time of paradigms lost and paradigms regained. Anthropologist/English professor James Clifford contends we are condemned to "a pervasive condition of off-centeredness."[19]

Naming, Claiming, Framing
Naming

Our problem has also been one of consciousness--remaining as conscious as possible of living in a culture off its hinges and receiving into our being the higher order of reality now emerging. Since 1945 theologians, historians, sociologists, and cultural critics have been trying to tell us, in a variety of throat-clearing and even throat-cutting ways, that the Christian church is going through another dramatic transition in its history--an image shift in consciousness identity, morale, mission, and evangelism as profound and as transforming as the Roman emperor Constantine's baptism, the schism between Eastern (Orthodox) and Western (Roman Catholic) Christianity, Martin Luther's ninety-five theses, the emergence of an Enlightenment faith. Simply to name Dean M. Kelley, Martin E. Marty, Robert Bellah, Christopher Lasch, Wade Clark Roof, Huston Smith, Charles Y. Glock, William McKinney, Peter Hodgson, and Robert Wuthnow is to humanize the litany of warnings about the revolutionary new realities confronting the culturally established churches in America.

Historian of ideas Allan Megill is one scholar for whom the metaphors of global revolution and cultural crisis do not serve. He critiques the "prophets of extremity" and the advocates of the crisis metaphor for obfuscating the issues involved. Every historian knows the appeal of the turnstile theory. Every age proclaims itself in one way or another at the "turning point in history," a turnpike of accelerated change on which everyone is undergoing a "crisis in meaning" or a "crisis in consciousness." We can all get a little too pleased with our knowledge, with our place in history, with our living, as Eve is supposed to have said to Adam as they left Eden, "in a time of great transition." Paleontologist/geologist/philosopher/Jesuit priest Pierre Teilhard de Chardin, however, argues that there are times when humanity is actually perched on some chronological fulcrum: "But there are moments when this impression of transformation becomes accentuated and is thus particularly justified."[20] That is why in the end even Megill gives up. After all the objections have been registered, the turnstile still turns stubbornly, he admits, as uncertainty: "For we do live in an age of uncertainty.... Crisis, for all its faults, is perhaps the best metaphor for inculcating a sense of this uncertainty."[21]

———————————————— 66 ————————————————

Religion is to spirituality as ideology is to thought.
Critic/educator Arnold Rampersad[b]

———————————————— 99 ————————————————

John Wesley, guiding light behind the international "Evangelical Revival" in the eighteenth century, talked about his conversion as a time when he felt his "heart strangely warmed." This is precisely the kind of experiences eighteenth-century Britishers had when they heard Wesley and other leaders of the First Great Awakening preach. At that same time, day laborers in America dropped their tools and walked off their jobs to hear English Methodist/evangelist George Whitefield and New Jersey Presbyterian/revivalist Gilbert Tennent preach. Theologian/educator Charles G. Finney, the founder of modern revivalism, talked about his conversion as a time when he felt his heart rushed by "waves and waves of liquid love." This is precisely the kind of experiences nineteenth-century Christians had when they heard Finney and other leaders of the Second Great Awakening preach.

———————————————— 66 ————————————————

Light . . . light, visible reminder of invisible light.
Twentieth century's most modern and most traditional poet/
most influential and most influenced writer T.S. Eliot

———————————————— 99 ————————————————

Have you ever given, or heard, a Wesley or an Edwards sermon from the pulpit on Heritage Sunday? Remember the reaction? Will you do it again? Have you ever given or heard a Finney sermon from the pulpit? The only thing these sermons move people to these days is the door. Why? Because a fundamental transformation in human consciousness and cosmology has taken place. The reigning worldview is breaking down all around us, as a new understanding of life is springing forth. Christians have not yet faced up to **naming** the consequences of this change on the Christian consciousness. If the truth be known, we are still trying to use Wesley's and Edwards's and Finney's methods and secrets, like a box of old keys, with predictable results.[22]

Worse and Worse of Better and Better

One example: The United Methodist Church boasts the best-trained, hardest-working, most motivated clergy it has ever seen. But The United Methodist Church is getting fewer and fewer results from its clergy than ever before. Why? Because we are geared up for a world-we-have-lost ministry. We are captivated by a world-that-is-no-more syndrome. Our appeals and ambitions center in "recapturing what we have lost" rather than in stepping forward to meet the challenges of what we have gained. The United Methodist Church's stubborn identity anxieties, its inappropriate displays of anger, its self-mutilation and suicide attempts, its tendency to push away those who love it, its impulsivity and frantic efforts to avoid abandonment, are only a few indications that the church itself may be afflicted with continuing borderline behavior.

The church does not have the option of standing safely by and watching these changes take place without taking part. One of the cardinal planks in quantum theory is that it is impossible to be an observer. Quantum theorist/ Nobel laureate Werner Heisenberg's 1927 Uncertainty Principle states simply that the observer alters the observed by the very act of observation.[23] Princeton physicist/atomic energy consultant/television narrator John Archibald Wheeler suggests we replace the term "observer" with "participator," since how any event turns out depends in large measure on the consciousness of the observer/participant. The universe, as Wheeler puts it, may "in some strange sense be 'brought into being' by the participation of those who participate."[24] If the truth be known, the church is most commonly a participant within a world of Wesley/Edwards sermons, a negative, reactionary, retrogressive participant within the spectrum of possibilities during the era in which God has chosen it to serve.

Contemporary Christian concepts and conducts of life are operating out of an antiquated cosmology and cosmogony. We are not living our own story. The Christian Church stands at one of the great turning points of history, a "cultural revolution"[25] as challenging as any the church has witnessed. State Department official/antitechnologist Francis Fukuyama has looked at only a political region where the pace of change is torrid and reached a conclusion he captured in the title of his celebrated article, "The End of History?"[26] Similarly, political commentator/columnist/baseball philosopher George F. Will declared the year 1989 to be the "most startling, interesting, promising and consequential year, ever."[27]

Science and technology can create, and in our case have already created, intellectual and cultural changes that are more radical than anything politics can produce. For this reason Michael H. Hart, in his book *The One Hundred: A Ranking of the Most Influential Persons in History* (1978), places Isaac Newton higher on the list than Jesus of Nazareth.[28] Hart is very wrong about this, but he is right in reminding us of the consequences of not claiming new worldviews for Christ. Even the Sermon on the Mount, minister/biblical scholar Hans Dieter Betz has argued forcefully, is Jesus' answer to the problem of reasserting God's presence and power at a time of collapsing cosmologies and mythic cosmogonic shifts.[29]

―――――――――――――――― 66 ――――――――――――――――

It will remain remarkable,
in whatever way our future concepts may develop,
that the very study of the external world led to the conclusion
that the content of the consciousness is an ultimate reality.

Nobel laureate/mathematical physicist Eugene P. Wigner[c]

―――――――――――――――― 99 ――――――――――――――――

What happens when antiquated worldviews and conceptual metaphors are clung to in the face of their declining moral and intellectual force is not hard to predict. The name of The United Methodist professional journal that is designed to keep its ministry up-to-date and contemporary speaks volumes about the church's preparedness to minister to the high-energy, high-speed, high-flex culture of the twenty-first century: *Circuit Rider*. If the truth be told, a church filled with yesterday's people is precisely what ministerial leadership has been trained for. Every Sunday morning, an urban culture of electronic circuitry and technological wizardry is expected to step into an ecclesiastical time warp because the church's leaders have lapsed into automatic-pilot mode. Global paradigm shifts are leaving denominations in the dust.

The Western Christian church has undergone at least three revolutionary periods of topsy-turvy upheaval and uproar.[30] I am sketching these shifts in paradigm traditions somewhat more sharply than they were in practice. But not by much. The first civilizational bifurcation point was reached during the Reformation, when Protestantism as a theological system, liberalism as a political system, objectivism/positivism/reductionism as a scientific system, and capitalism as an economic system began to emerge. Seventeenth-century western Europe is most often taken to be the birthplace of the modern world.

The second paradigm shift or bifurcation point occurred during the Enlightenment, which challenged the supernatural, suprahistorical character of religious faith with the principle of historicism and ushered in fullblown the era known as "modern."

We are right now in the midst of the third major challenge to religious faith in Western Christian history. The modern Age of Enlightenment culture, now over three centuries old, has lost its sense of purpose. Ministry today is taking place in the lengthening shadow of ideas and norms characteristic of the eighteenth-century Deists-Rationalists. In the words of philosopher/educator Frederik Ferré, "The most important fact about our current historical situation is hard to accept: that our modern world is in its last days ... and that we are--ready or not, like it or not--entering a turbulent period of transition to a very different world of postmodernity."[31] To cut a long story short (I and many others have elaborated elsewhere on this transition from premodernism to modernism to postmodernism),[32] the world of modernity will linger in the same way industrialism continues in the postindustrial world--as a junkyard of dented dreams.[33]

Suffice it here to say that "postmodernism" is an unfortunate but necessary word. First used in 1949 in architectural circles, then adopted in painting and dance, it describes what it isn't, not what it is. For that very reason "postmodern" (or even "transmodern," a word I almost decided to use throughout this book) is the perfect word to characterize contemporaneity and the early society of the twenty-first century. It acknowledges that we are living indeed in a transitional period still in rebellion against canonical modernism. It refuses the premature naming of this period of history in anything but "post" terms--postsecular, postcritical, postcivilizational, post-Enlightenment, post-Constantinian, post-Darwinian, postbureaucratic, postliberal, postmodern. Postmodernism suggests the truth that we do not yet know what we shall be; that our age is, in Catholic theologian/University of Chicago professor David Tracy's words, "the age that cannot name itself."[34] "Postmodernism" nicely conveys the sense of passage in the grey dawn of a new morning. When history is passing through a tunnel, people **need** tunnel vision and transitional strategies and open-ended thinking.

Two Sides to the Same Coin

There is no single or perpetual answer. No human perspective can be absolute. Physics was the first science to perceive the polycentric nature of reality in which simple structures of a center and periphery, of front and back, are replaced by multiple models marked by inclusion and paradox, all of which are limited. Quantum spirituality is lived out in an everywhere center and nowhere circumference. The modern world was built on dialectics--the *complexia oppositorum* of lawyer/Geneva reformer/theologian John Calvin, the thesis/antithesis of German idealist/philosopher Georg Hegel. The modern world moved dialectically, by conflict and contradiction and controversy. The postmodern world being born is not a bipolar worldview of either/or's but a double helix, Möbius-strip[35] culture of both-

and's, the *coincidentia oppositorum* (coinciding opposites) in fifteenth-century prelate/philosopher Nicholas of Cusa's mystical phrasing, the *conjunctio oppositorum* in Carl Jung's thinking.

People are moving on the continuum, and I speak here of a macrame of complimentary, not conflicting or contradictory energies, from systematic to narrative, from conceptual to perceptual, from mechanistic to organic, from monolithic to biolithic, from being to becoming, from existential to transpersonal, from math to image, from nothing-but to as-if, from product to process, from linear to field, from establishment to movement, from hierarchy to network, from private to public, from reductionism to holism, from structure-oriented thinking to process-oriented thinking, from denominational to ecclesial, from means to ends, from theory to fiction, from national to multinational, from eclectic to ecologic, from common sense to intuition, from emotion to volition, from action to character, from divine power to divine presence, from what we know to how we know, from "how much we have" (quantity) to "what we have" (quality), from win/lose to win/win, from authoritarian/bureaucratic to cooperative/charismatic, from literalism to multidimensionalism, from system to story, from religious to spiritual, from epic to lyric, from "Here I stand" to "This way we walk."[36]

Some of God's last words to us in the Bible are these: "Behold, I make all things new" (Rev. 21:5 RSV). Reading the signs requires reading between the lines in this "overlap of the ages." It means naming this time in which we are living for what it is: a "Third Wave" civilization, as newspaper correspondent/business consultant/futurist Alvin Toffler calls it;[37] a "third wave of the Spirit," as missiologist/evangelist David B. Barrett calls it[38]--a new tidal wave of truth, rushing past us and crushing us unless we go to the second part of "reading the signs."

Claiming

Third-wavers **claim** the time in which we live for God and the gospel. They learn to ride the revolutionary waves inundating us this moment, seizing the global initiative in ministries using audio (radio and cassettes), video (television, movies), print (books, magazines), and software. New Lights take courage from Ilya Prigogine's "laws of dissipative structures" (for which he received a Nobel Prize in 1977). These laws of biological and social transformation say basically that things have to fall apart in disequilibrium, instability, and turbulence before they can come together to take systems down new paths of development. Claiming this culture for God requires the irreversible exchange of energy between the gospel and the postmodern world. To bring Christ in communication with the world means proclaiming an old-fashioned gospel in new-fangled ways.

In the conceptual vocabulary of the Brussels School theory of change, the "perturbed" circumstances of the contemporary church can be called a singular moment or a bifurcation point. All living systems have the capacity for creating new self-organizations. This capacity is activated when a single fluctuation, adding its strength to the constantly fluctuating sub-systems, destabilizes the preexisting organization. The mysterious moment at which this revolution happens is called a singular moment or a bifurcation point. From this moment on, it is inherently impossible to predict whether the whole system will collapse into chaos or will recreate itself into the higher order and level of coherence Prigogine calls a "dissipative structure."[39] What is predictable is that without instabilities and transitions, without movement away from equilibrium structures, there is no possibility for the formation of new dynamic communities and states of matter--dissipative structures.

66

I feel in myself a life so luminous
that it might enlighten a world,
and yet I am shut up in a sort of mineral.
Nineteenth-century French novelist/printer/typefounder Honoré de Balzac

---
99

We sing these words of Charles Wesley, but we sing them in what Prigogine would call a "sleepwalker's" state: "To serve the present age/ [Our] calling to fulfill."[40] Welsh theologian/researcher Rowan Williams calls sleepwalking "the totalitarian mentality."[41] The totalitarian mentality is reflected in the number one bumper sticker in America, "Shit Happens." Whenever the flight from individual responsibility takes the conviction that nothing we do or want is going to make a difference, that things are largely out of our control and even out of the control of those bringing about the destruction, then you have the mentality of totalitarianism. Totalitarianism is the belief that someone else, or something else, is deciding what will happen to you; that your "fluctuation" makes no difference. Totalitarianism is, in Williams's words,

> the loss of the capacity to "mourn"--to draw on reserves of compassion that help us to re-affirm values, feeling the enormity of pain and death and violence, and feeling it because we have a richer and better hope. . . . When there is no time or energy to mourn because there is so much to mourn for, hopelessness takes over, accompanied by the lack of a sense of responsibility.[42]

Some of the fastest growing movements in the world are fundamentalist and totalitarian.

The **claiming** phase of reading the signs is where we "wake up" (Prigogine) and claim the changes going on as moral issues, as spiritual problems, as "something to do with power, vision, understanding, and choice, with the ways in which we decide to make sense of our lives."[43] We have become escape artists of the real world, evacuees from history. We run from one church to another, one minister to another, one fad to another, one secular theology to another, one addiction to another, in the hope of finding some exit from our deepening identity anxieties. When bailing out from reality doesn't work, there are unleashed either the forces of helplessness, hostility, and paranoia, or the full-blown psychopathological forces of violence, delusions, nihilism, and catatonia. Claiming the day for God means coming together around new images, structures, and symbols, giving up our avoidance mechanisms and "evasive fantasies" of "circuit riders," "main lines," and "establishment religion"--evasive, covered-wagon fantasies that must be, in Williams's words, "brought to judgment before we can be brought to grace."[44]

Paradoxy

---------------- 66 ----------------

The plural of paradox is paradise.

Pastor/composer Jaime Potter-Miller[d]

---------------- 99 ----------------

Claiming this culture for God means claiming paradoxy over orthodoxy as postmodernism's fundamental cultural category and intellectual phenomenon.[45] The word "paradoxy" is derived from two Greek words--*pará* meaning "beyond or beside" and *doxy* meaning "belief." A paradox is a linear contradiction but a harmony in truth. A paradox is an echoing pun on differentiations and oppositions which are metaphysically one. In *Some Paradoxes of Paul* (1974), theologian/biblical scholar Edmund B. Keller tells of how the disciples' response to Jesus' ministry "We have seen strange things today" (Luke 5:26 RSV) literally translates as "We have seen paradoxes today."[46] The sixteenth-century reformer/humanist/spiritualist Sebastian Franck built his theology on paradoxes he found in the Bible. He ended up with "280 paradoxes on wondrous sayings," as one of his most important texts has now been titled.[47]

Paradoxes, scholars inform us, are "associated with crises in thought and with revolutionary advances."[48] Niels Bohr is reported to have made it a dictum that "No paradox, no progress." The early Christians said to one another, "We have seen paradoxes this day"--strength in weakness (2 Cor. 12:9), living through dying (John 12:24), wisdom through foolishness (1 Cor. 1:25), self-confidence in self-emptying (Phil.2:7,9), exaltation in humility (Matt. 23:12), seeing by gazing at the unseen (2 Cor.4:18), human freedom in divine sovereignty, "reaching the goal by giving up the attempt to reach it,"[49] and so on. Ever since quantum mechanics was discovered in 1926, modern mathematicians and scientists working in the fields of special and general relativity, as well as quantum theory and materials science, have been presenting to one another, almost daily, a cross country of particle-wave paradoxes--for example, the nature of an object changing the moment an observer changes; the liquid state of solid gold particles; the reliability of Newtonian mechanics to fly us to the moon but the unreliability, indeed, the falsity of Newtonian mechanics to describe reality; the contradictory descriptions of subatomic behavior that are simultaneously true. Two classic quantum problems are even known as paradoxes: the Einstein-Podolsky-Rosen paradox (1935) and Schrödinger's quantum cat paradox (1935). The postmodern circuits of meaning are complex, pluralizing, and most of all, giddily paradoxical.

---------------------------------- 66 ----------------------------------

. . . May God us keep
From Single vision & Newton's sleep!

Poet/engraver/painter William Blake[e]

Nature and Nature's laws lay hid in night:
God said, let Newton be! and all was light.

Poet/translator Alexander Pope[f]

It did not last: the Devil howling 'Ho!
Let Einstein be!' restored the status quo.

Poet/editor/architect Sir John C. Squire[g]

---------------------------------- 99 ----------------------------------

Not only did modernization not yield single, determinate meanings; its multiple meanings became intrinsically paradoxical. The postmodern world comes to life in its paradoxes. One scholar has placed at the heart of postmodernism the complex of attitudes associated with the "visionary" and the "apocalyptic," working either separately or together.[50] Indeed, the key to living in the New Light is negotiating this crisscross of paradoxes. A few of these visionary/apocalyptic inconcinnities follow:

First, modernization introduced the world to the "global village" of Canadian communications theorist/devout Roman Catholic Marshall McLuhan. But the modern world is dying because the closer together we come, the farther apart we feel. Propinquity does not mean community. To the contrary, proximity often brings with it the breakdown of community life. Increasing numbers of contacts means decreasing amounts of time spent connecting. As we know the citizens in our global village better, the number of strangers in our one village gets larger than ever before. As the world gets smaller and smaller, the spans between people get bigger and bigger, and the differences between regions get wider and wider. As technology brings humans closer together in electronic ways, it pushes humans farther and farther away from one another in ways of intimacy and trust. That is one reason why horror sells. Of the thirty-three novels on the *New York Times* bestseller list at the time I am writing this sentence, fifteen are either horror, creep, or murder mysteries. Second only to children's movies in videos purchased are slasher movies. Over one million Americans read regularly one or more of the big four horror fan magazines: *Fangoria, Deep Red, Horror Fan, Gorezone.* A patient sneaked out of the Veterans Administration Hospital in Dayton, Ohio, on 14 June 1989, and was never heard from again . . . until in mid-August some kids playing in a wooded area of the grounds found his badly decomposed and decapitated body. Hurriedly they then went to a nearby McDonald's, bought some hamburgers and fries, and brought their lunch back to the body; they picnicked around the remains for forty minutes, and then notified authorities of what they had stumbled upon. Bodily mutilation and gore used to turn stomachs and make us sick. Now it turns us on and makes us hungry. Our churches are dying because they are less an experience of relatedness, wholeness, and authenticity than of simulation, segmentation, and atomization. There are not enough "touch me" congregations in this hands off, horror culture.

Second, modernization introduced the world to standards of hygiene and health that keep larger percentages of the population alive longer at the same time that modernity drains old age of meaning and deprives the elderly of purpose and vocation. Longer life spans make it possible for people to enjoy more years of retirement. But escalating costs of health care and inflation make the economics of a longer life one of life's greatest challenges. The suicide rate for America's elderly (sixty-five and older), according to federal statistics that are acknowledged to be underestimated, increased by 25 percent between 1981 and 1986.

Third, modernization introduced the world to a science-based culture that was reductionist, determinist, and materialist. What the modern world did, however, was to make all of us into objectivists and relativists at the same time. Modernization introduced the world to the scientific enterprise, which holds that nothing is worthy of investigation unless it can be quantified and measured. Yet the more moderns attempted to quantify and measure reality, the more ignorant they became about reality (this is the essence of Werner Heisenberg's Uncertainty Principle).

---- 66 ----

All Cretans are liars.

Enterprise commander/intergalactic explorer Captain Kirk[h]

---- 99 ----

Fourth, modernization introduced the world to a high-tech, high-flex culture where flesh is flaunted at every turn. But the modern world is dying because the more skin is exposed, the less we feel truly touched, truly known, truly embraced. The more the love-making, the less love is made. The more plugged-in we become to FAXs, PCs, VCRs, and CDs, the more tuned out we are to genuine experience. Twenty-five percent of America's children five years of age, who will be high school seniors as we begin the twenty-first century, now live below the federal poverty line, the highest proportion in thirty years. Eighteen percent of these five-year-olds were born out of wedlock--the highest proportion in this century. Half of them now live with single parents, a figure that will increase to 75 percent by the time they reach eighteen. Twenty-five percent of America's female teenagers will get pregnant, the highest teen pregnancy rate in the industrialized world. Every day forty teenage girls in the United States give birth to their third child.

Fifth, modernization introduced the world to "miracle drugs" and medical technologies that have transformed physicians into a new priest-hood and patients into "clients." Yet the modern world is dying because modernity and its priestcraft makes people sick--from CDs, or civilization diseases (cancer, heart disease, diabetes, neuropathies), from EIs, or environmental illnesses (chemical hypersensitivity, total allergy syndrome, etc.), from IIs, or iatrogenic illnesses (medically induced diseases). Every modern pill contains its own risk-benefit equation. CDs, EIs, and IIs are the modern equivalents of coal miners' canaries--warning signals that the nest we call Planet Earth is becoming an increasingly toxic place in which to live.

Sixth, modernization introduced the world to labor-saving technologies and bureaucratic hermeneutics. Yet the more money we possess to "enjoy life," the less time there is for enjoyment. Those most able to afford leisure amenities--boats, RVs, pools, second homes--can least afford the time for leisure. Similarly, in our ecclesiocracies, the more their mechanisms pro-duce uniformity, the more the churches mouth pluralism, the more their mechanisms produce uniformity, the more the churches mouth pluralism, and on and on.

---------------------------- **"** ----------------------------

More "Eagles" drive America's expanding road networks . . .
than fly in the nation's polluted skies;
and more "Cougars" pass the night in its proliferating garages
than in its shrinking forests.

Worldwatch Institute researcher/environmentalist Alan Durning[i]

---------------------------- **"** ----------------------------

Seventh, modernization introduced the world to "information explo-sion" and "information technology," with the amount of knowledge dou-bling exponentially every seven years. Yet the modern world is dying because the major cultural reality is one of shrinkage in cultural informa-tion, as the Coca-Cola-zation (and Americanization) of the planet homoge-nizes cultures under McDonald's arches, as the depopulation of America's farms diminishes local color and customs.[51] The modern world is dying because the major biological reality is one of shrinkage in biological information, as we are living in a day of species extinction and loss of biological information that defaces the image of Christ etched in creation. The modern world is dying because the major technological reality is one of spreading "disinformation," as the half-life of a technical scientific education is now less than seven years.

Eighth, modernization introduced the world to the modern university and knowledge industry. Yet as historian/editor/publisher Conrad Cherry has shown so graphically, our institutions of higher education are tied together structurally and prevented from falling apart by the segmenting strings of specialization and professionalization. Or in Cherry's more cogent way of putting it, "The paradox which is the modern university is that it is an institution which holds together and continues to exist in large measure by its decentering motion springing from the Enlightenment perspective."[52]

Ninth, modernization introduced the world to what social ethicist/social scientist Gibson Winter calls "one of the wealthiest, if not the wealthiest, system of production in the history of humankind." Yet at the same time millions are now dying of starvation, with from thirty-three to thirty-four million people in the United States alone existing in poverty.[53]

Framing

The **claiming** stage of reading the signs must be followed by the **framing** stage. It is not simply people's television screens that are scrambled and garbled. Postmoderns are open to almost anyone, or anything, that can frame a clear picture for their lives. The drug problem in this country is partly an attempt to turn white-outs into white-light experiences.

The United States Treasury Department informs us that in this country there is so much trafficking in drugs using large bills (Americans spend more money on cocaine than on education) that there is a greater than 50 percent chance that if you have a $100 bill on you right now, there are trace elements of cocaine on it, enough cocaine, in fact, that if it were in your system it would bar you from sports contests. A few years ago there was so much laundering of drug money in Miami banks that an average of thirty-five micrograms of cocaine adhered to every bank note in Miami. An estimated 75 percent of all convicted felons have drugs in their bloodstream when a crime is committed. Drug consumption outpaces growth in every other area of human enterprise, except the arms trade. With 5 percent of the world's people, the United States consumes 50 percent of the world's dangerous drugs. The world's most prescribed drugs? Benzodiazepine tranquilizers with the brand names Valium and Librium. The world's most popular drug? Alcohol. The sickness treated by the three best-selling drugs in America? Stress.

But postmodern people have not become less spiritual. They are both less religious and more spiritual, less oriented toward "organized religion" (the church has yet to comprehend how this culture hears this phrase) and more disposed toward what used to be known as "spiritual things." But postmodern people have not become less spiritual. In his acceptance speech upon receiving the "Communicator of the Decade" award, public television producer Bill Moyers announced his belief that "the search for what it means to be spiritual is the story not just of the decade but of the century." Musical genius/"fusion" creator/cool jazz trumpeter Miles Davis explains in his autobiography why he "believes in being spiritual" but is not "into" organized religion. "Because I personally don't like a lot of things that are happening in organized religion. It don't seem too spiritual to me, but more about money and power, and I can't go for that."[54]

By failing to comprehend the fact that people's definition of religion is no longer simply the denomination to which they belong, all those sociologists who lectured us on secularization theory, as sociologist/theologian David Martin persistently warned, led us astray. Postmoderns are not less interested in religion than ever before. Indeed, they are exploring new religious experiences like never before. The church has simply given them a less interesting religion than ever before. The "unchurched" (an ugly word) are actually more religious than they were a decade ago, their 2,500 metaphysical bookstores bursting with religious exotica and esoterica.[55] Oldline Christianity has entered a glacial age of coldness and despair, exuding all the beauty of ice, in the midst of a spiritual heat wave.

New Age piety is arguably the most powerful and widespread force affecting our culture today partly because it "reprimitivizes" religion, in historian/holistic health pioneer Catherine Albanese's wonderful phrase, opening it up to the personal, the universal, and the mystical.[56] This is also the appeal of the new theological Orient-ation, the "new paganism," and "satanism." After 150 years of mission work in one area of northern Indiana, there are now fifteen United Methodist churches. After ten years of mission work in this same geographical area, there are now seven "Churches of Satan," thriving congregations with Satan church schools.

Yuppies, Buppies, Guppies, Grumpies, Snags, and Dinks

Oldline sermons are oral souvenirs from a bye-gone era. Our pulpits resemble antique phonographic needles stuck in a deep groove, a repeating record of scratched songs filled with second-hand stories without power, second-rate images without focus, and second-run Muzak with the nostalgic sentiment of the swan song. Our ministries are all too often "a sleepy land, where, under the same wheel/The same old rut would deepen year by year."

The church is soaked and saturated in what theologian/Wesley professor Diedre Kriewald calls "old faith language."

Religious leadership must end its intellectual and imaginative failure to think through what it is doing in the light of the new, emerging cosmology, which is hospitable to spirit-matter theories and mindbody experiences. The postmodern world has been sacralized, not secularized. We do not live in a "society of unbelief." Surgeon/poet/professor/novelist Richard Selzer captures the postmodern mentality with eloquent force:

My entire life has been one long search for faith. I haven't found it. I do not believe in God. Having said that, . . . I want you to know that I love the idea of God. I love piety. Without it, you lead your life unmoored, in a state of isolation. You are a tiny speck in a vast universe. I'm jealous, frankly. I feel as though I've missed out on the greatest thing that can happen to a person--faith in God. It must be wonderful.[57]

The postmodern era is not an age of doubt and deicide. It's an age of goddifiers and god-shops. Postmoderns are enchanted and haunted by divinities, by all sorts of divine "salt substitutes" that flood the market. Postmoderns are escaping from a spiritual vacuum and are turning to pseudopriests and counterfeit spiritualities in unprecedented numbers. Almost half a million have now purchased a "channeled message" from the Holy Spirit, predictably titled (given its origination from two New York professors) *A Course in Miracles* (1975). Within a one-block radius in Santa Fe, New Mexico, there are the following: an art gallery called Spirit Art, a natural fiber store called Spirit Clothes, a shoe store selling "Easy Spirit Shockblockers," and a coffee shop where one can buy such disparate magazines as *Gnosis, Sojourners, Connexions, Regeneration Newsletter, New Age Journal*, new cross-disciplinary periodicals like *Design Spirit*, and Free Spirit Publishing Company products.

There is a yearning for a sacred way of living on the Earth. Postmoderns are hungrier for spirituality than ever before, and enjoying it less in their churches and synagogues. That is why postmoderns can easily get swept away by the gospel buccaneering of fundamentalism. Or they look to Spielbergian gurus to teach them about the ark of the covenant or the holy grail. Or they succumb to the salvation promises of the looking-good and feeling-good industry. Or they are given to measuring their spiritual well-being in terms of the sum of their private parts or their credit card transactions. Or they revolt against a one-dimensional worldview through New Age astrology, ufology, Urantia, channeling, fire-walking, "Psychic Fairies," crystals, "big foot," Marian visions, and "Vivation professionals." It is embarrassingly predictable that the fool's paradise of New Age Pied Pipers has become "the major alternative in America's spiritual life."[58]

Postmoderns are desperate for theological education, so on weekends they descend on America's largest downtown hotels and dig deep into their pockets to sit at the feet of flaky pseudoscientific "channelers" like Lazaris (pronounced Luh-ZAR-us) and patina-thin pop-spiritual thinkers like Shirley MacLaine. Yuppies (young urban professionals), buppies (black yuppies), guppies (Green yuppies), grumpies (grim, ruthless, upwardly mobile professionals), snags (sensitive New Age guys), and dinks (dual-income, no-kid couples) are yearning for coherence in their splintered lives. Shards of memory about a once-coherent story bring them, self-conscious and clumsy, to the churches of "organized religion," as romantic and unused for postmoderns as the ruins of medieval churches or the Batman cathedral.

English country vicar/television writer/theologian Peter Mullen believes there is nothing pastors do that is more depressing or dispiriting than ritualizing the rites of passage of the unchurched--their baptisms, weddings, and funerals.[59] The unchurched look to the church for morsels of meaning and experience but leave our sanctuaries still in pain from the pitifully thin gruel they obtain there. Lightweight fare sits heavily on the soul's stomach. Even if we could set the whole story at one seating, telling all would reveal little. The common memory has been shattered, the connections between story and source broken.

---- **66** ----

What he was, he was.
What he is fated to become
Depends on us.

Remembering his death,
How we choose to live
Will decide its meaning.

Spanish Civil War stretcher-bearer/Oxford professor/poet W.H. Auden[j]

---- **99** ----

People are searching for someone, for anyone, to **frame** an orthodoxy on the other side of paradox. Not for the correct set of beliefs. Nor for some generally accepted principles by which to live a straight, upright, proper life that fits in with prevailing patterns of belief and behavior. The modern world displaced the concept of orthodoxy itself--whether in music or art, religion or politics. Few ideas became normative enough during the modern era to warrant the title of an orthodoxy.

The orthodoxy on the other side of paradox to which the signs of the times speak is that orthodoxy that will **frame** a religious picture of an alternative future, that will **frame** regular, right rituals and life-transforming experiences of worship,[60] that will **frame** ordered but discordant doxologies of praise that do more than kneel to secular power.

Economist/seer/birdwatcher Robert Heilbroner liked to say that when forecasts based on economic theory failed, he and his colleagues took to telling stories. It is time for the church to take to telling stories again. Stories are, in French philosopher/Chicago professor Paul Ricoeur's reflection, "models for the redescription of the world." The orthodoxy on the other side of paradoxy will articulate a postmodern story of what it means to be a Christian. It does this canonically by establishing biblical concords --finding ways of making biblical events become concordant in the postmodern mind, identifying oneself with biblical figures, and helping perceptual antennae become more acutely attuned to picking up biblical information, images, and mysteries. It helps the New Adam and the New Eve to come to know the Bible, not as an object, as novelist/playwright/critic Gabriel Josipovici states so beautifully, but as a friend.[61]

―――――――――――――― **66** ――――――――――――――

A man is always a teller of tales,
he lives surrounded by his stories and the stories of others,
he sees everything that happens to him through them;
and he tries to live his own life as if he were telling a story.

Novelist/philosopher Jean-Paul Sartre[k]

Like the DNA strings of the genome,
or the amino acid strings of the antibody,
we humans are always stringing things together.
Even the cosmologists are belatedly getting into strings.

Neurophysiologist/professor William H. Calvin[l]

―――――――――――――― **99** ――――――――――――――

The three Great Commandments taught by Jesus Christ, while they may not "give people ideas" (as the good-natured grump said of Moses' decalogue of don'ts), give postmoderns celebrations and mysteries and stories on the **other** side of paradox.

First: "Hear, O Israel: The Lord our God, the Lord is one; and you shall love the Lord your God" (Mark 12:29-30 RSV). The starting point for postparadoxy orthodoxy is here: the first of the Three Great Commandments. It is a word that hits a nerve in every era; it is a thought that beheaded monarchs; it is a belief for which martyrs went to the stake; it is a celebration that showers the earth with shooting stars and that still today turns the world upside down.

There is one God who created one world, a uni-verse of interstellar galaxies, Planet-Earth gardens, and lifeform genes in which spiritual forces, especially love, triumph above all else. A high-flex, high-tech culture associates religion with the invisible, and the invisible with the inconsequential. Physicists teach us, however, that if anything, the invisible ought to be associated with power. A fundamental mystery of quantum fields is their astonishing vacuum energies. Nothing is more invisible or seemingly impotent than a vacuum. Yet one thimbleful of vacuum contains more energy than all the atoms in this very visible, thirteen billion light-year universe.[62]

Second: "Love your neighbor as yourself" (Matt. 22:39 RSV). Every time Jesus mentioned the first Great Commandment, he quoted the second from Leviticus 19:18. The postmodern world, where to be an American means to be individualistic, materialistic, democratic, needs a new understanding of neighboring, of the relationship of part to whole, of self to community.

"To love is to accept that one might die another death before one dies one's own" is how Marianne Wiggins's novel *John Dollar* expresses the essence of this postparadoxy orthodoxy.[63] God designed us to stand on our own. But not to stand alone. We are called to be as "distinct as the billows," as an old saying puts it, "but one as the sea." The second Great Commandment beckons us into living together in order to avoid dying together.

Third: "Love one another; even as I have loved you" (John 13:34 RSV). And how has God loved us? In the famous words of John 3:16, God so loved that God gave; or in the need-to-be famous words of Paul's hymn (Phil. 2:6-11), God so loved that there was the self-emptying of Christ--a love of loss and recovery, of agony and ecstasy, of pain and healing, of giving and receiving. The story of the life of Jesus is the story of loving others as God loves. The last of the three Great Commandments is the same as the Matthew 6 "kingdom principle"--seek first the kingdom (Christ) and all else will be added. Too much of the church is seeking revitalization when it should be seeking Christ. A revitalized church without Christ would be an anti-Christ. Christ is the church's only life.

In short, the orthodoxy on the other side of paradoxy plays the pedal notes of the gospel in a postmodern key, a harmonic sidestep here, a rhythmic doubletake there. It alters our angle of perception a bit to enable us to see and to speak the same things differently. It provides us with the reference points from which to challenge our own postmodern culture. Most critically, in a culture where text has ceased to be the key metaphor --it is now the story--a quantum spirituality will compose a master narrative, or what history of religions professor/Riverdale Center for Religious Research director Thomas Berry and Werner Heisenberg call "the New Story," Ilya Prigogine and Isabelle Stengers "the new description" of postmodern life.[64] Indeed, at this very moment a New Light movement is already mediating a transitional map of the moral universe amidst immense social and scientific change. The result is less a theology than a story that synthesizes science and philosophy with deep religious perceptions and sensibilities.

Mainline or Mainstream?

For America's once mainline, now oldline, soon-to-be "sideline" (Richard John Neuhaus) congregations, the stakes are high during this last decade of the twentieth century. "Mainline" is a railroad term that refers to the principal track on which the biggest train pulled into town, as contrasted with a "branch line" or "side track." The church is filled with a we-had-it-then-we-don't-have-it-now spirit of nostalgia for those whistle-blowing days when people would drive for miles to sit at some railway crossing just to be there when the big locomotive passed by. Happily, the church's elitist mainline days are gone forever. The metaphor of train-lines no longer fits the postmodern story-lines.

"Mainstream," on the other hand, is a riverboat term that refers to that part of the waterway where the strongest currents flowed. The church's mainstream days have just begun, but only if a New Light apologetic successfully calls the church to a biblically reformed, scientifically informed spiritual pilgrimage that can take as its interpretive model not only John Bunyan's *Pilgrim's Progress* (1678), or Lewis Carroll's *Alice in Wonderland* (1865), but also Gene Rodenberry's "Star Trek" (1966) or George Lucas' *Star Wars* (1977).

When Giants Learn to Dance (1989) and *Communities of Discourse* (1989) sit as uneasily together along the banks of a very swift river as do *Pilgrim's Progress* and *Star Wars*. Appearing within months of each another, both books trawl the choppy waters of Heraclitus's eternally changing river ("You can never step into the same river twice"), though from very different directions. By the time Kanter and Wuthnow come out of the water to reflect on their discoveries, they have both reached remarkably similar conclusions about the nature of social and historical change.

Rosabeth Moss Kanter is an economist, management theorist, and business professor at Harvard Business School. She is committed to returning new life to "mainstream" corporate life in America. Her research into surging economic currents convinces her that all "mainstreams" get clogged up, silted over, and dried out without the presence of vital "newstreams." Her book *When Giants Learn to Dance* is an eloquent appeal for the emergence of "newstream" ventures and outlooks that cut new channels and seek out different causeways than have worked in the past. All newstreams are "pains in the neck" to mainstreams, she admits. The needs of the two are very different (mainstream strokes are more backstroke and breaststroke, newstream strokes more freestyle and floating with the flow). The logic of the two is often contradictory (mainstreams prize security and conventional methods; newstreams prize high-risk tactics and explore-the-deep-end strategies). Newstreams are by their very nature "uncertain, bumpy, boat-rocking, controversial, knowledge-intense, and independent." But for all the mainstream/newstream tensions and cross currents, unless mainstreams can encourage a variety of newstreams to emerge without forcing them out of the mainstream, unless mainstreams can provide leaders with an opportunity to swim in both streams at once, any mainstream is as good as dead.[65]

Robert Wuthnow is a social scientist and historian of American religion at Princeton University. He, too, is committed to helping America's mainstream religious institutions understand the historical and sociological predicament in which they currently find themselves. In *Communities of Discourse*, perhaps the most significant contribution to the discussion of faith and social environment since H. Richard Niebuhr's *Christ and Culture*, Wuthnow charts the vectors of the difficult passage through history of three very different periods of cultural change: the Reformation, the Enlightenment, and the rise of European socialism. Each era was inaugurated when reformers were able to crack the relevance/identity dilemma, or what Wuthnow calls the "problem of articulation": They must "draw resources, insights, and inspiration" from their times so that they can "reflect it, speak to it, and make themselves relevant to it." Yet, at the same time, they must "also remain autonomous enough from their social environment to acquire a broader, even universal and timeless appeal."[66] What makes possible this "enigmatic" but emblematic culturing of movements is what he calls "communities of discourse," or what one reviewer cleverly dubbed as "social petri dishes" in which new ideas or "cultural products" can be carefully cultured.[67]

———————————————— 66 ————————————————

Objection des athées: "Mais nous n'avons nulle limiére."
The atheist's plea: "But we have no light."

Christian apologist/calculator inventor Blaise Pascal[m]

The one thing that frightens Satan
is to see a light in your heart.

Sufi proverb[n]

———————————————— 99 ————————————————

In a yet unpublished essay on the emergence of the Evangelical Enlightenment in America, historian/theologian Mark Noll comes independently to the same conclusions as Kanter and Wuthnow. On the one hand the church must master the dominant "interpretive systems of the day" if it is to be effective in proclaiming the gospel. It must be willing to use the "conceptual language" appropriate to its times, and it must not be afraid of the interplay between the gospel and the images and expressions of the surrounding culture. On the other hand, if the gospel is not to be in bondage to its own historicity, it must develop evaluative critiques of, and safeguards against, the corrupting contingent encroachments of the "primary interpretive systems."[68]

The challenge of a quantum spirituality's in-but-not-of the world posture is how to get close enough to postmodernity to grasp its exciting, emergent social, economic, and cultural realities, while, at the same time, standing far enough away for skinning and dissecting the protean spirit of postmodernism. It is only because of "newstream channels," "communities of discourse," and what I am calling "New Light communities" that the mainstream church can be well-briefed enough to stand up to the postmodern world and exalt the gospel while at the same time transcending this postmodern place and being at odds with the times. Ironically, it is only the historical perspective that helps postmodern Christians not be themselves. For the gospel is born out of as well as within all time.

Old Lights and New Lights

Historian/biographer William G. McLoughlin has written one of the most provocative studies of American religious history published in this century. In *Revivals, Awakenings, and Reform* (1978), he shows how each of the five Great Awakenings in American history has been dominated by two different types of leadership, which transcend liberal and conservative, modern and traditional, distinctions--both of them powerful, both of them persuasive for large numbers of people: Old Lights and New Lights.[69] Similarly, in their compelling investigation of our contemporary "out of joint" condition, possessing a mind-set fit for the eighteenth century while playing with the "toys" of the twenty-first, psychologist/ecologist Robert Ornstein and biologist/ecologist Paul Ehrlich distinguish between an "old minded" versus "new minded" approach to the planetary crisis.[70]

The metaphysic and metaphor of "light" is a privileged one. The Big Bang has also been called the "Primal Flash." The first words of God recorded in the Bible were "Let there be light" (Gen. 1:3). The one-word summary Jesus gave of himself was "I am the light of the world" (John 8:12). The relationship of Jesus to God is summarized in the phrase "light from light." Jonathan Edwards defined true religion as "a divine light in the souls of the saints."[71] He understood the role of the clergy to be "ministers of light" preaching "sermons of light."[72] God gave the natural world the light of the sun. God gave the spiritual world the light of Jesus Christ, "love's pure light" as we sing on Christmas Eve, whose rays are received and reflected by ministers of the gospel.[73]

───────────────── 66 ─────────────────

In your light we see light.

Shepherd/warrior/king David

Every generous act of giving, with every perfect gift,
is from above, coming down from the Father of lights.

Servant of God/pastor/saint James[o]

───────────────── 99 ─────────────────

Physicist John Archibald Wheeler, called by some the planet's greatest living cosmologist, advises those who want to take the mystery out of the phrase "quantum theory" to call it the "hunk theory of light."[74] Yet "light is the great mystery" in contemporary physics, philosopher/interviewer/Rutgers professor Renée Weber observes.[75] Light is also the metaphor for the great mystery of consciousness,[76] a one-word field of study now flourishing in virtually every area of human inquiry. Wheeler notwithstanding, more than enough mystery remains in the metaphor of light to make it the most promising image for ministry. Physical qualities like light, once thought to be continuous, are now seen as discrete and granular.

Quantum spirituality might also be called "the hunk theory of light," with three discrete "hunks" or leadership functions inherent in the theological understanding of ministry as light. To be a minister of light is, first, to impart the divine illumination oneself. This means more than simply "reflecting" the light, as poet/editor Ron Loewinsohn points out so incisively in his study of Edwards' use of light-sight metaphors: "The soul of a regenerate man is something like a mirror, but is more like a lamp, itself a source of light, an energy which is the fruit of an active process of burning."[77] Second, it is to refresh and delight those who have been in darkness. The best way to bathe a room with light is to open a window or turn on a switch. Ministry is opening windows and turning on switches all the time. Third, it is to direct people out of shadowy regions onto paths of light and to resist those forces that are trying to turn out the lights completely.

———————————— 66 ————————————

*I have often referred to myself
as an outsider on the inside of science.
The Keepers of the flame may say correctly
that they have no use for such outsiders.
Well, they don't, but science does.*

Maverick scientist/DNA researcher/literary stylist Erwin Chargaff[P]

———————————— 99 ————————————

Both Old Lights and New Lights perform the three theological functions of light. Neither lack chlorophyll. Unlike those mossbacked Christians whose fungoid faith shrivels under illumination, both Old Lights and New Lights grow and thrive in the light. The difference is the kind of light that supports them, and the kind of light they allow to pass through them. David Bohm's distinction between "transparentism" (a transparence with respect to the whole) versus "obscurantism" (obscuring the whole) captures the essential contrast between Old Lights and New Lights.[78] Old Light versus New Light is the difference between repetition and experimentation, between mirroring light and molding light, between gate keeping and channel opening, between going to seed and coming of age, between not being able to say good-bye and saying hello.

Both Old and New Lights, confronting in their own day the world being built by the Enlightenment, found it wanting. But while New Lights molded out of the past a future in the present, Old Lights simply mirrored the past in the present. For example, the two theological factions that emerged from the First Great Awakening were embodied by Old Light Charles Chauncey and New Light Jonathan Edwards. Both personified Enlightenment values. Both were critical of the church that the Enlightenment created. Both recast life issues in terms of individual and community, hierarchy and democracy, independence and centralization--productive terms for eighteenth-century New Englanders. The difference was that Edwards did so in ways that transcended old boundaries (see his *Some Thoughts Concerning the Present Revival of Religion in New England*, 1742) and ushered us into a new historical landscape. Chauncey's psychology, however, remained medieval (see his *Seasonable Thoughts on the State of Religion*, 1743), locked in modes of thought and action that owed little to the movement of history and changing experiences, that were not much given to the breaking of molds. In the words of the current dean of American religious historians, Edwin Scott Gaustad, "Although both [Chauncey] and Edwards were concerned with separating the wheat from the chaff, the attention of the one [Edwards] was fixed on the wheat, the other on the chaff."[79]

Today's Old Lights are the valedictorians of culture, their lives an elegy for an expiring or moribund mental world. Protecting the old from the new, the forces of order from the irruptions of the Spirit, Old Lights come in both fundamentalist and New Age varieties. They are known by their almost despairing end-of-an-era exercises in hand wringing, nail biting, whistleblowing, red flag waving. They often exhibit a cynical criticism of the postmodern scene or grimace at a menacing technological future. Their response to change is narrow and dogmatic. Their moral panic would return us to ancient beliefs after this destructive historical interlude with modernism, or Christianity, or whatever. That is why the Old Light vision of the future is rigid with old stuff--icebergs of anachronisms like dousing, witchcraft, animism, astrology, "neo-paganism" (aka New Ageism), or literalism, demonology, and bibliomancy (á la fundamentalism). For Old Lights it is not bliss in this dawn to be alive. Old Lights include such noted antimodernists as "architect"/radio buff Lewis Mumford, who warns us against machines; social critic/theological analyst Jacques Ellul, who warns us against technique; philosopher/educator/editor Allan Bloom, who warns us against electronic culture; poet/novelist/philosopher Georges Bataille, who warns us against deprivation; lecturer/activist Jeremy Rifkin, who keeps warning us against the fear of the month--biotechnology, computer culture, and so on; Baptist minister/editor/seminary dean Harold Lindsell, who warns us against liberalism; democratic socialist/political activist Michael Harrington, who warns us against conservatism; pastor/lobbyist/ university administrator/bootlegger's grandson Jerry Falwell, who used to warn us against communist conspiracies; Russian artillery captain/political prisoner/Nobel novelist Alexander Solzhenitsyn, who used to warn us against Soviet totalitarianism.

Old Lights are revivalists of the old. Their movements are defensive in nature, often constituting classic examples of letting the dead bury the living. Old Lights include the resurgent fundamentalists in every religion who put a freeze on history and fortify their adherents against the "new dark age" in which they are forced to live.[80] "Back to the Bible," Old Lights shout; "back to the Koran," Old Lights thunder. But not everything Old Lights say is wrong. Much is right. Even a stopped clock is right twice a day, the old adage reminds us.

New Light Credo as Science-Art

The other wave of spiritual energy inundating the planet comes through New Lights. In the same way New Light Jonathan Edwards met modernity head-on, and thus was enabled to speak to the ills of his society, so today's New Light movement meets the postmodern era head-on, confronting its revolutioning re-formulations and directing a devastating critique against its accommodations of religious truth to scientific knowledge.

In one sense the whole of this book is an extended meditation on the nature of true New Light leadership and on how more of these voices of the third millennium might emanate from America's churches and synagogues. One of the biggest unsolved problems in astronomy today is the case of the "missing mass" and "missing light." The most potentially powerful and massive compounds of our universe--comprising 90 percent or more of the mass of the cosmos--is hidden in the heavens.[81] The church has the same missing-light, missing-mass problem.

—————————— **"** ——————————

*The mismatch of our brains with our environments
has been produced by millennia of effort,
by the skill, ingenuity, and drive of our species--
by the very minds that are now out of step
with the world they live in.*

Psychologist/prophet Robert Ornstein and biologist/prophet Paul Ehrlich[q]

—————————— **"** ——————————

Not to batter the point at the beginning, New Lights can perhaps best be introduced by means of consul-general/ambassador/Oriental and African Studies Institute director Sir Reader Bullard's five criteria for the makings of a great scholar/scientist and art historian/television host Sir Kenneth Clark's five standards of a true artistic masterpiece. New Light leadership in the postmodern era will need to be an art-science: both hard science and high art. It is time once again to trot out the ancient, even "tired," topic of the arts and sciences, which educational psychologist/social behaviorist Jerome Bruner likens to "the faint lavender of old closets whose family gowns and dress suits and old uniforms are too interesting to throw away yet plainly not suited to modern living, brought out only on special occasions."[82] Philosophy, technology, and theology are bringing this "once tired topic" of science and the humanities alive again.

In Bullard's estimation, the first necessity in the making of a great scientist/scholar is insatiable curiosity. English poet/dramatist John Milton once compared truth to an entity sliced into a thousand fragments and scattered to the four winds. "From that time ever since," Milton continued, "the sad friends of truth such as durst appear, imitating the careful search that Isis made for . . . Osiris, went up and down gathering up limb by limb still as they could find them. We have not yet found them all, Lords and Commons, nor ever shall doe, till her Master's second coming."[83] Since truth is never found in one piece, the pursuit of truth requires insatiable curiosity.

"
---

*I am entirely certain that historians
should read more novels and poems,
look at more buildings and paintings,
and listen to more music.
I am almost as sure that students of literature and art
should read more history.*

American cultural historian/social critic Nelson Manfred Blake[r]

"

New Lights are holists, not reductionists, in their busybody curiosity about the world and its workings. In the eyes of modernity, New Light theology may appear to ramble in fields of scholarship overgrown in odd learning. That is because holistic theology is a many-sided, multicurved theology of comprehensive vision. Its readiness to enter unchartered waters is matched only by their willingness to trudge shorelines in search of cultural artifacts that have been beached, washed up on self-made islands of neglect and despair. Intellectually adventurous and wide-ranging, New Lights roam everywhere and browse anything, beachcombing for the telltale detail in everything from biography, buildings, billboards, and bumper stickers. Novelist/poet/professor Maya Angelou calls this a "catholic kind of read-ing, and catholic kind of storing."[84] A New Light leader is one whose being is both antennae and transmitter, picking up the various signals and vibrations emanating from the social, political, economic, and cultural realms. Open to and absorbent of popular culture, New Light mental cam-eras click when others are stashed away, in an omnivorous devourment of quenchless curiosity.

47

Just as the writers Jonathan Edwards venerated most were the two architects of the modern world--scientist Isaac Newton and philosopher/rhetoricist John Locke (Edwards confessed to reading them "more greedily than a miser gathering handfuls of gold")--so the greatest literature, music, art, philosophy, and science of the postmodern era will be the natural habitat of New Light leaders. Ideally New Lights will encounter in the original the best minds of their day, but this is less important than their wide-angled awareness of what is happening all around them. Voltaire, the popularizer of Newton in France, observed, "Very few people read Newton because it is necessary to be learned to understand him. But everybody talks about him."[85] What might be termed "filtered familiarity" with diverse and hybrid genres is a benchmark of the New Light movement.

Second, there needs to be a burning, all-consuming interest in one's subject. Philosopher Eric Voegelin's word "cosmion" refers to "a well ordered thing that has the character of the universe." New Lights offer up themselves as the cosmions of a mind-of-Christ consciousness. As a cosmion incarnating the cells of a new body, New Lights will function as transitional vessels through which transforming energy can renew the divine image in the world, moving postmoderns from one state of embodiment to another.[86]

———————————— 66 ————————————

Humor is the last stage of existential awareness before faith.

The world's first postmodern theologian/Danish philosopher Soren Kierkegaard[s]

———————————— 99 ————————————

Third, a mass of accurate learning must be lightly borne. No one knows just how much heavy scholarship lies behind the New Light touch. Quantum spirituality takes an earthed posture toward itself and others. The word "earth" comes from the Latin *humus*, from which we get our words "human" and "humility." Theologian/economist/ethicist Max Stackhouse talks of the need for theology to live more humbly, or in what he terms a "humble confidence" that submits one's faith "to tests that one cannot control--to the judgment and evaluations not only of peers but of peoples who share little or nothing of one's religious commitments, gender, class, race, culture, or civilizational history."[87] Whether wisdom is defined in Socratic terms (the knowledge of ignorance) or in Patristic terms (the ignorance of knowledge), there is no cause for boasting. In the words of Paul, "There is no place for human pride in the presence of God. You are in Christ Jesus by God's act" (1 Cor. 1:29-30 NEB). The more New Lights shine, the more they realize their reflected glory.

Fourth, without an unfailing supply of energy for long-haul projects, the highest levels of achievement cannot be reached. In an energy world, where life is movement and every subject a verb, "endurance" is the survival word, not "patience" (the biblical concept is better translated "endurance" than "patience" anyway--consider the "endurance" of Job). Charisma inheres not in personal glamour or glory but in a kind of transcendental energy and zeal that permeates everyday life. The power of New Light charisma comes not from sacred office or ritual responsibilities but from a dynamic persona of personalities, plays, and performances that is part poetry, part dance; part sorcery, part science.

Fifth, a scientist/scholar will draw from a fund of humor, directed mainly at himself or herself. A woman called the British preacher/evangelist C. H. Spurgeon "unspiritual" for saying so many funny things in the pulpit. He responded to her criticism by telling her she shouldn't think so, if she only knew how many funny things he thought of in the pulpit and didn't say. The only true response to truth, the ancient Chinese suggested, was laughter. "If one does not laugh," they said, "it would not be the Tao."

Laughter issues in a lightness of heart and brightness of mind that gives to life invigorating and agitating grace. Without laughter in all its forms, the three energy patterns of the human emotional plane--love, anger, and fear --remain scrambled and dysfunctional. European literature scholar/writer Mikhal Bakhtin presents laughter as one of life's essential forms of truth. New Lights lead the world to new laughs and new truths.

New Light Credo as Art-Science

In Kenneth Clark's five-part formulation in *What Is a Masterpiece?* (1979), the first aesthetic judgment involves being "moved by the subject."[88] When Cambridge physicist/mathematician Paul Dirac was Visiting Professor at Moscow University in the fall of 1955, he was asked by the students to state his philosophy of physics. He wrote the following words on the blackboard, which have been preserved there to this day: "Physical Laws Should Have Mathematical Beauty." Because God made and selected the form of mathematics, Dirac argued, the mathematics of physics must be beautiful. Indeed, "it is more important to have beauty in one's equation than to have them fit experiment."[89]

─────────────── 66 ───────────────

Scientists talking about their own work
and that of other scientists
use the terms "beauty," "elegance," and "economy"
with the euphoria of praise more characteristically applied
to painting, music and poetry.

Art professor/film producer Judith Wechsler[l]

─────────────── 99 ───────────────

If the essence of modernity has been the loss of beauty, as author/

49

painter/storyteller Pierre Delattre argues,[90] New Light mindedness endows contemporary experience with epiphanic effects. Putting words and images together so they have spiritual and emotional consequences, as well as rational and empirical connections, is the essence of becoming New Lighted. In the presence of New Lights, people are made to feel harmonious and beautiful again. Quantum spirituality is more playing music or painting a picture, less performing arithmetic or quantifying an experiment.[91] The dialogue partner for postmodern theology is less philosophy than art, especially music.[92] It is this sense of aesthetics that gives New Light ministries and theologies a musicality, a symphonic rather than a monologic sound.

Second, a masterpiece is not "one person thick, but many persons thick," as Clark paraphrases Lethaby's famous observation.[93] In an important article on new leadership models, Suzanne W. Morse argues that emerging leadership patterns are not about one person but about communities of people engaged in the business of doing their work **together**.[94] The New Light movement, like the Bible, is more the result of collective than of individual endeavor. This shift in leadership from the individual to the community, or what campus minister/educational theorist G. Max Case identifies as the "group leadership" phenomenon, is one of the most radically new components of the New Light leadership style.

"Thickness" extends vertically in time, however, as well as horizontally in space. The New Light apologetic passes beyond modernity without leaving behind the truths of modernity. New Lights are as concerned about the direction postmodern society is headed in as Old Lights are. The difference is that Old Lights back into the future while New Lights face into the future, educated to work on uncertain territory, equipped to minister in danger zones, and able to steer a steady course through the eddies and currents of spiritual pollution that abound everywhere.

The New Light movement brings to bear the mind of Christ on a postmodern mind-set, rooting up renewal through such diffracted viewpoints and diverse, saintly instrumentalities as John Wesley's pen, Jonathan Edwards's brains, George Whitefield's lungs, Francis Asbury's horse, Charles G. Finney's eyes, Sojourner Truth's basket, Frances Willard's feet, Chief Seattle's blanket, John Muir's bag of bread crumbs, Albert Schweitzer's doctor's kit, John XXIII's windows, Mother Teresa's knees, Billy Graham's Bible, Martin Luther King, Jr.'s voice, . . . New Lights are able to re-create, in Clark's words, "traditional forms so that they become expressive of the artist's own epoch and yet keep a relationship with the past."[95]

Third, great works of art promote a "profound assertion of human values."[96] New Lights narrate with their lives the story of how to be in harmony with the great living system we call Planet Earth, how to respond to our universe religiously. The New Light movement takes on the world's greatest themes, less concerned with solving old problems within respectably "carpentered" academic categories of straight edges and right angles than with creating new scenarios of the sacred and "heritizing" the present with a well-rounded sense of tradition. New Lights often depart from Enlightenment ways of linear tidiness. For example, they have stopped exclusively "squaring the circle," "spelling it out," thinking "straight" or with a "level head," putting the record "straight," facing the future "squarely" and out-facing each other "fair and square," eating "three squares a day," searching for "the sum total" of the matter or "the bottom line"--because they do not always believe these straight-minded, stream-lined ways to be definitive of thinking.

New Lights buck the currents of modernity with a dissident piety that becomes not simply counterculture, but counter-church. The New Light movement is a minority movement within a religious subculture. Since moral neutrality is a negation of all values, the New Light movement feels the need to get things said, even unpopular things. It challenges the religion establishment's enthrallment to enthronement with a movement mentality and spirituality.[97] New Lights spend their lives looking for the kind of coherencies and larger frameworks people need for unifying human experience, listening for the drumbeat of the Word amid the downbeats of the world.

66

La science, la nouvelle noblesse! Le progrès.
Le monde marche! Pourquoi ne tournerait-il pas?
Science, the new nobility. Progress.
The world marches on! Why shouldn't it turn?

French poet/Dutch soldier/German circus manager/
Greek construction worker Jean Nicolas Arthur Rimbaud[u]

99

Fourth, masterpieces are "those large, elaborate works in which a painter has put in everything he knows in order to show his complete supremacy in his art."[98] Since postmodern religion arises at the crossroads --at the intersections where science and the humanities, symbol and structure, meet--New Lights will be some of the great sprawlers of scholarship: twenty-first century Bacons, prepared to take all knowledge as their province, and twenty-first century Wagners, prepared to synthesize all art (or what Wagner called *Gesamtkunstverk*). They will disavow the disciplinary barriers to knowledge at the same time they respect the knowledge that comes out of the disciplines themselves. New Lights can minister to the whole person because they can deal with wholes and are comfortable around wholes. Reeling from the objective odor coming from the cool spaces of abstractions and clinical detachments, New Light tendencies are attached, participatory, and thermionic (able to convert heat into electricity). A favorite saying of Nazi-resistance leader/nuclear physicist/Nobel laureate Niels Bohr was written in the eighteenth century by German poet Friedrich von Schiller: "Only wholeness leads to clarity/And truth lies in the abyss."[99] New Lights thus will wear no uniform. They will be virtually impossible to pin down on a spectrum of left to right. In a church and culture that expects everyone to wear a uniform, New Lights are not ideologically identifiable. They are disturbers of the false peace of all party platforms.

Breaking out of the clone syndrome, it is New Light's nature, as it was Jesus' and Paul's natures, to elude all definition. In words taken from self-educated/day laborer/social critic Colin Wilson's first book, the international bestseller *The Outsider* (1956), New Lights see "too deep and too much" to easily conform to the conventions of mass society.[100] British evangelical/biblical scholar James D.G. Dunn, in his essay "Was Jesus a Liberal? Was Paul a Heretic?" finally has to answer yes. Both Jesus and Paul were "outsiders," he writes, "people who did not fit neatly into the pigeon holes and categories of their time, people who challenge and break an old paradigm and round which a new paradigm coheres."[101] One time, on the issue of the resurrection, Jesus sides with the Pharisees against the Sadducees, who believed that only what was written in the law should be a part of faith. The Sadducees deemed Jesus too open to other perspectives, too willing to cross boundaries, too inclusive of others. At other times Jesus was castigated by the Pharisees for being too casual, even cavalier, toward the law--for example, sabbath observances (Mark 2:23-28), food laws, (Mark 7:1-5), and the Corban (Mark 7:10-13). The Pharisees rejected Jesus and attacked him for trying too hard, going too far in interpreting the law in the context of the day in which he lived. In short, Jesus was claimed by none of the factions of Judaism of his **day**--not the liberals, the evangelicals, or the fundamentalists, not the Essenes, the Pharisees, or the Sadducees.

66

The greatest tragedy of theology in the past three centuries
has been the divorce of the theologian
from the poet, the dancer, the musician, the painter,
the dramatist, the actress, the movie-maker.
French Dominican theologian/historian M.D. Chenu[v]

99

The aura of artistry carries with it marginality, austerity, and originality. The jolt of originality and multiplicity of perspectives denies the New Light apologetic easy satisfactions. Its "oddly godly" appearance, as someone has called it, makes sure that no one will like all it has to say. This is because modernism's either/or conceptual categories are crumbling, its familiar left-right dichotomies displaced, its hard-core party labels bankrupt. New Lights can be proud that they sustain values that confound the conventions if not drive the conventional daft. Whether one agrees with New Light thinking or not, at least there is something to argue about. In a world of disappearances, where the rarest thing around is clean, fresh air, New Lights bring to the church the air that can bring back the breath of life.

Finally, Clark's last assertion is that a masterpiece cannot escape using "the language of the day, however degraded it may seem." One of the distinctive features of postmodernism is the dissolution of distinctions between "high" culture and "mass" or popular culture.[102] For example, New Light preachers enter into an unusually intimate and "high" relationship with hearers through what might be termed "Vox Pop" preaching. The "high" style of "Vox Pop" preaching less abolishes the difference between high and low than rejects the exclusivity of "high culture" or highbrow communication for lick-the-bowl-of-life congress with the customs and voices of the people. This was one of the major complaints New Light revivalist Charles G. Finney had against the Old Lights, or what he called "Old School" clergy of his day: They mistakenly "took for granted that [their] hearers were theologians."[103] In the same way the artist of a masterpiece must become "absorbed by the spirit of the time in a way that has made his individual experiences universal,"[104] so New Light canvases provide color symphonies of information and images showing how one can be in touch but not in tune with postmodern culture in all its myriad forms, from rock videos to rock gardens.

Quantum spirituality involves a postmodern aesthetic steeped in metaphor, a style of administration as an embodiment of divine order, a style of management as more "design science" than "decision science." It is enormously suggestive that pioneer quantum electrodynamics researcher/ Los Alamos group leader/California Institute of Technology theoretical physicist/painter Richard Phillips Feynman, who before his death in 1988 was reportedly the smartest person alive, has had his writings arranged into verse form by an admiring colleague. New Lights have a love affair with language; they are poetic personalities not averse to verbal patterning and punning. Literature claims a major role in New Light communication of the gospel. New Lights also have a love affair with people wherever they are found; they are come-hither, prismatic personalities not averse to picking up, and not just with a pair of scholarly tongs, peoples' junk language of clichés, slang, slogans, catch-phrases, pious swearings.[105] A chief source of New Lights' power will inhere in their ability to imprint images--to offer people images for which they can live, by which they can die. To use Aristotle's phrase, they must be "masters of metaphor,"[106] yoking ideas together more imagistically, wit by wit, than logically, brick by brick. Or to adapt Walt Disney's charge to his "Disneyoids," they must become "imagineers," engineers of the image and imagination.

Sky in the Soul

The time is ripe for a quantum spiritual involution as earthshaking for theological and church life as Darwin's theory of evolution was for the biological sciences and philosophy and as the quantum revolution of the mid-1920s was for physics and technology. But it will not take place until the modernist obsession with microscopes, with insignificant "Everyman" and "pathographies,"[107] has been broken, permitting a renewed appreciation for telescopes that pinpoint the power of "a thousand points of light" shining in the darkness. The fashion of weak lights in the darkness, or what activist/philosopher/psychologist John Gardner calls "nonleadership," must end, and with it the tendency of specialization and professionalization to drain off "potential leaders into marvelously profitable nonleadership rolls."[108] New Light leadership is the resymbolization of the historic Christian landscape, the reenchantment of the Christian sky. New Lights put sky back into the soul.

"

So that from this we can deduce
that in the infinite distances
there must be a place
*there **must** be a place*
where all is light
and that the light from that high place
where all is light
simply hasn't got here yet . . .

Poet/playwright/editor Lawrence Ferlinghetti[w]

"

Modernity gave up stargazing. Greatness was not in good form. Ultramodernism was more interested in polished skeletons, or in holding the keys to closets with skeletons in them, than in flesh-and-blood "heroes." Actually, modernity wouldn't have known what to do with its loudly lamented lost heroes and "giants in the land" if it had them, which it did in abundance. New Lights are not heroes or giants. Rather they are what Irish novelist/linguistics master James Joyce called "epiphanies of the ordinary," luminaries who light with their lives paths to "the way, the truth, and the life," lodestars who orient others to the cosmos's dazzling constellations of mysteries and wonders. New Lights help others experience the light force of Light.

One "sign of the times" that such a New Light awakening is underway is that the church's daylight deprivation seems to be coming to an end. We are only beginning to understand the biomedical significance of moonlight and sunlight in determining every aspect of our health and well-being.[109] The key to the future is whether religious communities will continue to emerge from their indoor habits and confined environments and bathe themselves in light--the light less that of "What a friend we have in Jesus" than "What a friend Jesus has in us" (John 15:14), less of "Let nothing you dismay" than "Let something you dismay"--a light that shines less with the "faith in Christ" than with the "faith of Christ," a light that does not reflect the widespread agnosticisms that **believe in God** (both the Devil and 98 percent of the American people do that) but that rises in morning-stars of prayer and praise that **believe God**. Only then will the church cease being Old Light, no light, or out of light.

Image Intermezzo I: Pigeon-Walking

Have you ever noticed that pigeons walk funny? Passenger pigeons may now be extinct, but almost three hundred different kinds of other pigeons are thriving as never before. What does one do with an oversupply of street pigeons, called "diggs," and all the fleas, bugs, ticks, mites, rats and droppings they bring with them?

If one is a major metropolitan center like Detroit, one races them. If one is Bayonne, New Jersey, one passes a law forbidding "unlicensed" pigeons from flying over the city. If one is former Harvard mathematician/songwriter Tom Lehrer, one writes a song like "Poisoning Pigeons in the Park."

If one lives in an apartment in New York City, one experiments with birth control pellets, carbide shells and black rubber owls. If one is a resident of Montbeliard, France, one puts out alcohol-soaked feed in hopes that the pigeons can then be easily picked up and carted away.

If one is an ornithologist, one studies them. Charles Walcott, executive director of the Cornell Laboratory of Ornithology, has unearthed why pigeons walk funny. It seems that every pigeon is born with a couple of "handicaps."

The first involves sex--one of the biggest problems pigeons have in life is identifying the sex of other pigeons.[1] The second concerns walking--as long as pigeons are in motion, they cannot see their surroundings accurately. Pigeons have learned to compensate for this disability by developing a unique way of walking. They go so far, then abruptly stop, pivot, cock their heads, then start again. Walcott called my attention to a 1978 *Journal of Experimental Biology* article in which psychologist/educator/ornithologist B.J. Frost (Queen's University, Kingston, Ontario) speculates that the momentary stillness of their heads allows pigeons to become aware of movement around them, while the motion of their bobbing heads enables them to detect depth and distance. It is partly from this odd way of walking that we get the term "pigeon-toed."

We must not laugh at pigeons. We also have the exact same disability. We move too fast to see clearly. Our lives are so crowded, our calendars so gridlocked, that "to wrestle our desire another way, to face it around to see its eyes." The Greek word metanoia is nothing more than a word for pigeon-walking.

But one metanoia is not enough. Christians are a pigeon-toed people. We cannot go far without things getting out of focus, without life becoming blurred again, without needing more consciousness transformations.

The white dove of love and peace is nothing more than a glorified pigeon.

One of the greatest things pigeons can teach us is how to walk spiritually.

we cannot see and judge the movement of God around us unless we too learn to be pigeonlike-- to stop, pivot, gain perspective and then start again.

When Jesus called his first disciples, he found Peter and his fishing boat partners by the Sea of Galilee, hauling in their nets from the water onto dry land. His first word to them was "Repent. Believe the gospel. Follow me. I will make you fishers of men and women." The Greek word for "repent" is metanoia, which means literally "a change of mind" or "an about face." In other words, one day you are walking in a certain direction. Then a metanoic experience happens, and you find yourself re-turning and facing a totally new direction--a new way of living and walking in the world. Poet/mythologist/ psychotherapist Sheila Moon describes the self-sense process as one of "turning," as learning

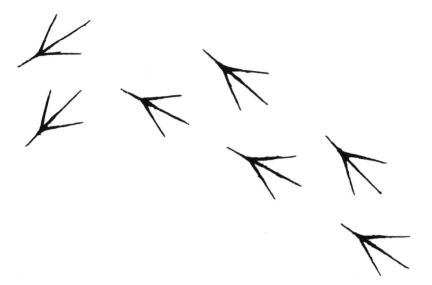

LOGOS

THE FIRE OF ENERGY: "THE WORD . . ."

Spiritmatters

A long time ago an English professor proposed to his class the two fundamental questions of metaphysics, summarizing in shorthand fashion the legendary debate between two philosophers, the Irishman George Berkeley and the Scotsman David Hume, one of whom appeared to have demolished matter (Berkeley) and the other to have demolished mind (Hume). The examination was as follows--with answers.

1. What is mind? Answer--No matter.
2. What is matter? Answer--Never mind.

Therewith the spirituality of the Enlightenment: The metaphysics that divided spirit and matter, the theology that separated the energies of thought from the energies of things,[1] the technology that edited out the existence of "consciousness" and "spirit," the philosophy that specialized exclusively in the "mind" and "matter" components. Therewith also the negative addictions of modernity: The way energy can become motion, the way matter can become materialism.

Herewith the spirituality of postmodern apologetics: A new sensibility, featuring a mindbody metaphysics that makes something out of nothing. "To put the conclusion crudely," British astronomer/Quaker Sir Arthur Eddington wrote, "the stuff of the world is mind-stuff."[2] Mind and body are identical, not because the mind is the body in disguise, but because the body is the mind in disguise.[3] Matter is the energy of Spirit. Ultimately, all that exists is spirit. What you see is the least of what there is. Or as Paul put it in his great statement about true reality: "What is seen is transient, what is unseen is eternal" (2 Cor.4:18 REB).[4]

Quantum spirituality begins not in the heights, nor out in the breadths, but by going down to the innermost depths, where "deep calls to deep" (Ps. 42:7 NRSV). In other words, a New Light apologetic begins by providing a biblical critique of postmodernism's horizontality, its antagonism (so apparent in its art) to notions of discoverable depth, its preference for flatness, its drifting about in the shallows. From a biblical perspective, that which is lowest, closest to earth, and deepest in heart, is that which is highest, closest to God, and uppermost in mind.[5]

---------------------------- **"** ----------------------------

Everything becomes fire, and from fire everything is born.
Oracular philosopher/nobleman/Heraclitus of Ephesus[a]

---------------------------- **"** ----------------------------

From the dawn of philosophy in Greek thought, the soul was conceived as fire. Postmodernism's starting point is not with matter but with spirit, with energy, with fire and the unity of spirit and matter. The greatest contribution of quantum physics to postmodern spirituality is its reorienting us to the role of spirit; its bringing together the "great opposites" energy and matter, mind and body; its bringing to an end the binary, adversarial reading of reality.

Quantum spirituality has already made more headway into the medical community than into the church, which persists in avoiding the physics of this century and rests content with the trotting out (again and again) of the old physics. In fact, some have called the mindbody movement the "third revolution" in Western medicine--the first being the advent of surgery, the second the discovery of penicillin. Every instance of matter is the expression of a spiritual reality.

The Risk of Seeing Double

Great souls have depth, and begin in depth. As early as 500 B.C., the pre-Socratic philosopher Heraclitus, the first to use *Logos* as a term for the underlying coherence of the cosmos, brought together spirit and the depth dimension in his concept of "the deep": "You could not discover the limits of the soul [*psyche*]/even if you traveled every road so deep is its measure [*logos*]." Quantum spirituality does more than join together as one two words in all their complexity and nuance: **energymatter, mindbody, spirit-matter** (as Teilhard de Chardin called it). It also argues that the deep matters of faith begin in the realization of what Albert Einstein called "the law of the equivalence of mass and energy." Depth is achieved only by looking at two points at once: emotion and thought, intuition and reason, energy and matter, feminine and masculine, subject and object, community and individual, chance and necessity, mind and body.[6] The modern era preferred looking at life with one eye closed.

Doubleness of perception evidences unity of vision and "singlemindedness" (Col. 3:22 NEB). In its tiresome head versus heart debates, the modern world cast asunder what God put together. The result was its poverty of body and soul, its chronic difficulty with living in depth, its measurement of growth in terms of breadth not depth. Indeed, energy without depth became the American formula for success. Without reconnecting what should never have been disconnected, without putting an end to this sibling rivalry, faith cannot find its depth perception or "implicate order" (David Bohm). Depth is the source and unity of both energy and matter.

———————————— 66 ————————————

I am spirit masquerading in matter's form. . . .
I cherish the illusion of being substance,
yet I am as much the spatial nothingness of atoms.
I am as empty and as potent as the space between stars.
Electromagnetic waves slice through me;
I am a specter cleft by swords.

Scientist/soldier/conservationist/aviator Charles A. Lindbergh[b]

———————————— 99 ————————————

The word "physics" comes from the Greek word *physis*, meaning "matter." Physics is the study of the structure of matter. Quantum physics is now the reigning theory of the structure of matter. It began in the first quarter of the twentieth century with the rather inconvenient discovery that matter doesn't really exist. Matter is basically a field of energy in motion. Science has now broken out of the substance paradigm that looks outside in, denying that physicists' particles are either waves or particles (both are "things"). Looking inside out, scientists are now affirming that particles are events. Matter is more a process than a substance, more "alert" (Prigogine) and "alive" (Bohm) than static and inert, more an activity than an aggregation, more an energy event than a building material.

This quantum principle of subatomic physics was feebly foreshadowed in the seventeenth-century philosophy of Benedict Spinoza and his remarkable "double aspect" theory of mind-matter relation in which mind and matter are different aspects of the same fundamental reality. We now know better. As one scholar summarized Oxford historian/philosopher R.G. Collingwood's exorcism of "the ghost in the machine": "Body and mind are not two different aspects of man; each is the whole of man as understood from the perspective of different orders of enquiry."[7] Energy and matter are two expressions of the same higher order of reality, with the difference between them only one of degree and pedigree: The latter is devolved from the former. The Bible does not say "In the beginning was the flesh and the flesh made words." Spirit comes first. "You must be born of spirit," Jesus said to Nicodemus (cf. John 3:5).

Spirit Shadows

Every religion has a "root metaphor" that gives it depth and substance. For the Chinese it is *Tao*. For the Indians it is *Dharma*. For the Egyptians it is *Ma'at*. For the Jews it is *Berith* or *Torah*. For the Christians it is *Logos*.

──────────────── 66 ────────────────

For the logos on high plays,
stirring the whole cosmos back and forth, as it wills,
into shapes of every kind.

"The Theologian"/bishop/saint Gregory of Nazianzus[c]

──────────────── 99 ────────────────

Logos is central to understanding the Creator and the creation.[8] *Logos* embraces a wide range of meaning. For the Stoics, *logos* spelled the character and coherence of the cosmos, its reason or thought. For Philo, *logos* was the mediator between Creator and creation, the divine mode of revelation and creation. For the Hebrews, *dabar* was the "word," or "event" or "thing" or "matter" that created the world. For late Jewish thought, *Logos* was personified as Sophia or Wisdom--the cosmic breath, the eternal emanating light, God's agent in creation. *Logos* was also the combined personification of Torah and Sophia--the way, the truth, and the life.[9] For the Apostle John, *logos* was the "word of life," the "Word [that] became flesh" (John 1:14 NRSV), the source of light and truth. For the Apostle Paul, *logos* was God incarnate in Jesus Christ. For Justin Martyr, *logos* was the power at work in a fragmentary way through all creation, culminating in Jesus Christ. In short, *Logos* stands in the Jewish and Christian traditions for the mind of God, the thought of God.

The metaphysic metaphors of Western culture have shifted. In the medieval period, the universe was seen as the "great organism." In the modern period, the universe became (thanks to the scientific and industrial revolutions) the "great machine." In the postmodern period, there seem to be many metaphysic metaphors. But one of the most central surely is "the great consciousness" or the "great thought"--"thought" that is defined as the word "to think" is constructed in Chinese calligraphy: by putting "brain" and "heart" together.[10]

Thought or consciousness are now part of the theories of matter. Physicist David Bohm formulates the question this way: "Whether matter is rather crude and mechanical or whether it gets more and more subtle and becomes indistinguishable from what people have called mind."[11] There is a reason why it is difficult to find in the Bible clear distinctions between thoughts and things.

Consciousness is even more than a causal reality. The ultimate reality of the universe appears to be consciousness, out of which energymatter arises. Zoologist/evolutionary biologist Conrad H. Waddington ventured in 1975 that almost nothing is known of the properties of matter, and not enough has changed since that time to say much more. Indeed, Aristotle conceived of God as "thought thinking itself." Human minds are individual, but not singular or separated. They connect at some mysterious level not accessible to ordinary conscious awareness. God is the Spirit of the universe, the consciousness of the cosmos: its energy, its information, its thought.

Metanoia can mean, literally, "after thought." What metanoia does is turn our minds after the mind of God, transform our consciousness so that it is connected to the divine consciousness, tune us into a *logos* logic. In other words, metanoia enables a metanoized self to think God's afterthoughts. Metanoia bestows on the believer a *Logos*-Christ consciousness, a *logos* logic that is based not on dialectic and struggle, but on harmony and wholeness.

―――――――――― 66 ――――――――――

The same creative energeia [energy] of God
that created matter and worked in that matter
to bring forth plant life and then animal life
also finally brought forth human beings.
Speculative theologian/rhetoricist/bishop Gregory of Nyssa[d]

―――――――――― 99 ――――――――――

Ideas of the mind not only matter, ideas of the mind move matter, even become matter, as epistemologist/Oxford philosopher Henry Habberley Price argued in 1953 in his controversial thesis that every idea is "psychokinetic"--it materializes in some shape or form.[12] The matter of faith is embodiment. Every spirit casts a shadow. Especially God's Spirit. The shadows of the Holy Spirit are consciousness cultures called "church" and "nature."

Scottish pastor/Princeton theologian George S. Hendry steers us in the depth direction in his exploration of the connections between the Incarnate *Logos* and the Creator *Logos*: "It is the concept of God as Spirit which best enables us to grasp, in some measure at least, the identity of the *Logos* in incarnation and creation, on which the New Testament lays stress." The Spirit does three things in the Bible. First, the Spirit creates and conceives. Second, the Spirit embodies--the greatest embodiment of Spirit being the incarnation, which is replicated in the church, the body of the *Logos*-Christ, and which has cosmic dimensions in the creation of a world conceived when the "Spirit moved over the face of the waters." Third, the Spirit goes out, emanating and undulating in what Hendry calls a "dual movement"--"it loses itself in its opposite, and fulfills itself by bringing its opposite to fulfillment in itself."

But if we look at the *Logos* incarnate as paradigm of the Spirit, we can see it is not the character of Spirit either to keep itself to itself or to replicate itself, but to go out from itself, to embody itself, to lose itself in that which is remotest from itself, in order to unite that other with itself.[13]

The fundamental heresy of our time is the first spiritual law of modernism: "The trees move the wind." Not only does *logos* logic teach a different spiritual law, "The wind moves the trees." The trees teach the same law as they bow and bend each time the wind passes by.[14] Few pictures are more pathetic than those depicting the time the church has spent mooching about the technism of the modern imagination, the materialist aesthetic of the modern mind.

---------------------------------- **"** ----------------------------------

In a sense, the whole of creation
may be said to be a movement between two involutions--
Spirit in which all is involved and out of which
all evolves or devolves downward to the other pole of Matter,
Matter in which also all is involved and out of which
all evolves upward to the other pole of Spirit.

Yogin/nationalist/poet Sri Aurobindo[e]

---------------------------------- **"** ----------------------------------

The modernist mantras "Trust the process," "The System works," and "Follow logic wherever it leads," for example, have muscled to the ground the church's underdeveloped, atrophying abilities to "Trust the Spirit" and "Follow the Spirit wherever she leads." Few tales are more tragic than those told by moderns in their employment of rational arguments to defy rational thought. France's leading contemporary intellectual/social anthropologist Claude Levi-Straus's portrait of the Enlightenment as the portal to Adolph Hitler demonstrates the affinities between the words "rational" and "rationalize," and the abilities of reason, pushed to extremes of sovereignty and sufficiency, to create unreason.[15]

The barbarism of Democritian-Newtonian billiard ball rationality has been graphically portrayed since 1945 in the "rational" thinking of defense professionals strategizing the use of nuclear weapons. Scholars of the Holocaust have called our attention to the ghastly consequences of modernity's assumption that it could solve its perceived problems through rational means alone. Logic can lead from truth to falsehood faster than a car can lead to a car accident.

The most powerful forces in the universe are spiritual: the energies of divine unconditional love. The Bible teaches that God is "spirit" or "energy." But the energy of divine love was assembled in matter in the human form of the *Logos*-Christ. Jesus is God's most sublime manifestation of energymatter: "This is love: not that we loved God but that God loved us" (1 John 4:10); and again, "We love because God first loved us" (1 John 4:19). Faith in God through Jesus Christ means being transformed by the energy of God into the likeness of the *Logos*-Christ. The most important question any of us will ever answer in life, the question that we "who live the life that is a race to death" (as Dante puts the paradox of evolution and entropy) must answer, and answer more than once, is this: Who is Jesus Christ?

66

If we had chlorophyll we should feed on light, like the trees.
Christ is our chlorophyll.

Factory worker/farm servant/philosopher Simone Weil[f]

99

But how does one say "Jesus" in a postmodern world? The basic theological issues in the *Logos/Pathos* dimensions of faith are incarnational ones. The creative processes of the cosmos were consummated in the Jesus event, transforming the very structure of our existence. Jesus of Nazareth, the culmination of energymatter, prehended our possibilities in God. The energy of divine unconditional love was most formatively and fully expressed in the matter that emerged to consciousness from a cave in Bethlehem one silent night, one holy night.

Conversion as an Energetic Field:
A Case Study of John Wesley

For John Wesley the "sum of Christian sanctification," the "height and depth of perfection," is "all comprised in that one word--love." In almost every sermon Wesley delivered there is mention of love in one form or another. Love means that the forces most to be reckoned with in the universe are spiritual, not material.

The 250th anniversary of the Aldersgate myth, where John Wesley is supposed to have begun the true answering of the question "Who is Jesus Christ" has come and gone. Historians celebrated the event by returning to Wesley's journals and coming away from them with a greatly reduced sense of the importance of the "Aldersgate experience" in Wesley's spiritual life. The luster of the legend has proved hard to tarnish, however, in the popular religious mind. If anything, the Aldersgate myth has become even more of a dominant discourse and is now seen as never before as a normative convoy for the church's spiritual renewal. One reason may be because the soul of this late modern/early postmodern culture of compliance and consumption is remarkably similar to the supposed state of Wesley's soul when he got up on the morning of 24 May 1738. A self-help society that cannot come to grips with an anti-self-help gospel seems to need to turn again and again to this more-than-twice-told tale and re-enact what transpired between 5:00 A.M., which is when Wesley customarily arose for prayer, and that evening "about a quarter before nine," one of the most famous clock-checks in the history of Christianity.

---------------------------------- 66 ----------------------------------

I have come to set fire to the earth.

Rabbi/Messiah Jesus[8]

---------------------------------- 99 ----------------------------------

For thirty-six years, according to the standard Aldersgate mythology, Wesley had built his life on the grunt theory of grace, the spiritual fallacy that it does good to do good, the salvation methodology that approaches grace as a project to be managed and completed rather than a gift to be received and enjoyed. Wesley had been groaning and goading himself into goodness, which he, like John Bunyan's Pilgrim, mistook for a suburb of the Celestial City, or what theologians call a state of grace. This mistaking of Morality, Legality, and Civility for Faith, Hope, and Charity nearly cost both John Bunyan's Christian and John Wesley their lives. In other words, Wesley mistook moralism for Christianity. He sought an experience of God through attainment, not attunement--to be a do-gooder (doing good) rather than a good doer (good doing). He sought to achieve a state of "grace by good" rather than become "good by grace."

The difference between "grace by good" and "good by grace" is more than the placement of words.[16] It is the difference between a hounding, impulsive, look-what-we-can-do-and-experience activism (*Circuibat benefaciendo*: "He went about doing good") versus a holy ambition "to be like God" (the literal meaning of the word "good") through a releasing of oneself to what the Orthodox tradition calls the "uncreated energies" by which we reach *theosis*: "For it is by grace you have been saved, through faith . . . not by works, so that no one can boast" (Eph. 2:8-9 NIV).

The difference between a theology of "do-goodism" and a theology of good doing is the difference between the word "Christian" as a value term that characterizes someone's goodness ("No one is good but God alone" Luke 18:19 RSV) versus a morally neutral term defining someone's faith and consciousness. Poet/journalist/humorist/screen writer Samuel Hoffenstein satirized our preference for the question "Does he lead a good life?" over the question "Does he lead a Christian life?" in this light-hearted presentation of what it means to lead a good life:

. . . kind to women, children, worms

To speak of God in the highest terms,
To help spell words like 'tetrahedral,'
To show respect for a cathedral.

No matter how hard Wesley tried to "do good," lead a "good life," and merit righteousness, he lacked the assurance of God's mercy and the joy of grace. He was missing what he would later describe as the witness of God's Spirit with his own spirit, that he was a child of God. Or as he confided to his *Journal*, "Does all I ever did or can know, say, give, do, or suffer, justify me in His sight?"[17]

66

Humanity is the mould to break away from,
the crust to break through the coal to break into fire,
the atom to be split.

Poet/playwright/stonemason Robinson Jeffers[h]

99

On 24 May Wesley got out of bed and practiced the ancient rite of "sortilege." Pastors call it today the "lucky dip" method of Bible reading. Wesley referred to it as the "at-random-rule" method of devotions. He opened his Greek New Testament to where it would, and his finger plopped on 2 Peter 1:4: "There are given unto us exceeding great and precious promises, even that ye should be partakers of the divine nature." He interpreted this as a divine sign eliciting high expectations for what the day might bring. Later in the morning, when he snatched a few minutes for a quick devotional period, he opened his Bible, again according to the "at-random-rule." This time his finger fell on Mark 12:34: "Thou art not far from the Kingdom of God." Again, Wesley wondered what God could possibly have in mind for him that day, and his expectant soul began to uncoil from the entangled folds of its faith. "In the afternoon I was asked to go to St. Paul's," his *Journal* reads. By whom? No one knows. By God, perhaps. But at St. Paul's he listened as Psalm 130 was sung, and his whole being clung to these words: "O Israel trust on the Lord: for with the Lord there is mercy,

and with him is plenteous redemption. And he shall redeem Israel from all her sins." In the evening he went "very unwillingly" to a society meeting on Aldersgate Street. During the meeting a lay person (Christ was disclosed to Wesley by the laity) read Luther's preface to Romans, and the rest has become legendary as one of the classic moments in Western Christian piety: About a quarter before nine, while he [Luther] was describing the change which God works in the heart through faith in Christ, I felt my heart strangely warmed. I felt I did trust in Christ, Christ alone for my salvation; and an assurance was given me that He had taken away **my** sins, even **mine**, and saved **me** from the law of sin and death.

I began to pray with all my might for those who had in more especial manner despitefully used me and persecuted me. I then testified openly to all there what I now first felt in my heart.[18]

Wesley had spent his whole life educating people, and himself, in the *Logos* of God and of Jesus Christ. But *Logos* for him was reason and logic. As a child of the Enlightenment, John Wesley, like Jonathan Edwards (who called reason the "candle of the Lord"),[19] and like us, was shaped by a hierarchy of reason and emotion that finds graphic expression in our language. We "fall" in love. We "slip" into a passion. We "delve" into our subconscious. We never "delve" into reason. We never "slip" into logic. We never "fall" into analysis. The higher self is associated with logic and analysis, the lower self with intuition and feeling. The effect of this Enlightenment hierarchy, against which the Romantic movement of the early nineteenth century was a reaction, was registered in economist/philosopher John Stuart Mill's autobiographical complaint that "the habit of analysis has a tendency to wear away the feelings."[20] Romanticism tried, but failed, to achieve a better balance and dynamic between thought and emotion, mind and body.

————————————— **66** —————————————

We reason deeply when we forcibly feel.
Governess/school teacher/pioneer women's rightist Mary Wollstonecraft[i]
If you don't feel it you will never attain it.
If it does not press out of the soul . . .
Poet/novelist/dramatist/last "universal" man Johann Wolfgang Goethe[j]

————————————— **99** —————————————

What tradition supposes Wesley to have discovered at Aldersgate is that *Logos* is an energy-releasing event. Energy flows are absolutely indispensable to the emergence of life, whether biological or spiritual. Just as farmers are said to provide only 5 percent of the energy necessary to produce crops--the energy of nature provides the other 95 percent--so general reason or *logos* provides only the energy of receptivity in the divine-human encounter that leads to *Logos*. God provides the rest by other means. It does not take much to release life's higher energies. That "tiny bit of energy" encapsulated in one apple seed, David Bohm observes, is sufficient to mold "the energy and nutrients [that] come from the sun, the air, the soil, the water, and the wind" to produce an apple tree and not "a dog or a cat or whatever."[21] Faith is not a moral enterprise: "Whoever seeks to gain his life will lose it" (Luke 17:33 RSV). Faith is an energy-releasing event that raises life to a higher power, that elevates *logos* to *Logos*,[22] that grows a self into a unique soul.

---**"**---

O sages standing in God's holy fire
As in the gold mosaic of a wall,
Come from the holy fire, perne in a gyre,
And be the singing-masters of my soul.
Consume my heart away; sick with desire
And fastened to a dying animal
It knows not what it is; and gather me
Into the artifice of eternity.

Essayist/dramatist/poet William Butler Yeats[k]

---**"**---

Philosopher/physiologist/psychologist William James, in one of the great classics of western spirituality, identified the quality of faith with the quality of experiencing. The real depth of the religious life, said James, is experience.[23] Faith is knowing God from the inside out, or with what Wesley termed "the right heart."[24] According to the *Oxford English Dictionary*, "heart" has the widest possible meaning, including the functions of will as well as intellect and emotion. When Jonathan Edwards called faith a "heart religion," he did not mean that faith is dependent on experience but that faith is explored and energized through our experience, which is deeper than our reason. God imparts truths that breathe and thoughts that burn within the totality of experience.

Faith is not simply intellectual understanding, or an act of human intention, or following some salvation "how-to" manual, or assent to creedal formulations. Faith is not a matter of doing, or even being, but an experience of becoming. Experiencing is faith's most fundamental activity. Or, borrowing the vocabulary of Nobel laureate/physical chemist/classical pianist/art connoisseur Ilya Prigogine, faith is the creative movement of self-organizing processes that are better understood as verbs than as nouns.

Faith is the state of excitation of a set of metanoia-inducing, space-pervading fields--a consuming-fire transformation of consciousness that reorients one's ambitions, motives, presumptions, and energies. "Religion consists in an intercourse between ourselves and our Maker," America's greatest theologian contended.[25] Metanoia is the most transformative, explosive encounter one can have. In a metanoized self, a pilot light becomes a consuming flame. Theologian/feminist Sharon Welch describes it as a "epistemic shift" of consciousness.[26] Metanoia totally transforms one's life. It totally transforms the course of history.

Lady Chapel of London's Westminster Cathedral boasts a beautiful mosaic depicting Jesus' first miracle--the changing of water into wine at the wedding feast in Cana of Galilee (John 2:11). In the mosaic a man is pouring out tasteless, colorless, odorless water from one jug into another. But as the water touches the mouth of the second jug, it becomes a deep shade of purple, as if water were turning into fine wine, with its vibrant flavor, its rich sparkle and its delicate aroma, before your very eyes. Journalist/internationalist Jim Forest, who tells this story, relates how it had never occurred to him before seeing the mosaic that Jesus' "first sign," a "miracle of transformation," is the key to understanding everything in the gospels: "Jesus is constantly involved in transformation: water into wine, bread and wine into himself, blind eyes into seeing eyes, withered limbs into working limbs, guilt into forgiveness, strangers into neighbors, enemies into friends, slaves into free people, dead bodies into living bodies, crucifixion into resurrection, sorrow into joy."[27]

God claims everything one is. God claims every rationality. God claims every sensibility. Quantum spirituality is more than a structure of the intellect; it is more than a structure of emotion; it is more than a structure of human being. It is most importantly a structure of human becoming, a channeling of Christ energies through mindbody experience.[28] Jesus Christ gives us a new and different consciousness--a *logos* logic way of relating to the world--a new and different form of existence in everything from ethics to eschatology. What Wesley discovered at Aldersgate is what poet/translator/educator Galway Kinnell anguishes over in these words: "When the head's gallows are hanging/A heart, a youth's cry is pain."[29]

Faith is the synergy of the most powerful united fields in the universe-- reason and emotion, mind and body, cognition and action, theory and practice, object and subject, spirit and matter, spiritual and physical senses-- working together to form Christ consciousness experiences. Faith makes a metanoized mulch of all dichotomized selves and heals all discursive dualisms (one of the worst of which was "sacred" and "profane"), all disastrous separations that threaten our existence.

Deep Flow Experiences

Psychologists, anthropologists, and toyologists have converged in recent years in a flow model of understanding human enjoyment. Indeed, they have found in the "flow experience" the crucial component to a life of fulfillment and passion. An experience of flow is defined as "the holistic sensation that people feel when they act with total involvement." When one is "in flow," there is no separation of action and awareness, no raising of questions like "Why am I doing this?" or "What am I doing here?" Autotelic experiences such as rock climbing and rock dancing are flow activities because they channel the holistic experience of oneness and allthereness, of enjoying what one is doing regardless of whether external rewards come with the activity or not.[30]

Scientists have even begun dividing life into "deep flow" experiences, "microflow" activities, and nonflow states. "Deep flow" experiences include all ritual behavior in which doctrine becomes drama and the word is made flesh. "Microflow" activities encompass things that encourage flow states such as coffee breaks, television watching, and other brief encounters with total immersion in life. The absence in life of flow structures causes what is called "flow deprivation," with its attendant consequences of tiredness, sheepishness, decline in creativity, diminished alertness. When the church no longer becomes a flow structure, or has all the "rush" and intensity of a flow of molasses, there are high social and psychological costs that must be paid. People experience themselves, each other, and life as null, dull, and void. People become uncertain and guarded. For good reason, behavioral scientist/university administrator Mihaly Csikszentmihalyi titles his study of the flow experience *Beyond Boredom and Anxiety* (1975).[31]

———————————————— 66 ————————————————

When the bird and the book disagree, always believe the bird.
                                                    Birdwatcher's proverb

———————————————— 99 ————————————————

An energy event may or may not be a flow experience. Matter may or may not be enlivened. Alfred North Whitehead made it into an "ontological principle" that every event in life existed and should be approached as "an occasion of experience."[32] But it is up to us whether that **event** is made into a flow **experience** of seeing the thing in front of us, seeing it for the first time, and becoming a channel of God's grace. What athletes themselves call "the flow experience,"[33] what rock singer/actor/producer/composer Prince calls "getting up on the one," is the essence of living in the depth dimension.

The woman who touched Jesus' garment (Luke 8:43-48; Mark 5:25-34) defined the experience of flow and demonstrated the degree to which it is up to us whether "Christ" is only a flow word or a flow state. Every living organism, Australian biologist/geneticist Charles Birch insists, is composed of "events," not "things," with each event connected to every other event and the only real "event" being the whole endless process or "holomovement." Jesus is always an energy event. He excited people to transcend themselves and discover God. He energized people's faith and made it flow. But we decide whether Jesus becomes an event or an advent, a nominal encounter or a genuine flow experience.

The love of God is the most powerful energy field in the universe. But we determine whether we become one with Love's divine energies and activities. We decide, as rock star Prince puts it about his music, whether we allow ourselves to keep "getting up on the one" by hitting the beat and reaching the rhythmical flow of the "danceless dance," the "artless art," the "motionless movement."

Augustine said that we "know" only what we "love." Our popular language of knowledge, with its reflectaphors of give and take, submission and dominance, reveals the degree of sensuality that goes with "knowing"-- we "get into" this subject, we "get on top of" that topic. Without *Eros*, there can be no *Logos*. Mystic philosopher/"Buddha of American Zen"/philosophical entertainer Alan Watts called this life's "backward law": Fight to control the water, and you drown; it is only in relinquishing oneself to the water, letting go and receiving it, that you float and rise to the experience of flow.[34] "All to Jesus, I Surrender . . ." is how the hymnwriter Judson W. Van Deventer expressed it in 1896.

The Greek word translated as "power" in English is *dynamis*, from which we get the word "dynamo." Where divine activity is at work, there will be the dynamics of power, dynamics given by the Holy Spirit (of whom the Greek word *energeia* is used in the Second Testament). Jesus' power flowed from his dynamic person and personality. The energy that flows through the body, according to vibrational and bioenergy medicine, is the major healing component in any medical treatment. Monitoring equipment can actually register the healing effects of "touch therapy," as a nurse's holding of an intensive-care patient's hand can bring **measurable** stability to erratic heartbeats.[35]

"Some one touched me; for I noticed that power had gone out from me" (Luke 8:46 RSV), Jesus professed. The healing process involves the transfer of energy from one source to another, energy which can be blocked at either end by negative attitudes or unbelief. But only one woman had faith enough to act in faith, as a petitionary prayer reaches out in faith, to touch the hem of his garment. Only that one person was healed. Jesus called "faith" the "flow experience" of turning toward him in complete dependence, the metanoia of our fused, unseparated self: body and mind, action and intention.

"Who touched me?" Jesus asked. When the Apostle Thomas refused to believe, Jesus said, "Touch me." In some languages the word for "prayer" comes from the phrase "to stroke the face of God." Energy must be made flesh in a material way. There is no such ghost as an immaterial, bodiless Christianity. Sensitive to **her** body, the hemorrhaging woman felt pain even after twelve years of the deadening discharge. Sensitive to **his** body, Jesus felt pressed on all sides. New Light leadership will constantly be pressed into service, pressed on all sides, even pressed out of shape: "I felt strength go out of me."

There are a lot of pained and painfully needy people out there who will swarm around an energy source like flies. Flies throw up on their food to pre-digest it before they suck it in. Like flies, needy people will throw up their insides all over an energy source ("spilling one's guts") before they attempt to suck it in. They can't help themselves. In whatever manner energy sources resist being drawn in by the voracious appetites of human neediness, New Light energy will never allow need to get lost in the crowd, pain to get numbed over the years, or hurt to go untouched.

Fields transmit charges or disturbances. Something brushes you as it passes through your field. You don't know what the moving energy is, or who it is, but you've been touched. Sometimes we will "see" and heal human need. Other times we will release or receive healing energies without "seeing" or "knowing" who is in our field. But always we will touch and be touched--in prayer, in baptism, in greeting, in healing. Not to touch is to withhold grace and good and healing. To touch is to be close. To pray is to be so close to God that one can reach out and stroke the very face of God.

———————————————— 66 ————————————————

Every soul that touches yours--
Be it the slightest contact--
Gets therefrom some good;
Some little grace; one kindly thought;
One aspiration yet unfelt;
One bit of courage
For the darkening sky;
One gleam of faith
To brave the thickening ills of life;
One glimpse of brighter skies--
To make this life worth while
And heaven a surer heritage.

English novelist/book review editor/moralist George Eliot[1]

———————————————— 99 ————————————————

Science is now more respectful of subjective ways of knowing than ever before. There is no true knowledge without acknowledgement. Understanding comes **after**, not **before**, we have experienced. Or in the words of Peter Mullen, "There is no understanding without standing-under."[36] Faith is not a feeling. Faith is understanding, and mindbody experience is the ultimate way of knowing, whether it be knowing God or knowing another human being. Mindbody experience is the ultimate way of touching and healing: "With all [Christ's] energy, which so powerfully works in me" (Col. 1:29 NIV). Without faith transforming an energy event into a flow experience, hands grope in the dark, finding nothing to touch.

A stranger approached a little boy flying a kite so high it was out of sight. "What are you doing?" the stranger asked. "I'm flying a kite," the boy replied. "How do you know there is a kite?" "I can feel the pull of it" was the reply. How do we know there is a living Christ in a postmodern world?

We can sense the pull of the Christ consciousness. We can experience the depths, the energy, the ecstasy of life. We can see his face in the faces of those we touch, as Jacob was the first to notice: "To see your face is like seeing the face of God" (Gen. 33:10 RSV). Postmoderns feel in order to think.

Partly for this reason postmodern theological understandings need to be built on aesthetic categories, the most basic of which is beauty. Thirteenth-century scholastic philosopher/theologian/saint Thomas Aquinas defined beauty as a triangle of three interlocking, interacting components: radiance, harmony, and wholeness. Conversely, postmodern aesthetic theory needs to take into consideration theological categories, the most basic of which is love. Yale social psychologist/love scientist Robert J. Sternberg defines love as a triangle of three interlocking, interacting components: passion, commitment, intimacy.[37]

If postmodern apologetics is to be an exercise of aesthetic as well as theological judgment, there must be present what I like to call the three "beauty marks" of faith: the wholeness of intimacy, the harmony of commitment, the radiance of passion. The discussion that follows is an attempt at formulating a theological aesthetics in which the geometrics of triangular love and triangular beauty have been smoothed into an encircling and encompassing oneness.

The Mysticism of Flash Lights and Flood Lights

The words modern and skeptic went together in the same way postmodern and spiritual go together. Postmodern culture is hungry for the intimacy of psychospiritual transformations. It wants a "reenchantment of nature." It's aware of its ecstasy deprivation. It wants to know God "by heart." It wants to light an inner fire, the circulating force of divine energies flowing in and flowing out. The primal scream of postmodern spirituality is for primal experiences of God. George Gallup, Jr., believes that this is the most important discovery the Gallup Poll has uncovered since its founding in 1935. Religious experience is the focal point in faith development. One third of Americans profess to having religious experiences. In fact, a major reason people don't go to church is their belief that these religious experiences will not be taken seriously by the church.[38]

The tap roots of religious experience rest in the holy, as sociologist/antimodernist Lutheran Peter Berger points out so majestically in *The Sacred Canopy* (1967).[39] Sarah Lawrence College literature professor/mythologist Joseph Campbell captured the primacy of the flow experience in these words:

> People say that what we're seeking is a meaning for life. I don't think that's what we're really seeking. I think that what we are seeking is an experience of being alive, so that our life experiences

74

on the purely physical plane will have resources in their own innermost being and reality, so that we actually feel the rapture of being alive. That's what it's finally all about.[40] Unless human energies are released by an overwhelming and wholesome encounter with the numinous, "the rapture of being alive," faith's depths will barely be two inches deep, its roots dismissive of meaning. New Light leaders are bearers of the divine fire, connectors of the divine energy. They infuse the church with new energy by helping people get in touch with the limitless supply of Jesus energy that comes from the active, creative operation of God's continual incarnation in the world.

————————— 66 —————————

No heart is pure that is not passionate,
and no virtue is safe that is not enthusiastic.
Materialist philosopher/baron Paul Henry Thiry d'Holbach

————————— 99 —————————

One of the most paralyzing of contemporary delusions is that moderns lead lives rich and deep in real experience. To be sure, world religions scholar/sociologist Robert Bellah's contemporary classic *Habits of the Heart* (1985)[41] demonstrates repeatedly that Americans make feeling as the ultimate criterion of measurement for everything. From morals to money, the basis for decision-making in American popular culture is to consult one's feelings. Bellah has even discovered that the dominant reason moderns go to church is to feel good about themselves.

————————— 66 —————————

The world demanded awe,
because this was a voyage through the stars.
But he [astronaut John Glenn] couldn't feel it.
The backdrop of the event, the stage, the environment,
the true orbit . . . was not the vast reaches of the universe.
It was the simulations. Who could possibly understand this?
Novelist/journalist/Friendship VII chronicler Tom Wolfe[m]

————————— 99 —————————

Here is the rub, and the nub, of the modernist dilemma. Modernists wanted the feel of experience, not the real thing. French sociologist/philosopher Jean Baudrillard's sociological ontology of the transition from modernity to postmodernity even makes simulacrum the primary reality. "Simulation is master, and nostalgia, the phantasmal parodic rehabilitation of all lost referentials, alone remains." Life does not exist outside simulations of the real, and meaningful experiences of life are now symbolic exchanges and simulacra of reality. In other words, "the real thing" is now simulacrum.[42]

Further, what modernists got used to "feeling" was themselves, not creation or the Creator. Experience came to refer to human experience--getting in touch with one's "self"--rather than the unition experience of the whole, of the self with all that is outside the self, or of the experience of God, either from within or in everything without. This is why novelist Saul Bellow argues in *Mr. Sammler's Planet* (1969) that modern culture has become a culture of ideas and theories without "sensations and experiences."[43] Similarly, T.S. Eliot complains that "the trouble with the modern age is not merely the inability to believe certain things about God and man which our forefathers believed, but the inability to **feel** towards God and man as they did."

"

Now, therefore, can we find anew the power to name God in a mystical-prophetic way? That is theology's central postmodern question.

Priest/metaphysician/theologian David W. Tracy[n]

"

Mysticism, once cast to the sidelines of the Christian tradition, is now situated in postmodernist culture near the center. In part, the physics of David Bohm and Fritjof Capra are ways of responding to culture's having pushed it there.[44] In the words of one of the greatest theologians of the twentieth century, Jesuit philosopher of religion/dogmatist Karl Rahner, "The Christian of tomorrow will be a mystic, one who has experienced something, or he will be nothing."[45] Too many people are nothing, as our empty pews are shouting to us, because we give them neither an energy-fire experience of Christ nor the Christ of an energy-fire experience. We may help them apprehend reality through the rudiments of mystical specula-tions, but not the rapture of flow experiences. The words of Boston's Trinity Church preacher/Bishop of Massachusetts Phillips Brooks are as true now as they were when first spoken in 1907: "Much of our preaching is like delivering lectures on medicine to sick people." Mysticism (which Einstein called "cosmic religiosity") is metaphysics arrived at through mindbody ex-periences.[46] Mysticism begins in experience; it ends in theology. Without the heartfelt experience of a healing God, there can be no mystics.

Somewhere on the journey from Jerusalem to Jericho, there must be a Damascus Road. It does not matter whether these ambushing, energy-releasing experiences of God are of the intensity of a floodlight, or a flashlight. For each person the experience will be of different candlepower. But it must be genuinely **your** experience of God, it must have authentic theological content, and it must lead **you** into the common experience of community. One of the finest minds in American history, Jonathan Edwards, never could isolate or predict a single psychological symptom to coincide with the arrival of spiritual enlightenment or the metanoic moment of conversion. Nor can we.

Metanoic experiences are like a chain, the links separate but connected, with no chain possible without each link. Experiences of prevenient grace are the first links in the chain, with experiences of justifying grace and sanctifying grace the links necessary to make the chain complete and hold it together until the day of glorifying grace. One of the greatest challenges facing New Light leaders today is the presencing of Christ to Tom-peeping modernists[47] greedily looking for love without links, relationships without risks, rights without vows, new levels of consciousness without transformations of the old, ecstasy without encounter. The Enlightenment bias toward spectatorship created a voyeuristic religion.[48] The postmodern ubiquity of video reinforces these Tom-peeping tendencies, encouraging a simulacrum spirituality. But no matter how widely signs replace reality, every kind of voyeuristic ecstasis from the mundane leaves an aftertaste of shame.

Primal Screams and Passions

The Enlightenment traditions created a principled distance between objective scientific positions and the passions animating the world. Moderns became, like their watchmaker gods, technically precise, but passionless. Postmodern traditions, on the other hand, call for a "sensual science," which physiologist/MacArthur fellow/Michigan State University professor Robert S. Root-Bernstein defines as a holistic combination of analytic thinking with aesthetic sensibilities and personal experiences.[49] A postmodern faith that fires the imagination and releases energy is not based simply on distanced understanding of objective, intellectual truths. It is not assent to a body of principles and moral precepts. There is not much energy that emanates from abstract lovers.

Nor is New-Light mindedness simply a praxis pietatis which wants sanctification without justification. When Wesley felt at 8:45 P.M. the "spirit of God, descend upon [his] heart," he was being taught to love God, in the words of George Croly's 1867 hymn, "as thine angels love,/ One holy passion filling all my frame." If music and theology are inseparable, as Lutheran organist/Roman high mass composer J.S. Bach believed, it is time postmodern theologians began writing passion music.

New Light believers are a people possessed, bursting with energy that comes from a sensual experience of God's presence--and absence. New Light believers are a possessed people: Possessed by a higher power, possessed by a Christ consciousness that is a heartfelt knowledge of God's love and forgiveness; possessed by a "sober intoxication" (in the early words of Jewish philosopher/community leader Philo of Alexandria), even a "divine intoxication" (in the words of New England poet Emily Dickinson).

> Exultation is the going
> Of an inland soul to sea
> Past the houses--past the headlands--
> Into deep Eternity--
> Bred as we, among the mountains,
> Can the sailor understand
> The divine intoxication
> Of the first league out from land?[50]

A medieval book of devotion included this prayer entitled "Anima Christi." The last petition is startling in its claim:

> Soul of Christ, sanctify me;
> Body of Christ, rescue me;
> Water from the side of Christ, wash me;
> Splendour of the face of Christ, shine on me;
> Blood of Christ, intoxicate me.

“

*The essential in these times of moral misery
is to create enthusiasm.*

Painter/sculptor Pablo Picasso[o]

”

Quantum connectedness, or what physicist/epistemologist Abner Shimony meant when he introduced the term "passion-at-a-distance,"[51] opens up radically new understandings of our connectedness to Christ. Spatial separation in a quantum world does not involve isolation or even physical separation. In fact, differentiation implies not separation but "faster-than-light" (physicist Henry P. Stapp's phrase)[52] connection that achieves fundamental expression in a focal point. Our conversion to Christ and our becoming "members" of the body of Christ defy biblical or physical analysis in terms of autonomous, separately existing parts. "Passion-at-a-distance" means that the life and energy of Christ become our life's enthusiasm until we become "partakers of the divine nature" (2 Pet. 1:4). The word "enthusiasm" means, literally, "to be infused with god-force" (*entheos*).

The word "zeal" is derived from the Greek word meaning "to boil." A quantized faith boils up in the heart, and keeps others' faith at a boiling point. It takes more than one "conversion experience" in life to keep up "passion-at-a-distance," to maintain a faith that effervesces from the depths of being and endures to the end. Multiple conversions and deep-flow experiences can arise from the curious, the consequential and the otherwise uncommon moments of life. This has no more, or no less, to do with salvation than the heart has to do with pumping lifeblood into the organism. Mega- and micro-flow experiences are what keep the fire of ecstasy alive, the pot boiling, the heart hot, the rapture alive.

—————————————— **66** ——————————————

Nothing is so contagious as enthusiasm . . .
it is the genius of sincerity,
and truth accomplishes no victories without it.

Politician/novelist/dramatist Edward George Earle Bulwer-Lytton

—————————————— **99** ——————————————

Of course, the subtlest form of "works righteousness" is the notion that we are "saved" by our religious experience. God has not redeemed us by doing something in us. God has redeemed us by doing something for us in the person of Jesus Christ. Grace is not a subjective event but an objective reality. Nevertheless, that objective reality takes on multidimensional life and power, polymathic vitality and victory, only when it is mediated, registered, claimed, and connected.

—————————————— **66** ——————————————

A legitimate fear that one's work will be dismissed
if it is afflicted by "subjectivity"
leads many [modern scholars] to write
with as little personal character or self reference as possible.
The "I" vanishes from the written page altogether. . . .
The most intimate variety of self-reference
that the prevailing style of scholarly writing allows
is contained in the comforting phrase,
"Our findings show that . . ."
Yes, here are people we can trust.

Political scientist/social critic/whalewatcher Langdon Winner[p]

—————————————— **99** ——————————————

One of physicist Niels Bohr's most revolutionary insights is that no phenomenon is a phenomenon until it is a **registered** and **experienced** phenomenon. Called the Complimentarity Principle, it generalized Werner Heisenberg's Uncertainity Principle. Split-beam and double-slit experiments unveiled the paradox of the quantum phenomenon: "No elementary quantum phenomenon is a phenomenon until it is a registered phenomenon."[53] Whereas the modern era was oblivious to the impurity and unneutrality of method, the Complimentarity Principle has given rise to a participatory methodology that factors into one's research identification with what is being observed.

Philosopher Henryk Skolimowski calls this new scientific method the "yoga of participation," which he believes complements the West's "yoga of objectivity."[54] Postmodern science no longer consists in putting as much distance as possible between the object and subject, between the known and the knower. Even sociologists like Clifford Geertz, through the concept of "reflexivity," argue the notion that the observer is part of the observation. Indeed, if David Bohm's theory of the implicate/explicate order is true (a theory that went Heisenberg/Bohr one better), there is no distance at all between the observer and the observed. The two are inseparable. The observer is the observed.

In the same way as "observer-participancy" constitutes the creative building material of the universe, so "observer-participancy" forms the very basic building blocks of the Christian life. We live both physically and spiritually in a "participating universe" (physicist/cosmologist John Archibald Wheeler). Energy events are not predictably patterned. They may occur years or even decades after one is "converted." This is one reason spiritual leaders throughout church history have encouraged people to keep journals and written accounts of their experiences (Wesley even excerpted from them in his own *Journal*). These reflections could then be studied by the community, analyzed by the individual, and properly interpreted. In many ways, Albert Einstein unveiled an important spiritual maxim in his musing that "experience is not what happens to you, but what you do with what happens to you." Life lived in the depth dimension knows the energy-connecting power of fire experiences.

Energy-Fire

Fire is always falling from heaven. If the universe is a "green dragon," as physicist/cosmologist Brian Swimme would have it,[55] New Lights are the dragon's breath. New Light apologetics point the way to new "Aldersgates" where fire may be found. New Lights are filled with fire, and breathing fire, because the gospel opens up the mystical possibility, in philosopher/social critic/essayist/poet Simone Weil's words, of a "real contact, person-to-person, here below, between a human being and God." At "Aldersgate" Wesley discovered a Creator who is "crazy in love" with creation, using fourteenth-century mystic/saint Catherine of Sienna's phrasing. At "Aldersgate" Wesley discovered that people are "capable of God," that God created people with the quantum capacity to be in an igniting connectedness with God. At "Aldersgate" Wesley discovered that all religious communication is motivated by an energy consciousness and flow experience of divine reality. Or in Peter Berger's terms, true religion is "an experience in which metahuman reality is injected into human life."[56]

At "Aldersgate" Wesley discovered that the power of truth in the Scriptures is in the human interaction with divine transactions, with God's initiating disclosures of incendiary consequences. The Bible does not impose abstract ideas on our minds, or interject arguments into our thinking. What the Bible demands is human interaction with biblical experience. What the Bible elicits is a concrete confrontation and encounter between humans and God which ends up, as T.S. Eliot puts it, "costing not less than everything."[57] At "Aldersgate" Wesley "put on the mind of Christ," inhabited the Christ consciousness.

66

God is fire which warms and kindles our hearts.
If we feel in our hearts the cold which comes from the devil--
for the devil is cold--let us pray to the Lord,
and he will come and warm our hearts with love for him
and love for our neighbor. And before the warmth of his face,
the cold of the enemy will be put to flight.

Russian Orthodox elder/saint Seraphim of Sarov

99

God did not send us a statement. God sent us a story. God did not send us love. God sent us God's only Son who loved. God did not send us a principle. God sent us a person who embodied those principles. Jesus did not say, "Follow the way." Jesus said, "I am the way" (John 14:6). The gospel is not the excitement of an idea (though it may begin that way). The gospel is the flow experience of a living person. The kingdom of God is not a place or a principle (which is what many physicists mean by "God"). The "kindom" of God is a person (Jesus Christ), and the "kindom" of God is a people (the Christbody community). We must have more than a principle within, regardless of what John Wesley's brother Charles's 1749 hymn says ("I Want a Principle Within"). We must have a person within. We must have a divine consciousness within. What John Wesley discovered over 250 years ago was that the gospel is made for persons, not persons for the gospel. Perhaps Jesus learned this the hard way from his father Joseph, a "man of principle" (Matt. 1:19). Persons are more precious than principles.

God still makes cold hearts, and cold planets, warm today, and God provides for their continual warming. God still makes churches that are so cold you could skate down the center aisle, as my mountain ancestors used to say, into churches so warm you could get steam cleaned. God still makes life, not a batch of pureed principles but a flaming "fire in the night."

On the night of 23 November 1654 the fire of God's redeeming presence burned deeply in the heart of seventeenth-century French scientist/philosopher Blaise Pascal, who gave us such things as the barometer and the adding machine. From that moment on he always kept a handwritten account of his "fire-in-the-night" experience sewn like a breast pocket into his clothing. An archdefender of reason, Pascal's deep devotion to Christ nevertheless led him to denounce, contra Descartes, rationalism as a disease of reason. Upon his death the scratch of paper he had touched and crinkled countless times but never showed anyone was opened to reveal:

From about half past ten in the evening until about half past twelve.
FIRE.
God of Abraham, God of Isaac, God of Jacob, not of the philosophers and scholars.

God is fire. People who have been touched from on high by the fires of the Almighty will get fired up. Nehemiah's secret of spiritual health--"The joy of the Lord is your strength" (Neh. 8:10)--is mirrored in the closing words of Pascal's memorial to that night: "Joy, joy, joy/Tears of joy."[58] When people asked Wesley why thousands came to hear him preach, he responded, "I set myself on fire and people come to watch me burn." Joseph Campbell calls love "the burning point of life." Fire is a natural, ecological, and spiritual force that, in its periodic occurrence, is absolutely indispensable in the perpetuation of plants, trees, and animals. But fire is no more key an element in the regeneration of forests than it is in the regeneration of faith.

"

We do not need a new religion or a new bible.
We need a new experience--a new feeling
of what it is to be "I."

Anglican priest/comparative philosopher/radio lecturer/television director Alan Watts[q]

"

Our bodies are nothing more than the human organization of energy-fire. Indeed, our bodies are almost entirely empty space, pervaded by families of energy states combining to create force fields. If somehow all the space separating matter in all the humans walking this planet could be removed, and the most elemental state of matter, atoms and nuclei, mashed to their most basic constituents, be they as some physicists believe the three families in the subatomic "particle Z"--the electron and electroneutrino, quarks ("up" and "down"), the muon and muon neutrino quarks ("charmed" and "strange"), and the tau particle and tau neutrino quarks ("top" and "bottom")--it would fill the container the size of one beach ball.[59]

What people see and feel in one another, what people fundamentally respond to, are the energies released by our mindbodies. Each and every atom and molecule makes a dynamic exchange of energy in a field of infinite energy. Through the synergy of the divine-human exchange of energies, an unbelievable field of healing and transforming energy is rounded up and released in the universe. Humans are constructed out of mutually attracting energy particles with positive and negative charges. Negative or neutral charges too often dominate human contacts. Positive charges in the church are about as rare as "strange matter"--positively charged lumps of quarks know as "quarknuggets"--is in the quantum world. "Consciousness is catching," psychologist/medical scholar/professor Frances E. Vaughan reminds us. Destructive, negative, constricting states of consciousness are caught as readily as creative, positive, expanding states of consciousness. All energy states are contagious.

John Wesley was a pioneer in medicine. One of the treatments he experimented with was electrical therapy. He believed that electrical treatments stimulated the healing properties of the body and counseled his people with this peculiar motto: "Be electrified daily."

The new electric machine provided the Wesley brothers with a metaphor for the mysterious attraction that drew Methodists together.

> Touched by the loadstone of Thy love,
> Let all our hearts agree,
> And never toward each other move,
> And ever move towards Thee.[60]

A magnet becomes a magnet only through the induction of an electric current. Prior to that it is only so much iron ore. What is it that makes iron ore into a magnet, that moves tiny iron filings from randomness into pattern? What is it that transforms postmodernist incarnations of New Lights into magnets for ministry? What is it that gives believers the electric current they need, that electrifies us daily?

---------------------------------- **"** ----------------------------------

We are the wire, God is the current.
Our only power is to let the current pass through us.
Of course, we have the power to interrupt it and say "no."
But nothing more.

Italian spiritual leader/theologian Carlo Carretto[r]

---------------------------------- **"** ----------------------------------

James Clerk Maxwell, a nineteenth-century physicist, sculptor, and photographer, discovered light to be a manifestation of electricity. New Lights believe and confess that what electrifies and magnetizes us is the love and grace of God. Our energy source is Christ. Everything we are, everyone we meet, is an organized system through which energy flows. New Lights are force fields of meaning through which the flow of energy takes the form of the love and grace of God. New Light leaders are energy connectors, open systems, transformational vortices who allow themselves first to receive, then channel the highest energies of love and truth coming into the planet. In an industrial culture tired of "punching in" and a technocratic culture desperate to get "plugged-in" (but plugging in to all the wrong energy outlets), New Lights connect people to the many positive sources of energy--from the sun to the soul--but especially to the most powerful energy source in the universe: Jesus Christ.

66

He that has united himself to God
acquires three great privileges: Omnipotence without power,
drunkenness without wine, and life without end.

Greek miner/novelist/poet/world traveler Nikos Kazantzakis

99

The energy requirements, both spiritual and physical, of the world have never been higher, while the energy level of the church has seldom been lower. One of the most indicting questions at Judgment Day, it has been suggested, will be when each of us is asked, "Why did you turn my gospel, the greatest source of energy this world has ever known, into something massively dull and solemnly boring?" Postmodernism is a culture for whom the word "God" is less an expletive than a sedative.

A magazine cartoon portrays a child playing with a construction kit. Noticing the great care with which the child is building, a parent asks, "What are you building?" The child whispers, "I've built a church." "But why are you whispering?" the parent responds. "Because everybody's asleep." A recent advertisement in another popular teenage-to-adult magazine, *Rolling Stone*, captured this tragic loss of energy-fire in the church:

> Religion is a boring subject. Agree? The opposition is more interesting, honest, exciting. One-year subscription, $6; sample, $1. Write: ***American Rationalist***, P.O. Box 994, St. Louis, MO 63188.

A Spirituality of Enjoyment

What the church has done is confuse a John-the-Baptist spirituality with a Jesus-Christ spirituality, a B minor faith with a G major faith. Or, in a phrasing more familiar to feminist spirituality, the church's orientation to suffering and death have made Christians "necrophilic" when God is calling us toward a biophilic faith that celebrates life and promotes good times.[61]

Jesus praised John the Baptist for being "a burning and shining light" (John 5:35). But John-the-Baptist spirituality is a B minor faith, a Christian faith lived out in the minor keys. It burns and shines solely for the spiritual. It "ponders nothing earthly minded." Like fakirs making beds of spikes for themselves, it deprecates the material and affirms the supremacy of the spiritual. Moroseness and morbidity may prepare the way for the Lord, but they are not the ways of the Lord. Indeed, this kind of faith often becomes little more than a voice crying in the wilderness.

One reason why "churches have a hard time competing with a good

Sunday brunch," in the words of ecofeminist/retreat leader Kathy Nickerson, is that few people are attracted to "Prophets Who Cannot Sing" as the title of a Coventry Patmore poem puts it. John-the-Baptist figures and fugues may appeal to those alienated from traditional expressions of Christianity. But Christians who see it as "still their fates/To warble tunes that nails might draw from slates"[62] make unattractive spiritual specimens. In the words of Norwegian playwright/essayist Henrik Ibsen's Julian:

> Have you looked closely at these Christians? Hollow-eyed, pale-cheeked, flat-breasted all; . . . They brood their lives away, unspurred by ambition; the sun shines for them, and they do not see it; the earth offers them its fullness, and they desire it not;--all their desire is to renounce and suffer, that they may come to die.[63]

New Lights have robust appetites for the pleasures of life--from sex to baseball.

---- **"** ----

Wer liebt nicht Weib, Wein, und Gesang
er bleibt ein Naar sein Leben lang.
Whoever does not love wife, wine, and song,
remains a fool his whole life long.

Protestant reformer/celebrator Martin Luther[s]

---- **"** ----

The early Christians succeeded so magnificently because they "outlived," "outloved," but also "outdined" the ancient world. How would you spend the evening if you thought you were going to die the next day? Jesus invited friends in for dinner. "I have eagerly desired to eat . . . with you before I suffer," he said to his closest friends (Luke 22:15 NIV). He invited them to join him for a small, intimate party, to take place in an upper room. They huddled together around a table, no doubt reminiscing and laughing about the other good meals they had enjoyed together. They broke bread together. They drank wine together. From this experience Jesus and his disciples dug deep wells of strength they would draw from in large draughts for the terrors of the next day.

Jesus ended his ministry hosting a party. He began his ministry, according to the Johannine chronology, attending a party in Cana of Galilee. Instead of showing up at the door with the gift of a bottle of wine, as moderns particularly are wont to do, he made 180 gallons of wine after he got there. The Jesus movement distinguished itself from the John-the-Baptist groups by not fasting (Mark 2:18-19). Jesus was always running off to dinner with someone--pairs, spares, strangers, odd couples. Luke 7:36 (NIV)--"One of the Pharisees [Simon] invited Jesus to have dinner with him"--is representative of dozens of verses scattered throughout the Gospels.

In fact, Strasbourg Second Testament professor/university president Étienne Trocmé and the contemporary Dutch Dominican/theologian Edward Schillebeeckx, make the case that the parables of Jesus were not delivered in his preaching to the crowds but when his disciples and others were gathered over a meal. The parables represent *Tischreden*, as the Germans call it, "table talk."[64] The parables were living witnesses to the biblical command "Taste and see that the Lord is good" (Ps. 34:8 RSV). As the wedding feast makes clear, the "glory of the Lord" can be tasted and danced. It comes in overabundance and is of the highest quality. The New Light apologetic strives to see and **taste** God's glory.

The shift in paradigm traditions from modern to postmodern has brought with it a shift from the top-down, logical, prediction/control ascetic *Tagesansicht* of the Apollonian to the bottom-up, intuitive, spontaneous/ celebrative poetic *Nachtansicht* of the Dionysian. There must be a balance between night and day, poetry and prose, as there was in Jesus' life. The symbol for postmodern science picked by Ilya Prigogine is the dance of Shiva. In the same way as the clock symbolized science in the seventeenth century and the thermal engine symbolized science in the nineteenth century, so dance--the transforming dance of Shiva, the dynamic principle in cosmology--captures the essence of the contemporary scientific enterprise.[65] With a flame in one hand and a musical drum in another, the dance of Shiva entails both demonstration and reconstruction (as postmodern philosophers would put it), both denunciation and annunciation (in the words of liberation theologians), both night and day.

"

Their death is Easter who make life their Lent.

Mathematician/gem collector/poet Coventry Patmore[t]

"

The church has yet to learn to dance, much less find its way in the dark. A Jesus-Christ faith knows the meaning of nails and thorns, of suffering and self-denial. But spiritual "disciplines," such as fasting and solitude, not to mention journaling and jogging, are less associated with penance and asceticism than with transformational exercises that sculpt the body and shape the soul into a work of art. Philosophical theologian/Franciscan priest Francis G. Baur and Canadian ecumenist/Paulist priest Thomas Ryan have reminded us, however, that the Greek verb *askein*, the root for our words "ascetic" and "asceticism," means "the artful shapening of a material." Precisely because the spiritual disciplines are nothing more than "the artful fashioning of life," they would argue that asceticism is necessary to mysticism. The spiritual person is the one who is "interested in and dedicated to the artful handling of the world, the artful shaping of one's self, and the artful forming of one's life into something beautiful for God."[66] Spiritual "disciplines" and economies such as "pommelling my body" (1 Cor. 9:27) and "straining for what lies ahead" (Phil. 3:13) exercise the mindbody that it might better receive the life-enhancing gifts of grace. Jesus fasted, not as a means of world renunciation or life-denying asceticism, but as a joyful exercise in strategic planning and preparing for what comes next. Jesus never reduced spirituality to training and technique.

―――――――――――― **❝** ――――――――――――

Even in heaven, they don't sing all the time.

Bookstore owner/publisher/novelist/poet Lawrence Ferlinghetti

―――――――――――― **❞** ――――――――――――

But a Jesus-Christ faith also knows how to "eat, drink, and be merry," a biblical expression usually used, surprisingly, with approval (see Eccles. 2:24, Luke 15:23). God so made the whole that what is good for the body, is good for the spirit. God so made the world that all prodigals are welcomed back home again to the sound of "music and dancing" (Luke 15:25 NRSV). We have inherited an image of a killjoy Jesus that could not be glummer. Jesus' contemporaries had an almost opposite image of him. They saw him experiencing happiness so much that they accused him of being "a glutton and a drunkard" (Matt. 11:19 NIV).

A Jesus-Christ faith challenges the lifestyle of both gluttonous pigs and abstemious prigs. The Apostle Paul attacked a group in one of his mission areas who championed the prohibitions "Do not handle, Do not touch, Do not taste" (Col. 2:21 RSV), because of their unnecessary impugning of the senses and the celebrative that one associates with John the Baptist. New Light congregations are places where postmoderns no longer have to shun the material in order to experience the spiritual.

The Lost Chord of Modernist Piety

A G natural faith has almost become the "lost chord"[67] in American religious life. The modern church has never gotten the biblical chronology right: John the Baptist came before, not after, Jesus. The modern era has never understood the Bachian chronology of the B minor Mass: The goal of the mass is a movement from B minor, the key of pain and suffering, to G major, the key of bliss and blessedness.[68] The modern era arpeggiated a gospel of celebration into a gospel of cerebration.

Early one morning a church office got a call asking to speak to the minister. "I'm sorry, he can't come to the phone right now," the secretary said. "He's celebrating." "He's what?" the voice at the other end of the line exclaimed. "What's he celebrating so early in the morning?" "He's celebrating Holy Communion," the secretary replied. How difficult it has been for modernists to reconcile "prayerful" with "playful" in their spiritual vocabulary. The Jewish and Christian traditions have a well-established branch of theology called "theodicy," which constructs a theology of pain and suffering. There is no branch of study for a theology of joy and celebration. There is, of course, "doxology." But for modern worshipers "doxology" is something done when money is collected and the offering plates returned to the front.

"

*In the beginning God **celebrated** the heavens and the earth.*

A child's interpretive reading of Genesis 1:1

"

The gospel enables postmoderns to serve God, in Luther's wonderful phrase, *hilari et libera voluntate*, "with a hilarious and free will." John Wesley is known for saying that "sour godliness is the Devil's religion." His early spiritual descendants, black and white, took him at his word. Black Methodists "got happy" in their faith. They even created a new verb, "happified," to describe the transforming power of the gospel.

Sit down! Lord, I can't sit down!
My soul's so happy that I can't sit down.

White and black Methodists were sometimes known as "shouting Methodists" because their life-affirming worship experiences erupted in shouts of praise and glory.

I'm not asham'd to own the Lord,
Nor to defend his holy word;
My soul has often been refresh'd
Among the shouting Methodist.

They pray, they sing, they preach the best,
And do the Devil most molest;
If Satan had his vicious way,
He'd kill and damn them all today.

They are despis'd by Satan's train,
Because they shout and preach so plain;
I'm bound to march to endless bliss,
And die a shouting Methodist.

We shout too much for Sinners here,
But when in Heav'n we do appear
Our shouts shall make the heav'ns ring
When all the saints shall join to sing.[69]

The gospel's "joy in truth" (Augustine), if truth be known, became for the medieval and modern eras a sour joy. In baseball player/sawdust trail evangelist Billy Sunday's words, "You would think that if some people laughed it would break their faces." Or: "To see some people you would

88

think that the essential [of] orthodox Christianity is to have a face so long you could eat oatmeal out of the end of a gas pipe."[70] It was mendicant friar/ seraphic saint Francis of Assisi who spoke tenderly of his "dear Lady Poverty" as "Madonna Poverty." Not Jesus. It was medieval culture that created the image of the poor and gentle and somber Jesus. Not the Bible. There is no excuse for a sadsack, wallflower spirituality. God's pantry is never bare. God's party is never dull.

One of postmoderns' biggest impediments to an energy-fire faith that can dance is getting rid of this modernist image of the humorless Christ and its party-pooper piety. The popular medieval religious poem *Cursor Mundi* says of Jesus: "That thrice he wept we find enough, but nere where he laughed." Someone as usually right as G.K. Chesterton could also be very wrong: "There was some one thing that was too great for God to show us when He walked upon our Earth," Chesterton wrote, "and I have some-times fancied that it was His mirth."

Francis of Assisi is a classic example of how short a slide it is from a G natural to a B minor faith. The modern church has been infatuated with the medieval glorification of St. Francis, oblivious to its own out-of-doors apostles like John Muir or Mary Austin who best incarnate an ecological ethics for today.[71] According to modernist composer/ornithologist Olivier Messiaen, Francis is the saint "who most clearly resembles Christ." Medie-valist/UCLA professor Lynn White, who blamed Christianity for the world's environmental collapse, suggested Francis of Assisi as "the patron saint for ecologists."[72] So also have process theologian/environmental ethicist John B. Cobb, Jr., and many others.[73]

Modernization's fascination with a saint who believed that the more violence one did to one's body, the closer one's spirit came to God, a saint who affirmed that "every creature proclaims: 'God made me for your sake, O man!'"[74] illustrates not only modernity's appalling historical ignorance about its own traditions (few know the rudiments of Christian faith, much less the difference between John Calvin and Italo Calvino, or more histori-cally the distinctions that pitted John Calvin against Sebastian Castellio) but also modernity's preference for spiritualities played in the minor keys.

Stories about Francis taming the wolf of Gubbio or making friends with a cicada are familiar. In fact, Catholic theologian/divinity school professor David Tracy has observed how "Francis now lives in common memory as something like the lost eighth member of Walt Disney's seven dwarfs, somewhere between Happy and Bashful."[75] Not so Disney-like is the story about the monastery cook who got into hot water because he soaked Francis's vegetables in hot water overnight. Francis was furious because the Bible says, "Take no thought for the morrow." Not so Disney-like is the story of how Francis carried a pouch of ashes on his belt wherever he went, so that if his food tasted too good, he would sprinkle some ashes on it because God would not be honored if he enjoyed the taste of what he was eating. "Man's enemy is his own flesh," St. Francis said. If Francis did not sufficiently starve and subject his body, he would put on a specially made belt of nails or a scratchy camel's hair shirt in which lived vermin and every kind of filth imaginable. When Francis's habit caught fire, he resisted those trying to put it out by screaming "Dearest brother, do not harm Brother Fire." Even after Francis received the stigmata on Mt. Alverno and repented of punishing his body so brutally, the forgiveness he sought was from "Brother Ass" (as he dubbed his body). Moderns liked this penitent obsessed with the E minor crucifixion key so much that they even invented for him a prayer, a "Prayer of St. Francis" which never existed before the twentieth century, a prayer to which Francis's name became attached most likely in 1936 because of a printer's error.[76]

Jesus himself, in one of the many examples of his humor, contrasted his non-repressive, nonascetic, life-affirming spirituality with that of the John the Baptists of the world, who think it unfortunate that our brains are attached to stomachs. Satirizing how sometimes neither receives a hearing, Jesus said,

> We played the flute for you,
>   and you did not dance;
> We sang a dirge,
>   and you did not mourn.
>
> (Matt. 11:17 NIV)

John the Baptist's B minor music, his funeral ethic with its fasting and flailing, its eating nothing but wild honey and locusts, its wearing nothing but a hair shirt, didn't appeal to you, Jesus is saying. But neither did my wedding ethic with its eating and drinking. What more do you want? God gave you a choice: B minor or G major keys; a funereal faith or a dance spirituality. You rejected both.

"

Jesus the dancers' master is,
A great skill at the dance is his,
He turns to the right, he turns to the left,
All must follow his teaching deft.

Twelfth-century abbot/monastic theologian/saint Bernard of Clairvaux[u]

"

No singing at a late nineteenth-century camp-meeting could bring forth more shouts of "Glory" and "Hallelujah" and "Praise the Lord" than when this song was sung:

> Lord, lift me up and let me stand
> By faith on heaven's tableland;
> A higher plane than I have found--
> Lord, plant my feet on higher ground.

It was written by Johnson Oatman, Jr., a composer more popular in the black than the white community. Born in 1856, ordained a Methodist preacher, during the course of his ministry Oatman composed over three thousand hymns, including "Count Your Blessings" and my favorite,

> There's not a friend like the lowly Jesus--
> No, not one! No, not one!
> None else could heal all our soul's diseases--
> No, not one! No, not one!
> Jesus knows all about our struggles,
> He will guide till the day is done;
> There's not a friend like the lowly Jesus--
> No, not one! no, not one!

Early in his career as a songwriter, Oatman made the following dedication in a Boston book.

> Let others sing of rights or wrongs,
> Sing anything that pleases;
> But while they're singing other songs,
> I'll sing a song for Jesus.

But for people to sing a song for Jesus, to be a fool for Jesus, to throw a party for Jesus, to give a witness for Jesus, requires an experience of Jesus. There is no road to truth that does not pass by way of experience.[77]

"

In singing and dancing is the voice of the law.

Japanese Zen master/painter/poet Hakuin

"

Moving Inward to Reach Upward

"Crying in the Chapel" was one of the most haunting songs rock-'n'-roll singer Elvis Presley ever sang. The last verse contains words Elvis himself could never take to heart:

> You'll search, and you'll search
> But you'll never find
> No way on earth to gain peace of mind.
> Take your troubles to the chapel,
> Get down on your knees and pray--
> Your burdens will be lighter,
> And you'll surely find the way.[78]

A starved soul, just like an empty belly, cannot be expected to have discriminating tastes. A starved soul will eat almost anything. Anything is what most moderns and postmoderns are eating, and becoming psychologically dependent on: Addictions to chemicals, drugs (especially food drugs like sugar, chocolate, caffeine), sex, self, shopping, money, power, food, chance. More people buy lottery tickets in America than vote.

Among my favorite poets is children's verse writer/satirist X. J. Kennedy. He is a member of a self-proclaimed literary "endangered species": poets who still write in rhyme and meter. The shortest poem in his collection called *Cross Ties* (1985) is a four line, sixteen word poem that does not rhyme:

> You touch me.
> One by one
> In each cell of my body
> A hearth comes on.[79]

Starved and stunted souls, restless and unearthed, are searching for the touch that will turn them on, the taste that will fill them up, the spark that will catch them on fire.

The economic world of ultramodernity is best understood in terms not of production but of consumption capitalism. As social life became shaped increasingly by a service and information economy in which conscious meaning in life came more from what people consumed than from what they produced, consumer interest also shifted from goods to experiences. The "good life" increasingly meant new, higher, and more meaningful experiences rather than more things and more goods.

An "experience industry"[80] has even enthroned status symbol experiences for selves to consume: fitness centers (Moore's Nautilus), electronic toys (Sharper Image), megaheroes in sports and entertainment (*People* magazine and "Entertainment Tonight"), travel tours ("Loveboat" cruises), New Age seminars, the drug trade (both legal and illegal). America's flourishing experience and reenchantment industries lead consumptive selves to touches that do indeed provide experiences, but alien touches and "satanic" experiences of ersatz bliss and stand-in meaning that light no enduring fires in the hearths of the soul.

The name Satan derives from the Hebrew common noun which suggests a constriction of flow, an obstruction of movement, a choked circulation of energy. Blocks in the gateway to the depths of transpersonal dimensions are frequently described and experienced as "knots": knots in the stomach, lumps in the throat, "knots in the heart" (an Indian Upanishad saying). Only when these knots that block the mindbody's free flow of awareness and energy are untied can the person be open to receiving the light-fire of Spirit. The "evil one" is Jesus' name for those knotting and blocking energies that would shape and subvert us into something less than God would have us be. Humans are the only species of life that have the capability of interfering with their God-given growth and development.

Raptures of the Deep

The "Fourth Instinct" is British psychologist/journalist/"Call My Bluff" panelist Arianna Stassinopoulous Huffington's name for it. Chemist/UCLA research professor Ronald K. Siegel, dubbed the "Leif Erikson" of pyschopharmacology, calls it the "Fourth Drive." "It" is the highest but in many ways the subtlest and most overlooked of the four basic human urges and impulses--the others being self and survival, power and material aggrandizement, and sex. In short, "it" is our drive and instinct toward God, our thirst for the spiritual dimension of being. Huffington would prefer to call this instinct the psychological path toward "radiance" or "wholeness" or "harmony." Siegel designates the Fourth Drive "a rational force that motivates the pursuit of intoxication." Carl Jung agreed, noting that a "craving for alcohol was the equivalent, on a low level, of the spiritual thirst of our being for wholeness."[81]

Whether expressed neurologically, psychologically, or psychopharmacologically, there is a fourth force that drives the human species to dance to a transcendent rhythm, to pine after flow experiences, to seek what deep sea divers call poetically "raptures of the deep."[82] When the Fourth Drive or the Fourth Instinct is isolated, belittled, or choked, the other three drives assume hegemonic, even demonic positions in the psyche. Sick selves are the result, and acute psychological distress causes all sorts of abuses to the human spirit and social order. Indeed, as the history of scuba diving reveals all too clearly, the result of these states of euphoria induced by high concentrations of nitrogen in the body ("nitrogen narcosis") can be deadly.

The Fourth Drive puts the other three drives in their proper place. It leads us beyond self, beyond power, beyond sexuality, and into others and God. Or, stated more theologically, people cannot experience the embrace of God's grace when their arms are tightly circled around other things. People cannot know the healing balm of the divine touch when their bodies are being stimulated and massaged by alien touches. That is why the Scriptures teach that whatever is blocking the circulation of love's energies, whatever is getting in our way, whatever we hold dearest to us that is constricting the flow experience of grace, must be let go.

——————————————— **"** ———————————————

God is the I of the universe.

Social credit exponent/mystic Alfred R. Orage[v]

——————————————— **"** ———————————————

For the Jericho tax collector Zacchaeus, and us, there is the **drive of self** and the experience of self, which all too often go by the name of experience of God. "The greatest love of all," one-time gospel singer Whitney Houston instructed a generation of kids in the 1980s, is "learning to love yourself."

Modernists' goals to be gods reduced the gospel to consumerist states of self-awareness, self-realization, self-reliance--to everything but self-transcendence. The essence of sin is not being less than you are but striving to be more than you are, the Promethean ambition of *Erimus Sicuti Deus* ("We shall be like God"). "You too will be like God," tantalized the serpent in the Garden of Eden (Gen. 3:5). "Let us make a name for ourselves," said the mortals in the land of Shinar (Gen. 11:4). Few evils are more insidious than self-creation and self-sufficiency, producing what used to be called "the energy of the flesh."

There is nothing wrong with the self's ambition to make a name for God. But modern selves aimed to make a name for themselves. One of the reasons Thomas Merton was attracted to Japanese and Chinese spiritualities was their correctives to the Western heritage of Cartesianism: "Descartes made a fetish out of the mirror in which the self finds itself. Zen shatters it."[83] Jesus did not go into the wilderness to find himself, or to learn more about himself, or to "center in" on himself. Jesus went into the wilderness to center in on God, to experience life on God's terms, and to summon the aggregate of collective experiences about warding off the powers and principalities of evil. Paul did not say in 2 Timothy 1:12, "I know who I am." Paul said: "I know whom I have believed."

Energy-fire experiences take us into ourselves only that we might reach outside of ourselves. Metanoia is a de-centering experience of connectedness and community. It is not an exercise in reciting what Jesus has done for me lately. Energy-fire ecstasy, more a buzz than a binge, takes us out of ourselves, literally. That is the meaning of the word "ecstatic." Niagara Falls is more than what little water I can catch from it in my cup. When Wesley felt his heart was strangely warmed, as historian/theologian James D. Nelson puts it, "his sensation was from outside himself and outside his kind; it was being done in him by God."

For the rich young ruler, and us, there is the **drive of material gratification**. The bumper sticker philosophy of the sixties was "Make Love, Not War." In the seventies and eighties it was "Make Money, Not War." This shopping-crazed culture, choking in its own luxuriance, is filled with those for whom a Porsche is the highest level of spiritual attainment imaginable, with those constantly courting new "religious" experiences that only money can buy. Some have even suggested that shopping is not only the postmodern equivalent of the cave dwellers' hunting and gathering rituals. It has also for some become "the unifying principle by which people structure days,"[84] and for many a social act that makes them feel normal and cheers them up. Adult Americans already average more time malling and shopping on Sunday than they do worshiping.[85] Even the word "Christian," as campus minister/religion professor Susan Brooks Thistlethwaite observes, has been made either into a mammonic adjective describing consumer products (Christian Yellow Pages, Christian bookstores, Christian music, etc.), or into cost-benefit calculations. Consumer thinking cannot seem to kiss bottom lines goodbye. Better **still** means better off.

For the Samaritan woman, and us, there is also the **drive of sex.** Experience became defined by modern youth as "sexperience"--torrid, transient sexual encounters. Love as it has prevailed lately in modern "Cosmopolitan" cultures was little more than a pelvic issue of two skins touching. In the AIDS-y eighties, it became even more remote than that. A couple of years ago the whole telephone system for one section of New York City went dead. The circuits of one telephone sex service became so clogged with hundreds of thousands of calls from around the world responding to their "Reach Out Don't Touch Someone" ads for aural sex that they overloaded and shut down. A new bumper sticker perhaps prophesies the nineties: "Make War, Not Love--It's Safer."

When Depth Becomes Hologram

There is no greater message the New Light apologetic can bring to the twenty-first century than the message of the "Fourth Drive": "Thou, Lord, dost make my lamp burn bright, and . . . lighten my darkness" (Ps. 18:28 NEB). The only touch with an energy charge sufficient to unclog our arteries and to channel the light of glory into every cell of the human body is the touch of Jesus Christ. Some of the most mind-bending, soul-expanding words in Scripture are these from the real Lord's Prayer in John 17:22-23 (NIV): "I have given them the glory that you gave me, that they may be one as we are one: I in them and you in me. May they be brought to complete unity to let the world know that you sent me [and believe]." Union precedes communion. "You in me, and I in you." Who could ask for anything more? What more do we expect?

New Light leaders turn people's attention to "thy courts": "A day in thy courts is better than a thousand elsewhere" (Ps. 84:10 RSV). To spend one moment in God's presence, in a complete theological and aesthetic awareness of our metanoic, theomorphic Oneness in Christ, is more of a holographic experience than any "turn-on" imaginable. Faith in Jesus Christ both increases one's capacity for living and expands the volume of life one can inhale into one's being.

———————————— **"** ————————————

Ignem Mittere in Terram
Cast Fire upon the Earth

Motto of the Jesuit Order

———————————— **"** ————————————

The depth dimension of energy-fire is captured by these words from "Veni, Creator Spiritus," flowing in and flowing out from New Light hearts to a choking world. The depth dimension of faith offers the possibility for postmoderns to get to the bottom of things while scratching their names from a bottom-line life.

O Holy Spirit, by whose breath
Life rises vibrant out of death:
Come to create, renew, inspire;
Come, kindle in our hearts your fire.

You are the seeker's sure resource,
Of burning love and living source,
Protector in the midst of strife,
The giver and the Lord of Life.

In you God's energy is shown,
To us your varied gifts made known.
Yours is the tongue and yours the ear.
Teach us to speak, teach us to hear.

Flood our dull senses with your light;
In mutual love our hearts unite.
Your pow'r the whole creation fills;
Confirm our weak, uncertain wills.

To postmodern ears, such a Hymn to Life is an endless amen, even the "Sound of the Great Amen."[86]

Image Intermezzo II: Whale-Watching

Jesus calls individuals. But he gathers individuals into community. Jesus and the church belong together. This is where the art of whale-watching comes in.

My favorite vacation spot is South Wellfleet, Massachusetts, on Cape Cod. On a dreary, overcast day, I like to visit Provincetown, climb the hundred-foot hill to visit the Pilgrim's Monument and Museum, and after examining artifacts and dioramas of whale lore, board the Portuguese Princess to go whale-watching. The ship's captain steers the boat into the Stellwagon Bank feeding grounds, and six to eight miles out the whale watch begins. Everyone scampers to the sides of the boat, leans over the railing, and peers out for what the naturalist/commentator calls "whaleprints." A whaleprint betrays the spot where a whale has sounded. If one looks long enough and far enough around the whaleprint (or what used to be called the "blow-wake"), one can see the whale surface again for another sounding.

Imagine the legendary hero/giant lumberjack Paul Bunyan walking on water and leaving footprints in the sea. That is what a whaleprint looks like. A whaleprint is an oily oasis of absolute stillness in the midst of an ocean of rollicking, billowing waves. No matter how turbulent the water or violent the waves, a whaleprint is so still, so serene, so smooth, that one could launch a toy sailboat on it without its being tossed about or blown over. Scientists tell us that a whaleprint is created by a combination of the whale displacing an amount of

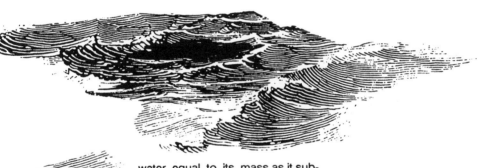

water equal to its mass as it submerges, and the action of its diving flukes, which create a churning column of water that literally rises and swells above the surface of the sea.

The church willy-nilly leaves a whaleprint on the surface of this planet. It too displaces an equal or greater amount of weight in this world. The question is, what kind of weight will it displace, and what kind of whaleprint will it leave? Too many people are scanning the horizon, peering for havens of peace in the midst of the violence and turbulence of our world, and not finding whaleprint communities of peace, love and forgiveness. Eyes only see more ripples, more waves, more tides.

God calls the church to be different, and to make a difference. God calls the church to leave whaleprints in its wake. The whaleprint is the voice of God upon the waters, speaking to a postmodern world: There is an oasis of serenity in your turbulent ocean.

PATHOS

THE LAND OF MATTER: "... WAS MADE FLESH"

The "mattering" of matter was perhaps Charles Wesley's greatest phrase: "Veiled in flesh the godhead see."[1] Matter is energy in motion, creating meaning-fields. What is spiritual becomes material. In the quantum theory of matter, energy can be made visible, particular, local, tangible. In an expanding steady-state universe, matter is also continuously and everywhere being created, at a rate of roughly one hydrogen atom per cubic meter every five billion years. Our life, our death--they all matter. Everything matters.

---- 66 ----

Matter and energy transform and transfer and translate . . .
Paulist priest/skier/ecumenist Thomas Ryan[a]

---- 99 ----

There is no matter without spirit. There is no flesh without word. The height dimension of faith teaches us that without the Word made flesh, there is no Word made power. In every epoch, however, the Word is made flesh differently. Energymatter is a dynamic process, a time continuum that interacts with and occupies space. But *Logos* materializes in *Pathos* in forms fundamental to, shapes revelatory of, the age.

As energy draws elements into specific matter, even giving rise to new properties of matter in the evolutionary process, a life-story takes shape that gives birth to a moral vision. A moral vision willy-nilly involves landedness-- a controlling mythos for artists, theologians, scientists, and other mythmakers whose interior landscapes derive spiritual energy from the mysteries and sublimities of portions of nature's external landscape. "Tell me the landscape in which you live, and I will tell you who you are" is a quotation from Spanish philosopher/journalist José Ortega y Gasset that theologian/historian/Americanist Belden C. Lane uses to paint his marvelous *Landscapes of the Sacred* (1988).[2] New Lights must get a feel for the lay of the land in the postmodern era.

In the modern period the moral energy in America came from New England landscapes dense with deciduous, carbon dioxide-fixing trees and townscapes forested with Christopher Wren steeples. This was "God's Country," as we liked to call it. Grinning renditions of "Down by the Old

Mill Stream," "Under the Shade of the Old Apple Tree," and "Under the Spreading Chestnut Tree" attest to the remarkable power of these old chestnuts and obsolete images to carry the nation's memories long after Longfellow's "spreading chestnut tree" was chopped down in 1876 and the once indispensible "old mill" was downgraded to a hat factory.[3] Masters of the nineteenth-century American landscape, popular artists such as George Inness, celebrated American innocence and promise through such widely reproduced pastoral paintings as *The Old Mill* (1849), *Autumn Oaks* (1875), and most spectacularly, the panoramic *Peace and Plenty* (1865).

"

The first thing to do is to choose a sacred place to live in . . .

Tahirussawichi, Pawnee tribe

"

For the postmodern period, the supposedly worthless desert is the relevant metaphor and reality. The Desert of the "Redskin" West is now contending for recognition alongside its heretofore more prominent myth-mate, the Village of the "Paleface" East. Landscapes of the desert Southwest press with special intensity on the consciousness of postmodern culture.

Throughout America's cultural history there has been an identification of wilderness landscapes with spirituality.[4] But the desert, "the loneliest land that ever came out of God's hand,"[5] is the wilderness landscape most freighted with spiritual significance, as ethnographer/naturist/mystic Mary Austin was one of the first to write about, in *The Land of Little Rain* (1903), and as novelist Edward Abbey taught in his apostolate for "the realm beyond the human."

Desert Spirituality

The landscape over which postmodernism presides, where postmoderns are most likely to take off their shoes, is the desert. The desert is now "God's Country," and with six million hectares of new desert forming each year (North Africa was once the granary of Europe), there is more and more of "God's Country" to which we can give ourselves. The landscape of Santa Fe (Spanish for "Holy Faith"), New Mexico, where there is a higher concentration of art colonies and galleries than any place in the nation except New York City and San Francisco, has become one symbol of postmodernism's holy faith, its "dancing ground of the sun" (the Native American name for "Santa Fe").

Postmodernism's shift of energy from North to South, from East to West, has led to material changes in the symbolic sources of faith and the structures in which faith takes form. For a people who feel cut loose and set adrift at the same time, the desert conveys modernity's simultaneous legacy of emancipation and alienation. The desolate landscape of American life finds expression in the harshness of the desert, the symbol of silence and survival and spiritual rebirth.

French sociologist/philosopher Jean Baudrillard portrays the desert as "an ecstatic critique of culture, an ecstatic form of disappearances."[6] The silence of "disappearance" and displacement has replaced the American dream. The desert discloses its mountains only at a lonely distance (educator/humorist/environmentalist Page Stegner refers to the mountain as the desert's "ecclesiastical display").[7] The modern era, congested with ideals and empty of space, has given way to the postmodern era, empty of ideals and congested with space and people. Postmoderns can only approach their mountains, their idealisms, from the distance of fifty miles. Postmoderns approach realism (which is fashionable in Southwest art) from the standpoint of the unreal. It is now the empty, inhospitable, strange places--the wilderness--that are the most necessary to the human spirit.[8]

---------------- 66 ----------------

A land of lost rivers, with little in it to love;
yet a land that once visited must be come back to, inevitably.

Poet/playwright/mystic/Indian rights advocate/conservationist Mary Austin[b]

---------------- 99 ----------------

New Light leadership is called to make straight a way in the wilderness (Isa.40:3), to show how the desert can now be trusted, not simply as a testing ground but as a "house of prayer"[9] and a healing stream for our souls. The energy organized into matter that we name "church" must add to its salvationist, "*Logos* Christology" tradition the life-giving "Spirit Christology" tradition of the wilderness sojourns. Indeed, the postmodern church is called into the desert, requiring a new reading and reappropriation of the exilic metaphors and images of the biblical passages and Desert Fathers. Theologian/urban missionary/Episcopal priest Ephraim Radner encourages the church to give up its "liberationist outlook" in favor of an "exilic ecclesiology," in these provocative words: "Rather than calling for the theocratic transformation of an entire society, much of the New Testament calls people out of an existing society into a theocratic alternative that is to continue in the midst of the larger society until the inbreaking of God's own action."[10] Belden C. Lane captures the essence of the desert's success as a teacher in these words: "Fierce landscapes offer none of the comforts of reason. At the extremities of geography, beyond the civilized precincts of all that is safe, we enter the dread terrain of our own extremities as conscious selves. Yet in that fearful ending we discover also a joyous new beginning."[11]

The desert is not propitious territory for the human species. It was designed with buzzards and lizards, not humans, in mind. It is by its very nature a habitat of immense ambivalence and liminality. The desert is a symbol of the ambivalence of existence in life and death, as Georgia O'Keefe's flowers and skulls so graphically portray.

But the desert is also a symbol of newstream communities, the postmodern *ecclesia*. The word *ecclesia* means literally those who are "called out" of the world, called "**out**" that they might better go "**in**" it. The desert is a symbol of stepping-out-to-come-back liminality; as demographic studies of the Southwest find that people from America's imploding urban spaces, lost in huge bureaucracies and businesses, de-sert to des-ert Sedona, Santa Fe, and other places for a point-zero period of subtraction and simplicity-- "deep breaths, deep sleep, and the communion of the stars," Mary Austin called it[12]--after which they return to metropolitan areas again. The desert is trial by fire; it takes fire to fight fire.

— 66 —

After the roar, after the fierce modern music
Of rivets and hammers and trams,
After the shout of the giant,
Youthful and brawling and strong
Building the cities of men,
Here is the desert of silence
Blinking and blind in the sun--
The old, old woman who mumbles her beads
And crumbles to stone.

New Mexico poet/editor Alice Corbin Henderson[c]

— 99 —

One cannot "succeed" in the desert, as modernism came to define success. One can only "survive" in the desert through dependence, vulnerability, and gratitude. Finding no spiritual peace or enjoyment in material saturation, postmoderns move to the desert for back-to-the-basics lessons in spiritual maturation. Like a line drawing, the desert strips away everything but the basics. It demands that we live on its terms if we are to survive. It opens the door to perception by removing all extraneous props from life.[13] The wilderness calls forth what educator/pastor Donald B. Rogers calls

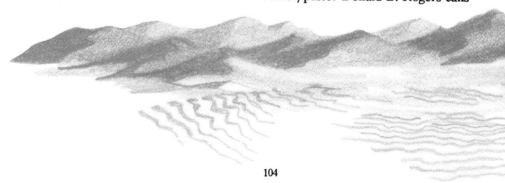

"coyote theology" at one time, at another time "weed theology."[14]

The desert is a transitional passage in the same way that postmodernism is a transitional passage. The desert will often test faith in the same way postmodernism will test faith. But both the desert and postmodernism can bring life into laserlike focus and into an encounter with God. The desert's very isolation and desolation inspire in postmoderns the need for others, for neighboring, for community.

The promise of the gospel is that New Lights can be at their fullest bloom even in the emptiness, the loneliness, the disappearances of the desert. The desert **can** blossom, in and of itself. Far from the desert being a barren, hostile place, it actually teems with life--from road runners to cactus to creosote to Native American tribes. But the desert can also blossom through what desert artist/"llama lady" Kirstin Hardenbrook calls "irrigated fields." New Lights must not be afraid of using technology in the desert, as the Israelis have done in the Sinai, for example, to create an arboreal environment, to instate a hydrologic cycle, so long as the motivation is not to lead us **out of** the wilderness but rather to help us be strong **within it.**

It Takes Two . . .

How high our faith reaches and how our faith reaches high are the domain of faith's second dimension--the sacramental spiral of the metanoized life toward heights of wholeness. The inner fires of personal encounter with God flicker and go cold without communal fanning. Or stated more theologically, the spiritual is only known "in, with, and under" the material.

---**“**---

It takes two to make a revelation.

University of Edinburgh divinity professor/
biblical scholar/chaplain to the Queen John Baillie[d]

---**”**---

Faith in a biblical sense is the physical stuff of spiritual existence. That is why Christian faith is attributable only to those who are members of a

community united by love for Christ. The *Logos* of divine energy becomes the *Pathos* of ecclesial matter in what the Bible names *koinonia* but we name "church."[15] The height dimension stands appropriately between the depth and the breadth, for it gives meaning and power to them both. *Pathos* mediates and sustains *Logos* experiences of God, and *Pathos* empowers and propels *Ethos* missions.

The Bible begins with the word *bet*. The first letter of the Hebrew Bible is the second letter of the Hebrew alphabet. When prefixed to the beginning of a word, *bet* is a simple preposition usually meaning "in," as in "In the beginning." But *bet* not only means "in." It also represents the plural, the conjunctive, the number "two." The Bible begins with two, just as all life begins with two--the human species starts as two, according to new research, and is not determined as one until a week or so after fertilization. One is nothing. Two is everything. One is not even a number. Two is the beginning of all numbers.

―――――――――――――――― 66 ――――――――――――――――

God makes things make themselves.

Twentieth-century Christianity's major voice/
philosopher/geologist Pierre Teilhard de Chardin

―――――――――――――――― 99 ――――――――――――――――

The Bible begins thus: "In the beginning, God." God what? God creates. We are made in the image of God, a God who creates. What is it that God creates? God creates creators and creator communities--a creator community of humans called Adam and Eve, a creator community of animals and plants called nature, a creator community of Hebrew slaves established with a Covenant at Sinai, a creator community of Jesus' disciples established with a Pentecost at Jerusalem. The biblical focus is on the community.

"Embodiment is the end of all God's works" is an eighteenth-century Friedrich Oetinger dictum.[16] Light may seem ethereal, but every physicist tells of its material embodiment.[17] An embodied self in the biblical sense is both individual and communal. Faith creates more than individual relationships with God. Faith creates plurals, starting with two creation stories. A Triune God creates communities. Indeed, God's signature way of addressing human problems is to create a community. What made the coming of the Holy Spirit at Pentecost so distinct from the Spirit's coming earlier among the prophets and other figures was, first, that at Pentecost the Holy Spirit came to stay and, second, that the Holy Spirit came with the stated mission of building a faith community we call the "church." The Holy Spirit, the God with us, is the God who builds communities.

To be alive with the fire of the Spirit, therefore, is to be part of the embodiment of Christ in the world and the setting of communities aflame with the Spirit's presence and fire. The oldest human institution is not the family, anthropologists tell us, but the community--the tribe, the clan, the village. Just as it was some form of community living that made humans "human," so it is some form of community living that makes Christians "Christian." Even Jesus is not presented in the gospels as some lonely prophet or lone messiah but as a master of a community of disciples who are charged collectively with carrying on his work. One cannot be a Christian any way save as a member of a community, a "household of faith." Christians, like birch trees, grow in clusters. They reach toward the sky together. They reach eternity together. At the Last Judgment, they are even judged together (Matt. 25:41-46).

66

The whole material universe is an expression and incarnation of the creative energy of God, as a book or a picture is the material expression of the creative soul of the artist.

Mystery novelist/theologian/dramatist Dorothy Sayers[e]

99

To become a new creature in Christ is to become a member (*membranes*) of a single organic entity. One cannot have one without the other. No eye, no ear, no foot, no hand has function or identity apart from the whole. One cannot fully be a Christian without a church. There is no true life outside of community. If we have learned one thing from the fields of semiotics and structuralism it is that all meaning is relational. Environmentalist/microbiologist René Dubos concludes that humans have a biological need to be part of a small group.

Community--Dead or Alive?

Modernism knew what it meant to be fruitful and multiply in almost every area except when it came to creating community. Community did not disappear completely in the modern era--there lingered symbolically the Italian piazza, the French café, the Spanish plaza, the Greek tavern, the English pub. But the fundamental fact of modern life became not its communal dimension but its privatization of life's pilgrimages, rites of passage and rituals. Religion was made into predominantly a private affair with little public meaning.[18] Little wonder, then, that the New Age movement bypasses the church almost completely except for joining God's actions in history.

In spite of all the "fellowship groups," "fellowship dinners," and "fellowship nights," and 320,000 church meetings a day, modernist American Christians still pulled their own way. Genuine community was often the hardest thing to come by. For, to sound another familiar theme, the ties that bind broke down in the modern era--witness the plight of the family, the church, the school, the union, the block club, the neighborhood pub, the political party. In their place was supposed to emerge a network of social institutions, a bureaucratic structure of community-based caring and socialization. The failure of this new social environment has generated a desperate "search for structure,"[19] especially among adolescents, and has led to "behavioral sink," a phrase anthropologist/archaeologist Edward T. Hall uses to describe the modern effect of overcrowding where we treat one another like objects and things.[20]

———————————— **66** ————————————

Nothing is itself taken alone. Things are
because of interrelations or interconnections.

Insurance lawyer/poet/essayist/playwright Wallace Stevens

———————————— **99** ————————————

The church is filled with faith's ferals, people who feel uncared for and alone out there, as uncared for and alone as the long, wiry figures of an Alberto Giacometti sculpture. Modern art is filled with "behavioral sink" expressions of moderns longing for love and community. So are the airwaves, filled with what someone has called "ad hoc electronic communalism" (AHEC), which includes call-in radio, telephone party linkages, porno phone lines, and television shopping. People are hungry for community; they are picking it up wherever they can find it. Americans spend more time alone than most other nationalities. This is partly because Americans conceive themselves as individuals dealing with strangers, a form of human transaction which entails complicated protocols and massive expenditures of psychic energy. Most people in history considered themselves as family members and conducted their business within the safe confines of bloodlines.[21] One way of writing the history of modern American religion would be to explore this search for surrogate bloodlines.

The Church's OBEs

Modern communities came to suffer from every kind of undernourishment. The sad state of modernism's "community life" is reflected in the phrases "financial community," "intelligence community," "community center," "community action," "community of nations," even "church community." American religious life is largely one vast wasteland of "OBEs"--out-of-body experiences. Christians have been successful in something their worst enemies have not been able to accomplish: keeping Christ out of his body, the church. The United Methodist Church, for example, thinks of itself as a "connectional church." Yet one of its major problems is that too many of its members are feeling dis-connected and unconnected, its dismembered spirituality void of every stitch and twitch of transpersonal connectedness. Media connections do not make up the difference, although new technology is likely to press our social connectedness further in directions heretofore unimaginable.

In summary: Since that day in the Garden of Eden when Eve asked Adam, "Do you love me?" and Adam replied, "Who else?" we have been learning the Genesis principle that it is not good that anyone should be alone. Why begin the Bible with *bet*? Because there is no singlefold creation. Plurals are basic to all that God creates. It takes plurals to love, to laugh, to worship, or to do anything else that makes life worth living. "It takes **two** to know **one**," Gregory Bateson once proposed.[22] All of creation, from bears to bodily organs, is created through this primal force of *bet*. Unitariness was the first thing God didn't like--"It is not good for man to be alone" (Gen. 2:18 NIV); "Two are better than one."

—————————————————— 66 ——————————————————

Few tools in our society
are designed for communal (or shared) ownership.
If they were designed for sharing,
rather than for individual use,
we believe they would change structurally, mechanically
and in material composition.

Industrial designers/better mousetrap inventors Victor Papanek and James Hennessey[f]

—————————————————— 99 ——————————————————

God creates in community--light and darkness, day and night, man and woman. We are what we are only because of our community of relationships. All those things that comprise what it means to be human are played out in the dimensions of community and tradition. There is no such thing as a "private individual." The Genesis principle of *bet* is clear: A free-standing human is not human. Or in the words of the Apostle Paul, who almost all the time spoke in communal categories,[23] no one lives to himself and no one dies to herself (Rom. 14:7). "We are members one of another" (Eph. 4:25 RSV). Even Jesus was not a solo performer. We have given insufficient thought to the function of the disciples in Jesus' life and to the kind of community they formed together. The communal nature of early Christian life, which manifested itself in the "house churches" headed by leaders like the women Nympha, Prisca, and Lydia, was thus an extension of Jesus' own personal incorporation into a community of faith.[24]

Yet God creates distinctiveness and separateness. There are two separations in creation: light from darkness and land from water. God separated the light from the darkness; God separated the cloud from the water, the sea from the sky. In spite of all the wholeness, things remain distinct, unique. Adam and Eve remain two, not one. Some separations are good and desirable. In microphysics, elementary matter or quanta are treated, not as particles (German physicist Max Planck and Albert Einstein) or waves (Scottish physicist James Clerk Maxwell and English physicist Thomas Young) or as wave/particles á la quantum field theory (Paul Dirac), but as continuous stacks of strings looping out into space with spaces between them. Quanta exist in community, but there are spaces and separations between communities of matter.

—————————————— 66 ——————————————

God guard me from the thoughts men think
In the mind alone;
He that sings a lasting song
Thinks in a marrow-bone.

Irish playwright/poet William Butler Yeats[8]

—————————————— 99 ——————————————

The Pauli Exclusion Principle, which stands at the heart of molecular, nuclear physics, explains why matter does not collapse on itself by asserting that no two electrons, protons, or neutrons can occupy exactly the same quantum state. There is an irreducible communal component to a quantum spirituality. But every person is uniquely incomparable and not interchangeable. At the atomic level of existence, every atom is different from every other atom. Electrons move around atomic nuclei trillions of times a second, vibrating in dumbbell-shaped regions called "spheres"; likewise cells, composed of trillions of atoms, are each unique, with patterns in their membrane surfaces as complex as fingerprints, which show up on photographs taken by electron microscopes.[25]

The corporeal dimension of the spiritual world has been reinforced by scientists' finding a social dimension to the natural and physical world. "Cellular" used to be an expression for a cut-off and isolated existence, a mere unit in larger structures. Scientists today use it in exactly the opposite sense, since cellular existence itself is a complex community of microorganisms. Similarly, quarks, the fundamental building blocks of matter, exist in community. One quark is no quark. At the very foundations of the universe, at the most fundamental and sensitive levels of the atomic and subatomic, physics has unveiled the truth that there is a relational, communal, interdependent, and interpenetrating structure to reality. Even galaxies group together in clusters, astronomers tell us; some small clusters contain ten or twenty galaxies, while others contain as many as a thousand galaxies. The first rule of neurosurgery, according to neurosurgeon Michael Salcman, who spends his life with hands in other people's heads, is "Don't ever pull on anything. Not ever. You don't know what it's attached to. It might be attached to something that's attached to something that's attached to the soul."[26]

The Wholeness Principle

What economist/theosophist Anna F. Lemkow calls "the wholeness principle"[27] pervades all of life. Strictly speaking, there is no separate identity called "self." One person is no person. I cannot exist alone. We take on identity only in relation to community. In fact, humans are so interconnected that one person can directly affect another person's brain activity on an unconscious level. Studies have documented how as one person's brain activity diminishes, so too does the other person's.[28] The opposite is also the case. We need one another to get well. "Nightingale wards" were so named because hospital reformer/nurse Florence Nightingale did not like single rooms. Patients in single rooms did not interact with others, often languished unseen, and, as she suspected correctly, suffered more accidents (actually three times more accidents) than those in wards.

———————————— 66 ————————————

The meeting of two personalities
is like the contact of two chemical substances:
If there is any reaction, both are transformed.

Swiss psychiatrist/analytical psychologist Carl Gustav Jung

———————————— 99 ————————————

"Community" is a word that needs an adjective. The adjective is made all the more imperative by the lack of a Protestant theology of community. "Community" has become one of today's buzz words, so annoying and cloying that one reaches for the flyswatter every time the word makes its appearance. Whenever one talks of "community," a writer in *The New Republic* observes, the reference "is now almost always its opposite." In fact, "the language of real estate commercials and the sentiments of the miniseries sustain a fake community that's worse than none at all."[29]

John Wesley had a similar problem with the word "church." He felt "church" was used mostly by those who did not know what it meant, to represent an entity that did not exist: "A more ambiguous word than this, 'the Church,' is scarce to be found in the English language."[30] Biblical scholar/the *New Interpreter's Bible* editor Leander E. Keck characterizes Paul's entire letter-writing activity as "his struggle for a right understanding of what it means for Christians to be church."[31] New Lights must be very precise in their definition of "community." Not just any community will do. The Holy Spirit builds a particular kind of community with a particular kind of spirit.

First John 1:6 alerts the church to the fact that the gospel's adversaries will also make claims to *koinonia* connections and *koinonia* traditions. A community of "caring and sharing," a "community of togetherness," a "loving" community, are not adequate definitions of community. One could say the same thing about the Rotarians, Eastern Star, or even the Ku Klux Klan. A detailed study of the membership of the KKK in Knoxville, Tennessee, between 1915 and 1930 revealed that 71 percent of the members belonged to Baptist churches and 24 percent to Methodist churches. A KKK gathering, after a successful night ride, using the above criteria of "caring and sharing," "togetherness," and "love" would be a good example of community. Nazism was simply another quest for the homogenous community.

From Community to Connection

The new connections created out of the energies of God's Spirit will have a particular kind of "spirit." Spirit is indigenous to many kinds of community. We speak of "team spirit," "community spirit," "school spirit." The church is a community of Spirit that embodies the spirit of Jesus Christ. That is why the use of the adjectival "Christbody" community: The Church is connections of matter "of one heart and soul" (Acts 4:32 NRSV)[32] organized around the energies of self-sacrificing love. The community's distinctive way of looking at life, its distinctive style of doing ministry, is shaped by Jesus Christ. Australian biblical scholar/Fuller Seminary laity professor Robert Banks believes that Paul's most distinctive contribution was precisely this organic concept of community.[33]

―――――――――― **"** ――――――――――

[Theoretical physics classifies the world]
not into different groups of objects but into different groups
of connections. . . . The world thus appears
as a complicated tissue of events, in which connections
of different kinds alternate or overlap or combine
and thereby determine the texture of the whole.

Physicist/musician Werner Heisenberg

―――――――――― **"** ――――――――――

Paul's original definition of the church as the Body of Christ, a body/member metaphor he used rarely (1 Cor. 12:12-31; Rom. 12:4-5) except in a revolutionary way, is more than a figure of speech. "For Paul the body of Christ is not only on the table," Leander Keck writes fetchingly, "but also at the table" (cf. 1 Cor. 10:16-17).[34] In fact, ecumenist/theologian/prisoner/martyr Dietrich Bonhoeffer's ecclesiology, as presented in *Sanctorum Communio* (1930), is based on a Pauline understanding of the church as "Christ existing as the community."[35] South African church historian/Oxford chaplain Peter Hinchliff suggests that if we want to understand the real nature of the church, as Paul understood it, we should imagine "Jesus Christ of the gospels translated into a community. . . . It is Christ in his corporate and representational aspect."[36] The church is Christ's extended mind and body.

The oldest extant Christian homily has come down to us as the Second Letter of Clement. It was a sermon delivered in the first half of the second century and is included in the canon of the Syrian Christian church. What did the early church preach? "I do not suppose that you are ignorant that the living 'Church is the body of Christ.'" And again: "The living Church is the body of Christ."[37] The church stands on the front lines of the coming reign of God. Or as biblical scholar J. Christiaan Beker entitles his chapter on Paul's ecclesial thought, "The Church [is] the Dawning of the New Age."[38] The event of Jesus Christ spells the end of the old age and the beginning of the new age. The church then is the "beachhead of the new creation," in Beker's words, "the sign of the new age in the old world that is 'passing away'" (1 Cor. 7:31). It is for this reason that Paul recommends not only a "messianic life-style within the church but also a revolutionary impact on the values of the world, to which the church is sent out as agent of transformation and beachhead of the dawning kingdom of God."[39]

―――――――――――――― 66 ――――――――――――――

Only connect. . . .

"Gentle genius"/novelist/pianist E.M. Forster's magic phrase[h]

―――――――――――――― 99 ――――――――――――――

John Wesley's definition of the church, as elaborated in a sermon entitled "The Reformation of Manners," continues Paul's "high ecclesiology" and soma (body) emphasis on the unity of the church and the mutual interdependence of its members. It also states explicitly Paul's understanding of the vocation of the church: not for self-preservation but for world transformation. Wesley weaves the strand of individualism into the fabric of community in such a way that the depth, height, and breadth dimensions of faith are explicitly stated:

This is the original design of the church of Christ. It is a body of men compacted together in order, first, to save each his own soul [the depth dimension], then to assist each other in working out their salvation [the height dimension], and afterwards, as far as in them lies, to save all men from present and future misery; to overturn the kingdom of Satan, and set up the kingdom of Christ [the breadth dimension].[40]

Christian identity is multidimensional. Embodiment works both ways, including both individuation and aggregation, personity (as it were) built out of community, a yoking and splitting that Teilhard de Chardin called not only compatible but inseparable. In the words of biblical scholar Robin Scroggs, "The individual is not complete apart from the community; the community suffers loss if an individual leaves or does not participate."[41]

"I Can't Be Me Without You"

The relationship of the whole to the part (or "sub-wholes," as they are increasingly called), of the single cell to a multicellular organism, is at the heart of the contemporary mathematics of quantum theory. It is an incredibly complex field of inquiry. General systems theory teaches that the entirety of any system supersedes and cannot be explained by the attributes and realities of its component parts. The mind, in other words, is more than one hundred billion cells connected by a web of neurons. Authenticity in postmodern culture must reflect this integration and wholeness. New Light communities are based on the "different from" principle of transcendence: The whole is different from the sum of its parts. Transcendence is a relational concept.

---------- 66 ----------

Not Chaos-like, together crush'd and bruis'd,
But, as the world, harmoniously confused:
Where order in variety we see,
And where, tho' all things differ, all agree.

English satirist/poet Alexander Pope[i]

---------- 99 ----------

All religions have something to do with the whole, the totality. Parts have no existence apart from wholes. In the modern era religions largely succumbed to the Enlightenment's fragmented, fetishistic love for the part. This is the essence of sin: Mistaking the part for the whole, or separating the part from the whole. Sin is falling into the trap of synecdoche--taking a part for the whole (*pars pro toto*) or the whole for the part (*totum pro parte*), the sin of individualism and the sin of collectivism.

Modernism drank this draught of synecdoche to the dregs. Indeed, the modern era got more than a shade drunk in its passion for the individual. In almost every jeremiad sociologist/preacher Robert Bellah writes, there is this persistent weighing of the relationship between the individual and the community, with the latter found wanting. The Frenchman/anthropologist Louis Dumont comes theoretically close to equating modernity with the progressive triumph of individualism. International business and government consultant/organizational behavior and management professor David Kolb similarly defines the modernist ambition as "the attempt to institutionalize an individual or social subject free from traditional restrictions."[42] People who make fragments become fragments.

The modern state and the modern economy unleashed tremendous individualizing and collectivizing forces, depersonalizing people into both autonomous individuals and homogenous masses. Simultaneously, Christian communities became both collectivistic (fundamentalist subcultures that could not imagine what it would be like to have beliefs other than their own) and individualistic (liberal quests for personal fulfillment). Individualism and collectivism are equally sinful. God's "kindom" is neither an assortment of webs where each spider reigns supreme (anarchy) nor an ant hill where all function mindlessly and mechanistically (totalitarianism).

The New Light apologetic must come to terms with the "communal awakening" of postmodernity. Social ethicist/sociologist/prophet Gibson Winter calls this period of history a "Communal Age," with a tremendous nostalgia for community life manifesting itself in a society of "communalisms" (fundamentalist, private, public, democratic, and so forth).[43] Lutheran dean/theologian Mark R. Schwehn finds the "ascendancy of the community question above all others" so "striking" and "novel" that he portrays issues relating to community as "the most vital theme within contemporary intellectual life."[44] New Light leadership is fundamentally gathering communities together and building them up into a true body of Christ. A Christbody community will have its finger pointed at both the personal and the communal. It will protect the interests of the community at the same time it preserves the identity of the individual. It will make room for the rebel, the heretic, the virtue of nonconformity, at the same time it encourages discipleship, obedience, and the virtue of fidelity. It will realize that not all members of Christ's body are equal (in the words of the house of Israel's complaint, "The way of the Lord is not equal," Ezek. 18:29 KJV). But all are equal members. There must be a place for the individual within the community, and a place for the community within the individual.

"God sets the solitary in families," the Bible reads (Ps. 68:6 NKJV). God sets the individual in community. Individuals gain their identity by belonging to the covenant community of Israel and by incorporation into the body of Christ. Theologian/divinity school dean Bernard Loomer calls this solitariness and togetherness, each playing its role as a partner in destiny, the idea of the "communal individual."[45] A person is complete only in community. It is only in community that a person can be truly himself or herself. That is why Quakers will travel for miles to sit together in silence. Silence together is totally different from silence alone.

—————————————— 66 ——————————————

There is no knowing ourselves individually
until we know ourselves as a species.

Biologist/environmentalist Paul Shepard[j]

—————————————— 99 ——————————————

"I can't be **me** without **you**" is how one New Light pastor, Moses Dillard, puts it to his congregation. Individual identity is realized only when it is devoted to a greater whole. People are free and whole only when they belong to a living community, not when they are off on an island somewhere.

Without the whole, we lack the inner strength of selfhood and the outer strength of community.

The Coriolis Force

The connectionist model might also be dubbed the "Coriolis Force" of human fulfillment. The Coriolis Force, named after the French civil engineer Gaspard G. Coriolis, is a horizontally acting force that works in opposite directions in the Northern and Southern Hemispheres and partially governs rotational motions such as the vortex of draining water, which moves counterclockwise in the North, clockwise in the South. Humans are beings that find fulfillment in what appears on the surface to be dual directions--self and society, curling inward and thrusting outward. A human being, created in God's image, has as much of a dual aspect of particle (individual) and wave (community) as matter appears to have at the atomic level. This is why the Holy Spirit is called by Roman Catholic theologian Heribert Mühlen the divine "we" or the ecclesial "we." The Spirit is the person of the Trinity that "makes present to us the Father and Jesus," as well as being the person of the Trinity that "makes us the people of God, one with the Father and Son."[46]

——————————— 66 ———————————

You cannot have well people on a sick planet.

Priest/mystic Thomas Berry

——————————— 99 ———————————

The health of every individual depends on the health of the entire global community, and vice versa. Or in terms of the holographic paradigm, the information of the whole is stored in every part of the plate. London physicist David Bohm writes of the enfolding of the whole in every part as the presence of an "implicate order," where there are retained individual identity and functioning while the shared identity of the larger organism is embodied. The Apostle Paul struggled with this issue in 1 Corinthians 12 and 13. He concluded that individual gifts are for the purpose of building up the community in love. The individual is the quantized state of the community, the unfolding of the whole in the part in which there is an undivided (i.e., "individual") consciousness with the community.

The modern world tried to make the individual coherent apart from community. It was more prone than any era before it to emphasize the propaganda of the part over the reality of the whole. Some sociologists have even argued that mass society actually built stronger individual identities because individuals were forced to make decisions among an array of options, whereas traditionally choices had been made for the individual.

The danger of evaporating the individual self in the "wholeness" of the group is one of the key differences between the New Age movement and the New Light movement. Both reject individualism. But New Age posits in its place a cosmic Oneness. Fritjof Capra celebrates the time when "all individuality dissolves into universal and differentiated oneness." Hence the New Age madness of "You are god."

Not so New Lights. The Christian tradition has invested heavily in the process of individual identity formation. It never sacrifices the individual for the community. Indeed, individuals often have access to deeper truths than the established authorities and larger communities. But this access is combined with, not opposed to, membership in the community. Community deepens and harmonizes the individuality of each member. Mathematician/philosopher Alfred North Whitehead pointed this out in his illustration of the cathedral of Chartres, whose sculptured figures on the cathedral porch retain their individuality while adding beauty to the whole.

Robinson Crusoe Selves

The discovery of truth moved in the modern era toward the privacy of individual illumination and away from community, tradition, and authority. America's romance with "individual salvation," which maximized self-interest and dis-membered spirituality, began with the Puritan heresy making the individual self, not the communal individual or the social self, the sole interpreter of God's word. Through his epistemology and ethics Immanuel Kant did more than almost any modern figure to enthrone the autonomous individual at the center of the universe.

——————————— **66** ———————————

But as it is, they desire a better [community],
that is, a heavenly one.
Second Testament letter of unknown authorship[k]

——————————— **99** ———————————

Swiss Reformed pastor/neo-orthodox theologian Emil Brunner has pointed out how the figure of Daniel Defoe's *Robinson Crusoe* (1719), an Enlightenment bestseller, symbolized modernism's philosophy of life. "It is the idea of the self-sufficient individual, to whose existence the coming of a second and third individual does not essentially bring anything new." Add to this social philosopher/political economist Adam Smith's eighteenth-century law that said if one did well for oneself, one did well for the community, and it is not hard to see how we have arrived at the self-directed religion Robert Bellah identifies in *Habits of the Heart* (1985) as "Sheilaism," where it is every man for himself, every woman for herself, and no one wanting to owe anybody anything.[47] As early as the eighteenth century, Wesley accused Methodists of spending time in their class meetings "looking at their own navels."

French sociologist/philosopher Émile Durkheim, who pioneered our understanding of religion in its most elementary form as a way of getting people to relate to one another, calls these captain-of-his soul, master-of-her-fate notions "the cult of the individual." "The apogee of the individual" is how engineer/writer/film director Alain Robbe-Grillet describes the passing age. His novels contain people who have no personal names, as his act of protest against the mechanized, impersonal, alienating world of extreme individualism. Author/critic Lionel Trilling's *Sincerity and Authenticity* (1972) discusses how the Polonius axiom "This above all, to thine own self be true" has been reinterpreted by moderns to mean being faithful to one's feelings, however fluctuating and unreliable they may be. New York City police report that increasing numbers of drivers simply ignore red lights, stop signs, and barricades.[48] In a world devoid of communal restraints, people are ceasing to feel any sort of group obligation or covenant. Their own wishes are paramount. Community without individuality becomes oppressive. Individuality without community becomes anarchic.

Relational Energy

One of the most revolutionary developments of the postmodern era is its rethinking of the ideas of self, person, and consciousness. Perhaps the most important contribution to this rethinking, indeed one of the most revolutionary developments in psychology since Freud's psychoanalysis, is family psychiatrist/consultant John Bowlby's three-volume *Attachment and Loss* (1969-1980).[49] Neurologist/psychologist/mythmaker/moralist for modernity Sigmund Freud portrayed the isolated individual wrestling with forces within and without as the "mature ego." Client-centered (not theory-driven) therapist/humanist Carl Rogers, whom scholars cite as the most influential psychologist in American history, talked about the "self system" as the goal of psychological development. Carl Jung described "individuation" as the process of becoming a whole self through the integration of the conscious and the unconscious mind. Biologist/developmental psychologist Jean Piaget's "learning theory" soft pedaled education as a communal activity and focused instead on the solo child's developmental needs as a

singular learner reaching the higher ground of personal autonomy and abstract thought.

In contrast, Bowlby's "attachment theory" presents a model of human fulfillment that stands the three schools of Western psychology--behaviorism (introduced by advertising executive/environmentalist/psychologist John B. Watson in 1913), psychoanalysis, and humanistic psychology--on their heads. It is based on the proposition that we are not lonely islands or unitary selves. Indeed, it is only when we accept the contradictions within ourselves, and others, and when we engage in interpersonal relationships that we can fully realize our own uniquenesses and individual personalities. Lev Semenovich Vygotsky, called by physicist/philosopher Stephen Toulmin the "Mozart of psychology," provides an attachment model of education as a communal activity involving adults sharing a culture with children through the "loan of consciousness."[50] For both Bowlby and Vygotsky the self is like art. In the visual arts color, line, and form are nothing but the energy of light that takes visual shape. The energy given off by art is in the community of color, line, and form existing in relationship to each other and to their subject.

---------------------------- **"** ----------------------------

The individual is universal and the universal is individual.
The word "individual" means undivided,
so we could say that very few individuals have ever existed.
We could call them dividuals.
Individuality is only possible if it unfolds from wholeness.
Theoretical physicist/music listener/art viewer/walker David Bohm[1]

---------------------------- **"** ----------------------------

In other words, selfhood, like art, is relational energy. Its creative energies inhere in radiating relationships with others. The conception moderns had of the self as an island has been overturned by a postmodern conception of self as a wave, especially of a self that makes waves. Just as every wave in a field has a certain quantized energy proportional to its frequency, so too every "whole" individual is a quantized outgrowth of the whole, enfolding and upholding the whole at every moment. Christians

depend on others for spiritual sustenance, including the very formation of their faith.

Information Utilities and In-formational Theology

Canadian cultural historian/mass-communications theorist Marshall McLuhan predicted in 1964 something that has come true--the economic ascendancy and implosion of information.[51] According to official estimates, 70 percent of the gross national product will come from service industry activity by the year 2000.[52] One of the most telling power phrases in contemporary English language is the one promising inside information: "in the know." Its obverse side is equally revealing, if damning: "didn't know." Even the expanding "underclass" is defined as much by access to social sources of information as by economic status. Communities of discourse may revolve around the yarns of yesteryear. But not around yesterday's disintegrating Yaltas of organization and power. What is the number one source of capital and power in postmodern society? Information-driven/knowledge-based innovation.

"

Information is proud that it has learned so much:
Wisdom is humble that it knows no more.

Eighteenth-century satirist/poet William Cowper[m]

"

Information-become-knowledge-become-wisdom is the supreme source of power in what newspaper correspondent/futurist Alvin Toffler calls the emerging "super-symbolic, knowledge-driven" economy.[53] The Johannine phrase "the truth shall make you free" (John 8:32) testifies to the power of being informed to transform human history or to liberate history from the bondage of ignorance. Unfortunately, in postmodern society the relationships of information to knowledge, and of knowledge to wisdom, are unclear and confused. What is worse, the accumulation of information and/or the pursuit of knowledge have superseded wisdom as the end of human efforts.[54] The devolution of wisdom into knowledge into information may be the supreme source of degeneration in postmodern society.[55] A character in philosopher/political activist/writer Simone de Beauvoir's *Les Belles Images* (1966) asks when the decline began in those "truly human values of dignity, brotherliness and generosity which gave life a unique savor." She answers: "The day knowledge was preferred to wisdom and mere usefulness to beauty."[56]

What is it that energymatter mainly does? It transmits and codifies information. But information and knowledge are themselves communal categories. No person really "sees" another person, Gregory Bateson points out, using the classic 1943 Adelbert Ames experiment.[57] What we "see" are information bits and sensory bytes that we then assemble and make into a picture image. No human being is "seen" by another human being in exactly the same way.

Selfmade intellectual/millionaire/MIT professor Edward Fredkin, who works in the interface between computer science and physics, presents this position most radically. Some physicists contend that information is a derivative of energymatter. Others say that energy, matter, and information constitute a scientific trinity of equals. Fredkin argues that information is more fundamental than either energy or matter. In fact, Fredkin believes that energymatter consists basically of bits--binary units of information like one finds in computers and calculators. What is deoxyribonucleic acid (DNA), the energymatter of heredity, but information? This makes the universe, and everything in it, basically an information-processing system.[58]

———————————————— 66 ————————————————

[Information] is the difference that makes the difference.
Biologist/epistemologist Gregory Bateson
*[Information] is the difference of form
that makes a difference of content or meaning.*
Physicist/conversationalist David Bohm

———————————————— 99 ————————————————

Church communities of the future, rooted in this postmodern time and high-tech place, must give some attention to the process and transformation of information in its inner and communal life. Information is both a biological principle **and** a theological concept. The modern world began with a religious Re-formation. The postmodern world begins with a religious In-formation.

According to the *Oxford English Dictionary*, to inform means "to give form to, put into form and shape." The purpose of the church is to give form to, to put into form and shape, the energymatter known as Jesus Christ. New Light leaders, therefore, are in-formational connectors helping the body of Christ to become an in-formed church, an in-formational community. In-formational communities exercise both informative and performative functions. The informative function is to impart ideas and to communicate concepts necessary for the life of the individual and the community. The performative function is to involve the hearers in the processes of in-formation: to change attitudes, to inspire participation, to make good things happen.

The human mind has a low "bite rate." We are slow in taking in data when it comes dribbling in. Yet at the same time the human mind has a "high resolution." When information is set in a wider context, placed in larger patterns and purposes, the human mind can absorb almost limitless amounts of information because it can turn that data into knowledge. If learning is knowledge transmission, wisdom is knowledge transaction. In a world where people are suffering from information anxiety, their minds mere storage bins stuffed with unstrung beads of information and false information, people need help in selecting which bits of facts, figures, and forecasts to drop into the waste bin and which to pick up to make into jewelry and clothing. Immense media coverage does not guarantee illumination or real insight.

New Light leadership helps patches of information become cloaks of knowledge. Information brokering is central to creating community in postmodern culture, not to mention achieving synergic states of group consciousness. Association of Theological Schools president/divinity school dean Jim L. Waits, in his address at the seventy-fifth anniversary of the founding of Emory University's Candler School of Theology, calls for clergy to move from their "learned ministry" model to a "knowledgeable ministry" model. "Knowledge ministry" helps information become "alive in the consciousness," as Einstein put it. Knowledge ministers bring people the reliable base of information and bigger picture of life that they need: The knowledge and wisdom that can "speak articulately on the significant issues of public life and community that affect us all."[59]

Christbody communities must come to be seen as thermodynamic units in which the rules of the conservation and degradation of energy apply. Some preachers almost unwittingly do an energy analysis of a congregation, assessing the energy charge of a room, pinpointing the energy flow, and drawing strength from those hot spots from which energy emanates most powerfully. Trinity College dean/Canterbury Cathedral honorary canon/ theologian John Bowker, one of the few to think along the same lines as Waits, argues that "the process and transmission of information, in the human case, is so important that it has never been left to chance: It is channelled, protected and organized in ways which require systems for those purposes."[60]

Reluctance to see communities of faith as information-processing systems and the refusal to assist people in exploring and critiquing the unexamined metaphors by which they live helps explain why oldline communities are in such a state of entropic decline and disarray. Yet entropies of information produce variety within a species as well as new species themselves. The second law of thermodynamics states that energymatter decomposes and, what is more, that the more entropy grows, the less the amount of usable energy. Since the total amount of energy and mass in the universe cannot change, the entropic consequence of the second law is known as evolution.

A major New Light undertaking is the designing of newstream communities that can be "in connection" and "in-formation" with the spirit of Christ. Christ will be embodied for the postmodern church in information.

The following are five gross premises of embodiment, without sufficient space spent on argument, that build anew the body of Christ for the postmodern era -- being "in connection" and "in-formation" with: (1) other Christians, (2) all creation, (3) one's ancestors and ancestral memories, (4) other faiths, (5) technology.[61]

With Other Christians:
The Energy of Betwixt and the Energy of Between

The first of these five untheorized observations is that New Light embodiment means to be "in connection" and "in-formation" with other Christians. Deeper feeling and higher relating go together. The church is fundamentally one being, one person, a comm-union whose cells are connected to one another within the information network called the Christ consciousness. No congregation or denomination can go it alone in being the body of Christ. No congregation or denomination is accountable only to itself. To be "in connection" and "in-formation" is to be related to other Christians and the shared culture of all Christians and to grow a set of organic relationships and coalitions around a common love for God and a common desire to do what Jesus did and go where Jesus went. The danger of bureaucratic models of the church, as opposed to organic ones, rests precisely here: One bureaucratizes something so that one need never interact with it.

——————————————— **66** ———————————————

The trouble with so many people
is that they know so many things that aren't so.
Editor/humorist/lecturer Artemus Ward [pseud.] Charles Farrar Browne

——————————————— **99** ———————————————

Communities have souls, not just individuals. The modern era downplayed a biblical doctrine of salvation that had this communal dimension. In contrast, the New Light movement is concerned about the salvation of ensouled communities as well as individual souls, and the salvation of community souls relating synergistically to one another. There is a difference between the energy of betwixt and the energy of between. The former is where two organisms bring their energies together to form a social energy state known as synergy, or what engineer/lecturer/writer Buckminster Fuller described as "doing more with less"; the latter is where several betwixt energies join together to create an exponential releasing of social states of energy. Through synergia (literally "working together with") the whole can be different from the sum of its parts. The power of community is the energy of between: The synergizing of synergies in which "one [shall] chase a thousand, and two [shall] put ten thousand to flight" (Deut. 32:30

RSV).

Instead of exploring new models of connectedness that multiply syner-gies--pluralist, adaptive, participative, cooperative, democratic structures and combinations--Old Lights are taking the road back to traditional community life, which was better at adding than at multiplying--homogene-ous, unchanging, sequential, competitive, pharaonic-sized organizational pyramids in which the whole stays the sum of its parts. Much of the ground leading to these new models has been trodden before. For example, Peter Kropotkin in his enduring classic *Mutual Aid* (1917), reveals that Russian zoologist/dean of St. Petersburg University/ professor Karl Fedorovich Kessler argued in 1880 that cooperation, not competition, was the major component of evolution.[62] Sociologist Alfie Kohn's *No Contest* (1986) provides sixty years of statistical validation from the human side of the natural world that cooperation and friendship are more productive and stable bases for social systems to work from than competition and aggres-sion.[63] Driven by the need to build anew, the New Light movement rescues from old communities the memories to cherish out of the memories to perish.[64]

With All of Nature: Priests of Creation

Second, New Light embodiment means to be "in connection" and "in-formation" with all of creation. New Light communities extend the sense of connectionalism to creation and see themselves as members of an ecologi-cal community encompassing the whole of creation. "This is my body" is not an anthropocentric metaphor. Theologian/feminist critic Sallie McFague has argued persuasively for seeing Earth, in a very real sense, as much as a part of the body of Christ as humans.[65] We are all earthlings. Indeed, in the biblical view of creation human earthlings do not stand at the apex of God's handiwork. Above us are the angels. The medieval great chain of being preserved this emphasis by placing humans at the midpoint, not at the peak. The world of nature has an identity and purpose apart from human benefit. But we constitute together a cosmic body of Christ.[66]

In an ecological model of the church, the earth is not separate from us; indeed, we are in symbiotic relationship with the earth. Creation spirituality is of tremendous help here in weaning us from this homocentric warp.[67] Jonathan Edwards believed that "the beauties of nature are really emana-tions or shadows of the excellencies of the Son of God."[68] So woven together are the destinies of heaven and earth that it is impossible for us to sin against one part of the body without doing damage to the whole body. No one suffers alone, as Pythagoras perceived when he said that if there is but one suffering soul in the universe, all other souls will be affected with suffering until that one suffering soul is restored to health.[69] An ecological model of community is something on which even sociobiologists can agree with Christians. Edward O. Wilson argues that we humans require life around us, that we cannot do without the living world any more than we can do without food or sleep, because our ancestors who survived were the ones who harmonized with what was around them. With nothing around us, we die.

—————————————— 66 ——————————————

God, you are my God, I pine for you;
my heart thirsts for you,
my body longs for you,
as a land parched, dreary and waterless.

Wilderness sojourner/psalmist David[n]

—————————————— 99 ——————————————

Quantum spirituality bonds us to all creation as well as to other members of the human family. New Light pastors are what Arthur Peacocke calls "priests of creation"[70]--earth ministers who can relate the realm of nature to God, who can help nurture a brother-sister relationship with the living organism called Planet Earth. This entails a radical doctrine of embodiment of God in the very substance of creation. The *Oxford Diction-ary of the Christian Church* (1974) identifies the difference between panthe-ism and pan-entheism: Pantheism is "the belief or theory that God and the universe are identical"; panentheism is "the belief that the Being of God includes and penetrates the whole universe, so that every part of it exists in Him, but . . . that His Being is more than, and is not exhausted by, the Uni-verse."[71] New Light spirituality does more than settle for the created order, as many forms of New Age pantheism do. But a spirituality that is not in some way entheistic (whether pan- or trans-), that does not extend to the spirit-matter of the cosmos, is not Christian. A quantum spirituality can in no way define God out of existence.

With Ancestors in the Faith: Life-Biomass

Third, New Light embodiment means to be "in connection" and "in-formation" with ancestors and ancestral memories. One of the most significant things that can be said about New Lights is that they know their ancestors--not in the name of individual fulfillment, as in so much New Age raiding and raping of others' religious traditions (while at the same time reaping little benefit from its own) but for the sake of communal identity and integrity. In the same way earth is now receiving light from that Big-Bang moment when the stars first clapped together, so the church must allow in light from its first ancestors, who have now become as numerous as the stars.

In the doctrine that Jesus "descended to the dead," the early Christians extended the gospel's boundless compassion even to those who had already died. The greatest Eastern Orthodox theologian of the twentieth century, Georges Florovsky calls this the church's "ecumenicity in time," which needs to exist alongside its "ecumenicity in space." Unfortunately, relations with the dead are no longer normative features of the church's existence. In earlier days we were able to make concrete connections in time through doctrines like purgatory, or the solemn reminder of the churchyard ceme-tery, or, in rarer cases, the coffins of prominent parishioners and lionized preachers buried under the sanctuary floor. The closest moderns came to extending connectionalism in time was on ETC Sundays (Easter, Thanks-giving, Christmas) or memorial dedications, when bulletins listed who gave Easter lilies, Thanksgiving baskets, Christmas poinsettias, or memorial con-tributions--all of which inserted into sacred space an economic criteria for remembrance.

— **66** —

An investigation of just [a single gram] of earth revealed
that an astounding number of small organisms lived there:
among other things 30,000 protozoa, 50,000 algae,
400,000 fungi and 2.5 billion bacteria.

Norwegian ecophilosopher/semanticist Arne Næss[o]

— **99** —

What the metaphor of "brain" was to moderns, "genes" will be for postmoderns.[72] An organismic view of congregational life connects churches to the rest of nature. Organisms produce and reproduce themselves through autocatalytic networks of relationship, one of the most significant of which is genetic information. Organisms are constructed as storehouses of genetic information and intelligence. Ecologist/ornithologist Eugene Odum uses the term "biomass" to refer to the knowledge that is stored in the cells and the genes. Living matter or "life-biomass" is the stored information of the universe, which is of more complexity and sophistication than that contained in all the libraries of the world. Organisms preserve their own history, just as the universe itself contains its own history.

Unfortunately, humans use only 2 percent to at most 50 percent of their genetic potential, still less of their "life-biomass."[73] If most of a human organism's rich, useful gene pool of information never gets used, how much more of a congregation's genes and memes goes forever begging. "Memes," a term first coined by Richard Dawkins, refers to culturally transmitted ideas and customs which have been implanted in the human brain by social interaction and historical development.

One of the first things New Light leadership does is to learn the genetic/memetic endowment and environment of a community. Future leadership will be built on epigenesis: The formation of an organism out of genetic/

memetic characteristics more than generic principles, but an organism that advances in complexity of form and structure. Of course, much information transmitted through the genetic code is common to us all. We hold 99.9 percent of our genes in common with other humans, which is why we can know a great deal about one another even before we have ever met.

But every organism also is coded. No community's story is plotless. In fact, each instance or part of energy matter encodes an image of the whole. Biochemist/plant physiologist Rupert Sheldrake's intriguing but controversial hypothesis known as "morphic resonance" proposes that human learning processes are "morphogenic fields." In the same way animals solve maze-running puzzles more swiftly and easily the more often animals of that type have been faced by, and outfaced, such puzzles in the past, so community learning patterns are established and strengthened by the traditions and repetitions of the past.[74] For this reason some memes are more infectious than others.

Every community means a great deal more than it says; its encoded meanings are inaccessible to those who have not consulted the archive of the given organism's evolutionary history. While every organism is informed by much more than its genetic code, organisms are reluctant to incorporate new energy that is not processed in genetically compatible DNA languages. That is why so many capable pastors, careful not to fall into traps, tumble into them anyway, oblivious to the coded nature of conversations and debates. Without conducting as full a roll-call as possible of the organism's genetic make-up, no community will give up its secrets or bare open its heart to epigenetic challenges that make possible the emergence of new structures which cannot be explained in terms merely of genetic inheritance or memetic expression. "Insider" information helps create new visions for the future.

———————————— 66 ————————————

Land, then, is not merely soil; it is a fountain of energy flowing through a circuit of soils, plants, and animals.
Conservationist/game warden Aldo Leopold[P]

———————————— 99 ————————————

The treasury of a people's memory is often best found in their musicality, however hidden. What songs make their lips quiver, their spines shiver? Biblical scholar/literary critic Gil Bailie argues that every community listens to a "sound track." Indeed, the gospel is being drowned out today by implants of alien sound tracks into the brain. What sound track communities listen to determines what they hear, what they see, what they do.[75] New Light leaders check out the background music to a community's life before making any moves. Only after understanding each community's unique cadence and rhythm, do they even begin contemplating interrupting that sound track, much less changing it.

In short, decoding a community's genetic/memetic hereditaments is the first task of New Light leadership. But in addition to genetic/memetic ones, organisms have two other self-regulatory processes: the metabolic and the neural. Assessments of the intellectual and emotional capacities of a congregation (neural) and its physical strength and energy levels (metabolic) are critical in-formational components that must be gathered before launching any organism down newstreams. Once cracked, a community's code of words, behaviors, and mannerisms can then be recoded into a more convincing and transformative consciousness, given the range of the community's metabolic and neural resources available at any one time. Without recoding for fresh journeys down newstreams, a community's hopes--its feelings, its interpretations, its ambitions--remain a stagnant pool.

When leadership goes with the genes and persuades an organism to extend its consciousness to the whole and go beyond the body's lifetime, mountains move. When one goes against the genes and lives within the memory of the isolated part, even staying inside the confines of its metabolic and neural structures, molehills stop movement. Transcendence, not to mention splicing defective genes, is impossible without connecting and cracking a community's genetic/memetic code.

---------------------------- 66 ----------------------------

When history dies, the future has no children.

Chinese proverb

---------------------------- 99 ----------------------------

The interconnectivity of memory, tradition, and land is a form of extending connectedness to ancestors. When eighteenth century England's premier woman religious thinker/"Mother of Methodism" Susannah Wesley on her deathbed called for her children to stand around her and sing, she conveyed more than a love of music or a joy that triumphed over a time when few found anything to sing about. Susannah Wesley, through that request, symbolized her belief in the communion of saints, the sense that Christians belong to a throng of believers, some of whom reside in this world and some in the next. New Light communities preach "the faith that was once for all entrusted to the saints," (Jude 3 NRSV). They are communities "of the quick and the dead," with connections that extend backwards in history as well as forward to the future.

Through the "great cloud of witnesses" (Heb. 11), the rush of history fills every place where Christians gather. More than anything else the presence of that cloud makes sanctuaries smell holy. Ninety percent of the universe's mass is invisible, felt only through gravity. The "cloud of witnesses" is the "dark matter,"[76] the invisible mass of the church. Dark matter constitutes the old age quality to New Light communities. For it has been in those pews that generation after generation has worshiped, endowing that space with sacredness. A Society of Friends report on the sacredness of buildings puts it succinctly: "Places and things do not hallow people, but the enduring faith of people may hallow places."

Indeed, the proud amnesia of the modern church became hostile to "horizontal" models of relationship with the dead, where they were seen as neighbors to the living, and substituted instead "vertical" models of connectedness that led the dead away from the living and the earth. The severing of our relationship with both our ancestry and our posterity has been so complete that we are now proving ourselves to be the greatest enemies of both. The modern world forgot that it could harm the dead as well as jeopardize the future. New Light communities are dedicated to being, in economist/educator/pacifist Kenneth Boulding's marvelous phrase, "good ancestors to the people of tomorrow."

─────────────── **"** ───────────────

World views, in fact, are not very often exclusive.
Most of us carry two or three around with us all the time.

Jewish-Christian scholar/Second Testament theologian E.P. Sanders[q]

─────────────── **"** ───────────────

The New Light movement casts spiritual nets wider in time as well as space, recovering public traditions that can place communities in an ancestral stream. New Light leaders see their role as one of providing what Aldo Leopold called "split-rail experiences," provoking our awareness of the genetic endowment as well as re-enacting the uniqueness of those "split-rail values" unique to the community.[77] Historian/publisher/theologian/Duke professor David C. Steinmetz argues forcefully in his probing study of the teaching office of the church that solidarity between the living and the dead has theological content to it. "Ministers have been ordained to transmit a message which they did not compose and which they dare not alter. They have been called, not to improvise their assignment, but fulfill a role prescribed for them by someone else."[78] Echoing what Paul said to the Corinthians--"What, did the word of God originate with you . . .?"--Steinmetz then quotes pastor/systematic theologian Carl Michaelson, who told his seminary students that "they ought to preach the faith of the Church even if they could not claim the whole of that faith for themselves."[79]

Tradition, of course, does not transmit only truth and morality but also falsehood and wrong values. Each generation is called to advance the tradition, which is the church's transformative function, not simply to perpetuate indiscriminately whatever is passed on. But if we are not to deprive posterity of a history, the context of our proclamation must not be our own deliberations and expectations, nor, as Steinmetz puts it, the "half-understood context of the last article we happen to have read," but the gospel of Jesus Christ as this is testified by scripture and transmitted by the tradition of the church.

John Calvin put this forcefully: "Those then who have been ordained to declare the word of God, let them know that God has not at all appointed them to put forward their own notions, and to say just what seems good to themselves."[80] The work of the church did not begin with us. It will not end with us. We are carrying on the work of those who have gone before. A Christbody community is an ancestral community. Paul had a conception of Christians as being members of a heavenly church as well as of a local church. Indeed, the local church for Paul was a temporal manifestation of God's eternal commonwealth.

With Other Religions: The Nuclear Threat

Fourth, New Light embodiment means to be "in connection" and "in-formation" with other faiths. To be in-formation means to know each other's songs almost as well as one knows them oneself, and to enlarge the community to include those whose conceptions of God differ from ours in form. To be in connection means to be able to sing, not only selected stanzas, but all the verses.

There is another "nuclear peril" that is almost as dangerous as the technological one moderns became accustomed to fearing. Social anthropologist/provost Sir Edmund Leach was the first to point out this sociological "nuclear peril" when he gave the Reith Lectures in 1967.[81] Modern horizons have been so narrowed, modern interests so confined, that we can know too much about those immediately around us and not enough about others, thus losing the mystery, wonder, and diversity that a broader context and extended family circle brought to earlier Christians. Modern nuclear families "stew in their own juice," as process theologian/Anglican priest Norman Pittenger puts it; so too do modern nuclear congregations. We must enlarge the family circle if our churches are to become nuclear-free zones.

Just as physicists cannot understand truth by one model alone--that is, either the wave nature of light or the particle nature of light--so one model may not suffice to understand God completely. In fact, Bohr's Complimentarity Principle, which he used the yin/yang imbalances to symbolize, says that both features can't be brought into existence at the same time even though both are true. One can be a faithful disciple of Jesus Christ without denying the flickers of the sacred in followers of Yahweh, or Kali, or Krishna.

A globalization of evangelism "in connection" with others, and a globally "in-formed" gospel, is capable of talking across the fence with Hindu, Buddhist, Sikh, Muslim--people from other so called "new" religious traditions ("new" only to us)--without assumption of superiority and power. One Caribbean theologian has called this the "decolonization of theology."[82] It will take a decolonized theology for Christians to appreciate the genuineness of others' faiths, and to see and celebrate what is good, beautiful, and true in their beliefs without any illusions that down deep we all are believers in the same thing.

The American denomination boasting the most "decolonized" official proposal for guidelines for effective interfaith witness is the Southern Baptist Convention. The recommended draft of these "guidelines" emphasized "not judging, not convincing, but witnessing." "Witnessing" was defined as having to listen, "genuinely to run the risk of opening yourself to another person and to his beliefs." The "guidelines" also warned against comparing the best of one tradition with the worst in another. "Recognize the ideal in all faiths, and the fact that most believers do not attain the ideals of their faith." Sadly, the final document adopted by the Home Mission Board of the Southern Baptist Convention excised all the above statements.[83]

The knowledge of the environments of other religions is a spiritual duty as well as an intellectual necessity for the formation of our own religious heritage. The Christian religion does not speak with one voice any more than the religions of the world speak with one voice. The tide of an exoticized and orientalized theology is already at flood stage in New Age thinking partly because of modernist Christianity's theological xenophobia, especially during the Pacific Wave. Modernism's unpretty contempt of and dishevelled spirit of disregard towards other religious traditions reflected its shadow familiarity with its own traditions. In his book on creative singlehood, seminary president/professor of theology and personality sciences John Landgraf makes it a **"prime** requisite to being well-married to another person is being **well-married to oneself."**[84] An example of East-West integration that is less a subversion of the Christian tradition than an homage to it is the flourishing field of study known as transpersonal psychology, where the West's emphasis on material processes of self-realization become mutually dependent on the East's emphasis on consciousness journeys of self-annihilation.

The interfaith embodiment of a quantum spirituality is based not on the Enlightenment search for what the world religions hold in common but on the multitudinousness and uniqueness of each particular vision of truth. The particles known as protons and neutrons are themselves made up of more basic particles called quarks. Quarks come in at least six "flavors"--up, down, strange, charm, bottom (or beauty), and top (or truth) quarks. Each "flavor" of quark also comes in three varieties of "color"--red, green, and blue. It is "color" that is the source of the strong force that keeps the quarks together. Without knowing one another's "colors," our spiritual journey is little more than monochromatic busywork, an attention to the isolated and ephemeral designed to distract the believer from the height of faith's vision.

With Natural Technology:
Sonar TVs and Electronic Bibles

Finally, New Light embodiment means to be "in connection" and "information" with technology. The modern era got hoaxed into believing that science and technology were its best hopes. The postmodern era has a more ironist than positivist view of technological change--the Hydra always grows new heads. The progress of technology does not increase human happiness. New technologies will not save us. But neither will art, poetry, and music save us. The arts integrate experience; the sciences help us to understand experience. Neither is sufficient to create a metanoized life, a decentered self. The postmodern sense of community is now multi-dimensional. Only the whole can save us.

This is a point of some importance as postmodern culture moves from an industrial economy to an information technology and world economy, especially since the church appears to prefer to work in a way opposite to that of the global labor force (both in the manufacturing and the information-services sectors), which is spending most of its time handling and processing information. Science and technology comprise at least half of postmodern culture, with the church investing little of its energies in these areas except for periodic sloganish outbursts of critical concern.

The grand transformation of our communications systems, the spread of automation, the growth of data-bases, the development of the cashless society: All promise heightened possibilities for the church as a connectional community. It simply will not do to resurrect the Luddite spirit and rhetorically or in any other way smash the computer, bash the "goggle-box," crash the idaphores, as the original Luddites in 1812 did to the new technology of cropping frames. Energymatter willy-nilly finds a technological home. Poet/novelist/farmer Wendell Berry composes his diatribes against the computer on a 1956 Royal Standard typewriter. Churches would have to get rid of their cars, their telephones, their books--even that beloved anachronism, the mimeograph machine--if their practices lived up to some of their antitechnology talk, much of which endlessly, and often tediously, reinvents the wheel. Although some within oldline denominations have been among the first to take advantage of computer networking, by and large, the church's preference for the technologically archaic and defiantly drab in hardware, software, and fleshware is unbecoming a follower of Christ.

A New Light apologetic must be technologically aware. It must be open to combining spirituality and technology in ways that do not, as the New Age movement's "push button meditation" audiotapes are prone to do, violate the integrity of the Christian faith[85] or bear false witness to those searching for a quick "fix" on self-fulfillment. Technological change can endanger community life, especially when we so mindlessly "sleepwalk through the process of reconstituting the conditions of human existence," as political scientist/educator Langdon Winner puts it so well.[86] But the advent of new technologies like cable television and electronic networks and teleconferencing may actually make the gospel more accessible and human relationships more human. Technology can be a friend of faith when it enables members, at the mere flick of the remote control button, to interact with intelligent discussions and presentations of the issues that immediately face us or to communicate the good news more effectively to a culture in which more and more people are handling keyboards better than books. To a public increasingly alienated from written culture, the printed word lags behind at every corner of postmodern advancement.

Media ministries, telemarketing, and direct mail may be high risk tactics where the church "can win big or lose big," as one marketing professional puts it.[87] But the church has no alternative but to use the technological resources of the day to the glory of God. In his day John Wesley made pioneering use of low-cost movable type to print mass tracts, pamphlets, and books. Every New Light movement in church history has been facilitated by utilizing the dominant media forms of the age. The traditional door-knocking model of "pastoral calling," for example, has only limited application to postmodern culture where home visitation requires a substantial expenditure of psychological and physical resources by everyone involved. The greatest "calling" ministries today are done by telephone. Part of the appeal of New Age thinking is its openness to the mystical uses of technology, including brain machines ("Techno-Zen"). The computer breakthrough known as cyperspace or "virtual reality" holds out the possibility of facilitating higher modes of meditation and consciousness.[88] A moving chapel service at the seminary where I work connected worshipers in Dayton with people from around the world through the shared prayers of an Ecunet computer community projected onto a large screen in the sanctuary.[89]

─────────────────────── 66 ───────────────────────

The body of a living organism is its technology;
the technology of an organism is its body.
Historian/poet/philosopher Frederick Turner[r]

─────────────────────── 99 ───────────────────────

A haze of fear need not engulf the melding of spirituality and technology. All of creation belongs to God. As co-creators with God, inventing new forms of energymatter (information) is a part of the ongoing work of creation. The car (or computer) can even be seen to be as much a species as a horse. "It just has a more complicated sex life," Kenneth Boulding insists.[90] To be sure, there is tremendous destructive power in technology. All energymatter transformations generate entropy. The nail-biting truth is that there is also tremendous destructive potential in the energymatter organism known as the church.

The Church's "Swimming in Newstreams"

The biggest contribution newstream communities make to a postmodern church may be to show how a sharp sense of Christbody community can be felt in the world in radically new ecclesial forms. In order for New Lights to make a difference, however, the religious establishment must come face to face with its mechanisms of homeostasis and homeorhesis.

The term "homeostasis" was first coined by neurologist/physiologist Walter B. Cannon. It refers to the tendency of any organism to remain the same and to keep structuring itself to prevent change. "Homeorhesis," on the other hand, describes the tendency of an organism's processes to "continue in their original patterns, even if temporarily disturbed."[91] The paradox of nature is that when organisms settle for bland permanence rather than asserting change, homeostasis and homeorhesis destabilize structures and values.

No structure of any superorganism is permanent. Dionysius the Pseudo-Areopagite first coined the term "hierarchy" in his treatises on *Celestial Hierarchy* and on *Ecclesiastical Hierarchy*. "Hierarchy" for Dionysius meant, however, "the orderly arrangement of all sacred things taken together." The purpose of all hierarchical arrangements, of whatever form, was "assimilation and oneness with God," a spiritual ascent that made possible "the continued love of God and divine things, a life divinely sanctified into oneness with Him."[92] Hierarchy today means something vastly different. Hierarchy today means mostly bureaucracy and technology, rigid pyramidal monopolies of information and power chosen by the modern world as its way of organizing human beings into a "holy and harmonious order," as Dionysius first put it.[93]

As power stations of matter, bureaucracies no longer work. Particular social forms are shaped by metaphors of the mind and by systems of communication, production, and transportation. Global paradigm shifts in thinking, technological revolutions, and cultural "de-massifications" (Toffler) have already rendered bureaucratic monopolies like denominations an anachronism. The alienation and antagonism postmoderns feel from and toward highly ordered, centralized structures of religion and politics are only dimly appreciated by those inside these modernist structures of human association. Bureaucratized structures, elaborate "cubbyhole" and "channel" controls, ladder-climbing, risk-averse systems of rewards, authoritarian models of organization--all worked as long as the controlling metaphor for the church was a stable establishment structure of procedures, principles, stone, marble, steel, glass, brick, mortar. As Greek philosopher Plato first put it, ships at sea can only be steered to reach their destination by a single captain and an obedient crew. When the metaphor for the church becomes a living, moving organism of flesh and blood, connective tissues and membranes, structural designs to the ordering of the ecclesial community that lead to negations of spirit need to be redrawn.[94] But the ensuing body will still be hierarchical, for hierarchy is one of the built-in principles of spiritual and biological evolution.

The essence of "mass democracy" was bureaucracy. The essence of "mosaic democracy" is free association and decentralization. Philosopher/political critic Paul Goodman's classic definition of decentralization captures postmodernism's need for more human-scale associations: "Decentralizing is increasing the number of centers of decision-making and the number of initiators of policy; increasing the awareness by individuals of the whole function in which they are involved; and establishing as much face-to-face association with decision-makers as possible."[95] The paraphernalia of postmodern congregational life must be based on a mosaic of models and a plurality of styles that are more oriented toward charismatic (Paul's Rules of the Spirit) than to bureaucratic procedures (*Robert's Rules of Order*); more adept at letting people and things have their head than always trying to keep people and things "under control"; more prone to prophesy ways forward and exercise communal foresight than to move ahead under the procedural banner of long-range or strategic planning; more likely to make decisions based on faith than on feasibility; more susceptible to vision quests and voyages that inhabit futures than ventures based on "find-a-need-and-fill-it" programs and strategies; more eager, as internationalist educator/theologian John C. Wagner puts it, to go "surfing" than "rowing."

— 66 —

All that is ugly in this twentieth-century civilization,
comes from plans. Plans are ugly. . . .
That's why there is no architecture,
because there are blueprints.
Art model/ceramicist/one of film world's greatest directors Jean Renoir[5]

— 99 —

The difference between the two is illustrated in Edward T. Hall's description of how Pueblos in New Mexico go about building a house. The first thing Pueblos do is to select the land. Then they get the money (or the relatives' cooperation and resources). Then they get the right thoughts. They wait to build until everyone concerned has the right thoughts, thoughts that they believe are as important a part of a house as brick and mortar. Having the right thoughts brings people together. It adds to group cohesiveness and solidarity. When a Pueblo Indian builds a house, it reaffirms the group. When a white man builds a house, the last consideration in the owner's mind is reaffirming the group. In fact, much of house building in America is precisely designed to contribute to feelings of envy on the part of associates, friends, and neighbors.

Mansions Not Made with Hands

Postmodern society is wanting to become more organic, not less. The first question is how organic are Christians willing to allow their churches to be? How much spiritualizing of matter will be allowed to take place?

Simply the titles of two of the most influential books in helping American business plan for economic life in the twenty-first century say how bullish economic theorists have become in bureaucratic china shops: management consultant Tom Peters's *Thriving on Chaos* (1987) and management psychologist Rosabeth Moss Kanter's *When Giants Learn to Dance* (1989). Both of these management manuals chronicle a "revolution" in the workplace that is using energy concepts to move organizations beyond the highly centralized, bureaucratic "corpocracy culture" of the industrial era.

"Organetics" is the term one scholar uses to describe this new organizational model of energy processes and system of energy dynamics.[96] Peters and Kanter are not the only ones searching for organic structures that will produce the synergy of harmonious interaction and move toward wholeness. Many are finding them in a fitness regimen of "downsizing," "demassing," and "decentralizing" that places a premium on movement models of leadership over establishment or managerial models. Corporate leaders are now encouraged less to set agendas and follow goals and objectives than to bring forth visions and inhabit dreams. To emphasize mutual collaboration over competition,[97] alliances over adversarial systems, synergetic feedback over chains of command, participatory decision making over pyramidal/top-down decrees, vision management over crisis management, arms-length arrangements over elaborate goal setting and problem solving objectives, some companies have even appointed "synergy czars" and "synergy centers" to symbolize their commitment to more value-creating, relationship-building structures.[98]

66

The first problem with "organized religion"
is that it's too organized.

Banker/seminary trustee F.G. ("Moe") Cavin

99

Revolutionary changes in the way America does business are already in the wings, rendering the modern corpocracy an archaic and decrepit institution. How much more then does the church need to reexamine its incorporated ways of thinking, especially as they have born fruit in that highly bureaucratized and centralized structure known as the "ecclesiocracy." The church must become a high synergy culture. Synergistic living is reached when information sharing and group consciousness results in the organism's performing feats that the same number of individuals, working separately, could not do. In synergy the whole multiplies the power of the parts. The parts are not in conflict with the whole.

Where there is no vision, there is division.[99] Where there is vision, there is little need for legalistic systems, intricate divisions of labor, job descriptions, chains of command, and lines of authority. One of the major ironies of our times is the way in which economic communities are often way in front of religious communities in showing how there can be true discernment of spirits, accurate ascertainment of the "sense of the meeting" (as the Friends would put it), consensus building without striving for consensus blocking movement, and moving forward through collective "preparedness"[100] rather than bureaucratic planning. The section that follows is an attempt to allow prophecy to take the place of precision-planning, position-taking, and interpretation-in-the-interest-of-a-theory.

The "X Factor"

Sports journalist/novelist George Plimpton has written a book about that "mysterious component" which, when added to the athlete's natural ability, gives that player "a kind of boost, like an afterburner kicking in," a "psychic energy" that makes the whole greater than the sum of its parts. He calls it the "X Factor" and describes it in terms of a combination of adrenaline, intelligence, confidence, concentration, and discipline.[101] For Christians the difference between an ordinary community and an extraordinary, life-producing organism is one word: Christ. Christ is the "X Factor," the church's "Plus Factor," the "Inner Power" that transforms an assemblage of individuals into a synergic community of healing and love.

If the church is to become a synergic space, it must first be Christianized. It must meet the ABCDE involutions of the "X Factor." The ABCDE rule for synergic Christbody inter-connections and in-formation is as follows: Alterity, Bonding, Critical Mass, Dirt, Euphonics. The ABCDE involutions, when placed in a biblical framework, represent evolutionary steps to higher spirituality and the ecclesiastics of synergy.

Alterity: Otherness Rituals

The church must provide postmoderns with an alterity of rituals by which they can turn and tune to one another and feel connected to the cosmos. The church has scarcely even begun to harness the radical height-ening of diverse ritual needs expressed by postmodernity, in its quest of the four ways of being fully alive and fully human--the sensory, the mystical, the transpsychic, and the mythic. We need not unpack these in detail here but note only that without ritual expression these four different modes of being are distilled out of life, and with them the how/who/where/why questions of existence.

It would be a mistake to think of ritual as merely transmissive of the old. Ritual is not a Dead Sea of customs and conventions, a stagnating of traditions in heavily salted ceremonies deposited from collective knowl-edge. Scholars of ritual experience are uniform in their judgment that ritual traditions provide openings, holes, spaces into which the new can emerge and even amend the old. Rituals tune the organism, integrating and organizing its multitude of vibrations and energies into communal actions of enormous power. One has only to look at the communal ritual systems of Nazi Germany, which led to mass enslavement, to see the power for both good and bad resident in ritual maps of reality.

Rituals of worship create and center the Christian community. Ritual helps people scale the heights and plumb the depths of their existence. Worship is among the greatest cultural achievements of humanity in that its shafts of light illumine the landscape afresh and reveal strikingly new and important features unseen by previous generations. The forces and powers involved in worship, both communal and private, are some of the most mysterious in the universe. Theologian/bishop/saint Ignatius writing to the Ephesians counseled them, "Don't forsake the gathering of yourselves together for worship. For when you worship Satan's power is broken."[102] At least for Paul, the "coming together" of the community is primarily for wor-ship.[103]

---------------------------------- **66** ----------------------------------

No city or house divided against itself will stand.

Second Testament teacher/prophet Jesus son of God

Their heart is divided: now shall they perish.

First Testament prophet/teacher Hosea son of Beeri[t]

---------------------------------- **99** ----------------------------------

Tragically, our worship has about it the tang less of salt than of saltpeter. We have made worship into a consumptive experience of listening to sermons and singers. We have insisted that one worship style, and one devotional pattern--that of the "mainstream" Western tradition--fit the whole Christian world. Our worship is written and conducted as if it were a dead language, its musty elegance lugubriously resuscitated for the sake of a few fossils from the fifties whose theology of food is still pot luck in an era when home-made, from-scratch, covered dishes have become almost as difficult to produce as hand-hewn covered wagons. One only needs to contrast our organization of energies toward the exploration of outer space and the event-horizons of the universe with our same organization of energies toward the exploration of inner space in worship and prayer. We are not nearly as intelligent or inspired in our interior life of meditation and worship as we are in our outer ways of invention and discovery. Sacred theater today has become other-denying, wearisome worship, afraid of free play, antagonistic to alterities, able only to sing all the old songs and cry all the old tears.

The fastest growing types of churches in the United States are "megachurches"–mostly interdenominational, "market-driven" or "service-driven" congregations who allegedly understand the comprehensive appeal of the shopping mall's choice-culture of convenience, speed, and options. In 1984 only one hundred churches averaged more than two thousand in attendance on Sunday. In five years that number has quadrupled. There are now ten thousand churches that have a weekly average attendance of one thousand or more, one thousand churches with two thousand or more people attending each week. Oldline Protestantism, its budgets groaning under the strain of maintaining citadels of the establishment, is now fashionably into criticizing the megachurch phenomenon as a symptom of America's "growthmania" (which assumes an automatic connection between size and value, between growth and viability, between mass and matter), and a symbol of the compromises oldliners are not willing to make to reach this culture for Christ.

66

$$391,581x2^{216,193}-1$$

The largest known prime number (it has 65,087 digits)

99

To be sure, the concepts of mass and matter are fundamentally distinct in physics. Light is matter but has zero rest mass. The Church's titanic spirit, which continues to take it the way of the Titanic, is proof of what happens when mass and matter are confused. American society is filled with institutional violations of what editor/lecturer Kirkpatrick Sale calls "the Beanstalk Principle," the notion that there is a certain limit or optimal mass size that varies from one thing to another beyond which matter ought not to grow.[104]

Yet consultants/sociologists Robert Buford and Fred Smith of Leadership Network, a church consulting firm, describe the secret of success for these megachurches in terms of their being more concerned about the church's roles than its rolls. These churches grow not because of "growthmania" but because "they see themselves as delivery systems rather than as accumulators of human capital."[105] Their goal is to educate and send people out in meaningful ministries, rather than to get people to come in to the church's forgettable mediocrities. They operate on the principle that, in the words of another megachurch consultant, "if your church cannot provide an excellent program . . . you would do the Body of Christ a service by not offering the program at all."[106] Furthermore, they ironically can be more intimate than small churches, many of which have sold out to American individualism, their pastors acting as private chaplains, and their churches serving as private chapels for individuals and families.

More than anything else, however, newstream congregations, whether megachurch or small church, offer rituals of communal and individual worship that build up the body of Christ, that edify the edifice. The Apostle Paul talks of the need "for the equipping of the saints for the work of ministry, for the edifying of the body of Christ" (Eph.4:12 NKJV). When the Bible talks about the edification of believers, "edify" does not mean intellectual enlightenment but the erection of a building--the building of believers into a body of Christ that is signified by variation, value, and metamorphosis more than growth and size. This is accomplished in a variety of ways.

First, there is a renewed role for the Bible as the book of the community and a new role for the community as an interpretive community of the book. In theologian/Yale educator David H. Kelsey's phrase, the church forms itself around the biblical writings "which . . . provide the images, concepts, principles, parables, etc., that serve to evoke, nurture, and correct the dispositions, beliefs, policies, emotions, etc., that are basic to the identities of members of the community and to the identity of the community itself."[107] In a postmodern culture, biblical authority takes on an entirely different character than it did in the modern period. Authority relationships are now more controlling than authority principles.[108]

———————————— **66** ————————————

Odd, the way the less the Bible is read,
the more it is translated.

Popular theologian/critic C.S. Lewis to playwright/poet/critic T.S. Eliot[u]

———————————— **99** ————————————

A New Light apologetic involves a postmodern relationship with the Bible, not as with an object but as with a "friend." This is less a posture of control and "criticism" than of listening and playing and imagining. As novelist/playwright/critic Gabriel Josipovici points out in *The Book of God: A Response to the Bible* (1988), we are the ones on the receiving end.[109] The modernist misreading of the Bible led to domination, oppression, and ideology. Further, the literal reading of the Bible was as lethal to the spirit as the higher critical readings were. Belief that the Bible is the Word of God, which became untenable in modern intellectual circles, must regain its pride of place in the church without losing touch with the nature of consciousness itself, which is contextual, perspectival, and partial.

Alterity of rituals around Bible study includes new understandings of how the Bible can be used devotionally. The modern period directed its attention to how the Bible, the "scholar's book," could be read scientifically. It was more concerned about interpreting the Bible than interpreting life from the standpoint of the Bible. The disciplines of both exegetical and devotional Bible study must be taught if New Light leaders are to pick out biblical passages that seem bland to the untrained eye and then peel those passages open, showing how they illumine an entire life.[110]

Devotionalism must not degenerate into a pop spirituality. But it must be open to new ways that both the "learned" and the "little ones" read the Bible, from listening to it on audiocassettes on the way to work to hand-held computer Bibles that fit into pockets and allow one to type in a key word or words, then zoom to the appropriate chapter and verse.[111] Devotional reading of the Scriptures must also be as systematic as exegetical study of the Scriptures. Both should begin early. Jerome Bruner's *Process of Education* (1961) argues that any subject can be taught to any child at any age in a form that is honest.[112]

The postmodernist challenge is to make the scriptorial pictorial, transforming biblical images into healing metaphors that become a curative medium of meditation and prayer. Biblical exegesis will then be less "breaking the text down" through word studies and more "trusting the whole" through a scalar field exegesis of the three different types of images-- metaphor, model, and myth. Form-critical analysis appears to be unable to address issues raised by, for example, the prophets' use of imagery.[113] Only in the life-style of a common life, however, do the Scriptures come fully alive with the power of snares broken, cords loosened, wounds healed, and prisoners freed.

―――――――――――――― 66 ――――――――――――――

When you fall, I fall
When you suffer, I suffer;
We are both in the same boat

Ojibwa chant to a slain deer

―――――――――――――― 99 ――――――――――――――

Psychologist/historiometrist Dean Keith Simonton's *Scientific Genius: A Psychology of Science* (1988)[114] traces *cogito to* its original meaning of "to shake together," which he builds into a model of ideas bouncing randomly off one another until they fall into configurations known as "eurekas" or "divine inspiration." This is precisely what happens when teamwork in studying the Bible is accented over individual learning. There is a role for daily personal Bible study as well as for conferencing study and small group discussion. But as the Puritans liked to put it, "The sparks are beaten forth by the flints striking together."

Second, newstream communities will develop ritualized systems of relationship between the human journey and the nature of things. In the modern era worship was demystified and denatured. Postmoderns are driven by desire to explore and celebrate an ever-deepening intimacy with the Great Mystery that is the universe. Liturgies of the earth--fire, land, wind, and water--can restore the biological and physical rhythms of the planet to our computer-programmed consciousness. Outdoor earth rituals can also provide worshipers with experiences of connectedness to all earthlings: What the Sioux Indians call the creeping people, the standing people, the flying people, and the swimming people. All earthlings must be incorporated into the body of Christ in more ways than just through the "blessing of the animals." We must find ritual ways to make earthlings' presence felt, their participation solicited, their voices heard, if the ideal of ecological worship is to be realized.

Bonding: Bonding or Bondage

The great need is for bonding in the church. In the same way that bondage (as in actor/rock singer Madonna's hit single "Spanky") is a perverted expression of the cultural search for bonding, cults are a perverted expression of the religious search for bonding. New Light leaders are bodybuilders who form and facilitate communities where a variety of spiritual gifts can be exercised and uplifted, bodybuilders who direct and connect people with Christ's energy and build synergy in their connectedness. John Wesley, one of the greatest bodybuilders in history, built his select bands, classes, societies, and mass gatherings by the biblical and fully-fleshed concept of "membership." The church that has been Christianized is an organic, intimate fellowship or network, not a political or bureaucratic organization.

For the attainment of synergic states of community, the meaning of membership and the quality of participation must be less rights based than duty based.[115] Community has now become as much something we choose and craft as something we inherit and preserve. When "choice" movements abound everywhere, it is sheer ignorance not to integrate elements of choice into understandings of church if the "church" is to be, using Joseph Campbell's terms, a "macrocosm" of the order of the universe, a "microcosm" of the order of the individual, and a "mesocosm" of the order of the society.[116]

At the same time, however, Christbody communities are not voluntary societies, volunteer organizations, human gatherings one forms and joins out of a community of self-interest. The danger is ever present that the church, in the words of continuing education expert/Christian Ministry

Resources founder/director James F. Cobble, Jr., rather than "existing as a community of believers who are building one another up in love," will "turn into a group of individuals who simply attend a common meeting. Certain beliefs may be held in common, but faith in God becomes a personal and private affair."[117] There is a vast difference between being individuals in crowds (or lone wolves in migrating packs) and communities vibrant with individuals. Individuals in crowds are people who like to do their own thing around people, and with people watching. The body of Christ is the last place on earth where people do their own thing. Christbody connections are where duty to others is ascendant over duty to self, where the gifts of the Spirit are used for the upbuilding of the community and not for the self. The church is a divine creation, an organism of which one is a living "member," that lives the life of Christ and incarnates, however imperfectly, Christ's real presence in the world.

Networking is the real nature of Nature as God made it. Hierarchical or centralized control structures are not how things will get done in the future. Networking is indispensable to disseminating information in a postmodern world. Postmodern religious communities will be constructed, less as independent separate parts, and more as networking centers and social organisms constituting an indivisible whole in which relations to other people and things are constitutive of actual entities. The behavior of the organism is not the product of the behavior of its parts except insofar as the behavior of the parts is partly the product of the structure or behavior of the organism. Part and whole, individual and community, are relationally constituted by each other through dramatic feedback systems and connected units, part dependent on part, such as mass gatherings, face-to-face communities, and small groups.

The history of social creatures reveals three "design limits" or ranges of "magic" numbers clustering around three basic kinds of human-scale communities: the barracks community, the backyard-fence community, and the bed-and-breakfast community.[118] The first, the barracks community, is the political community, with a "design limit" of some five thousand to ten thousand people. Most urban centers in the millennium before Christ, to the extent archaeologists can reconstruct the sites, were created out of population levels of between five thousand and ten thousand people. Most contemporary architects and city planners recommend this range as the preferred size of a community capable of promoting the full scope of economic, cultural, social, and psychological needs within walking distance. Anything larger and the social system tends to overload and burn itself out. The mass gatherings known as campmeetings in nineteenth-century America can be seen in this light as expressions of the need for experiences of political community even by those in the most isolated outback areas of the country. The need for mass gatherings in the postmodern era, whether in "Ichthus" youth festivals or urban camp-meeting "Heartwarmings," will in the future increase in importance.

The second basic kind of human-scale community is the face-to-face, backyard-fence community of neighbors, the primary communal unit through ten thousand years of history. Five hundred seems to be the "magic" number for the optimum size of face-to-face community for non-magical reasons. Five hundred is the memory capacity of the human brain that enables us to know persons by face, by voice, and by name. Four hundred fifty feet is the optimal distance for recognizing a face, even in rough outline. Four hundred seventy-five is the adequate pool of people for mate-selection that is without in-breeding. Not surprisingly, five hundred is the maximum membership one pastor can serve effectively. Even then, the number of possible relationships with a congregation that size is almost 250,000. A community of one hundred people has been proposed as the "design limit" for human relationship if one expects substantive levels of interaction with every member of the community (potentially 4,950 different relationships).

— " —

*In a world of big aggregations of people
and strong pressures to aggregate,
the only hope is in finding small communities.*

Manufacturer/lecturer/educator Hallock B. Hoffman

— " —

The future of the postmodern church lies chiefly in its small, intimate bed-and-breakfast communities, the third human-scale community. For humans to feel secure there must be an intimate and supportive small group (Whig career politician/orator/scholar Edmund Burke called it "the little platoon"). Soldiers under gunfire behave courageously and sacrificially not because of "patriotism" or "orders" or "ideology" but under the constraints imposed by the cohesion of small intimate groups.[119] The postmodern church, besieged from all directions, will respond bravely and faithfully for precisely the same reasons. The good news is that modern communication makes possible even higher forms of group consciousness, "collective intelligence,"[120] and organic existence than ever before existed. Metanoized selves interact into small groups; metanoized groups interact into larger

honeycombed communities; and the possibilities multiply exponentially.

Gallup poll after Gallup poll presents an ugly picture of people not finding help in dealing with life crises from organized religion or religious professionals. This is partly because the modern church's "big-is-beautiful" mentality came to not like to "think small." It minimized small group studies. It overlooked biblical mandates (e.g., Rom. 12:10; Eph. 5:21; 1 Cor. 12:25; Phil. 2:2-4) for the guidance and attunement of small groups. It underestimated the strong internal communications and decision-making processes facilitated by small groups. It sacrificed the "communal discernment of spirits" to personal discernment, and in so doing became nervous around communal encounters with God.

There is perhaps no better illustration of how the church's understanding of connectionalism has changed from a "connectional people" to a "connectional structure" than in the plight of United Methodism's small group experiences. Small groups for Wesley were intimate gatherings at which members held each other accountable, pointed out shortcomings, encouraged spiritual growth, and bore each other's burdens. Small groups today are committees through which the maintenance demands of the denomination sap much of the church's energy and vitality.

For the majority of human evolution we lived in small groups--not alone, or in crowds (the human brain has difficulty with density), but in small groups. As Jesus' band of disciples demonstrated, small groups enlarge opportunities for communication, interdependence, and shared symbolic experiences. They also focus the power of God for those outside the community to behold. Small groups are greenhouses for spiritual photosynthesis or the storing of the sun's energy in sugar that can then be transformed into starches, fats, and proteins to build the body and do the work of mission. An embodiment spirituality cultivates not an individual morality but a connectional morality.

There is a geological law that the hardest and most chemically stable rocks always come to the surface as the softer ones weather and wear away. Rustum Roy calls this the "protrusion of the fundament." He suggests that the inescapable power of small groups in human existence is a sociological "protrusion of this fundament," a corresponding social-psychological law to the law of physical chemistry that presents the number twelve as the maximum coordination number--the maximum number of atoms that can

be packed around a central atom to touch it.[121]

Among the best metaphors for this new understanding of bonding are the harmonic vertical motions, roped-together rituals, and daring initiatives of mountaineering,[122] all of which revolve around teamwork. Behavioral scientist Mihaly Csikszentmihalyi's investigation of mountain climbing, which George Leigh Mallory, the legendary climber of Mount Everest in the 1920s, called an art form, reveals the mythical and spiritual dimensions of the sport. After John Muir's 1873 climb up Mount Ritter, which had been a deeply spiritual experience, he wrote that "Christianity and Mountainanity are streams from the same fountain."[123]

"

Never doubt that a small group
of thoughtful committed citizens can change the world.
Indeed, it is the only thing that ever has.

Anthropologist/seminary trustee Margaret Mead[v]

"

In many ways it is the mountains that turn the pages of the gospel. Jesus spent his first thirty years in a valley that lay cradled among hills. Six of the most significant events in Jesus' ministry occur in mountain settings. His ministry began at the Mountain of the Temptation, traditionally thought to be the barren rocky peaks west of Jericho known as Jebel-Quarantal. From the basalt mount called the Horns of Hattin Jesus is supposed to have delivered the Beatitudes. The 9,232-foot mountain perpetually capped with snow, Mount Hermon, is the most likely candidate for the site of the transfiguration. The triumphal entry began on the Mount of Olives, the main hill east of Jerusalem; Gethsemane lay on its lower western slope. Olives, where Jesus preached his last sermon, was also the scene of the ascension. Finally, the site of the crucifixion is alleged to be outside Jerusalem on a hill called Golgotha, also known as Calvary's Mount. Jesus lived all his life in close relationship with the mountains.

So must we. We must become umbilically attached to other members of Christ's body, as the five people in mountaineering are attached to the same rope. Mountain climbers will scrape against one another, get tangled up in troubles of someone else's making, get vexed at the stones being kicked their way, and even come not to like some of the other climbers. "Where two or three are gathered together," an old saying has it, "there is Beelzebub in the midst of them." But New Lights will draw on the "staying power" of the Holy Spirit to "stay together."

In workshop leader/sociologist Parker Palmer's spirituality of community, endurance is called "staying at the table."[124] One Palmer axiom of community life, formulated just a year after joining an intentional community, states: "Community is that place where the person you least want to live with always lives." His corollary law is that "When that person moves away, someone else arrives immediately to take his or her place."[125] To those who criticize the church for its lethargy, its timidity, its conservatism, its defensiveness, its boredom, university chaplain/educator/prolific author William H. Willimon asks, "Really, now, what do these Docetists expect from so earthly, so human an institution?"[126] But beyond these feelings is the awareness that mountain climbers are inextricably tied together. They comprise what the Germans call a *Schicksalsgemeinschaft*, a "fate community" that rises or falls together. Mountaineers share a common destiny. They "die climbing."

"

Mountain climbers always help each other.

Sherpa/mountaineer/silent inspirer Norgay Tenzing

"

A Christbody community shares a common nervous system. Or, in the words of an old Zulu proverb, "When a thorn is stuck in the foot, the whole body stoops to pick it out." When one member of the body suffers, all suffer. Once again the Apostle Paul gives us the right words, "We, though many, are one body in Christ, and individually members one of another" (Rom.12:5 RSV). True bonding takes place when nothing need ever be said; pain is felt by the others; the entire organism sends its healing resources to that part of the body in need and in pain.

Critical Mass: Critical Mass Democracy

In New Light communities the concept of critical mass is replacing that of majority rule or consensus building as the newstream of decision making. In nonlinear connections small inputs can effect tremendous changes. The fundamental premise of critical mass movement is that the personal investment of passion and commitment counts for something. Indeed it can carry weight that overrides the indifference and boredom of the majority. A minority of concerned, committed Christians can and should have a bigger impact on the whole than a large number of apathetic and bored church members who show up at congregational meetings to vote on their pet peeves and projects. The church should not be run as a majoritarian democracy any more than every action of the American nation should be determined by Gallup polls and voting booths. In America we have a constitutional democracy with a Bill of Rights to protect the minority. In the church we have a prophetic democracy with discernment of spirits often to protect the majority.

Reaching critical mass means arriving at the number of people required to set off a chain reaction. You don't need very many. Armenian explorer/

philosopher/mystic Georges Gurdjieff argued that one hundred fully enlightened people would be all that was necessary to change the world. The transcendental meditation (TM) movement puts the number needed to move to critical mass at 2 percent; psychoanalyst Erich Fromm estimated 20 percent.[127] The means by which these small numbers are gathered are as much through the energies of play and leisure as through work and enlistment. The fundamental question of the nature of quantum fields, for example, is their mysterious vacuum energies.

———————————— 66 ————————————

Where two or three are gathered together,
there am I in the midst of them.

Jesus' formula for the principal of critical mass[w]

———————————— 99 ————————————

The power of small numbers can be seen in the analogy of the laser. What is laser light? It is simply ordinary light that is out of phase and on its own wavelength. Laser light is formed when a certain level is reached (called the laser threshold) of light quanta that are in phase with the wave that stimulated it, augmenting and amplifying the passing wave until a packet of quanta "lock into phase" and become "coherent." This issues in a powerful increase in the intensity of the light. In brief, laser light is coherent light. It is light whose quanta are "in-phase" with one another while the regular light all around it is vibrating "out-of-phase." The power of small groups is in their ability to develop the discipline to get people "in-phase" with the Christ consciousness and connected with one another.

Dirt: Striking Pay Dirt

Geography has been described as the science of dirt. Wholeness must be built on diversity, but diversity has its limits. For the church to recover and maintain its geographical and theological identity as a "peculiar people," it must come to terms with the principle of pay dirt, the fourth involution of the "X Factor."

Every generation inherits spiritual soil that has become either overgrown or overdeveloped with thorny places, hardened paths, and shallow spots. For the gospel to take root every generation of believers must themselves set about the task of striking pay dirt. It is the responsibility of every generation of Christians to invest deeply in the process of uprooting those things (habits, assumptions, questions, conflicts) that choke creativity; replanting those vital branches that have become uprooted; adding new topsoil to the shallow spots; aerating the hardened paths; and cleaning up the thorny, overgrown places. No generation of Christians can strike pay dirt for another generation. Every generation must strike pay dirt for itself.

This is nothing less than the continual process of Christianizing the church. Sometimes one has to get rid of the wrong kind of dirt before striking pay dirt. Research scholar/anthropologist Mary Tew Douglas defines this kind of dirt as "matter out of place."[128] There is some "matter" that is "out of place" in church. The cleaning-off, clearing-out operations that free space for God to work afresh is every generation's task. Similarly, social anthropologist/administrator/educator/editor Edmund Leach in *Culture and Communication* (1976) says that "power is located in dirt," where "dirt" means anomalous boundary phenomena.[129] Boundaries are sources of power because they "test the spirits" (1 John 4:1). Without the common experience of the church's "we," as passed on by tradition, the "I" of subjective experience can be dangerously deceptive.

Few people have not experienced the auditory hallucination of hearing a phone ring while they are in the shower. We are prone to hear sounds that aren't there for two reasons. First, the "perceptual set" of our mind programs us to believe that someone always calls when we are in the shower. Second, the sound vibrations of the shower excite our sense organs. The end result is that we run out of the shower and drip all over the carpet to answer phones that aren't ringing.[130]

——————————— 66 ———————————

[Moses] held to his purpose,
like someone who could see the Invisible.

Anonymous Second Testament letter writer[x]

——————————— 99 ———————————

Because of the shifting terrain of the culture, where illusion and reality are forever colliding across theological categories and spiritual communities, postmoderns have proven themselves "willing to swallow an awful lot of chaff along with our whole-wheat," as Maureen O'Hara delightfully puts it.[131] A case in point is the way the New Age movement embraces Christianity while at the same time burglarizing ideas from "meditation, positive thinking, faith-healing, rolfing, dietary reform, environmentalism, mysticism, yoga, water cures, acupuncture, incense, astrology, Jungian psychology, biofeedback, extrasensory perception, spiritualism, vegetarianism, organic gardening, the theory of evolution, Reichian sex therapy, ancient mythologies, archaic nature cults, Sufism, Freemasonry, cabalistic lore, chiropractic, herbal medicine, hypnosis, and any number of other techniques designed to heighten awareness." The problem with such a bizarre concoction, observes all-occasions Jeremiah/sociopolitical historian Christopher Lasch, is that "though it can sometimes furnish temporary relief from the symptoms of spiritual distress, [it] cannot bring about the equivalent of a religious conversion, a real change of heart; nor can it bring about even an intellectual conversion to a new point of view capable of standing up against rigorous questioning."[132]

Boundary markers keep the church Christianized through open-ended investigations and healthy skepticism as well as testing and cleansing rituals that separate the wheat from the chaff and keep Christian categories clean. The need for boundary markers or dirt is the subject of what used to be called "Christian apologetics." A postmodern connectional church must also be a correctional church. The point is not to purge from the people's faith all traces of religious eclecticism but to lure them away from non-Christian spiritualisms, the occultisms, and the supernaturalisms that undercut the truth in every age of church history.[133] The church must identify continually what constitutes its "dirt," where its pay dirt is to be found, while keeping the insides of its formal community life clean from "matter out of place." Of course, some boundary markers, erected by one generation, must go in the next. For example, the strong modernist boundary separating the individual as "private" from the church as "public" must be abolished. But newstream communities will require identifiable religious boundaries if the Christian faith is to be life transforming and not ludicrously conforming, as it came to be in the modern church, where people revered the Bible but seldom read it; where people were unable to defend the faith because they didn't know what the tradition was; where people just leaped into line with whatever was cool, hip, and trendy.

Euphonics: Theology and Echology

The fifth involution in the "X Factor" is euphonics. Greek mathematician/philosopher Pythagoras thought of matter as the harmonics of the world. Contemporary physicists think of matter as standing waves in an open field. Matter is music. And music is the language of matter, the limerence of light.

———————————— 66 ————————————

May not Music be described as the Mathematic sense of sense,
Mathematic as Music of the reason?
the soul of each the same!
Thus the musician feels Mathematic,
the mathematician thinks Music--Music the dream,
Mathematic the working life--
each to receive its consummation from the other.

Mathematician/musician/poet Joseph J. Sylvester[y]

———————————— 99 ————————————

Little wonder, then, the marriage of the musical and scientific muses in the lives of so many scientists (e.g. French mathematician/audiophile Joseph Louis Lagrange, American chemist/pianist Charles Martin Hall, theoretical physicist/violin aficionado Albert Einstein).[134] The title of Douglas Hofstadter's book *Gödel, Escher, Bach: An Eternal Golden Braid* (1979) succinctly states this thesis about the innate connections between mathematics and music, science and art.

In Greek mythology Mercury was known as the inventor of the lyre, the creator through music of harmony in church and state. But Mercury also served as the winged messenger, the one who links heaven and earth. Those who link heaven and earth today had best understand the deeper message of Mercury: There are no euphorics without euphonics. Or to state the principle in the way sociologist/political economist/educator Max Weber would have preferred, it's hard anymore to have an enchantment without a chant.[135] Due to the impact of Einsteinian space-time wave mechanics, the media, and much else, postmodern culture has become once more, in Torontonian media theorist/St. Louis educator Marshall McLuhan's terms, "post-Euclidean" and "acoustic"--mosaic, simultaneous, in-depth, resonating.[136] Unlike organized religion, music does not have to beg for a living in the postmodern world.

Perhaps the best way to think of the role of music in postmodern culture is not as "music-as-expression," not even as "music-as-commodity,"[137] but as music-as-lifestyle, even music as "look." The lifestyle and look of music is absolutely central to increasing synergies in newstream congregations. Unless a New Light apologetic can transcribe into echological form a theological vision of life and community for the postmodern era, it will only be one discordant voice among many.

Cultural evidence is as everywhere evident as the aural tyranny in elevators, malls, phone lines, stores, offices, "boom cars," even ski slopes, that music is more than the top forty on the car radio. The U.S. Army blares rock-'n'-roll music (specifically Michael Jackson's "You're Bad") into Panamanian president/general Manuel Noriega's stronghold to drive him into Panama City's Vatican enclave. Some convenience stores and shopping malls insert classical tapes or Guy Lombardo records into their stores' sound-systems as "teen-repellent."[138] Police departments are beginning to plug some of history's greatest musical masterpieces--Beethoven's Ninth Symphony (1824), Richard Wagner's *Tristan und Isolde* (1856), Bach's Mass in B Minor (1749), Alban Berg's *Wozzeck* (1914)--into outdoor loudspeakers in crack-infested neighborhoods to drive away drug dealers. Church sanctuaries are being built according to requirements that place first what used to be an afterthought: sound. Business executives are advised, "If you have to address a noisy gathering, try playing music as the crowd gathers before the speech begins. When music stops abruptly, groups usually stop talking and turn to see what happened."[139] A 1989 sampling of Christian magazine readership by the Barna Research Group revealed that the southern gospel magazine *Singing News* is second only to *Guideposts* in Christian readership, with *Contemporary Christian Music* only slightly behind *Christianity Today* in popularity.[140] On the very day presidents George Bush and Mikhail Gorbachev announced their 30 May to June 3 1990 summit meeting, newspaper headlines across America read: "Michael Jackson Upstages Summit at White House."[141]

--**"**--

If the King loves music,
there is little wrong in the land.

Chinese nobleman/Confucian philosopher/sage Meng-Tzu

--**"**--

America's greatest religious thinker, Jonathan Edwards, advanced the thesis that "music, especially sacred music, has a powerful efficacy to soften the heart into tenderness, to harmonize the affections, and to give the mind a relish for objects of a superior character."[142] If Edwards were writing today, he would no doubt advance a stronger thesis: Music now is replacing the word as the universal medium of sensibilities and community life. Rhodes scholar/comparative literature professor George Steiner calls this the "musicalization of sensibility." He traces it to the hunger for community experiences of grace: "Unlike books, which are read alone, which cut one off in their imperative of attention, music can be listened to socially, [and] it offers the attractions of simultaneous intimate and familial or collective emotion."[143]

Music has become, as non-juror/bishop Jeremy Collier predicted in the eighteenth century, "almost as dangerous as Gunpowder; and it may be requires looking after no less than the Press or the Mint. 'Tis possible a publick Regulation might not be amiss."[144] Social reformer/philosopher Jean Jacques Rousseau sought in musical renovation (his own *Le Devin du Village* [1752], being an example) remedies to the state of social fragmentation of his day. Shortly before beginning *Tristan and Isolde*, composer/theorist Richard Wagner communicated to a friend his conviction that part of music's power "consists precisely in communicating the strangest and most unusual feelings to a listener in such a way that . . . he yields unresistingly, as it were, to an ingratiating allurement and thus involuntarily assimilates even what is most alien to his nature."[145]

Actually, we have yet to understand the effect of structures of sound on the mind. What we do know is that music has become one of the most pervasive, if not the most powerful, force in postmodern culture. Background noises and sounds have become as significant as the foregrounded plots and ploys. Music's powers are better compared to economic exchanges and mystical signals than to entertainment. Music helps us to be free; it moves the soul; it also may be, in the words of historian/philosopher/educator Oswald Spengler, "the only art that is capable of clearly expressing what we feel about God."

Newstream communities must find musical ways of building community and interpreting the faith to the postmodern generation.[146] Vibrations are the soul of matter. Every particle in the universe creates two things through its vibrations: light and sound. Electronics now lets us show how light is sound, and sound is color, by the creation of color symphonies from stereos. Every color has its own sound, and each sound its own color. New Light connections turn the body's bioelectric signals into musical conceptions of life,[147] creating vibrant mindbody melodies that make beautiful music unto the Lord. New Lights bring forth and harmonize with others the body's internal symphony of electric voices sounding at different frequencies and intensities. Music shares with ritual the task of harmonizing the emotions. That is why worship is so central to community life--it brings together music and ritual. Worship is the ritual of music speech.

―――――――――――― 66 ――――――――――――

When the angels in heaven listen to music,
and God is with them, they listen to Bach.
When God is away, they listen to Mozart.

German anti-Nazi leader/theologian/pastor Karl Barth

―――――――――――― 99 ――――――――――――

Two postmodern sages, one working at the interface of science and religion (Arthur Peacocke, director of the Ian Ramsey Center at Oxford), the other at the interface of science and economics (Peter Drucker, professor of social science and management at Claremont Graduate School), have a demonstrated penchant for comparing nature and management to a classical musical score. Peacocke portrays God's immanent activity in terms of Beethoven's presence in the Seventh Symphony, or the development of a Bach fugue out of a few brief notes. Drucker is attracted to the symphony orchestra as a model of the postentrepreneurial corporate structure.[148] The attractiveness of this image for understanding the interplay of the individual and the communal in connectional leadership is both irresistible and limited.[149]

"Orchestra" comes from the Greek. It refers to the place in the theater where the chorus danced. This is ultimately why postmoderns want to come to church--not simply to listen but to play and dance and record music and messages they do not fully understand. The church must be a place where people achieve unity from incompatible elements and contrasting notes, melodies, themes. In composer/conductor Gustav Mahler's famous comment to naturist/mythologist/composer Jean Sibelius, "The symphony must be like the world. It must contain everything." The church should be the place where people come to sing and dance and jerk the world out of its indifference and injustice. It is a place of "symmetry"--of pleasurable, rich repetitions ("symmetry" comes from the union of the Greek roots *sym* ["to gather"] and *metria* ["measurable repetition or motion"]). It is a place of "symphony"--of dramatic harmonizations (again "symphony" comes from *sym* ["to gather"] and *phonia* ["harmonious sounds"]). In other words, a New Light church is a place where new music is composed and celebrated, where the dancer and the dance become one.

The orchestral image is also useful insofar as it helps us define new models of pastoral leadership. Orchestral conducting is a mostly nontraditional model of ministry, although Moses is introduced in Revelation as a heavenly composer or choirmaster (Rev. 15:3). In letters to the early churches Paul identified more than two dozen different ministries--administration, service, teaching, pastoring, giving encouragement, and so on. Each candidate for ordination has more facility in one ministry, on one instrument, than the others. The role of the conductor, however, is not to play any instrument. Mahlers and Mehtas of ministry help others play the instruments God has give them. In the modern era many pastors came to see themselves as one-man/one-woman bands. In the postmodern era pastoral leadership must see itself as conducting the "charisms," or "gifts," or ministries of a community.

Seminaries are places that educate leaders to play many instruments, to the end of not playing any at all but of calling forth and teaching and directing others as they play their instruments. Mozart matched parts to voices; today religious leadership tries to match voices to parts. Perhaps our communities would be better served if seminaries stopped educating leaders in how to fit individuals into "job descriptions" and instead educated them on to how to mix and match team responsibilities to fit persons.

―――――――――――― 66 ――――――――――――

Within and around the earth, within and around the hills,
within and around the mountain,
your authority returns to you.

A Tewa Prayer[2]

―――――――――――― 99 ――――――――――――

Conducting is not a weak image of leadership, as the "enablement" model of the 1960s and 1970s made it seem. A biography of the international celebrity/nineteenth-century opera composer Guiseppi Verdi tells of his hatred of hand organs. Few things in life Verdi disliked more than hand organs. In fact, when he died three hundred hand organs were found stored in his basement, testimonies to his one-man crusade to rid the world of an instrument that, to his ears, sounded out of tune most of the time and, worst of all, was played in a tired tempo because when the person turning the handle got tired, the tempo would slow down. One day Verdi stumbled upon an organ grinder on the street with a flea-bitten monkey holding a tin cup. As Verdi passed by, he tapped the organ grinder vigorously on the shoulder, saying, "The tempo! Pick it up, man, pick it up!" Then he continued down the street holding his hands over his ears. Days later Verdi happened upon the same organ grinder, but the man had a whole new look. He was wearing a new suit. The organ was polished. The monkey had been given a bath and looked healthy and happy. As Verdi moved closer to the unexpected scene, he saw a big sign the man had attached to the organ. It read: "Master Musician. Studied with Verdi." If postmoderns are to clean up their acts, if they are to be able to say they've studied with the Master, they first must have been touched and called forth by a master teacher.

If anything, calling forth people's God-given gifts and enabling them to flourish is almost a prima donna model of leadership, at the least requiring the talents and energies of a pulpit/podium virtuoso. Violinist/conductor Eugene Ormandy became so caught up in conducting the Philadelphia Orchestra one evening that he threw his right arm out of joint. Conducting is a high-energy occupation.

—————————————— 66 ——————————————

. . . Some to church repair,
Not for the doctrine, but the music there.

English poet/satirist/witticist Alexander Pope[aa]

—————————————— 99 ——————————————

Conducting charisms is also a servant occupation. Watching the directions and hearing the interpretations of the conductor are significant. But they are not everything. The music is everything. For over twenty-five years a conductor presided over one of the world's great symphonies. When the conductor died, the orchestra scheduled a memorial concert. The concert hall was filled to capacity. The orchestra played the entire evening's repertoire of rapturous music without once a conductor appearing on the podium. The empty podium was the most memorable part of that memorable evening. "For twenty-five years he taught us to honor the will of the composer. Because we did that tonight, we were able to play together."

Pastors help people to play together, to make beautiful music together, by honoring together the Scriptures and by living and playing as a community in the light of God's continuing revelation. The great conductor/"most gifted executive musician" Sir Thomas Beecham, founder of Beecham Opera Company (1923), the London Philharmonic (1932), and the Royal Philharmonic (1946), traveled to a certain city to appear as a guest conductor. During the first rehearsal, he quickly noticed that the orchestra was not well trained. As the rehearsal continued, it became more and more frustrating for Beecham. He finally had to stop the musicians for a third time at a certain place in the score. One of the musicians protested: "Well, just how do you want us to play?" Sir Thomas looked at him and calmly suggested, "Together!"[150]

Even playing together, however, does not address a second postmodern danger. This is the presumption of defining togetherness according to one's own precepts and not the Bible's. From the museum in Vienna where Beethoven's piano is sometimes on display, there comes the story of a young student, touring the country, who quickly ran over to the piano and started playing a few bars of something on it. Then she turned to an aghast attendant and asked, "What do some of the other pianists think of this instrument?" The guard informed her that pianist/statesman Ignace Paderewski had viewed the piano once. The young musician interrupted: "He must have played something most beautiful." "On the contrary," corrected the attendant, "Mr. Paderewski did not feel worthy of even touching it." Pastor/preacher Donald J. Shelby uses the sorry fate of pianist/conductor/composer George Gershwin's Second Rhapsody for Orchestra with Piano after his death in 1937 to illustrate the dangers of postmodern hubris. Gershwin's editors, convinced they could improve on his original 1931 score, literally tore up the rich orchestral parts, destroyed them, and inserted their own lines and harmonies. It was due to the faithfulness of symphony conductor/music director Michael Tilson Thomas and the love of the composer's brother/lyricist Ira Gershwin that the original conductor's score was rescued from obscure files in the Library of Congress and restored to reveal the composer's artistic genius. Postmoderns are prone to treat Scripture as those editors treated Gershwin's music. When we supplant God's original intentions with our presumptions, violence is done both to the Scriptures and to ourselves.

— 66 —

You can't always trust what the pulpit says, . . .
but you can always depend upon what the organ says.

Industrialist/philanthropist Andrew Carnegie[bb]

— 99 —

The biggest contribution New Light leaders can make is not in calling forth people's technical mastery of their specialized skills and gifts, vital as that is. It is not even in showing people how to read the composer's score accurately and quickly and interpret it sensitively and faithfully, important as that is. The conductor's biggest assignment is to get people not just to perform themselves but to learn and listen to the other parts of the orchestra, working together with others' areas of responsibility and disciplining their own sound accordingly. An orchestra of individual virtuoso talents, each maestro only listening to his or her own performance, is a cacophony, not a symphony. Pastoral leadership gathers people together to enjoy and celebrate making beautiful music unto the Lord, playing and knowing in common what they can never know and play alone.

There are serious problems with the orchestral model, however. The first is that the classical idiom should serve as only one postmodernist reference among many. Once classical becomes canonical in worship, the people lose music's powers of both freshness and diversity. Granted, when a Who's Who in Music has categories for a variety of artists, including "classical" and "light classical," and places former Beatles member/composer Paul McCartney in the latter,[151] it is helpful to realize that one generation's "contemporary" sound is another generation's "classical." But when defined historically and in a less relaxed sense, the classical idiom is one of the least exportable models of community, and one of the least international forms of musical expression. For example, two of the most famous "classical" instruments, piano and organ, are expensive and difficult to make. They are also not very transportable when compared to the four truly transcultural musical instruments: guitar, flute, drum, and synthesizer.

"

The man that hath no music in himself,
Nor is not mov'd with concord of sweet sounds,
Is fit for treasons, stratagems, and spoils;
The motions of his spirit are dull as night
And his affections dark as Erebus.
Let no such man be trusted. Mark the music.

Poet/playwright/plantsman William Shakespeare[cc]

"

In the same way as New Light leaders must balance their own instruments with the instrumentation of their sections as well as the interests of all the 105-plus orchestra members--New Romantic school composer/conductor Richard Strauss warned aspiring conductors "Never look encouragingly at the brass"[152]--they must also function in many roles simultaneously when it comes to musical styles. New Lights display openness toward the artistically new and solicitude for the welfare of the old. There is more than one way of worshiping, and there is more than one way of bringing spirit out of matter.

The five most significant forces in the history of music are French chanson, Italian baroque opera, Viennese symphony, American jazz, and American rock. Norwegian "ecophilosopher"/farmer/mechanic/mountaineer/musician Sigmund Kvaloy insists that postmoderns be able to play different types of music for different social arrangements.[153] The classical model is one that is "governed from the outside." In practice time, which is alone, one reads sheet music, learns metronomic beats, counts and subdivides bars, and prepares for group practice, when the conductor, alone holding the whole score, walks in and replaces the metronome. If one doesn't comply with the stick or go with the plan, there is a loss of face and security.

New Light communities are able to cope creatively with a diversity of nonclassical genres of community life. New Light leaders must be able to punch in and enjoy a variety of musical styles as well as play multiple leadership roles: classical, jazz, rhythm and blues, country and western, southern gospel, space age, rap. In the jazz band, for example, every member has the same importance. Without any conductor, jazz musicians are challenged to "swing" with the rhythm, find the flowing wholeness, and get in touch with music's "forces in motion." A jazz musician's doom is counting, keeping track of bar lines and beats, or memorizing improvisation. Jazz functions especially well as an international language. At a jam session in Tokyo, a saxophonist can sit down with a trumpeter from Argentina, a drummer from Moscow, a clarinetist from Sweden, and a bassist from Nigeria. Soon everyone will be "swimming in the same river" of flow.

Every jazz musician has a moment of creativity or scat made possible by painstaking and disciplined practice and profound musical intelligence. Jazz music no less than classical requires the most sophisticated technical equipment, highest levels of mastery, and most expert musical knowledge of harmonics, scales, tone, phrasing, rhythm, and dynamics. Discipline is the sine qua non of all creative outbursts of the artistic spirit. Without disciplined practice, every believer settles for less. But "practice" is not a means to an end, or a medium of perfection but a preparation for receptivity, an orienting of one's being to receive God.

―――――――――――――――――― 66 ――――――――――――――――――

A song is anything that can walk by itself.

Composer/guitarist/folk-rock singer Bob Dylan[dd]

―――――――――――――――――― 99 ――――――――――――――――――

From the family of instrumentalist/composer Fritz Kreisler comes a compelling story of one of the greatest violinists who ever lived. Kreisler hated to practice. He loved to perform. His wife, concerned about the stewardship of his gift, constantly urged him to spend more time in practice, while he devised excuses, until the issue became a thorn in the flesh of their marriage. As his brilliant career began "to withdraw into winter's quarters" (an Argentinean idiom that means to go into retirement), a huge testimonial banquet was arranged for Kreisler. Admirers came from all over the world to pay him tribute. Kreisler beamed when he was introduced as "the world's greatest living musician." Turning to his wife amid the promenade of praise, he said, "Did you ever hear such adoration?" She replied quickly, symbolizing how fast a change it is, without practice, from the *ludique* to the *tragique*, "Fritz, think what they would have said if you had practiced." A disciplined life and the daily doing of unpleasant "chores" are as imperative in the jazz idiom as in the classical. Without disciplines in its life together, a community settles for less as surely as a bird who only walks, a cat who only crawls.

The notion that God may enjoy nothing better at times than to listen to jazz saxophonist/composer Charlie Parker or rock-'n'-roll singer Elvis Presley or country-western singer/seminary trustee Willie Nelson offends the modern sensibility that sits the "sacred" squarely side by side with the "classical." A battalion of prejudices greets the introduction of electronic synthesizers in worship for precisely this reason. Just as the present-day piano is the successor to the aristocratic harpsichord (except its strings are struck rather than plucked), the synthesizer is the successor to the majestic organ which is nothing but a twelfth- or thirteenth-century synthesizer of sound, through pipes instead of electronics. The piano is here to stay. The organ is here to stay. The synthesizer is here to stay. But the dearth of new piano literature and organ compositions testifies to the inadequacy of sound constructed and organized in the traditional manner to satisfy the creative yearnings of contemporary composers. "Serious" pianists and organists, like "serious" worshipers, are more "ingenious antiquarians and painstaking curators" of a bygone age than original artists.[154]

No matter how much we might prefer otherwise, God is not conducting the drama of postmodern lives today through Bach or Buxtehude or Baroque culture. Bono Vox, lead singer and lyricist of the Irish rock band U2, is a New Light believer who writes music with a social conscience: Songs warning against drugs and dealing with death, hate, suffering, and the environment. His Grammy Award-winning album *The Joshua Tree* has sold fourteen million copies. Similar things could also be said about Bruce Cockburn, Clash, Tracy Chapman, Midnight Oil, Russ Taff, and The Call. The environmental movement is making rapid headway among the younger generation because Greenpeace, Friends of the Earth, and other environmental groups have turned to rock musicians like Sting, Peter Garrett, XTC, and Paul McCartney to transmit environmental messages.[155] In a letter to the editor of *Greenpeace*, fifteen-year-old Becky Loop of Caldwell, Idaho, testified to how she first became sensitized to ecological issues:

listening to groups like REM, U2 and Midnight Oil. I joined Greenpeace at an REM concert. If I had parents who didn't allow me to listen to any kind of music with a beat, I wouldn't know or care about anything but my own life, and I wouldn't be inspired to make the world a better place. Please open your ears.[156]

"Classical" church music survives in most American churches in much the same way that musical genius/pianist/composer Igor Stravinsky said Hungarian composer/pianist Franz Liszt's tone poems "survive" in concert halls: "only by constantly renewed neglect."

If one does not hear the music, it has been said, the dancers will seem mad. So much of postmodern culture seems sheer "madness" to the church because it will not hear its music. Not to open one's ears to the music of the day is to close off one of the most powerful means of communicating the gospel and to close down the closest thing humans have to a universal language. Already, postmodern popular music is less "rock" than "space" (aka Mannheim Steamroller). The rock era, born in 1956 with Elvis Presley, represents a fairly conservative attempt at traditional music-making in the face of momentous revolutions in technology and economics. By the 1980s rock music was on the wane.

Not all musical expression is worthy of human ears. Not every musical trend should be baptized into the faith. Satan, and Satan's protege the satyr, are both master musicians: The devil plays the violin, the satyr the lyre or pipe. Punk music is a mean manifestation of the negationist, iconoclastic, anarchic impulses in postmodern culture, for example, and deserves our disrespect. Seminary trustee/children's lobbyist/institute director Tipper Gore is prophetic in warning of the dangers of opening up our mental and spiritual intake valves to musical fantasies of gore and sexual violence.[157]

The eighteenth century Evangelical Awakening that John and Charles Wesley participated in "unleashed one wild wave of religious hysteria" and irrational "enthusiasm" after another. Through their poetry and music, however, the Wesleys directed many of those wild energies into constructive channels and visions of the future. The Wesleys published at least fifty-seven hymn collections during their lifetime, all of which were designed to be devotional books for the people to memorize, all of which gave rise to a new form of religious art and public worship that has captured the hearts of the people down to this day: hymnsinging. The differences between the revolutionary developments of the Awakening and today's deformation in music are at least twofold.

First, the Wesleys wrote music for the people to sing that, while fresh and contemporary, at the same time called on the commonplace. As English instructor/hymnologist Martha Winburn England puts it, "The trail of Wesley tunes would lead our day from Lincoln Center to City Center, from Broadway to Tin Pan Alley, from the Rare Book Room of Union Theological Seminary to some very red lights indeed."[158] Hymns, to be real hymns, must be fresh expressions of the spirituality of the people. This was at the heart of the Wesleyan revolutionizing of Protestant hymnody. Methodism was the only religious denomination in America, church historian/seminary

librarian Norman Kansfield has determined, to require its pastors to spend a specified amount of time each day (e.g., five hours per day in 1784) in reading and study.[159] The Wesleyan New Light movement insisted on leadership that mastered and meted out the dominant media forms of the day.

Postmodern leaders must be disciplined in spending required time not just with books and films, the popular cultural forms most beloved by academics, but also with radio, television, cassettes, videos, and compact disks. Like the piano and organ, the book is here to stay. But so too is electronic communication. Pop videos are particularly postmodern inventions: Aesthetics and economics, art and advertising, are one and the same. The challenge of pop videos has been how to create on a small screen the intimacy and community of a live event. It is a challenge the church has yet to comprehend, much less meet.

Squirm Appeal

Second, postmoderns no longer come simply to hear the music played by the orchestra. Postmoderns come to sing and dance and learn new dances. The great Anna Pavlova was asked after a performance: "What did you mean by that dance?" She is said to have replied, "If I could say it, do you think I would have danced it?"[160] In his masterful study of *The Prophets* (1962), Hasidic scholar/philosopher/ethicist/mysticist Abraham Heschel speaks of the "pathos" of God, by which he means God as Supreme Artist and we as artists in God's image. The church must come to see communal sensibility as an artistic exercise. Our churches must become art colonies, schools of the dance, sanctuaries of entrainment. For too long they have been auditoriums for the consumption of entertainment, or when put on by church cartels, "infotainment": passive listening to sermons, passive listening to singers and instruments, passive responding to liturgies.[161] The participatory moments of modernist worship are times of bodies standing rigid in place behind bolted-down pews, tightly clutching hymnbooks. The last thing worship is designed to do is let real feelings out.

Hymnbooks were originally intended to be devotional books that

people kept at home and used for personal and family prayer, theological study, and hymn memorization. Worship should give full measure to the body and free all its senses, whether in the form of body prayers and praise, guided visualizations and meditative iconography, or interactive preaching and overhead projector hymnsinging. The use of musical and visual motifs in worship help to complete the circle of one's being.

The collapse of the professional paradigm for ministry appears to some as anticlericalism. But "clergy" and "lay" categories are fundamentally an establishment's division of labor, not a New Light movement's preoccupation. If anything, modernist worship drove bigger wedges between pulpit and pew than almost any other era of worship had. That is why clergy downsizing can mean lay upgrading if the change represents a triumph of spirit over structure, a transition in resource mobilization and empowerment that taps more into personal initiative, team relationships, and cooperative communication than "formal" institutional mechanisms, managerial control channels, organizational charts, and structural maintenance.

———————————— 66 ————————————

Somewhere . . . is a continual music.
Termites make percussive sounds to each other
by beating their heads against the floor. . . .
Almost anything that an animal can employ to make a sound
is put to use. . . . [Bats] have been heard to produce,
while hanging at rest upside down in the depths of the woods,
strange, solitary, and lovely bell-like notes. . . .
Fish make sounds by clicking their teeth. . . .
Leeches have been heard to tap rhythmically on leaves. . . .
Even earthworms make sounds,
faint staccato notes in regular clusters.
Toads sing to each other.

Neurologist/pathologist/biologist/poet Lewis Thomas[ee]

———————————— 99 ————————————

The difference in "lay" levels of contribution and satisfaction between the church as a centralized, efficient worship/workplace and an alive spiritual organism dancing to the rhythm of sanctification (or what some call "divinization," others "christification," still other "celestification") can be seen in a story that came out of the annual Los Angeles combined choir performance of Bach's *St. Matthew Passion* (1729). Choir members were anticipating the event with more than the customary enthusiasm because the great Leopold Stokowski was scheduled to conduct the several hundred singers and orchestra. At the dress rehearsal Stokowski concluded the practice by tapping for silence and then saying:

Well, I guess you know the notes well enough. But the spirit is lacking. I want each of you to sit down tonight with your Bible and read St. Matthew's account of the life of Christ. Try to grasp it all. Who knows--perhaps that message is just what our listeners need in a time of doubt and despair. Then let's come back to our performance and try to convey to our audience the meaning and inspiration of these sacred words.

For the same reason some concert pianists memorize their music away from the keyboard so as to avoid the predicament in which their fingers "know" the music but their souls do not, so too did Stokowski want his musicians to "know" the music in the most basic biblical sense. Choir members confessed that "we singers were startled to hear this advice from the worldly, debonair, Stokowski. But we did as we were told. The next day we sang our hearts out for him."[162]

Postmoderns want to sing their hearts out. But their parts must be heard in concert with one another, just as the various voices in a fugue, or in rock-'n'-roll, respond to one another and play off against one another simultaneously.

Every age builds its cathedrals. Postmodern communities, like premodern pyramids, early modern cathedrals, and modern films, required the individual skills of many people collaborating for their completion.[163] Community is the highest collective form of divine cocreativity.

Image Intermezzo III: Wave-Riding

The individual and community synergize for mission. Waves are the product of wind and water. This is where wave-riding comes in. When I was in high school, I earned money during the summer by lifeguarding at various Christian camps in the Adirondack Mountains. One summer I worked at Sacandaga Bible Conference in Broadalbin, New York. Included in my job description was the task of taking teenagers on speedboat rides every afternoon. It was a tough assignment, but somebody had to do it. I quickly learned that there are two kinds of teenagers who go to Christian camps. There are those who, when the engine is revved up and the throttle let out, stand in the middle of the boat straddling the bounce across the waves while yelling, "Faster, faster." These are the wave-riders, and you can see the exhilaration and excitement in their faces. Then there are a whole other crew of campers who are not at the center of the boat, but are leaning over the sides of the boat, clinging for dear life, hoping and praying that this wonderful experience will soon be over. These are the boat-huggers. You can tell this type from the looks of fear and panic in their faces, as well from some other physiological symptoms best described no further. Boat-huggers and wave-riders: two very different types of mission for the church.

God calls the church to leave the harbor, lift anchor, and launch out into the joy and risk of the deep sea. Our mission is not to hug harbors, or drop anchors where it is safe, or cheer as other boats sail into the deep. The place for the church is on the high seas--where it is turbulent, where it is dangerous, where storms gather with their fiercest intensity. In early

Christian art the church was portrayed as a boat driven upon a perilous sea.

Jesus made this very clear to his disciples in Mark's account of Jesus rebuking the storm. One evening an exhausted Jesus was sleeping on the little seat placed at the stern of Peter's boat when a sudden squall arose on the Sea of Galilee, notorious for its storms. As the splashing waves broke upon the boat and the disciples found themselves bailing water, they panicked and rushed to the stern of the boat where Jesus was sleeping. Shaking him violently, they cried out despairingly, "Master, the tempest is raging. The billows are blasting high. Don't you care we are sinking?" Brushing off sleep, Jesus arose, went briskly to the side of the boat, stretched out his arm, and spoke peace to the storm: "Peace, be still."

What a magic moment! What a privilege to have witnessed one of the most spectacular miracles of Jesus' ministry, his subduing the waves and wind with the mere sound of his voice. What a thrill to have been there for such an event. But Jesus turned to his disciples angrily and rebuked them: "Where is your faith?" (Luke 8:25 RSV). They had missed the real blessing. What could have been more of a thrill than witnessing this miracle of Jesus calming the storm? The miracle Jesus wanted to show them was not the miracle of calming the storm, but the miracle of calming them in the storm.[1] Think what it would have been like to have experienced the miracle of wave-riding, the joy of knowing that no matter how fierce the storm, no matter how many crises in your cruises, nothing of ultimate harm could happen to you as long as you were in the boat with Jesus. With Jesus in our midst, there is nothing to fear.

Jesus never promised to speak peace to every storm in our lives. In fact, Jesus' dictum to his disciples in Mark 13 was basically "in the world you shall have tribulation." But Jesus did promise to speak peace to us in every storm. One of the most beautiful prayers ever written is the traditional prayer of the Breton fisherman: "O God, thy sea is so great and my boat is so small." Jesus is calling the church to be a community of wave-riders--people who will lift anchor from whatever holds them in life's harbors; people who will sail off into the high seas of ministry and mission; people who will believe that even when God does not calm the storms, God will calm them in the storms; people who will know that to voyage with Jesus is to enjoy peace even in storm-tossed experiences. The storms came upon the house built on rock no different from the house built on sand. But it stood. The point is not to avoid storms but to stand through storms with Christ.

As John Wesley was making his way to Georgia from England aboard the merchant ship Simmonds in 1735, he watched in total amazement as a community of Moravian passengers continued to worship God and sing in the midst of an Atlantic storm, as if nothing were happening. Wesley marveled at this kind of faith. Then he asked God to help him develop a faith for when the big storms blow. If more people were to see that kind of faith today, there would be a population explosion of wave-riding believers.

THE WIND OF SPACE "... AND DWELT AMONG US ..."

The church is a spatial force. Space and energymatter have coevolved. The creation and perception of space, the breadth dimension, govern a religion's worldviews in more ways than even "structuralism" has appreciated--an academic fashion that streetcar conductor/librarian/television critic Clive James has dubbed "the greatest invention since pig Latin. It can make an idiot sound unfathomable."[1] For Isaac Newton, as for all moderns after him, space is the "sensorium of God," the dimension in which God does God's best and most absolute work. For Christians living in North America, a land vast in space, identity is most often expressed in spatial terms.[2]

"

The truth of space is time.
German theologian/dialectic philosopher Georg Hegel's maxim.
The truth of time is space.
Brazilian Lutheran pastor/theologian Vítor Westhelle's maxim[a]

"

After energy becomes matter, the Word is made flesh, space must be occupied, and incarnation come to dwell among us. Spirituality is a spatial and thus public matter, not a private concern. But space has no identity apart from energymatter. "Space is three dimensional," mathematician/geometrist/physicist/pioneer relativity theorist Hermann Minkowski writes, "with the three pairs of directions length, breadth and height." Where and what should be the space of the postmodern church? What should be a New Light apologetic's way of relating to external space?

Geomantic Missions

There is a new science of place-making, first developed in Germany in the 1930s and in Britain in the 1960s, that is attracting widespread attention among architects and builders. It is called geomancy which means literally "sacred geometry." It can be better defined, in the words of geomancer Richard Anderson, as "the act of finding the right time and place for human activities."[3]

These questions were asked of Jesus: "Is this the right time?" "Is this the right place?" Pentecost announces that the Holy Spirit enables every time to be the right time, every place to be the right place. Now is the right time and the right place for the evangelization of the gospel. Postmodern missions must have a geomantic imagination and geomantic design. What I am calling a geomantic style of evangelization will ensure harmonious habitation patterns as the gospel interconnects and interacts with all life- and landforms.

The geomantic evangelization of New Light ministry will be based on a revolutionary visionary space. New Lights go not to those who want them the most but to those who need them the most. Like the father in the parable who raced to embrace in love and forgiveness his prodigal son, New Lights will race to embrace in love and forgiveness those in need, whoever they are and wherever they have broken down.

Who Are the Lepers?

John Wesley was among the first figures in modern Christian history to portray the missional task of the church as the establishment of global space for the gospel.[4] His geomantic principle was an updating of St. Francis' exploiting of religion's centrifugal forces--"The world is our cloister": "The world is my parish." The fundamental purpose of any religious community is not to seek and serve itself but to create a geomantic *Ethos* of hospitality and friendship for the world's increasing numbers of "lepers," and to provide spiritual and cultural space for mission in a world that destroys space for everything that does not end in material attainment and status advancement. Without a sense of transforming mission, the church is limited in space. Unfortunately, the spatial bias of the contemporary church has been toward the inside and away from the outside, toward itself and away from the created world. Space in modern America came to have private but little public meaning.

In the Bible, no other disease is accorded equal prominence with leprosy.[5] It has such ritual and theological significance that Jesus not only touched those suffering from leprosy (Mark 1:41), he also instructed his disciples to go out two by two and "cleanse lepers" (Matt. 10:8). Quantum spirituality confronts the dark alleys, the hidden niches and street corners of "Filth and Wine" (Fifth and Vine), where lepers live. The breadth dimension of faith, where energymatter occupies space, challenges Christians to take their theology for a walk. The moral transformation of *Ethos* attends the religious transformation of *Logos-Pathos*. Instead of faith living with its back to the streets, Jesus expects us to march our theology up and down the streets of life, relating the gospel to what is seen in all its glory and gore. A space full of sweetness and light, of dopey optimism and pollyanna promise, is not the biblical *Ethos* for ministry. Faith must become streetwise.

Our world is filled with lepers--not simply the fifteen million people today who suffer from leprosy's rotting limbs and running sores but also those suffering the modern-day plagues, at the sight of which we pull up and cry, "Leper! Leper!" as we back away in disgust and distrust. Lepers are the people and principalities forgotten and let go by a society that prefers romance to reality, those whom we abandon physically and, what is even more devastating, those we abandon spiritually and emotionally. The fate of lepers is like that of Naaman, the Syrian general whose story gets recorded in the First Testament. In spite of all of his gifts, his position, his authority, everything was negated by this one sentence: "But Naaman was a leper."

Naming the lepers too often is little more than a tour of the poor and homeless, little more than a cleansing bath in guilt, little more than scrubbing our missions off with buff-buzz words like "oppressed" and "dispossessed," which temporarily washes away our omissions. A New Light apologetic needs to locate lepers as Jesus understood them--sectors of society that the world abandons because it needs to abandon them, because their presence is a threat to the establishment's peace of mind and sense of order. For example, Eden Earth, once our mother, has now become one of our lepers. The present plight of our global condition calls for a new theology of human nature, not simply the human nature issues of original sin but also issues of what Thomas Berry calls "human-earth relations," which explore the interaction between humans and their natural environment. No wonder New Lights sometimes get controversial and end up offending everybody. Mary's *Magnificat* contains more social and political dynamite than Jefferson's *Declaration* and Marx's *Manifesto* put together.

66

God cannot prevent the fall of a sparrow
without unmaking the world.

Physicist/vibration researcher/musician Sir Brian Pippard[b]

99

"Pinged"

When nations find the presence of diplomats offensive or undesirable, there is an internationally recognized procedure for having such persons "pinged" (declared *persona non grata*) and for getting rid of them. We too have "pinged" members of our society, marked them *persona non grata* by figments of modern prejudice and indifference, and are constantly finding new and furtive ways of getting rid of them. Modern evangelism focused its concern on "nonbelievers" and let drift to its peripheral vision the oppressed "nonpersons" of the world, as Gustavo Gutiérrez has argued so persuasively.[6] The *Ethos* dimension of faith can be defined as that space-turned-to-place where lepers know themselves loved and accepted, where lepers feel the touch of God healing them, transfiguring them, and changing them "from glory to glory." Postmodern believers are people who, when they wish to experience the touch of God's hand, touch a leper.

Paul Brand is a world-renowned surgeon who devoted much of his life to reconstructing clawed fingers, twisted hands, and deformed feet at the leper hospital in Vellore, India. One Christmas he was guest of honor at a party in the dormitory where the lepers lived while they waited their turn for surgery. After a long day in the operating room, Dr. Brand came to the party and was immediately asked to speak. Exhausted and empty of ideas, he breathed a prayer for the winds of God's Spirit to speak through him. As he rose, he was struck by the sight of the lepers' hands--some half-hidden in concealment, most grotesque in their disfigurement.

"How I would love," he began, "to have had the chance to meet Christ and study his hands! But, knowing what he was like, I can almost picture them.". . . The carpenter's [hands], rough, tough, gnarled; the healer's, sensitive, compassionate; the crucified hands, marred, yes even **clawed.**

"And then there were his resurrected hands. . . .Why did he want to keep the wounds of his humanity? He carried the marks of suffering so he could continue to understand the needs of those suffering. He wanted to be forever one with us."

Silently, one by one, the lepers lifted their hands high. They were the same stumps, scars, and claws as before. Yet they were not the same. No one now tried to conceal them, for they had acquired a new dignity.[7]

The notion that some people are more valuable than others, or what might be called the modern myth of the disposable person, is one of the more toxic wastes of modern society. The sacred value of each person is diminishing as the technological value of certain persons is rising. Our world is bleeding from a thousand different veins because of this erosion of the more decent and humane qualities of human life and the sustained abuse of the weak and innocent. We live in a lifeboat society where those who are weak, or uneducated or deformed or unwanted are perceived as having less of a right to consume the earth's resources than the strong, intelligent, beautiful, or loved.

ULKs, CTDs, WOGs

Our hospitals are filled with patients nicknamed "ULKs," "CTDs," and "WOGs": ULK is a nursing acronym found written on hospital charts identifying Down's syndrome babies--it means "ugly looking kid"; CTD is physician medicalese for patients on the precipice of death--it means "circling the drain"; WOGs is a clerical acronym used by some religious leaders for people suffering from AIDs--it means "wrath of God syndrome."[8] ULKs, CTDs, and WOGs are examples of people deemed disposable. They are a few of the ones targeted to be the first thrown overboard. If the truth be known, many of them have been tossed out already. But they do not go alone. New Lights count with pride the times they also have been given the "Jonah's lift" over the side.

66

A man searches for bones and scraps in the dump site.
Now shall I write about the infinite?
A worker falls from the roof, dies, and will no longer
*   eat his lunch.*
Should I then talk about the fourth dimension?

Peruvian poet/novelist Cesár Vallejo[c]

99

At Amiens in medieval France, the leper was required to stand in a grave while the priest threw three spadefuls of earth on his or her head.[9] In other more merciful communities, the dirt was pitched toward the feet. But such rituals, including the infamous "lepers' mass" in which the diseased were reckoned "as one dead," did not go out with the medieval period. The same stigma, segregation, and deprivation can still be found attached to today's lepers. Tragicomic novelist/sardonic humorist/word coiner Kurt Vonnegut calls this the "star syndrome," the notion that some people, by virtue of what they do, who they are, and what they have, can be, and indeed exist to be, sacrificed like pawns on a chess board to ensure the survival of the stars. The "star syndrome" is but an updated version of the Nazi doctrine of *lebensunwertes Leben* ("life that is not worthy of life").

"If you're not good for something," we say, "you're good for nothing." The Bible begins with a different set of values: "Behold, it [is] very good" (Gen.1:31 RSV). Life itself, being itself, is valuable, whether it is good for anything or not. God created us as "human **beings**," not "human **doings**." The belief that certain people are expendable is morally reprehensible. The church's greatest spatial heresy is its failure to walk the road with lepers, its diminished sense of the indivisibility of humanity and of God's endowment of each member of creation with sacred worth and dignity--its refusal to recognize that we need the ULKs, CTDs, and WOGs of this world more than they need us.

John Wesley spent eighty-eight years answering the question, "Who are the lepers?" in a consistent and compelling way. The Evangelical Revival began as a mission to lepers, to social outcasts, to political untouchables, to religious pariahs. Jonathan Edwards, in his double role as chief architect and chief critic of the American Awakening, insisted on "fruits" as a major "distinguishing mark" of true spiritual transformation: "As when we see a tree excessively full of leaves, we find so much less fruit; and when a cloud arises with an excessive degree of wind we have the less rain."[10] One of Wesley's favorite sermon texts was Isaiah 55:1: "Ho, every one that thirsteth, come ye to the waters" (KJV). Wesley's opposition to the theological elitism of predestination overflowed into an opposition to social elitism. "God is not willing that any should perish," Wesley wrote on 20 May 1739, quoting from 2 Peter 3:9, "but that all should come to repentance." In God's eyes there is no objective division of social space into deformed or beautiful, sick or healthy, nasty or nice, Down's syndrome or EGC (exceptionally gifted child). There are only children of God whom Christ loves and for whom Christ died.

——————————————— **"** ———————————————

. . . Space is God. And it is indeed clear to me
that all the space there is, not proper to the body,
all the space there is without the bounds of the creation,
all the space there was before the creation,
is God Himself.

Great Awakening preacher/philosopher Jonathan Edwards

——————————————— **"** ———————————————

If God were discriminating in the economy of grace, we would all be in trouble. Transcendentalist/preacher/poet/essayist Ralph Waldo Emerson observed this a century ago: "There is a crack in everything God made." No matter how clear the glass, it is full of tiny cracks that can suddenly shoot across at shattering speeds. If glass were flawless, it would be much stronger than steel. At the start of one of Billy Sunday's revival campaigns, he asked the mayor to send him a list of all the people who needed special prayer. The mayor sent over to him the city directory.

One way or another, we are all cracked. We all distort the light. We have no cause to boast. For this reason, Georgian short storyist/novelist Flannery O'Connor spent much of her life writing reminders to the Christian community of its special responsibility to the ugly, offensive, abandoned, expendable members of society. For this reason, Guggenheim fellow/artist Diane Arbus spent much of her life photographing those "pinged" by society--the deformed, shopping-bag ladies, drunks, derelicts, dwarfs, the mentally deficient. What the soul is to the body, declared the anonymous author of *Ad Diognetum* in the second century, the Christian is to the world. Christians are to be the world's soul--its conscience, its compassion, its salt. We are to keep the world from rotting.

On 21 May 1771 physical scientist/Cambridge divinity professor Thomas Rutherford heard Wesley preaching from Hebrews 8:10-12, where it reads, "For all shall know me, from the least to the greatest." Wesley's sermon emphasized that God's way is to begin with the least and then move to the greatest. All true awakenings of God's Spirit have begun with a similar maxim for mission. In New Light space there is no separation between evangelism and social justice, between evangelizing the lost and, in the unforgettable words of poet/author/organizer Meridel LeSueur, "remembering the dismembered." The Christian heart is an organ that has one beat.

Empty-Shoulders/Open-Doors/Full-Tables Geometrics

Throughout the Christian tradition, processions and pilgrimages were religious acts most conducive to releasing curative energies and health-giving, redeeming powers. The church must be healed of its spatial heresy, its endless round and rigmarole of splitting mission into spiritual space and material space resulting in useless space. Each year some ten thousand new books and articles on evangelism appear, which perpetuate these insidious distinctions between the "personal gospel" and the "social gospel." Perhaps the healing of space can be aided by the parable of an imaginary pilgrimage down a modern Jericho Road.

―――――――――――― 66 ――――――――――――

Hospitality to strangers
is greater than reverence for the name of God.

Old Hebrew proverb

―――――――――――― 99 ――――――――――――

You are driving your car late one winter evening down a desolate, country road. Suddenly the car jerks, sputters, and stalls out. The next ten minutes are spent turning on the ignition, to no avail. Now even the battery is dead. The temperature inside the car is now approaching the freezing conditions outside. You bundle up, put on your gloves, and step out the door to hail down some passing motorist. For fifteen minutes you wait for a motorist to pass, without even one sight of headlights in the distance. The only light comes from a darkened farmhouse, about five hundred yards ahead. There is one window illuminated in the back of the house. It is after midnight, the light in the house suddenly goes out. But you have no choice. The winds are too strong, the cold too piercing, the hands too numb. As you come closer and closer to the porch steps, your hands warm up from the sweat of fear until, by the time you make a trembling fist to knock on the door, the fur lining your glove has become soaked. The house seems so dead, and the door knock goes unanswered so long, that you begin to wonder if the window really was lit. Then the door begins to creak open. Without looking up you blurt out all your apologies about the late hour and your problems about a broken-down car. But before you can say very much you hear these words, the best and most beautiful words a stranger could

173

possibly hear in a situation like that: "Come inside. Don't be afraid. We're Christians here."[11]

This world is filled with people left out in the cold--broken down in life physically, emotionally, socially, economically. Geomantic evangelization is an open invitation for strangers to come inside, even without warning, always certain of welcome. In the early church, one could travel among Near Eastern cities as a stranger, come into a new city, identify oneself as a Christian, and be greeted as a brother and receive hospitality, University pastor/biblical literature scholar Wayne Meeks has written.[12] When the church extends what might be called an empty-shoulders/open-doors/full-tables hospitality to all guests (and therefore to God) to come in from the cold, the spatial heresy of the church will have been smashed, and its rolling-stone missionary career halted.

Front Porches, Town Squares, Rocking Chairs

There is only one problem with this parable. It doesn't exactly work. First, it is a rural road. By the year 2000, 94 percent of the American population will live outside of rural areas. By the year 2000, with the cities of the world growing at a rate of eight million people a month, there will be five hundred "world-class" cities, with half the world's population living in cities. To be sure, the city as we know it has become archaic and decrepit. Gridlock, to mention but one example, is grinding it to a standstill. The Bible, some wag has suggested, is as relevant today as it was yesterday. For example, consider Noah's taking forty days to find a place to park.

But, the cities of the future will no doubt be new creations, human-scale communities in which people spend as much time "cocooning" by the fireplace as on nights on the town. Whether large (metropolitan) or small (micropolitan), future cities will be made up of villages full of front porches, town squares, and rocking chairs, where people can live and work and shop in the same vicinity. The insanity of sprawling tract suburbs, a world built by work-bound men and homebound women that can function only if there are cars to drive and nonworking women for chauffeurs,[13] is more and more made painfully clear by the "dumbbell" existence of its adults (a long, grueling commute between work at one end, home at the other) and by the "latchkey" existence of its children.

The fastest growing communities in the country are the "urban villages," "edge cities," and "technoburbs" where jobs are close to people's homes. SmallCity USA is even proving irresistible to retirees. The workplace will be the neighborhood of the twenty-first century. Future cities will also probably be less workplaces than hometowns for various niche neighborhoods based on socioeconomic, cultural, and ethnic lines.

What is clear is that the postmodern church must end its institutional and visual idolatry of rural life. The church must rid itself of its antiurban *ethos*. Twenty-eight thousand people live in the John Hancock building in Chicago every day. No denomination knows what to do with them. No church I know of is more at home on wormhole, ten-lane freeways than on sidewalks and country roads. In fact, America's oldline denominations are so out of their element in the culture where the masses live that, to give but one example, 40 percent of all Presbyterians in Chicago (population 3.1 million) attend one church--the thirty-five-hundred-member Fourth Presbyterian Church.[14] Some futurists claim we are moving from a world made up of countries to a world made up of cities. They believe that within the lifetime of our kids people won't understand what "country" means. Approximately 250 million people lived in the world when Jesus was born, most of them in rural areas. But Jesus was born in the city--Bethlehem. Jesus grew up in a city--Nazareth. Jesus was crucified and resurrected in a city he loved and wept over--Jerusalem.[15] The Bible begins in a garden, the Eden of the Book of Genesis. But the Bible ends in a city, the New Jerusalem of the book of Revelation.[16]

————————————————— **66** —————————————————

It does not matter where I am, Kowloon or Hong Kong-side;
around me always . . . the huge endless stir of the place,
the roar of the traffic, the passing of the ships,
the comings and goings of the ferries,
combine into one gigantic sensation of communal energy.
For the most part, I know very well, it is not energy expended
in any very high flown purpose,
but still its ceaseless rumble and motion move me,
and I sit there gnawing my chicken,
drinking my San Miguel beer from the can,
more or less entranced.

Newspaper correspondent/editor/novelist Jan Morris[d]

————————————————— **99** —————————————————

"On the Road Again . . ."

The second problem with the parable is that geomantic evangelization means being on the road again, always on the road again. The wind wanders, carrying us on quests and journeys through what Martin Luther called hells of despair, purgatories of uncertainty, heavens of assurance. The ends of the earth are where a pilgrim people ought to be.[17] Geomantic evangelization is not sitting at home, waiting for vehicles to break down outside the church's doors. Scholars estimate that Wesley traveled between 3,000 and 4,500 miles per year; preached at least two sermons per day, and from 1748 to 1790 traveled 225,000 miles and preached over 40,000 sermons. When someone criticized Wesley for leading such a "vagabond life," he replied, "Why, indeed it is not pleasing to flesh and blood; and I would not do it if I did not believe there was another world." Hebrews 13:13 speaks of going "outside the camp" to meet Christ. Who lived outside the camp? The outsider, the alien, the foreigner, the stranger. A quantum spirituality does not just travel on the road; it lives on the road, forever on the move both in terms of space and social context, never finding a place for itself in any culture. The true definition of "catholicity," nineteenth-century German theologian/philosopher Friedrich Schleiermacher wrote, is the pursuit of Christianity's completion by helping it find true expression in every culture and every time. In such a life hospitality to strangers is necessary for survival.

The Five Spiritual Laws of Systems Dynamics

If "Follow me" means "Hit the road," then postmoderns must learn certain geometrics of the Jericho highway. The postmodern geometry of evangelization is not of the character of the "four spiritual laws" that Old Lights have used to evangelize the gospel, "spiritual laws" that allegedly govern the relationship of God to humans in fashion parallel to the Enlightenment's physical laws that govern the physical universe.[18] Rather, these spiritual laws are more like the winds that blow in faith's breadth dimension. Collectively they constitute the *Ethos*, the weather pattern in which the locomotion of a geomantic mission takes place.

————————————— 66 —————————————

Cars today are almost the exact equivalent of the great Gothic cathedrals . . . the supreme creation of an era, conceived with passion by unknown artists, and consumed in image if not in usage by whole population which appropriate them as purely magical objects.
Semiologist/pianist/watercolor painter/television watcher Roland Barthes[e]

————————————— 99 —————————————

Whether America's oldline churches disintegrate or are reorganized through the formation of dissipative structures depends largely on how well they follow these five essential principles of locomotion governing dynamic living/open systems. Anthropologist Gregory Bateson calls the new resystematization of knowledge known as "general systems theory" and its impact on contemporary thought "the biggest bite out of the Tree of Knowledge in two thousand years."[19] That may be. But so far systems theory is so theoretically self-conscious, its academic heavy-breathing so ponderous and off-putting, its worrying every point to within an inch of its life so exhausting, that it has yet to transform significantly the modernist style of systematic theology into a postmodern living systems approach to theology.

Systems theology differs from systematic theology in the same way the world of a field naturalist differs from that of a molecular biologist. First, systematic theology tried bringing the study of God under rational control by segmenting and quantifying the participants in the theological system, whether reductively or deconstructively. Systems theology, on the other hand, is a holistic approach to the dynamics of God that seeks to increase wisdom about how God works, toward the end of more harmonious, systemic interactions with God.

Second, the objective of systems theology is not the erection of one *summa theologia* á la Karl Barth or Paul Tillich or Carl F.H. Henry but the establishment of an "ecology of models."[20] These road rules for autocatalytic pathways that distinguish living/open systems from artificial/closed systems are quintuplets, members of the same family.[21] They are less five separate laws of directional change than one unifying law. If certain ones are favored to the exclusion of the others, postmodern missions to lepers will get blown astray. The road rules are (1) You can't steer a parked car, (2) You can't drive forward without a rear view mirror, (3) You can't pass in the slow lane, (4) You can't repair a car while it's still in motion, and (5) You can't run on empty. I use the image of the car because it is, along with the country house, America's most characteristic social artifact.

Road Rule
#1
You Can't Steer a Parked Car.

The road to hell is said to be paved with good intentions. How many thousands of miles of blacktop has the church put down bridging the diseased, depraved, destitute ditches of life with spans of goodness, truth, and beauty? Why then isn't there more of Christ in our world? Why is the human race an endangered species, engendering such urgent need for acts of conservation? Why does it seem that Planet Earth itself has AIDs, humans' fire-snuffing, land-raping, air-polluting, sea-poisoning, our energy-sapping, matter-spoiling, space-constricting, time-distorting ways uncontrolled and unchecked?

One reason is because stock-taking is preferred to risk-taking. The church has been putting itself through pre-flight paces when it should have been living a risk-laden life. How many Christians are sitting in front of the wheel, keys in hand, frustrated by the meager precision of prevision, waiting for the "this-is-the-way-walk-in-it" (Isa. 30:21) word, searching for clearer directions, and arguing over the quickest way to go. The Smucker sisters, elderly Mennonite folk artists from West Liberty, Ohio, embroider this road-rule on pillows: "You can't plow a field by turning it over in your mind."

Every time you make a move, you take a risk.
Actor/television producer/host ("Let's Make a Deal") Monty Hall

---

You can't steer a parked car. "A closed system glides towards its equilibrium state, stalls out, and stops there."[22] A closed system moves toward more perfect organization, control, equilibrium, sustainability and predictability, all of which are euphemisms for death and stagnation--or in systems language the state of perfect maintainability and structure with no destabilizing features. One of modernism's most balmy notions was that health and preservation were to be found in predictability and sustainability, that order and chaos were mutually exclusive correlates. Even the most elementary use of systems observation (not to mention sexual reproduction) reveals just the opposite. Dynamic reality is a bubbling cauldron of disorder, irreversible changes, disequilibrium, and instability. Open systems resist thermodynamic equilibrium. They demonstrate a dynamic openness to risk-taking exchange with their environments. It is only when organisms risk entropy, when systems risk the possibility of running down, falling apart, and crashing, that they become dynamic vehicles for God to use for world transformation. Energy connectors and life forces bring chaos before harmony.

No faces would ever age, no skin would ever wrinkle, if no one ever went out into the sun, if no one ever showed an emotion. But what a price to pay to look young. It is only when New Lights risk getting on with it, even when they don't feel like "getting," even when they're not "on," and even when they're not quite sure what the "it" is, that life comes into focus, lepers can be seen, the postmodernist future is defogged, and missional road maps can be made to make sense. It is only in the act of trusting that we discover God's trustworthiness. It is only in giving up the security that sustains and maintains that the universe can truly sustain and maintain us.

The problem is, of course, this is exactly the opposite of the way in which the drivers of the earth's five hundred million motor vehicles in use each day (one for every ten human beings) want to operate. Moderns have been taught not to move until we know where we're going--not only where we're going, but what we're liable to have to go through to get there. We don't want it said of us what historian/folklorist/poet Carl Sandburg's song said about Kalamazoo: "We don't know where we're going but we're on our way." We want to be able to plan ahead, to predict, to exercise control, to be efficient.

Marshall McLuhan, while teaching at the University of Toronto, became embroiled in the dispute over whether to allow the expressway to be shot through the heart of the city. He wrote the then premier of Ontario a letter in which he gave this wonderful aphorism about life lived in the global village: "Mere concern with efficient traffic flow is a cloacal obsession that sends the city down the drain."

———————————— 66 ————————————

It's not so hard--you push down the accelerator and turn left.
Racecar driver Bill Vokovich, when asked how he won the Indianapolis 500

———————————— 99 ————————————

The truth is, of course, that what postmoderns find on the road is unpredictable, inefficient, and uncontrollable. Destinations and destinies are not always in a one-to-one relationship. Moses went up to the top of the mountain to escape and came down with marching orders. The modern world is like a Mack truck without brakes careening down the hill at seventy miles per hour. It is out of control, leaving behind dented vehicles and broken lives. "If someone is going to stop it, they have to jump on it."[23] How can New Lights wrest the wheel away from the lunatics and Looney Tunes who have steered the twentieth century? How can New Lights diminish the destruction on the highway of history when modern culture will not apply biblical brakes to slow it down? Perhaps by recalling and if need be relearning skills hardwired into our cerebellum when we were but children. Perhaps by listening to our children, who often impart valuable information in unexpected ways. Perhaps by relearning the secret of "taking a chance on God" that children show while riding simple things like bicycles and leaping off of swings into our arms: Security in insecurity, stability in instability, safety in danger, control in vulnerability, life in death, steadiness in speed (the faster a bicycle's wheels turn--they work like gyroscopes--the steadier the bike).

Yet we persist in the ineradicable stupidity and lethal folly of our modernist quest for control and security. Before we even take our foot off the brake and venture out into the frenzied, traffic-choked freeways of open-systems existence, we want to take out all the failure insurance that money can buy that there will be no accidents, no breakdowns, no collisions, no tailspins. There is no such failure insurance, and so we sit there in a closed system, afraid of the exchanging of energy or matter with its environment. The road forward is blocked by the big perpendicular, an absorbing preoccupation with the possessive pronoun. This is where the fear of spending one's life in the closed system of a parked car functions as a starter switch. Once the car is in motion, we no longer need the switch and can set it aside. Fear often gets us to begin a trust relationship with God. It can give us that kick start from a dead stop.

The one certainty of a life lived on the Jericho Road is that it will encounter roadblocks and wrong turns, that it will take bumpy rides down back alleys and blind alleys as well as boulevards. If everything is coming your way, you're probably in the wrong lane. There is a poster outside sociobiologist Edward O. Wilson's office: A frog is perched dangerously out on a limb; the caption reads, "All progress has resulted from those who took unpopular positions." Every driver of a car knows there are more uphill roads than there are downhill roads. The only way to handle a tailspin is to steer into it, otherwise the car goes wild. The first law of the Jericho highway's systems dynamics encourages failure, facilitates disequilibrium, steers into change. But New Lights fail fast and fail forward, careful not to oversteer in making corrections.

Road rule number one also brings with it a corollary law, the ultimate law of hope. The road's last turn will be the best.

Road Rule
#2
You Can't Drive Forward Without a Rearview Mirror

Every age must fix its rearview mirror to fit its frame and angle of vision. Road rule number two teaches postmoderns never to move without first looking over their shoulder at the past and locating themselves within a living tradition. New Lights have a backward way of moving forward. Traditional theological concepts, symbols, and conceits, far from obstructing a postmodern vision, provide the very models, myths, and metaphors for articulating it.[24] Tradition is not the inert burden modernism made it out to be. Backward looking and forward thinking can be mutualities of motion.

The second rule of locomotion in systems theory is that the whole space-time process structure needs to be in vertical as well as horizontal relationship with its parts. If a dynamic exchange with the environment is a constant in open systems, that exchange must be defined vertically as well as horizontally. The interactive relationship of the whole with the environment (called by many the "S/E field" or systems/environment field) includes the system's establishment of a positive interrelationship of communication and trust between the internal parts or subsystems themselves. One of the most important of these vertical parts or subsystems is memory. Even the simplest chemical reaction systems have a form of memory, which is bypassed or blocked at the peril of the organism. Hence road rule number two for the locomotion of open systems. You can't drive forward without a rear-view mirror.

Instructions for the assembling of a certain make of Japanese motorcycle begin: "Before assembling motorcycle, obtain peace of mind." Thanks to their rearview mirrors, New Lights can live and drive historically, a major source of mental centering and stillness. The more still the center, the more accurately the wheel spins, the more calm the ride.

Tradition is the only stable way organisms can move through time. In the modern era rearview mirrors became like glove compartments--vestigial structures kept for cosmetic reasons and used for functions that had little to do with their original purpose. The rearview mirror became a handy place for moderns to hang ornaments and trophies like dice and garters, or to look at themselves. In his poem "Of Modern Poetry," Wallace Stevens has the line "Its past was a souvenir." Our past has become precisely that: A souvenir, some memento of a trip long ago, we take off the shelf periodically to dust or to fondle as it rekindles nostalgic memories.

―――――――――――――― **66** ――――――――――――――

Save by the Old Road none obtain the new,
And from the Ancient Hills alone we catch the view.
Compleat Victorian/chemist/farmer/astronomer/librarian/poet Coventry Patmore[f]

―――――――――――――― **99** ――――――――――――――

The result of a souvenir past has been an iconoclastic modernity that had nothing in sight in its rearview mirror. Florentine freedom sympathizer/poet Elizabeth Barrett Browning pointed out graphically the problem of an empty rearview mirror in her "Casa Guidi Windows," written during the abortive Italian revolution of 1848:

If we tried
To sink the past beneath our feet, be sure
The future would not stand[25]

Because the past sank in the modern consciousness; because we have not, in the prophet Jeremiah's words, stood by the roads, and looked, and asked for the ancient paths, where the good way is (cf. Jer. 6:16), the future is in danger of not standing through these transitional days when clock culture is giving way to computer culture. The New Light apologetic looks to the past to sanctify the present.

The cultural significance of the computer can be compared only to the technology of the clock in the seventeenth century and the craft technologies of the potter and weaver for the ancient world. A defining technology for our age, the computer has already proven its power to redefine our relationship to nature, to reality, and to the past. Computer culture makes conversations with our ancestors and visits to ancestral places increasingly difficult. English mathematician/logician/inventor of computers Alan Turing predicted some twenty-five years ago the emergence of the "Computer Man":

A mind-set derived from the binary number system, which totally lives in a quantifiable present.[26] This makes devices like rearview mirrors all the more necessary. Even car manufacturers have sensed a growing need for a consciousness of what lays behind us, as the number of rearview mirrors standard on a car has gone from one to three. History transports us through time like travel transports us through space. It is the human time machine whereby we see new scenes, hear new voices, and feel new sensations. Historian/historiographer Michael W. Kammen, in his marvelous book *Selvages and Biases* (1987), accents the identity value of a life rich in contacts with the past:

> First, history helps us to achieve self-knowledge and thereby a clearer sense of identity. Second, it helps us to acquire moral knowledge and thereby enables us to make sensibly informed value judgments. Third, it improves our understanding of the actual relationship between past and present, as well as the potential relationship between present and future.[27]

We easily exaggerate our distance from the past. Indeed, the past has a way of catching us from behind, even overtaking us. A car's right-side-view mirror reminds us of this every time we look at it: "Objects in mirror are closer than they appear." Historian/mathematician/moral scientist F.W. Maitland summed up in twelve words the importance of memory in a philosophy of life: "Life is short, and history is the longest of all the arts." Reverence for the old gives open systems a readiness for the new.

─────────────── **66** ───────────────

In every moment there is also a new possibility
arising out of the totality of what is given for that moment.
Australian/biologist Charles Birch and American/process theologian John B. Cobb, Jr.[8]

─────────────── **99** ───────────────

Christians can get trapped by the debates of the past. Already, postmodernism's pasty use of the past, especially fashionable in its architecture, is nostalgic and whimsical. If Jacques Derrida "stands as a successor to the Kabbalah"[28] ("Kabbalah" means something handed down by tradition), it is not to hand on the tradition to the next generation but to handle and fondle the tradition as an end in itself.

We can also be too attached, make too much sense of, the past. Much of the past was as nonsensical as the present. A too living past may create a dying present by smothering innovation and creativity. One can love the past, without living **in** it, while learning **from** it. It is history that instructs us in the nature of what ethicist/theologian/clergyman Reinhold Niebuhr called "ironic evil"--the tendency for our virtues to become vices, our strengths weaknesses, our wisdom folly.

Spiritual power lies in transitions. Quantum spirituality is a movement spirituality in which power is released not in the "repose" of the past, nor in the motion of the moment, but in the transition from one energy state to another, from a past into a future, from a future into a present.[29]

**Road Rule
#3
You Can't Pass In The Slow Lane**

Unfortunately, according to the second Law of Thermodynamics, every time you transfer energy from one form to another (the first Law of Thermodynamics states simply that energy has many forms--thermal, electrical, mechanical, and so forth), useful energy is lost. Information theory, however, recasts the second law in ways that reverse the customary assessments of increasing disorder, or entropy, in the universe. Entropy and information are complementary quantities. According to Bell Laboratory scientist/mathematician Claude Elwood Shannon--whose 1948 paper entitled "The Mathematical Theory of Communication" defined information as possibilities for making a series of choices from among a set of alternatives--the greater the distance from thermodynamic equilibrium, that is, the more intense and constant the exchange and interaction with the environment, the greater the information and transformation that comes to the system. The more orderly and organized a system is, the more predictability and redundancy it carries, and thus the less information one stands to gain from it. Its very orderliness reflects its low information content. Conversely, the more a system behaves in a surprising and unorderly fashion the more information is conveyed by it.[30] In other words, at faster speeds and greater distances from stabilized states come larger amounts of information, creativity, and transformation. The more disorder within a system, the more information; the more information, paradoxically, the greater the potential for structure and order. At zero miles per hour there is perfect organization and minimum information. At sixty-five miles per hour there is imperfect organization and maximum information. The higher the living organism, the faster it evolves. From the standpoint of nature, the worst thing we can do is to slow down.

This third road rule of living systems ties together people as diverse as Michelangelo, Margaret Thatcher, and Mother. Michelangelo was often so absorbed in his work that he forgot to eat; Margaret Thatcher has been known to forget to sleep; my mother used to say to the three of us boys of a morning, "Get up and get moving. Better to wear out your shoes than your sheets."

The most basic, biblical sense of mission--and a favorite of John Wesley's--is best expressed in the words of the Hebrew Preacher: "Whatever task lies to your hand, do it with all your might" (Eccles. 9:10 NEB). Or as Jonathan Edwards phrased it in one of his seventy resolutions, "Resolved, to live with all my might, while I do live."[31] Whatever we do, we ought to throw ourselves into it and give it everything we've got. This is what may be called the "Jehu" method of driving a car. The Bible says Jehu was a charioteer who drove "furiously" (2 Kings 9:20 RSV). My mountaineer ancestors picked this phrase up--"You crazy Jehu"--and used it as an epithet to level at drivers who drove "furiously" down the highway. Those persons who made the greatest impact on history are the Jehus who drove "furiously" through life, who "read as they run" (Hab. 2:2). John Wesley's motto was "Though I am always in haste, I am never in a hurry." British lexicographer/conversationalist/critic Samuel Johnson tried to engage Wesley in "idle conversation" but complained that Wesley never stopped long enough in one place to have a decent conversation. He was always hasting off some place to do something he deemed more important. The world has been changed by people in a hurry.

The article in the Apostles' Creed about Christ coming to judge the quick and the dead, someone has pointed out, has special meaning for today's city driver, where you are either quick or you are dead. Because postmoderns are living in a state of relentless accelerando, the overdrive syndrome, we harbor this guilt that the faster we move, the further we go from God. Car phones, fax machines, overnight mail, high-energy physics, speed learning, time-based business strategies--all attest to the accelerated pace of postmodern highways.

"

*When you're driving 45, sing
"Highways Are Happy Ways."
When you're driving 55, sing
"I'm but a Stranger Here,
Heaven Is My Home."
When you're driving 65, sing
"Nearer My God to Thee."
When you're driving 75, sing
"When the Roll Is Called Up Yonder,
I'll Be There"
When you're driving 85, sing
"Lord, I'm Coming Home."*

Anonymous poem often found engraved on back of calling cards

"

But speed need not equal danger. Brakes dragging all the time is not good driving. If anything, the real danger can come from those who toot along in the slow lane, oblivious to others on the road. One of my favorite bumper stickers I spotted in Florida: "When I get old, I'm going to move up North and drive slow." Too many Christians are going through life stuck in first gear, never reaching cruising speed. Too many organisms are idling through life, spending their time in neutral, swept along by the conditions that prevail in the heavens and highways. To many people are like Charlie Brown. Sitting in front of Lucy's famous doc-in-a-nickel-box booth, psychiatrist Lucy soothes him with the comparison of life to driving on an expressway. "Some people love the fast lane. . . . Some people can't resist the passing lanes. . . . Others are content to stay in the slow lane. . . . On the freeway of life, Charlie Brown, where are you driving?" The last frame of the comic strip has Charlie Brown looking straight at you and saying, "I think I missed the exit about ten miles back."

The paradox is that the slowest way to pass through life can be in overdrive. There is a little-known phenomenon of relativity that scientists call "time dilation." It says that the faster you go, the slower time appears to go, until theoretically, time virtually stops for systems that approach the universal speed limit of 299,792,458 meters a second (the speed of light in a vacuum known as "c"). Speed does more than shrink our world. It also expands it.

The fast lane can be the Lord's lane if God is in the driver's seat. Sometimes the disciples literally could not keep up with Jesus. He wore them out. Holocaust survivor/Jewish theologian/storyteller Elie Wiesel's wife was chatting with an admiring crowd a few summers ago. "Your husband appears at times so driven, so consumed by a mission," she was told. "I know that people think Elie Wiesel is driven," she admitted, "but if he is, I know one thing: He is not the one doing the driving." Whether speed is good or bad hinges on this issue of control.

---------------- 66 ----------------

Great art thou, O Lord, and marvelous are thy works,
and there is no word which suffices to hymn thy wonders.
Orthodox Office of Baptism

---------------- 99 ----------------

There is in our world today such an endemic and epidemic small-mindedness. We have such puny ambitions, such pygmy expectations. How frustrating it must be for God, who made us but a little lower than the angels, when all we see ourselves is but a little higher than the apes. History is in tow to the imagination. And our imaginations are rotting and mildewing in mediocrity. Charles F. Kettering, the inventor of the self-starter, said this: "Nothing ever arose to touch the skies unless there was one person who dreamed that it should, believed that it could, and willed that it must." The missionary call of shoemaker/orientalist William Carey did not recommend slavish adherence to speed limits: "Expect great things from God;

attempt great things for God."

There are authoritative aerotechnical tests which prove that a bumblebee cannot fly due to the shape and weight of its body in relation to total wing area. But bumblebees don't know this. They keep right on flying anyway, flapping their short wings an incredible 160 times a second and consuming an astonishing caloric equivalent of 180 candy bars an hour. Quantum spirituality prepares the believer to face reality like the bumblebee: Staying blissfully aloft, not knowing what other people supposedly know (i.e., "It can't be done") but just doing it anyway.

The graveside ritual includes words that tie us to the most distant reaches of the universe: "Ashes to ashes, dust to dust." Each person must decide which he or she will leave behind: the dust of decaying matter or the ashes of transforming energy. Physicists tell us that certain elements in our bodies (like the phosphorus in our bones) were created at early stages in the evolution of our galaxy, then cycled throughout the lifetime of several stars before appearing in the earth's crust and finding a home in our body. As Dallas physician/diagnostician Larry Dossey puts it, "Our roots go deep; we are anchored in the stars."[32] Indeed, from a chemical standpoint we are formed out of the ashes of dead stars. New Light endings are as their beginnings: They leave behind ashes, not dust.

Road Rule
#4
You Can't Repair the Car While It's Still in Motion.

Indian spiritual leader/civil disobedience advocate/hand spinner Mahatma Gandhi once said, "There is more to life than increasing its speed." A lot of people are **going** nowhere at sixty-five miles per hour. The are **getting** nowhere in high gear. They keep going only to keep from stopping. The speed of the fast lane must never become sought for its own sake. When movement becomes an end in itself, and space a consumable commodity, we forget why we entered the fast lane to begin with--to pass our past; to travel farther into a leperless future than any of our forebears had gone before; to pursue our vision-quest of "the way, the truth, and the life" on behalf of all creation.

But there is exhaustion as well as exhilaration in the fast lane. One of the worst things any driver can do is to try to repair the vehicle while stepping on the gas. Systems that strive to change themselves while in use undergo tremendous stress. We must all know when to get over, to slow ourselves down, to seek maintenance, and to let other passing motorists pass us. As Samuel Johnson said to poet/playwright/novelist Oliver Goldsmith, "No man is obliged to do as much as he can do. A man is to have a part of his life to himself. . . . Privacy is the condition of our being able to be in public." Without "being-time" and "fallow-time" and "waste-time" we suffer downtime or do time one way or another. A social worker chronicled her round-the-clock efforts among the sick and homeless, her becoming "weary in well-doing" (Jung calls this inflation), until she abandoned the highway for secluded arbors by the side of the road. For her own survival she took to the trees, lived on nuts and whole wheat grain with the squirrels, and wrote a book with the uninflated title: *When Helping You Is Hurting Me: Escaping the Messiah Trap* (1988).[33]

——————————————— 66 ———————————————

Here lies the body of John Blake,
who stepped on the gas instead of the brake.

Tombstone epitaph in Uniontown, Pennsylvania

——————————————— 99 ———————————————

Disturbances in an energy field require constant self-stabilization or "autopoiesis," a systems term that means "the characteristic of living systems to continuously renew themselves and to regulate this process in such a way that the integrity of their structure is maintained."[34] How systems deal with entropy depends on whether they are maintained and regenerated or disintegrated. In the past evolution favored organisms with quick reflexes. Biologist Paul Ehrlich and psychologist Robert Ornstein make a strong case for organisms now "expanding our perceptions by adding 'slow reflexes' to their behavioral repertoire."[35]

The need for solitude, for contemplation, for leisure and recreation, not only is indispensable for our personal well-being and self-stabilization. James M. Yates, who is a master at making systems theory comprehensible, illustrates "co-stabilization" by pointing to the way the atmosphere responds to human pollution. It depletes its ozone layer, which will tend to eliminate the culprits who are upsetting its delicate steady state.[36] Without repairs, which in systems language can take the form of exporting, importing, or converting energy, no system can exist in dynamic relationship with its field. Without repairs no car can stay on the road, much less race at truly mind-numbing speeds.

Changing oil, inflating tires, and managing waste products are also imperative ingredients in our creativity and adaptation to the paradigm shifts taking place in our world right now. Working late, never stopping, fear of mechanics and service stations keep us addicted to the old order and rutted in old ways of doing and seeing things. Austrian physicist/tapestry weaver Erwin Schrödinger got his Nobel Prize in 1931 for the Principle of Indeterminacy. He is credited with "the greatest six-month burst of creativity in scientific history." What preceded this unparalleled period of productivity, which gave us, among other things, Schrödinger's wave equation (called by mathematician/physicist Arnold Sommerfeld "the most astonishing among all the astonishing discoveries of the twentieth century"), was a two-and-a-half week Christmas vacation at a villa in the Swiss Alpine town of Arosa.[37]

New realms of consciousness open to us more when we are quiet and attentive than when we are busy about many things. In the Christian tradition resting and play begin the week rather than end it because they are the basis of all creative life. Without play, without repairs, without maintenance, we don't have the creativity or energy to break out of the old patterns and see things in new and fresh ways. We don't have time to ponder the lessons of the past. We don't learn how to shift gears without stripping gears.

────────────────── 66 ──────────────────

Stillness and tranquility set things in order in the universe.
Ancient Chinese/Taoist classic *Tao Te Ching*
The problem is to stay away from writing, not to get at it.
First American poet laureate/novelist/critic Robert Penn Warren[h]

────────────────── 99 ──────────────────

Creativity that is revolutionary requires this violent, energy-sapping action of breaking away and breaking the rules. Normally one does not hug the yellow line. But driving conditions sometimes develop--fog, car accidents--when one must hug the yellow line and indeed cross it if one is to proceed. Walt Disney, while a "realist," always insisted that his animators know how and when to break the rules. The exigencies of the road may be such that New Light creativity most resembles that of the Macedonian general Alexander. In 333 b.c. Alexander studied the Gordian knot that everyone else had unsuccessfully tried to untie, pulled out his sword, sliced the knot in half, and became king of Asia because he slipped free of preconceived ideas and local traffic laws.

Uovo di Colombo is an Italian expression (as well as a German proverb) that refers to a "simple, obvious idea that doesn't occur to the person who could use it the most." It translates literally as "Columbus's egg," and refers to the alleged creativity of the Italian navigator/explorer Christopher Columbus (the story most likely is about the Italian architect/goldsmith/councilman Filippo Brunelleschi), who, when told that going to India by sailing due west was as foolish and impossible as balancing an egg on either end, did precisely that--by bashing the egg's end in and standing it upright. The world's most creative advances often come after the violent smashing of preconceptions, the established "order," and assumptions most taken for granted.

Road Rule
#5
You Can't Run On Empty

Everyone has to have fuel. Fuel is what propels life forward. It is what transforms a dead machine into a throbbing, pulsating missional force in running order, reborn anew for every generation. Fuel is, in other words, the energy of faith. Everyone has to have faith in something. There is no such thing as an infidel. Whatever gets you up in the morning, whatever gets you excited about life, that is your faith. There are people without enough fuel to do their work in life. Then there are people who try to get by on the fumes of faith. But neither go far. Both eventually, or quickly, stall out of life. Or worse. Nothing is more volatile or unstable than fumes.

———————————————— 66 ————————————————

When we consider
the extreme instability of our bodily structure,
its readiness for disturbance
by the slightest application of external forces, . . .
its persistence through many decades
seems almost miraculous. The wonder increases
when we realize that the system is open,
engaging in free exchange with the outer world,
and that the structure itself is not permanent,
but is being continuously broken down by the wear and tear
of action, and as continuously built up again
by processes of repair.

Physiologist/pioneer trauma researcher/medical school
professor/wood worker/musician Walter B. Cannon[i]

———————————————— 99 ————————————————

Although open systems are self-regulating and self-stabilizing, any organism will deteriorate without a persistent source of free energy. In systems language this energy that can be used for fuel to run the system is called negentropy. There is something fundamentally entropy-producing and destabilizing about the energy of faith. Boundary regulation controls the level of negentropy--energy, information or material--that is necessary for the maintenance of the open system. An excess of energy dissipated to the environment and the system can no longer be maintained. A deficit of entropy and the same happens. Boundary regulations do not just let in elements from one environment to another--the gas station to the car. They also keep elements in a specified part of the system without entering other parts--the gas pump to the fuel tank. Surfeits and deficits of free energy are the very stuff of life itself. They lead to the collapse of maladjusted, "old guard" subsystems and the inclusion of complicated feedback systems, what chemists call "auto-catalytic steps," or in cybernetic terms "positive feedback loops," reinforcing informed adaptation by bringing the organism to and even beyond its threshold of self-stabilization.

"

Le coeur a ses raisons que la raison ne connoist point.
The heart has its own reasons
which Reason does not know.

Mathematical genius/scientist/philosopher Blaise Pascal[j]

"

Moderns are confused by the bewildering variety of fuels or negentropies out there from which to choose. "Feeding on free energy" is the most important decision in life. What fuel will we select? If the fuel we fill up on is pleasure, the result of the decision is automatic entropy: The ride will be unpleasant. If the fuel we select is material wealth, the result of the decision is automatic entropy: The weight of meaninglessness will crush and crash us. If the fuel we select is success, or self, the result of the decision is automatic entropy: We will never make it past life's "surface distortions"--Washington, D.C., jargon for potholes. If the fuel we select can be described in these words from one Ira Gershwin song, "Who cares if banks fail in Yonkers/ Long as you gotta kiss that conquers," the result of the decision is automatic entropy: We will spend our lives in the night of nothingness.

But if the fuel we fill up on is the free energy of faith in Jesus Christ, we will travel down the Jericho Road, far from thermodynamic equilibrium but singing and laughing, inviting to join us the lepers abandoned by the side of the road and the strangers broken-down on the road's shoulders from bad, entropic fuel.

Celebrating One Another's Strangeness

The shape of evangelization on the road will have the wrong geometrics unless its spatial imagination revolves around the outsiders, the strangers, the lepers. Philosopher/ethicist/clown Tom W. Boyd provides us with a splendid typology of outsiders in his phenomenology of play. First are the "idealized outsiders," those larger than life figures that range beyond the scope of our jealousy. Second are the "alienated outsiders," members of marginal groups (ethnic minorities, homosexuals, the handicapped) who are forced into outsiderhood. Third are the "intentional outsiders," those who have chosen for whatever reasons to stand apart, even if it means self-destruction. Fourth are the "innocent outsiders," the clowns, who playfully symbolize our twin desires to "stand out" and "blend in."[38]

There are three levels to the definition of "stranger." First, strangers may be people either inside or outside the church. A member, encouraged to be more friendly by her pastor, approached a person she did not recognize and asked, "Are you a stranger here?" The reply: "Yes. I have been a stranger in this church for thirty-two years." We are all "talking to a stranger," as John Hopkins' 1967 four-part teleplay of one day in the life of a family puts it. The entire world is one vast "company of strangers," as the title of a 1981 book by Parker J. Palmer puts it.[39] The church is a company of strangers where God is the host.

Second, strangers may also be those forces, visible or invisible, and those technologies, hard and soft, that alarm us. "Transcentury technology," which Moscow is calling "the Third Revolution," could radically alter the global economy. Biogenetics, nanotechnology, and vapor-phase technology are gathering revolutionary momentum. Artificial intelligence is already present in fifth-generation computers. Social thinkers such as E.F. Schumacher, Herman Daly, John Todd, and Amory and Hunter Lovins have found themselves swept up in a busy marathon of lectures, exhibitions, and conferences, explaining their promising scenarios of (respectively) alternative technologies, steady state economies, and attentive community designs. All the while we in the church have spent our time humming and hahing about computers. The possibility of building a computer with consciousness as well as intelligence is explained in computer scientist/pianist/composer Douglas R. Hofstadter's *Gödel, Escher, Bach: An Eternal Golden Braid* (1979).[40] The ruckus raised by the new technological environment created by a single generation--from nuts and bolts to gallium arsenide, from telegraphs to helix and holography, from metal pipes to light pipes, from flash lights to laser beams--is a domestic squabble. And, in fact, some of the greatest insights are born out of disagreements among siblings and friends.

―――――――――――――― 66 ――――――――――――――

Let not the prayer of the stranger
find entrance before Thee, O Lord.

An old Hebrew prayer

―――――――――――――― 99 ――――――――――――――

Third, strangers may also be the strangers within, including one's own body, as John Steward Collis's book *Living with a Stranger* (1979) argues so eloquently, and school master/literature professor/lecturer G. Wilson Knight's book *Symbol of Man: On Body-Soul for Stage and Studio* (1979) portrays so beautifully in these words: "Man has, in effect, been reduced on every level to heads and hands sticking out from clothes. The simple truth is that we have regarded the body as evil; and, as a result, have no real intuition of 'soul'."[41]

Evangelization cannot go into a geomantic dynamic unless each one of these "strangers" is present and accounted for. To be sure, fear of the stranger is real. A four-dimensional faith does not harbor romantic, nostalgic views of the stranger. Strangers **are** dangerous. Patrick Keifert observes how in contemporary culture public spaces,[42] especially in urban settings, are thought to be cold, violent, and dangerous. As a result, we live in a society afraid of strangers. "We rush through these spaces encased in bubbles of silence. When we stop someone on the street for directions, we say, 'Excuse me,' since we believe we have broken into their sacred, private bubble."[43]

66

All churches are one, and the unity of the churches is shown by their peaceful intercommunion, the title of brethren, and the bond of hospitality.

Theologian/defender of the faith Tertullian[k]

99

Wesley's most famous quotation portrays the world as his parish. But the world in which we live does not have the **feel** of a parish. Parishes are familiar and friendly places. Parishes should feel the opposite of what is out there in the "corporations and organizations and institutions that loom large on the horizons of our world."[44] Ministry with strangers may be as dangerous nowadays as it has been at any time in history. But Jesus anticipated the danger, even predicted it. In giving us the Jericho Road model of evangelization, he chose the road that was a synonym for gangs of robbers, rapists, ruffians, and other criminals.

Fear of the stranger is learned, as well as culturally conditioned. As Marshall McLuhan was the first to observe, Europeans go outside to get away and go inside to be friendly. Americans go inside to get alone and go outside to be friendly. We teach our children to be cautious around strangers, even, as children's writer/poet Irma Joyce rhythmically warns, to "never talk to strangers"[45]. We drill in our teenagers not to thumb a ride or pick up hitchhikers. We encourage our elderly to walk in groups. Even our greatest writers warn us of strangers. J.R.R. Tolkien, in *The Lord of the Rings* (1956),[46] tells us that an unknown face is a thing to be feared. Actor/ meteorologist/novelist/playwright Albert Camus's *The Stranger* (1942)[47] portrays the "stranger" as a murderer. The stranger in river pilot/prospector/humorist Mark Twain's short story "The Mysterious Stranger" (1916) turns out to be Satan.[48] The early Christians had to overcome their distrust and suspicion of the Gentiles, and did so through one of the least understood phenomena of the early church: The phenomenon of the house church, an important feature of early Christian hospitality. Paul's letters presuppose this feature of church life, and the book of Acts abounds with stories of homes as outposts for the spread of the gospel. New Lights transcend fear of the stranger, that they may take seriously what Michael Ignatieff calls the "needs of strangers."[49]

The Greek concept of the stranger is expressed in the word *xenos*, an almost oxymoronic word that means both "foreigner" and "guest." The Latin concept of the stranger is expressed in the word *hospes*, which connotes a relationship between a guest and a host. Geomantic evangelization is turning *xenos* into *hospes*. Or as international theologian/spiritual director Henri Nouwen phrases it, evangelization is converting *hostis* ("foreigner") into *hospes*.[50] The distinguishing characteristic of a Christian in the early church? Philoxeny, or a "lover of strangers"--the original meaning of the word "hospitality." The distinguishing characteristic of a Christian leader in the early church? *Philoxenos,* or a "lover of hospitality," as Titus 1:8 reads. The postmodern church must move from xenophoby to philoxeny. The stranger is not the murderer, not the traitor, not Satan. Jesus tells us that the stranger is none other than Jesus himself!

The only basis for evaluation on Judgment Day Jesus deemed worth mentioning was the geometry of our behavior toward strangers. An *Ethos* of social solidarity is why the damning of Diotrephes in 3 John 9-10 is so severe.[51] He refused while on earth hospitality to strangers, which is the final condemnation when in heaven. The Sodomites were despised not only because of their sexual deviancy but because they were known as "haters of strangers."[52] In the same way inhospitality to strangers is "hateful to God," so hospitality is equated with faith and piety by early church fathers such as Clement of Rome. For some contemporary moral philosophers like John Feinberg, failure to help strangers should be criminal.[53] For New Lights, welcoming strangers is a sacred obligation.

"Open your homes to strangers," commanded Paul. (Rom. 12:13)
"Open your homes to each other, without complaining," directed Peter. (1 Pet. 4:9)
"Open your homes to welcome strangers," said the writer of the Hebrews. (Heb. 13:2)
"Open your tables to hungry enemies," Paul even goes so far as to say. (Rom. 12:20)

Six Protocols of Postmodern Evangelization

It is not only people who are known by the company they keep. Information, ideas, and arguments are also drawn to one another. In the postmodern prospectus for geomantic evangelization, six protocols of spatial mission cluster together and must be enumerated before developing further this empty-shoulders/open-doors/full-tables theology: (1) New

Light leaders will be "playing away," in this postmodern culture, (2) New
Light evangelization is hearing God's story, (3) New Light evangelization is
something natural and generous, (4) Evangelization is not technique, (5)
Evangelization's essence is not the transmission of information, (6) Postmon-
dern evangelization must be less one-on-one than two-by-two.

#1 New Light Leaders Will Be "Playing Away" in this Postmodern Culture

Coincident with the theological transformations taking place is a
sociological change that has ushered in a new ecclesial situation. As far as
I can tell, Bishop/*Honest to God* John A.T. Robinson was the first to use the
sportine analogy of "playing away" to describe the current missionary
condition of the post-Constantinian church. It is a vital metaphor, and one
that New Light leaders would do well to develop as part of their mission to
postmodern society. Ecumenist/theologian/Paulist priest Thomas Ryan,
who has already contributed greatly toward a "spirituality for sports," as he
calls it, persuasively argues that "Churches should encourage play on all
levels as part of their mission of evangelization in contemporary society."[54]
By "playing away" Robinson meant that modernization's shifts in the mythic
structures and sociological scaffolding of belief once and for all ended the
Constantinian captivity of the church. From now on, the church no longer
will be playing home games to home crowds. The social climate and
intellectual atmosphere in which the world church operates is now either
apathetic or unsympathetic to the church's gospel--either its goals or its
games. In other words, the Eurocentric church no longer enjoys the home
court advantage.[55]

New Light and Old Light leaders have made differing adjustments to
this diasporist discipleship, to always being on the road. The "away strategy"
preferred by many Old Lights is to try to recover the home court advantage,
decry their "away situation," and desire to return to precritical forms of
faith. The best of the Old Lights have perceived properly that the best way
to "play away" is to play one's own game. But sociologically Old Lights have
been drawn into playing the culture's game and accepting its terms as much
as New Lights have. Theologian/evangelism professor William J. Abraham
portrays "modern evangelism" as basically a "kind of entrepreneurial
industry organized, funded, and run like a modern corporation."

Decisions are generally made on a technical and pragmatic basis.
There is a heavy emphasis on organization over against genuine
community. Much attention and money is given to public relations,
advertising, and commercial enterprises like tapes, records, and
books. Evangelists offer friendship and love for sale through radio
and television, and educational credentials are used as passwords
into the lives of the gullible. The whole operation depends on a
personality rather than on serious preaching. Ministry is reduced to

messages and miracles transmitted through the airwaves on the latest technology from Japan.[56]

The race to be "with it," Old Lights have found, quickly becomes old hat.

The "away strategy" preferred by most Old and New Lights, however, has been either the "best offense is a good defense" approach or the "we can play their game" approach--either battening down the hatches, bracing oneself against the onslaughts of postmodernity, and pealing forth ageless myths ("singing the Lord's song in a strange land"), or taking the world with deadly seriousness, submerging oneself in the world, and losing oneself in outreach and identity ("singing a strange song in the Lord's land").[57] Our game legs may want to give the game away. But it is only God's game to give.

It was this last strategy that had the most disastrous effect in the modern era. It is one thing to resist the reactionary Old Light tendency to get "hooked on a game of life that has nothing to do with the way the universe is going," as R. Buckminster Fuller once put it. It is another to give up one's game entirely to play another. The more the church sought to find itself in and serve modernity, the more soulless modern political and social life, the more naked the public square (in Richard John Neuhaus's words), the less public the American republic. The more the moral infrastructure of the church learned to see itself as transformative of the social order and less transmissive of theology and truth, the more the church abdicated positions of moral leadership in terms of its own inner and intellectual life, the more rigid and ideological the church became in terms of its outer life and social/political agenda. Either the church had nothing to say and was saying it in the realm of theology (one is reminded of printmaker/avant garde composer/teacher John Cage's "I have nothing to say, I am saying it, and that is poetry"); or the church left nothing to be said in the realm of politics, with modernism's contestant theologies looking more and more like ideologies replete with identikits packed tightly with ideological rectitude, didactic rantings, and certificates of merit and doctrinal clearance given to those who follow the party line of some "ist" or "ism."

The need for a new "away strategy" among postmodern Christians is apparent from the paradox of the oldline denominations' position in the postmodern world: The more the church believes the culture's propaganda, the less the culture believes the church's gospel. Relevance has a life span of zero. Its birth cries and death wails are indistinguishable. It is time for New Lights to come to terms with themselves as distinctively spiritual leaders, offering a faith that is not sold out or cut down to the size of the world's current *Weltanschauung*. "Playing away" means the church must reconceive itself as a resistance movement and come to terms with the socially disruptive power of the gospel.

At the same time, however, New Light movements must capture the spirit of the times without being captured by or capitulating to it. If New Lights will spend postmodernity "playing away" in the culture, they had better learn, better than ever before, their own texts and traditions and aesthetics. Any team plays best when it plays its own game. The more denominational differences are marginalized, for example, the more ingenious we must become in making John Calvin and Martin Luther and John Wesley live among us as contemporaries. New Lights are people who live by understanding the nature of their environment rather than fighting against it. They are trend-setters, not tread-followers in scholarship and ethics, always living on the "cutting edge" while being acclimated to the weather patterns of a life lived in the midst of a faith climate rather than a culture climate. New Lights had also better be prepared in this post-Constantinian world for a new missionary age of "witnesses" and "martyrs."

#2 New Light Evangelization Is Hearing God's Story, Not Our Story

Self-introduction has been the most common, and most dangerous, form of evangelism. New Light evangelization is based on receiving more than giving--whether it be strangers or Christ. John Wesley, like the Apostle Paul, was remarkably reluctant to recount his Aldersgate experience. In the vast corpus of his writings, he only mentions Aldersgate twice. The more real and integrated an energy event is in one's life, the less one needs to talk about it, the more one can help others to see where their energy events are taking place.

---- **"** ----

To be witnesses is to go wherever the Spirit of God is at work and there demand that the Son of God be acknowledged.

Sri Lankan college principal/ecumenist/pastor D.T. Niles[1]

---- **"** ----

Missions begins with a theology of receiving and then moves to a theology of giving. Receiving diversity in how God's story may be told in a variety of ways is the beginning of geomantic evangelization. New Lights demonstrate openness to the options people have in following Jesus. As the Hebrews expressed it, God is a God of many names (*Elohim, Shaddai, Yod Hey Vav [YHWH], Adoni, Ehyeh, Echad, Ani, Ayin*).[58] God will be who God will be, and who God will be is controlled by God's calendar and God's Spirit. In the words of China's greatest Protestant leader of the twentieth century, Bishop K.H. Ting, "Evangelism not only brings Christ to men and women--it brings Christ out of them, so that people at both ends of the line of communication are receivers of the gospel."[59]

The possibilities for world evangelization are enormous. People are open to God. People are eager to talk about God. But for a culture that believes in God but not in organized religion, it is the height of folly to give them organized religion and not God, to give them our story and not God's story. It is God's story, not some personal or denominational adventure, that is our "great commission."

#3 New Light Evangelization Is Something Natural and Generous, Not Contrived or Commissioned

It is not duty, but delight. Christian Reformed Church missionary/ theology of missions professor Harry R. Boer contends that "the view of evangelism as first and foremost a Christian duty required by the Great Commission of Matthew 28:19-20 is no older than the last century, prior to which the mainspring of evangelism among lay Christians was the natural-ness of sharing Christ with one's neighbor out of sheer inner excitement over the new life of hope one has found."[60] In days of early Christianity, and in every day of revival, the spread of the gospel took place by word of mouth. The church's mission exploded not because it had a sure-fire program or strategic plan, not because it took its duty more seriously at one time or another, not because it had documents people could read, but because early Christian messengers (*keryks*) voiced Christ's message (*kerygma*), because believers began "gossiping the gospel"[61] to their neighbors. In the earliest days of the history of the church these first Christians gossiped the gospel spontaneously throughout the territories of the Mediterranean world. Augustine called first-century evangelism "one loving heart setting another on fire." William James used to say, "Come, let us gossip about the universe." Theologians are people who specialize in gossip about God.

#4 Evangelization Is Not Technique, but Grace.

Evangelization is not a form of advertising. The trouble ad-evangelism has gotten the church into can be seen in any Christian bookstore, with its Jesus Junk, Holy Hardware, and Holy Gauche.[62] Too much of modern evangelism has been skillful public relations, little more than Welcome Wagon programs and "Jesus Saves" slogans. The loss of common grace, which makes evangelism "professional" or "technical," can be seen in the specializing role of greeters and ushers in modern gathering rites.

There are two great teachers of hospitality evangelism in our time: "Miss Manners" (Judith Martin) and "the Frugal Gourmet" (Jeff Smith). Both attest to the interconnectedness of spiritual and social grace.[63] Both help us formulate a theology of the Table in which every meal is of religious significance.

#5 Evangelization's Essence Is Not the Transmission of Information but the Presencing of Christ

The evangelists of the early church certainly shared information about Christ, but only as a step toward making Christ's "presence" present. The eucharistic sacrament embodies this sacramental sense of evangelization: God comes to **us in our** coming to the stranger. "I was a stranger and you welcomed me, reads Matthew 25:35 (RSV). Philip is called "the Evangelist." Why? Because he mediated God's presence. His life became the "real presence" of Christ. The old news of his life changed into the good news of Christ and into gospel for the stranger: bread for the hungry, health for the sick, sight for the blind, liberty for the oppressed.

The biblical writers came to see that God attaches a promise to the presence of the stranger. It is the very promise of God's presence. The examples were everywhere before them: Abraham receiving three mysterious strangers at his camp in the Negev (Gen. 18:1-3); Lot extending care to the angel visitors (Gen. 19:1-3); Laban welcoming Abraham's servant (Gen. 24:31); Rahab opening her home to the Israeli spies (Josh. 2:1); Martha opening her home to Jesus (Luke 10:38); Lydia sheltering Paul and Silas (Acts 16:15); even the barbarians, Paul said, "lodged us three days courteously" (Acts 28:7).[64] Most significant of all is the coming of Jesus as a guest to the world.

There is a Hell, Michigan. There is also a Paradise, Michigan. There is a United Methodist church in Paradise. There is no United Methodist church in Hell. Here is precisely our greatest problem of evangelization. What we know something about is an evangelism in reverse--a friends-evangelism rather than a strangers-evangelism. There is an old missions saying that goes like this: Too many Christians share their faith with one another and have fellowship with the world when it ought to be the other way around. Too many Christians express their faith in Paradise, and keep silence in Hell when they should keep more silence in Paradise and speak their faith in Hell.

#6 Postmodern Evangelization Must Be Less One-on-One than Two-by-Two

From among the disciples, "the Lord appointed seventy-two others and sent them two by two ahead of him to every town and place where he was about to go" (Luke 10:1 NIV). If evangelization has something to do with helping people give up the alienation and isolation of their individualistic self-obsessions and become part of the body of Christ, if missions move *Logos* into *Pathos*, then evangelization must have an *Ethos* of space in which its style and structure embodies a geomantic style and structure of living where "we are members one of another" (Eph. 4:25 RSV). In other words, geomantic evangelization means hospitality evangelism.[65] Or as ecclesiologist/Villanova University professor Bernard P. Prusak puts it, "hospitality is a sacramental expression of *koinonia*."[66]

Three "I's" of Hospitality Evangelism

Hospitality evangelism occurs in three "I" stages: invitation, introduction, initiation. These are three ancient artforms, neglected but not obsolete greeting rituals that in earlier traditions were practiced almost unawares. Each one of these stages in ancient hospitality incorporates one of the three essential ingredients in postmodern evangelization: invitation, *diakonia* and humble service; introduction, *kerygma* and proclamation; initiation, *koinonia* and community. The evangelical synergy of *kerygma*, *koinonia* and *diakonia* sets evangelization in an eschatological context.[67]

Invitation

First, there is the **Invitation**, the searching for strangers that motivates *diakonia*. God's power is an invitational power. We do not **have** to come. Where the Bible says, "Compel them to come in," the original Greek word does not convey the sense of forcing them in but rather of urgently **inviting** them to "come in." Jesus' sense of urgency was expressed in his forbidding the Oriental custom of lengthy oral greetings and salutations, which were often accompanied by kneeling, embracing, and kissing. In Luke 10:4, when Jesus sent out the seventy-two, he told them not to engage in such elaborate amenities because they were time consuming and diverted attention from the immediate needs of the mission field.

---------------------- **"** ----------------------

Thou hast made me known to friends whom I knew not.
Thou hast brought the distant near
and made a [friend] of the stranger

Poet/philosopher Marcus Aurelius[m]

---------------------- **"** ----------------------

Few members of oldline denominations have sent even one invitation to come and meet Jesus. New Light pastor/Bridgeport, West Virginian Dale Waters observes how we in the church are "better at reading menus than inviting people in for dinner." Postmoderns are being taught like never before to respect with one's absence those things for which one's presence has not been requested. No one wants to go where one's not invited. We want, but wait, to be invited. Even God waits for our invitation. That is the meaning of *paraklesis*--which literally means to invite or "call to one's side" (see Acts 8:31; 28:14). New Lights must do evangelization the old-fashioned way: Ask people. One out of four American adults not presently attending church would go with someone to church if asked. Or, in statistical terms, fifteen to eighteen million American adults are waiting for a personal invitation.[68]

I discovered how much of a lost art an invitation is the first time I used RSVP with seminary students. Most simply did not know what an RSVP meant on an invitation to dinner from the president of the seminary. Invitation is more important today than ever before because religion is seen as something private and personal. Things private and personal are those things to which we can only be invited.

In hospitality evangelism the Scriptures are the invitation. Invitation has a more extensive meaning than periodic. It is more expansive than a single event. Invitations are long-standing, indeed, lifelong events. The last invitation offered by the Holy Spirit is the one in the book of the Apocalypse (22:17 RSV): "The Spirit and the Bride say, 'Come.' And let him who hears say, 'Come.' And let him who is thirsty come, let him who desires take the water of life without price." God's Spirit did not say to John, "Only tell those who are educated and cultured, 'Come.'" The Bible did not say to us, "Tell only those who are wealthy and enterprising, 'Come.'" The church is not told to tell those who are only loving and forgiving, "Come." The only directive is "Whosoever will . . . , 'Come.'" Faith is an invitation from God to new life in Christ: Come! Faith is an invitation from God to get in out of the cold: Come! "Faith is an invitation to become lovers," Kings College senior resident/theologian Norman Pittenger has written.

The postmodern church is a community that sends out invitations to the world to "Come as you are." This does not mean that in receiving us Jesus approves of us as we are. Acceptance and approval are not the same thing. But whether we approve or not, the church is always to accept, always to invite in. Second Peter 2:7-8 even calls Abraham's nephew Lot "righteous" at the same time he is known for being weak, morally depraved and drunken. How can Lot be accounted an "upright man" (Wisd. of Sol. 10:6 NJB) and saved out of Sodom? It was his "hospitality and piety," his willingness to shelter and feed strangers visiting Sodom with even the worst of motives, that saved him.

Biblical scholar Chan-Hie Kim, while working at the Upper Room Chapel, studied the structure and format of twenty-five ancient invitations (Greek documents written on papyrus found in Egypt), invitations that in his words "could have very likely been used to invite people to the dinners mentioned in the New Testament."[69] What he discovered about the nature of these invitations has direct application to hospitality evangelism. First, the occasion for the celebration was clearly stated in the invitation. There were no surprise parties. Everyone knew why he or she was being asked to come.

Second, each invitation was short and succinct--indeed, short and succinct enough to put into **one** sentence. But that one sentence contained **eight** structural elements. The first structural element was an invitation verb. The most popular invitation verb in the Scriptures? **Come!**

"Come into the ark, you and all your household." (Gen. 7:1 NKJV)

"Come with us and we will treat you well." (Num. 10:29 NIV)

"Come now, let us reason together." (Isa. 1:18 NIV)

"Come, all you who are thirsty, come to the waters; and you who have no money, come, buy and eat!" (Isa. 55:1 NIV)

"Come, let us return to the Lord; . . . and he will heal us." (Hos. 6:1 NRSV)

"Come to me, all you that are weary and are carrying heavy burdens, and I will give you rest." (Matt. 11:28 NRSV)

"Come, you that are blessed by my Father, inherit the kingdom prepared for you." (Matt. 25:34 NRSV)

"Come; for all is now ready" (Luke 14:17 RSV)

Not by accident did some campmeeting spirituals begin with this very invitation verb: "Come, thou fount of every blessing . . ."; "Come, ye sinners poor and needy . . ."; "Come to Jesus, come and welcome . . ."; "Come, friends and relations . . ."; "Come, all ye young people . . ." Not by accident did some of the great hymn-writers of the church begin their songs in a similar vein: "Come thou almighty King" (anonymous); "Come weary traveller unknown" (Charles Wesley); "Come, ye faithful, raise the strain of triumphant gladness" (John of Damascus); "Come, we that love the Lord" (Isaac Watts); "Come, ye disconsolate, where'er ye languish" (Thomas Moore).

The other seven structural elements in every invitation were (2) the name of the invited guest, (3) the name of the host, (4) the purpose for the invitation, (5) the occasion, (6) the place, (7) the exact date, and (8) the precise time.[70] Immediately one is struck by the absence of any opening or closing salutation, surprising given the importance of the epistolary convention. Scholars have pondered why there was no opening or closing salutation, as well as why these invitations always refer to the hosts in the third person rather than the first. Their conclusion is simple, but it has profound implications for hospitality evangelism: Invitations were written by the hosts and then given to messengers to be read in front of the sought after guest.[71]

WE ARE THOSE MESSENGERS
CHRIST IS THE HOST
THE STRANGER IS THE GUEST

The two meals at which Jesus played the role of host, not guest, were the feeding of the five thousand (Luke 9) and the Last Supper (Luke 22). Invitation is inextricably attached to *diakonia* in hospitality evangelism because the role of the messenger in spreading Christ's invitation, "Come and Party!" announcing a messianic banquet of healing, redemption, and fulfillment, is the role of humble servanthood. It is to be at someone's beck and call. It is to do the work of someone else's bidding. It is to accept whoever shows up.

Preacher/editor/Princeton homiletics professor Thomas Long tells the story of staying at a hotel in a large city and being surprised to find, posted on the elevator door, a small handwritten notice that read, "Party tonight! Room 210. 8 p.m. Everyone invited." Professor Long said he could hardly picture who would throw such a party and for what reason, but he imagined that at 8 p.m., room 210 would be filled with an unlikely assortment of people--sales representatives, vacationers, motel employees, teenagers, and more.

Alas, the sign on the elevator door came down. It was replaced by a typewritten statement explaining that it had all been a hoax, a practical joke. It made more sense being a hoax than a reality, Long confessed, but in a way that was too bad and sad. For just a moment, those staying at that hotel were excited by the possibility that there just might be a party somewhere to which everyone was invited. Who they were or why they came wouldn't matter a bit. The only thing that would matter is that they showed up, and what happened to them after they arrived at the party. Perhaps if there is to be such a party, Long concludes, the church is going to have to throw it. An invitation to the world to come to our party, the best party anyone could ever attend, is the essence of what hospitality evangelism means. Or has the church forgotten how to throw a party?

Introduction

No one who regularly addresses groups of people would disagree with the observation that one of the hardest things about speaking in public today is surviving the introduction. Within recent months I have been introduced in the following ways, among others:

Those who have not heard Dr. Sweet will look forward to what he has to say.

President Sweet is the author of seven books, two of which are worth mentioning this morning.

Or there was this memorable blurb in the bulletin: "We are grateful tonight for the presence of Len Sweet, a sour guest preacher. Thanks for sharing our Lent with us." The second stage of hospitality evangelism involves **introduction**, or *kerygma*, treating the stranger as guest. It will help us to keep in mind as background information three customs surrounding introductions as the Bible knew them.

First, in ancient cultures, strangers were placed under the protection of an established member of the community who then acted as patron, as host, as friend, and as introducer to the other members of the community and most especially to the host of the celebration itself. To reject or to offend the stranger/guest was to offend and reject the protector/introducer/patron of the stranger.

Second, the custom of writing letters of recommendation to introduce traveling missionaries to churches along their way was widespread in the first century. In fact, a sizeable portion of the New Testament is precisely this: letters of introduction (see Rom. 16:1-2; 1 Cor. 16:15-18; Phil. 2:29-30; 4:2-3; 1 Thess. 5:12-13; Philem. 8-17; Heb. 13:23; 3 John 12). In writing the letter for the recommended, the writer is asking that the person being introduced be treated just as if the sender were present.

Third, a cardinal custom of ancient rituals of hospitality was that travelers might expect their basic needs of food and lodging to be met for a period of three days. The Christian ethic of hospitality, however, pushed the standards even higher. Since Jesus is the perfect host (John 13:1-12), even if the strangers arrived too late and were not entitled to food (i.e., after the evening meal), they were still hosted and taken care of (Luke 11:5-8). What is more, a stranger's benefits of responding to Christ's invitation were not just food and lodging but such refined and extravagant amenities as anointing, the kiss of peace, and foot-washing. Christians showed humility and respect even toward strangers through washing their feet. Basic to the ritual of introduction is the showing of service and respect to the strangers in our midst.

There is a vast difference between the introductions that take place in hospitality evangelism and the confused realities of the two evangelism strategies dominating American religion today: **Scared-Saved evangelism** and **Show-and-Tell evangelism**. As different as Scared-Saved and Show-and-Tell evangelism are, they share a common soul. The soul of modern evangelism is numbers, which are constantly brought up and printed for judgment, like a computer print-out. In fact, numbers are as much a preoccupation of oldline Protestantism, as Yale professor/parish church scholar Gaylord Noyce argues, as conversion statistics are for evangelicals and fundamentalists.[72] Yet as one philosopher of mathematics puts it, "'quantity' is very likely not an important philosophical category."[73]

Scared-Saved evangelism seeks to bring people into heaven by scaring the hell out of them. This strategy has not entered the church through the church growth movement. Boggle-eyed believers have always dipped their mental pens into the well of their imagination and come up with hideously vivid word pictures that would stand intrigue and suspense master/film producer Alfred Hitchcock's hair (what little there was of it) on end. One nineteenth-century itinerant complained of the way "Some people make hell their fence, and the devil their bully, to scare children into heaven." John Wesley himself was accused of verbally barbecuing his hearers over the coals of hell so vividly that unbelievers rushed to repent to avoid their dreadful fate. Preaching that would swing people "hair-hung and breeze shaken over the pit of hell," as they used to say, was very popular with Wesley's associates, especially during the early years of revival. Yet any reading of Wesley's sermons, with their emphasis on God's love, disputes this caricature.

Spirits so low and discouraged that they are without hope of heaven or fear of hell prove ultimately immune to Scared-Saved evangelism. So do people with living conditions so deplorable that they barely manage to get through the day, much less contemplate tomorrow. The fires of hell do not scare people who are living in freezers. By and large, however, Scared-Saved evangelism can be quite effective in populating the altar, especially with middle-class Americans. But in the process it populates the mind and spirit with wrong ideas.

First, it implicitly sanctions the presumption of the Inquisition: The notion that the end justifies the means, since it is fear and not love that is the basis of the appeal. Billy Sunday used to say that "it doesn't matter how I get a soul to heaven, so long as I get him there." It mattered to Jesus. We need read no further than four chapters into the Second Testament to find that out. It must matter to us.

Second, Scared-Saved evangelism gives people a twisted, tormented concept of God. Jesus was walking with his disciples one day and suddenly turned around to face them, asking, "What do you seek?" (John 1:37-38 RSV). In other words, Jesus wanted to know "What do you really want?" Later in John's Gospel, Jesus sadly answered his own question: "You seek me for the loaves and fishes"--"because you ate the bread and your hunger was satisfied" (John 6:26 NEB). One of the most forgotten principles of the Christian life is that of the uselessness of God--that God is not to be used as some passport out of perdition, or some cosmic bellhop, or some divine welfare state that gives unlimited benefits and never exacts taxes. It is not an easy prayer to say, but Martin Luther prayed it: "Oh, my Lord! If I worship thee from fear of hell, burn me in hell; and if I worship thee from hope of paradise, exclude me thence; but if I worship thee for thine own sake, then withhold not from me thine eternal beauty."

—————————— 66 ——————————

*Form is Soul, and doth
the Body make.*
Sixteenth-century poet/court clerk/sheriff Edmund Spenser[n]

—————————— 99 ——————————

Third, Scared-Saved evangelism shifts our attention from this world to another. A sense of eternity is certainly not inconsequential to the Christian, and everyone wants to go to heaven in as numerous a company as possible. But the biblical accent is not on our ability to answer the question, "If you were to die today where would you go?" but on our ability to answer another question: "If you were to die today, what would you have left undone for God?" Salvation is not a journey to heaven or a ride to paradise. Salvation is the explosive experience of God's redemptive love in community with others. Wesley called salvation "Heaven now," "the beginning of heaven," "walking in eternity," "tasting the power of the world to come." We do not love God so that God will save us. To love God is to be saved. We do not love

God so that we will go to heaven. To love God, on whichever side of the grave, is to be in heaven. The reality on which we stake our faith is not the assurance of heaven or insurance from hell, but the indwelling love of God.

In 1 John we are told "This is how we know..." Know what? That God will let us into heaven? "This is how we know we are in him" (1 John 2:5 NIV); "This is how we know that he lives in us" (1 John 3:24 NIV). Our assurance of faith is that God loves us, redeems us, and empowers us to live redemptive, abundant, and transforming lives. Our assurance is one of living in God, not living in glory.

Show-and-Tell evangelism is a much more civil and decorous evangelistic strategy than Scared-Saved evangelism, although it comes in hard-sell and soft-sell varieties. It too has a long line of ancestry in the Christian tradition, as exemplified by George Whitefield's ten-minute rule: Never converse over ten minutes with anyone without letting him or her know where you stand spiritually.

Show-and-Tell evangelism asks people to stop and "listen to what Jesus means" to them, or "Listen to what Jesus is doing" in their lives. Or more egotistically: "Listen to what Jesus is doing through me." Show-and-Tell evangelism is another name for self-introduction. Its effect can be illustrated by the story of the man who fell into a well and in his despair and panic promised to live a holy life if only God would get him out of this mess. Someone heard him screaming and praying, found a rope, and rescued him from a watery grave. He kept his promise, and his life was transformed. He was so thrilled at his new life in Christ that he began to go around pushing anyone he could into wells.

We push people into wells of our own making when evangelization becomes simply witnessing to our experience of God. We are not called to witness. We are called to *be* a witness. "You shall be my witnesses" reads Acts 1:8. When one *is* a witness rather than witnessing, the finger is pointed, not at oneself, but at God--at the God who justifies, sanctifies, and glorifies.

Show-and-Tell evangelism is a reflexive activity, since the narrator and the story are the same. Hospitality evangelism is a reflective activity. "Ye servants of God, **your** Master proclaim/And publish abroad, **his** wonderful name" is how Charles Wesley's hymn puts it, with a little added emphasis. Or in the words of Paul: "For what we preach is not ourselves, but Jesus Christ as Lord, with ourselves as your servants for Jesus' sake" (2 Cor. 4:5 RSV). One of my favorite eighteenth-century theologians, English devotional writer/spiritual director William Law, put it this way: "I invite all people to the marriage of the Lamb, but no one to myself."[74]

The difference, as precocious child poet/novelist/psychic Sylvia Plath might have phrased it, is the difference between the evangelism of the moon and the evangelism of the sun. When the moon shines, we say, "The moon is beautiful." But when the sun shines, we say, "How beautiful the earth is." Moon evangelism draws attention to its own reflected glory, to how much

God loves me and is working in my life. Sun evangelism draws attention to God, to how much God loves you, and to the ways God is there in your life.

— 66 —

One who is full of oneself has no room for God.

Contemporary folk saying

— 99 —

Evangelization is not "Come to church, we've got such a great minister," or "Come to church, we've got the fastest growing Sunday school in town," or "Come to church, you will not hear better music." Evangelization is "Come and see a man who told me everything I have ever done" (John 4:29 NRSV). Evangelization is "We have found the Messiah, come and see" (cf. John 1:41). And since evangelism is a holistic endeavor that encompasses justification, sanctification, and glorification--it does not separate itself off from social action as another task--evangelization is "Come, work with us in building up New Jerusalem."

Church management consultant/United Methodist minister Lyle E. Schaller's studies are famous for showing that the single most effective strategy for evangelization in helping bring new persons to Christ and the church is for church members to invite newcomers home for dinner, or to take them out for Sunday brunch. We did not need to wait for Lyle Schaller to tell us that. What we needed to do was read the Gospels. Why was Jesus always running off to dinner with strangers? Hospitality evangelism is entering people's lives on their turf and in their terms, getting them to talk about their pain and hurt, pointing them toward God's love and grace, then joining them in mission. We can't truly introduce someone to Jesus unless we first know the person well ourselves. Similarly, we can't carry people across the river of life on the back of our own experience. We can only show them where the stepping stones are and encourage them across.

In other words, geomantic evangelization is not an object we possess, a set of principles and pronouncements we elucidate, or a product we package and market as better at "meeting people's needs" for security of soul and peace of mind than any other brand of religion available today. Christianity is not a product, or principle, or possession that is offered by the evangelist. Christianity is Jesus Christ who is introduced by the messenger. A prospective bride, mired in the modern marvels of matrimonial ritual, writes to Miss Manners to ask, "I'm confused by the lists of household 'necessities' in the bridal magazines. What are the minimum essentials a bride needs to begin married life?" To which Miss Manners replies, "A bridegroom."

Hospitality evangelism is as simple and unadorned as beginning married life. All one needs are three things. First, all one needs is Jesus Christ. Second, all one needs is someone to call "Beloved." There were two great turning points in Jesus' life: baptism and transfiguration. Both times a voice from heaven named him "Beloved Son." The naming of people "Beloved Son"/"Beloved Daughter" can be turning points in people's lives. Third, all one needs is to be surrounded by two or three people: "If two of you agree . . ." and again "Where two or three are gathered together . . ." (Matt. 18:19,20 RSV). Hospitality evangelism has no more necessities than that.

———————————— 66 ————————————

Ah, great, sweet Lord, make Thou of little me
Only a soft reciprocal of Thee.
Mathematician/animal-lover/architectural theorist Coventry Patmore[o]

———————————— 99 ————————————

The only introduction necessary is this: Saying to someone, "John, here is Jesus. Jesus, here is John." We are being trained daily by our culture to introduce friends and strangers to beer ("This Bud's for you"), to cars ("It feels right"), to movies ("Have you seen . . . ?"). Postmoderns must be trained by churches to offer chance strangers, as well as close friends, Jesus Christ. They must also be prepared to make introductions to trees, to rocks, to whales, to waves.

The scene portrayed by physics and the biological sciences is a world dominated by random occurrences where no player knows the lines to speak before the moment itself. Geomantic evangelization presupposes, therefore, that we are experienced in Christ ("I know the one in whom I have put my trust," 2 Tim. 1:12 NRSV) so that we may personally introduce Christ. The greatest compliment anyone can pay a New Light Christian is not what we think it is. It is not "Praise be to God for Susan" but "Praise be to Susan for God."

In no way do New Lights diminish the importance of personal, verbal interaction. The issue is over the content of that personal, verbal interaction. One of the chief impediments to a vital faith is the notion that we can live our life so that it will speak and we won't have to. The problem here is, first, no life is good enough to speak for itself, and, second, attention is once again directed to one's life and not to the God who is already working through prevenient grace in other people's lives. While actions speak louder than words, words still speak, especially when the verbal and visual are brought together in expression. The church today confronts reverse hypocrisy. Whereas hypocrisy of old paraded faith before the world, hypocrisy of today plays down before others the faith that is there. The late Reader Harris, a brilliant British barrister and Pentecostal Christian, revealed the secret of his courtroom success: "When I have a poor case in court, I make a speech; but when I have a good case, I call the witness." The witness we are to make, however, is to introduce others to Jesus Christ, not to ourselves.

At funeral processions in the nineteenth century, they used to muffle the drums. Moderns still do this today with our tight-lipped, funereal faith.

New Lights learn to roll their faith across their tongues and put some teeth into evangelization. If we had worn our teeth down from talking so much, one could feel better about our gumming our way through gossiping the gospel. But in many cases our faith hasn't even begun to grow teeth to begin with.

"Teeth" is not our impeccable logic, or even our impeccable example. "Teeth" is our passion, our enthusiasm, our biting intensity of belief and trust. Every advancement in history has been the product of passion. David Hume, the famous eighteenth-century philosopher and empiricist, was once seen hurrying along a street. He was asked by a friend where he was going. "To hear George Whitefield preach," came the unexpected reply. His friend was stunned. "Surely you don't believe what Whitefield is preaching, do you?" "No," replied Hume. "But Whitefield does."

Introductions that draw people into the worship and adoration of God must take place in a sanctuary, not so much an architectural space as an atmospheric space, a spatial haven where the normal street rules of aggression and retaliation are suspended. The sanctuary syndrome of geomantic evangelization sets place apart for God; makes a particular space out of bounds to the world's way of thinking and acting. It is space where change can take place in us as well, not merely space where we can change strangers. Henri Nouwen insists on this powerfully in *Reaching Out* (1975), laying down a marker he calls "the paradox of hospitality":

> Hospitality is not to change people, but to offer them space where change can take place. It is not to bring men and women over to our side, but to offer freedom not disturbed by dividing lines. It is not to lead our neighbors into a corner where there are no alternatives left, but to open a wide spectrum of options for choice and commitment.... It is not a method of making our God and our way into the criteria of happiness, but the opening of an opportunity to others to their God and their way.[75]

Eastern Orthodox theologian Nikos Nissiotis robes the sanctuary syndrome in more academic garb:

> The Gospel does not offer an easy, unilateral or identical solution to be applied everywhere in exactly the same way. The churches are obliged to present it and link it to the given and changing social and cultural situations in which they live.... The essential thing about the universal nature of the Gospel message, which proclaims one faith in Christ, is that it is rooted in particularity.[76]

It is not our duty to change people's thinking to our way of thinking. It is not our job to change people's minds until they adopt our point of view. A real and lasting change of mind is metanoia, and that is a change God works in God's grace and time. After making the introduction, our job is to keep the conversation going between God and the stranger. We do not write the script. We do not put our words in God's mouth. We do help people open up to God's overtures; we do help people express themselves to God in the way they know best. Some of the greatest words missionary/theologian D.T. Niles ever uttered are these seldom-quoted ones:

To be evangelists is not an undertaking to spread Christianity. It is rather to be caught within the explosion of the Gospel. Christ is at work ... and in his working we are caught, impelled, given until we become part of the lives of those to whom we are sent.

In other words, New Light missionaries learn about Christ from the people to whom they minister. Geomantic evangelization is not merely teaching Christ to people, or persuading others to occupy your space with you. It is experiencing Christ in the envelopes of space in which the stranger exists. It is being taught Christ by the "beloved" to whom we are sent. It becomes, "like a U-Haul truck, an 'adventure in moving,'" Niles concludes.

As guests in the church's sanctuary, strangers need not divulge anything about their identity and history until after the invitation has been accepted, the introductions begun, and the celebrations in part enjoyed. Early patterns of hospitality required the guest to wear the mask of stranger, however eager one might be to shed it or to strip it off. Who one is--friend, kin, or foe--must remain unknown, a separate issue from the rites of hospitality. This forgotten feature of ancient protocols of hospitality must be reclaimed for geomantic evangelization to extend beyond "lifestyle enclaves," as phrased by Robert Bellah, describing those places where we go to find "our kind of people," as phrased by missiologist/church growth professor Peter Wagner in the most obscenely titled book on missions and church growth ever written.[77]

─────────────────── **66** ───────────────────

Hail guest, we ask not what thou art;
If friend, we greet thee, hand and heart;
If stranger, such no longer be;
If foe, our love shall conquer thee.

An old Welsh rhyme

─────────────────── **99** ───────────────────

Initiation

The third stage of hospitality evangelization is **Initiation**, the *koinonia* process whereby the stranger/guest becomes friend and family, whereby outsiders are redefined as no longer strangers, outcasts, or lepers. The entrance of the stranger into the intimacy of family life revolves around initiating into the presence of Christ, the host of hosts, who meets his people at table. Table was the centerpiece of Jesus' ministry. It became "the place for both experiencing and expressing *koinonia*," Bernard Prusak argues.[78]

The primary expression of hospitality evangelism is the meal, the table, the banquet--the ritual that grounded and defined Christbody community.

All guests are to be treated as if they were Christ. "The beginnings of Christian liturgy around the Lord's Table emphasized hospitality to the stranger."[79] By the parable of the great supper (Matt. 22:1-14), written late in the first century, it is clear that there could be an exclusive dimension to table communion. But as a symbol of salvation, hospitality as initiation was dispensed impartially to all, friends, strangers, even enemies, because salvation was dispensed freely to all alike. We live as a company of strangers, as a community of guests in God's house. We never become property owners or landlords who can decide the kind of people who get let in and the kind of people who get kept out. We are to receive every stranger the same way Christ received us. This process of making room for one another (not "move over" but "make room"), this making one another feel "at home" in God's house, this transforming of public space into public worship,[80] is our initiating one another into the body of Christ.

Hospitality evangelism knows the connection between liturgy and missions. There is nothing the church does that is more liturgical, more material, more evangelical, than breaking bread together around the Table. Indeed, the ritual component by which hospitality was most often defined was the "meal."[81] The Gospels, which are full of table scenarios, teach the breaking of bread as a sign of the coming of God's kingdom. The Table is the primary expression of and initiation into the hospitality of God's kingdom. In the early church foot-washing rituals were more acts of hospitality than acts of humility, but as Lutheran pastor/New Testament scholar/professor Arland J. Hultgren has so convincingly demonstrated, Jesus' washing of his disciples' feet in John 13:1-11 was a symbol of eschatological hospitality, a "receiving the disciples into the place to which he is going, the very house of his Father (14:2)."[82] The Table has more primacy and power than the Towel and Basin partly because it requires the sensuous involvement of one's entire being--smelling, hearing, seeing, feeling (a touchy subject), and tasting.

---- **66** ----

Jesus, in his friendship with outcasts and sinners,
is a model of friendship with God.
Jesus as parable enacts God's friendship with humanity.
The God of Jesus is the One who invites us to table
to eat together as friends.

Theologian/feminist Sallie McFague[P]

---- **99** ----

Throughout Christian history, and especially during those times when Christian communities functioned more as movements than as establishments, food became in many ways a surrogate form of institutional or national identity. The history of Methodism can almost be written as a history of initiation into the hospitality of the meal. There is an early Methodist proverb that the number of guests entertained at meals or religious gatherings must equal the number of puncheons in the floor (a puncheon was half of a split log, the flat side turned up to serve the place of a wide board). Early "Methodist taverns," which housed travelers and strangers, often made floor puncheons into one continuous bed. In later years, Methodists extended their generous hospitality by placing two beds in a room, with two and sometimes three guests in a bed.

Architectural historian/folklorist Dell Upton has explored the meaning of "southern hospitality" in his marvelous book, entitled *Holy Things and Profane: Anglican Parish Churches in Colonial Virginia* (1986).[83] He describes the interior and exterior architecture that made church space special and set apart, inculcating in worshipers feelings of hospitality toward God and one another through pulpits, altarpieces, chests, fonts, tables, textiles, communion plates. But most of all, "Hospitality was judged by the quality of one's table." The highest compliment eighteenth-century biographer/novelist Edward Kimber could pay Maryland hospitality was to refer to it as "Full Tables and Open Doors." High hospitality, even high cultures, meant good food in extravagance to the point of self-sacrifice. Less hospitality than that was worse than no hospitality at all. The French revolutionist/publicist/traveler Jean Pierce Brissot de Warville recorded George Washington's complaint that pre-Revolutionary Virginia hosts, no matter what their socioeconomic station, made it a point of honor to "send their guests home drunk."[84] According to Robert Beverley, author of a 1705 history of Virginia, "The poorest planter would sleep on a form or couch or even sit up all night to give his only bed to a traveler."[85] The best seats in the house, the best seats in the kingdom, go to the stranger.

Blessing, Breaking, and Distributing the Bread: These are the three parts to hospitality evangelism's initiation at Table. First, **blessing**: Ancient greetings were most often blessings. The holy kiss of welcome (1 Cor. 16:20) blessed the embrace of a common faith. The Ugaritic formula of greeting was built around this blessing: "Welfare be upon you." St. Francis of Assisi was known for his greeting/blessing, which he used everywhere and which he believed was given him by God: "The Lord give you peace." Jacob's struggle to obtain a blessing, which won him the name Israel, was really a quest for **more life**.[86] Unfortunately, modern forms of greeting have neither been life-giving, nor blessings, for that matter.

The "Ritual of Friendship," for example, is an odd grouping of words that ranks right up there with the oxymoron "Orthodox Christianity" and the tautology "Independent Baptist." When friendship needs to be ritualistically dragged into existence, forced into bloom like marigolds in March, there is need for something deeper than "friendship." Similarly, the introduction into modern liturgies of a segment called "Passing of the Peace" is the peace that passes my understanding. Either from the standpoint of those frozen in place trying to quick-thaw for two minutes of friendliness, or those whirling dervishes endangering anything or anyone in their path, the attitude is one of "Let's get this over with so we can get about the real work of worship."[87] Or in the words of Andrew Sullivan speaking in *The New Republic*, the "sign of peace" is "the Vatican II equivalent of that poignant moment in 'The Price is Right' when you realize you're the contestant: (Why is everybody smiling at me?)."[88]

Breaking: The breaking stage of table initiation is symbolized in the breaking of the bread and the pouring of the wine. One of the most striking phrases in all of Augustine's writings is this: "The deformity of Christ forms you. . . . If he had not been willing to be deformed, you would not have recovered the form you lost." Christ's body was broken, his blood poured out, so that we who hurt and fail, we who mock and even betray, we the forgetful and the forgotten, may still humbly repent, recover who we are, and kneel before the one who put us back together. It is precisely Christ's unstanchable wounds that empowers his body to heal other members of the body. It takes a thorn to recover a thorn. It takes bread that is broken to feed and heal a body that is broken.

Distributing the bread: Here is where we come to the heart of what it means to eat the body unworthily. If the bread and wine have not been distributed to all, if the lepers are not present at the meal, if we have not heard "the cry of the needy," if "every city and every diocese" has not built for the poor "houses of hospitality" (Council of Nicaea), if every family does not have "a room where Christ is welcomed in the person of the hungry and thirsty stranger" (St. John Chrysostom), then one takes nourishment at one's own risk.

— **66** —

When you give a dinner or a banquet, do not invite your friends or your brothers or your kinsmen or rich neighbors, lest they also invite you in return, and you be repaid. But when you give a feast, invite the poor, the maimed, the lame, the blind, and you will be blessed, because they cannot repay you. You will be repaid at the resurrection of the just.

Storyteller/dinner host Jesus the Christ[q]

— **99** —

As the postmodern church gets back on the road again, Jesus wants us to see with Samaritan eyes. The Levite "saw" the man lying half dead on the side of the road, but "crossed over" to the other side. Only the Samaritan truly "saw" the stranger--for only he was sensitive to human need. *Popular Science* feature writer/wildlife enthusiast Edwin Way Teale, who stumbled

one day upon a
bird beneath his
feet, observed how
"a thing may be
found many times
and still be lost.
You can walk right
by it time and time
again. It must be
recognized in
order to be seen."
This is the

geomantic evangelization of the church, the heart of hospitality evangelism:
To recognize Jesus when he comes to us, and to help others recognize Jesus
when he comes to them. "Brother, receive your sight. That was God who just
stopped by. Sister, receive your sight. That was God who just passed your
way." In on-the-road evangelization, we ourselves meet God in the stranger--
the stranger on the road to Emmaus, the stranger lying in the ditch on the
road to Jericho, the stranger hungry for bread and beauty. But many times
God, as at Emmaus, is revealed to us only **after** we have offered hospitality
to the stranger (Luke 24:29-31).

Greek philosopher/first Christian apologist Aristides, defending Christians before Roman emperor/world traveler Hadrian, gave this eyewitness
account of the earliest Christians' geomantic evangelization:

Christians love one another. They never fail to help widows and
orphans. If a man has something, he gives it freely to the man who
has nothing. If they see a stranger, Christians take him home and
treat him like a real brother. If someone is poor and there isn't
enough food to go around, they fast several days to give him the
food he needs. This is really a new kind of person. There is
something divine in them.[89]

Windily is how New Lights make space sacred, according to lexicographer/
Pulitzer poet/critic Richard Howard's lines:

If I tell you this place is holier
than others, I only mean
more holiness has run out of it.[90]

Image Intermezzo IV: Water-Striding

There is one more means of traveling that Christians are called to learn: the water insect art of water-striding. This re-turns Intermezzo IV back toward Intermezzo I. Jesus called his first disciples from a life of hauling things out of the water onto the dry land to a life of returning landed, stranded people to the water. He found fishermen hauling fish from the water onto dry land. But he called them to a metanoic life of dragging people from dry lands of lostness and loneliness, from barren deserts of despair and depression, from the wilderness of disappearances and death, into the water of new life in the Spirit.

God is an "ocean of love," confided Jonathan Edwards. No wonder the human body is over 50 percent saltwater. When we cry our tears are seawater. We are both a land and a water people. A crusty clump of swampland, humans are part saltwater and part minerals found in the crust of the earth. Humans are literally the earth come to consciousness. For this reason,

New Lights are amphibious leaders. Jesus calls his amphibious apostles to enter Peter's boat and embark on a quantum way of living. Jesus calls us into a new life and baptizes us a water people. But baptism means more than sticking one's toes in the water, or even getting one's feet wet in faith. In calling Peter, James and John into the water, Jesus called them to immerse themselves in the life of faith, to swim in the stream of the Spirit. Even more --at one point in Peter's life, Jesus called Peter to step out of the boat and walk on water.

The Christian life is more than one of wave-riding. It is also one of water-striding. In fact, in some southern states water-striders are known as "Jesus bugs" for precisely this reason. When water-striding becomes a way of life, **quantum spirituality** will be a reality. Philosopher/lyric poet/critic Samuel Taylor Coleridge illustrated the thinking process by the use of the same insect: "Most of my readers will have observed a small water-insect on the surface of rivulets, which throws a cinque-spotted shadow

fringed with prismatic colours on the sunny
bottom of the brook; and will have noticed,
how the little animal wins its way up against the
stream, by alternate pulses of active and passive
motion, now resisting the current, and now yielding
to it in order to gather strength and a momentary
fulcrum for a further propulsion. This is no unapt emblem
of the mind's self-experience in the act
of thinking."[1]

But like the bug,
attention is not drawn to the water-
striders themselves or to their
miraculous way of walking on
water. As Coleridge observed,
one only sees the shadows,
or four pulsating specks dancing on
the bottom of the creekbed. No one
ever really knows how much walking on water
it takes simply to crawl creekbeds.[2]

A water-striding faith does not show how big you are.
Only how great God is.

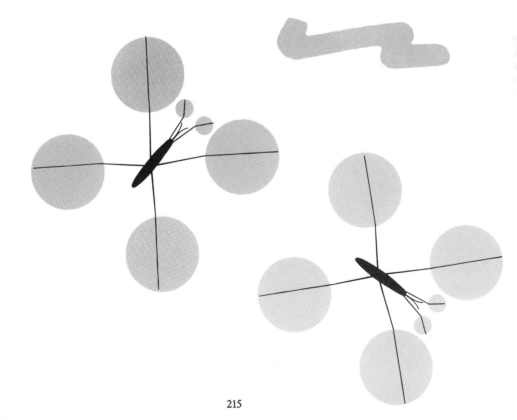

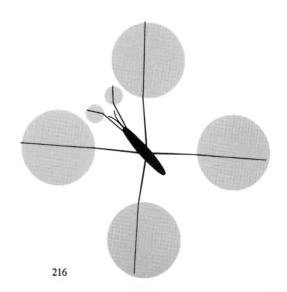

THE SEA OF TIME ". . . AND WE BEHELD GOD'S GLORY"

The "Community of Those Who Travel" is how the church was some-times designated in the fifteenth century. A postmodern apologetic is always on the move. As with all the ocean's "marueilous straunge Fishe," in the words of sixteenth-century sailors, motion forward is what keeps New Lights breathing. The image of the journey is decisive for postmodernism, ever on the way to Damascus.

Tragically, the church has created a world devoid of motion, a theological still life. "For my part," wrote Scottish essayist/poet Robert Louis Stevenson, "I travel not to go anywhere, but to go. I travel for travel's sake. The great affair is to move."[1] The great discovery of space apace time is that (also in the words of Stevenson) "the most beautiful adventures are not those we go to seek." In a world filled with Tom-peeping pleasures and television travelers, New Lights are the true world-travelers, the real water bearers, and water striders.

❝

To travel hopefully is a better thing than to arrive.

Adventurist/novelist Robert Louis Stevenson.[2]

❞

Where the Concrete Ends

Most of us are strollers on the sidewalks and boardwalks of life. We keep forever on the paved and familiar. We want to get where we are going without delays and obstructions. We want to go where others have gone and where the sidewalks and boardwalks lead. In case we stray off the sidewalk or boardwalk for one reason or another, society has posted plenty of snarling signs to get us back on again: "Keep Off the Grass"; "Don't Make Waves."

New-Light mindedness nudges postmoderns off the sidewalks onto the grass, fields, and forests, off the boardwalk onto the rocks, streams, and seas of life. To improvise on a phrase from the children's book *Where the Sidewalk Ends* (1974) by Shel Silverstein, "Where the Concrete Ends" is the beginning of what physicists call the "fourth dimension." One can get by with a sidewalk/boardwalk spirituality. Most moderns have lived their entire lives trapped in a three-dimensional consciousness. But Jesus revealed a fourth dimension of faith, a sea spirituality, a Spirit sensitivity, a sacramental consciousness of "something really wild in the universe."[2] In Ludwig Wittgenstein's words, *"Denk nicht, sodem schau!,"* (Don't think. Look).[3]

❝

Know that since God created human beings
and brought them out of nothingness into existence,
they have not stopped being travelers.

Thirteenth-century Islamic Sufi sage/mystic theologian Ibn al-'Arabi[b]

❞

For those who are nagged by the unadventurousness of their piety, for those with the courage to let rip in life and dive into the divine, for those courageous, reckless, and honest enough to explore faith's frontiers, for those willing to let logic off the leash, there is an alternative. There comes a time, as Danish philosopher/theologian Soren Kierkegaard said, when the Christian faith requires one to swim out fifty fathoms deep. A faith that takes off its shoes ventures into a cosmic ocean dense with magic, mystery, and miracle--the haunt of burning bushes and parting waters, angelophany and Arcimboldo effects, voices and dreams, deaths and resurrections.

For the church to get underway in the postmodern world, it must entrust itself to the guidance of the Spirit, leave the fixed space-times of Newtonian kinematics, and relearn the art of traveling across seas and continents and space-time fields that interact dynamically and unpredictably with energymatter. "Our favorite image of Time," novelist/playwright/ critic J.B. Priestley has observed "are of course all these tides, floods, rivers,' streams--anything, it appears, that suggests moving water."[4] Traveling takes time. The modern era seemed to have everything but time. Indeed, classical physics neglected the concept of time.

A culture, or a church, can be characterized by its attitude toward time. Time is the key to *Theos*, as relativity theory, which "temporalized" space, would suggest. New Lights must take the time, and allow space to become temporalized. They also must be daring and mobile enough to sail with Jesus through what liberationist/education philosopher Paulo Freire calls the "paschal passage."[5] New Lights must catch the waves of a spiritual Gulf Stream taking them into the unknown regions of what Nobel laureate/ philosopher/London School of Economics professor Karl Popper and electrical engineer/Stanford University professor Willis W. Harman call the "Spiritual Sciences."[6] Portugal's greatest modern poet, Fernando Pessoa, says that "sea both separates and links continents." So does the sea of time both separate and link the other three dimensions.

———————————————— 66 ————————————————

God exists now; this angel exists now;
and this motion exists now. The "now"
is either the same for all three, or it is one or the other.
If it is the same "now," then time, aevum, and eternity
are the same. And if the "nows" are different,
there will be several "nows," which seems absurd.

Anonymous thirteenth-century theologian[c]

———————————————— 99 ————————————————

Doing Time

There is an unseen world that pushes the seen world along. Philosopher/mathematician/college president/BASIC computer language inventor John G. Kemeny uses the illustration of a two-dimensional world trying to put behind bars a three-dimensional being. One moment the jailers would see their prisoner behind bars. But whenever the captive wanted to escape, all that would be necessary would be to assume momentarily some height and step out of jail, suddenly disappearing from view and then reappearing outside the jail.[7]

———————————————— 66 ————————————————

Time here becomes space.

German musicodramatist/poet/political philosopher Richard Wagner[d]

———————————————— 99 ————————————————

Space-time is the fourth dimension of a quantum spirituality. Albert Einstein brought space and time together. "Henceforth space by itself, and time by itself, are doomed to fade away into mere shadows," geometrist/ numbers theorist Hermann Minkowski writes, "and only a kind of union of the two will preserve an independent reality."[8] Einstein taught that time and space are "modes by which we think and not conditions in which we live." In space-time there is no before or after, no past or future, only moments of creativity in which the new can emerge in continuity with the old.

The fourth dimension stretches the domain of theology as much as that three-dimensional captive stretched the two-dimensional imaginations of those stunned, flat-world inhabitants. The fourth dimensional fusion between outer space and inner space can yield energy of the highest *Theos*. It can be the place of *basileia*--the communion of love *(koinonia agapes)* where we behold God's glory most resplendently.

One of the most distinctive features of Jesus' thought centered in his concept of time. Not only did Jesus have a strong consciousness of time as *kairos* (a definite point in time) as well as *chronos* (a duration or continuation of time), on three occasions Jesus spoke these words: "My time has not yet come." But as biblical scholar/storyteller/musician Thomas Boomershine has pointed out so forcefully, Jesus also had a sense of life as a path "through" time, in which God was not confined to working in linear fashion from past to present to future. Indeed, Jesus' concept of the reign of God or *basileia* (best defined as the future made present in Jesus Christ who himself is the *basileia* or realm of God) was one in which time flowed from the future into the past and then into the present, or from the future into the present and then into the past.

In the fourth dimension of space-time, all circular movements become a spiral. Nothing ever repeats itself, not even the earth's orbit around the sun. The spiral path is life's fundamental locomotion in the fourth dimension.[9] Jesus believed that God created in spiral and field as well as in linear fashion, from the future as well as from the past.

66

It is the theory which decides what we can observe.

Patent writer/cosmologist/physicist Albert Einstein

99

It is in this sense that what postmodern preachers must do in the pulpit is "time," according to Eugene L. Lowry, rather than what is most often done in the pulpit, which is "space."[10] The narrative, chronomantic shaping of suspenseful "time," rather than the conceptual organizing of logical "space" and chronological "time" is what will move postmoderns to metanoia experiences of justification, sanctification, and glorification. "Doing time" in the universe is the most incredibly mysterious, high-energy, high-speed, high-risk journey one can take. It may even take postmoderns to the dawning of a new sense of uniform, global time.[11]

A Peter Pan Piety?

John Wesley was never one to go lazily down ruts worn by his predecessors. He believed that most people's faith was a fairly pedestrian, terribly routine, ground-grazing affair. His followers were encouraged to leave the beaten paths in search of the strange, the supernatural, the highest regions of all God has to offer. Very soon these early Methodists came on the mysterious. Visitations from the Spirit sphere came not just in the form of "Old Jeffrey," the famous Wesley family ghost. They also came in the form of ecstatic visions and voices, shivers from another world that are common in the childhood days of religious movements. Royal clerk of the closet/moral philosopher/bishop Joseph Butler, one of the great theological figures of the eighteenth century and author of the classic *The Analogy of Religion* (1736), gratuitously warned Wesley about the dangers of "enthusiasm": "Sir, pretending to extraordinary revelations and gifts of the Holy Ghost is a horrid thing, a very horrid thing." Wesley never claimed direct revelations from God for himself, but he would no sooner give up the dreams and visions, paranormal and psychophysical or what the scholastics called the "preternatural," than the Bible. The theme of one of Wesley's last sermons, preached on 22 September 1790 at Bristol's Temple Church, was taken from Mark 9:23: "All things are possible to him that believeth" (KJV).

Moderns have tended to downplay such high expectations for fear of being seen as part of the Peter Pan School of Piety--a fairytale faith that has never grown up, that believes in magic wands and pixie dust, that takes flights of fancy into never-never lands far removed from the ground of common-sense experience. Moderns pride themselves instead on a down-to-earth, grown-up faith that is solidly anchored in reality, ruddered by reason, and propelled by God working through the scientific method. The fourth dimension is seen by modernizers as the fantasy realm of religious obscenity--faith caught *in flagrante delicto*.

---------------------------------- 66 ----------------------------------

[Theology and science]
have become companions in tribulation,
under the pressure of the ecological crisis
and the search for the new direction
which both must work for, if human beings and nature
are to survive at all on this earth.

German christologist/creation theologian Jürgen Moltmann[e]

---------------------------------- 99 ----------------------------------

One does not have to be a reader of science fiction to know about the fictions of science. At the very time the bloom is off the scientific rose, scientists themselves are more humbly realistic about what science can do, less confident that "everything can be explained" than are many Christians.[12] The five most influential philosophers of science in recent times--Sir Karl Popper, Paul K. Feyerabend, Thomas S. Kuhn, Alexander Koyré, and Imre Lakatos--all show that the natural sciences are a fallible and less exclusive guide in leading us to truth than we have commonly supposed. The leading edge of theoretical particle physics brings into focus science's methodological limitations, which prevent it from treating and interpreting important parts of the human enterprise. Postmodernist intellectuals like Jacques Derrida no longer take seriously normative notions of scientific discourse.

Because "global and existential meanings," as Huston Smith terms them, cannot be arrived at through the scientific method, science "fails in the face of all ultimate questions" (Karl Jaspers) and leaves "the problems of life . . . completely untouched" (Ludwig Wittgenstein).[13] Center for Philosophy of Science director/amateur historian Nicholas Rescher concludes that science "does not have exclusive rights to 'knowledge': Its province is far narrower than that of inquiring reason in general."[14] Geneticist/University of California professor Philip T. Spieth has written that "sound science without theology leaves us stranded with subjective values, no basis for morality, and no conception of purpose."[15] Geneticist/virologist/molecular biologist Gunther Stent is famous for his contention that science may now be close to the point of diminishing returns. The officially atheist Albert Einstein conceded that "science without religion is lame, religion without science is blind."[16] Biochemist Jeffrey Wicken confesses that "science's limitations must be pronounced again and again, like a mantra, as its necessary juggernaut marches on."[17] Scientists have become outspoken in their warnings about privileging the language of science.

In April 1974 the members of the American Psychiatric Association voted 5,584 to 3,810 to drop homosexuality as a disease. Investigation and the scientific method do not always shape science. Sometimes it is a show of hands. "Brain Trust" panelist/Salk Institute research professor/statistician Jacob Bronowski, in his influential study *Science and Human Values* (1956), reminds us that "there is today almost no scientific theory which was held" in the eighteenth century. Most often "today's theories flatly contradict" those of the Enlightenment: "Many contradict those of 1900. In cosmology, in quantum mechanics, in genetics, in the social sciences, who now holds beliefs that seemed firm sixty years ago?"[18]

When it comes to reliability, religious faith is no more vulnerable than science. Suffering leaves us in the dark about most of life's ultimate questions, and the "problem" of evil is as absorbing and unsolvable as French lawyer/legislator/mathematician Pierre de Fermat's last theorem, which has mystified mathematicians since its publication in 1670. Equally condemned to a special ignorance about the ultimate realities of the world, both science and religion have increasingly turned toward mystical insight for help. In the words of Sir Brian Pippard, "a physicist who rejects the testimony of saints and mystics is no better than a tone-deaf man deriding

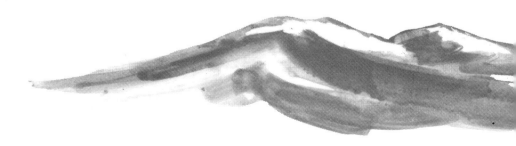

the power of music." The balance has now shifted, according to Ilya Prigogine and Isabelle Stengers, "toward a revival of mysticism . . . even in science itself, especially among cosmologists."[19]

Yet modernist intellectuals continue to subscribe to the monstrous falsehood that the scientific premise is the only route to truth. Leaving to science all wonder-working powers, modernist Christians have been open to the microchip miracles of technology at the same time that they resigned faith to the realms of the possible and appropriate. Modernists came to expect the spirit of high adventure and discovery to pervade the life of science, but not the life of the Spirit.

Unicorns, Leprechauns, Mermaids

There is no such thing as a grown-up faith. We have made a flatulent sentimentality out of one of the hardest of Jesus' "hard sayings": When one no longer has the faith of a child, one no longer has faith. Poet/essayist/diplomat James Russell Lowell, while walking past Boston's House for Incurable Children one day, said with a wink to his companion, "They'll get me in there some day." The House for Incurable Children is but another name for a Christbody community.

66

Trail dire e il fare c'è di mezzo il mare.
An ocean lies between saying and doing.

Italian proverb.

99

A first-grade student took almost an hour to walk home from school, a distance easily covered in no more than fifteen minutes. "Tomorrow afternoon you come straight home from school, young lady," her mother scolded, fearing for the child's safety. But the next day the same thing occurred. It took the child almost an hour to make the trip. "I thought I told you to come straight home," the mother said angrily. "That is what I did," responded the child. "Then what took you so long?" "Well, I stopped to talk to the squirrel in the tree. I watched a caterpillar cross the sidewalk and disappear into the grass. I looked at my reflection in a puddle of water. I

pretended I was a queen walking through my kingdom. Mommy, I did as you said, I came straight home."

For God, and children (and for science fantasist/feminist/fictionist Ursula K. LeGuin), the journey more than the arrival is the point of it all. "It is good to have an end to journey towards; but it is the journey that matters, in the end," is how LeGuin put it in *The Left Hand of Darkness* (1969).[20] Many times I have mentally contrasted my kids' impatience when we take trips in the car, their back-seat fidgeting and fighting, with my own childhood memories of family outings as fun-filled adventures packed with thrills and excitement. Then one day the difference became apparent. On my trips as a parent there is no stopping except for quick pit stops between the point of departure and the point of destination. But when my parents took us on trips, we would, with the unhurried wanderlust of the curious child, stop to pick flowers, collect rocks, climb hills, and picnic at wayside rest areas.

When humans build waterways, we build them straight as the birds fly. When God builds rivers and streams, they meander and wind, twist and turn like the dog in the poem who went along the road with "haphazard intent,"[21] caring as much for the trip as for the terminus. In the full work of creation, God did not always follow Fermat's principle whereby light takes the quickest path between two points. Nature scarcely admits the existence of a straight line. Nature has little use for mechanized, digitized time.

We are like too many of the pioneers who walked the distance from Missouri to Oregon in the mid-nineteenth century. Their diaries tell graphic stories about encounters with dust, rocks, ruts, and mud. But most of them are strangely silent about the vastness of the plains, the grandeur of the Rockies, the brilliance of the Western sky, or the very stars to which they had hitched their wagons. By not lifting their eyes from the path, the "Cortez effect" had taken over: No one surprised by the shock of the new; everyone yawning at the discovery of the unknown. If the children of the Oregon Trail had kept diaries, we would have found a different story. Their feet were no doubt stuck in the silt and slush, but their heads were in the stars.

"Neothany" is a word zoologist/biologist/paleontologist/curator Stephen Jay Gould uses to describe the way the evolutionary process holds onto childhood and youth. Neothanization is reflected in these verses found among the manuscripts on Spanish philosopher Miguel de Unamuno's desk when he died in 1936:

> Widen the door, Father,
> for I cannot enter.
> You made it for children,
> and I have grown up.
> If you do not widen the door,
> have pity and make me smaller.
> Take me back to that age

In which to live was to dream.[22]
The child is always on the side of faith; faith is always on the side of the child. If the childlikeness of faith goes away, faith goes flat. Its neothanic evolution gets stunted. It merely goes through motions. It gets bogged down. It gets fogged up.

The powers of adultish, pedestrian piety are well illustrated by fog. Scientists recently decided to determine just how much water there is in fog dense enough to shut down a major international airport, or descend upon and paralyze seven city blocks of a major metropolis. They calculated how much water there would be in that density of fog if it were fully condensed. What they discovered was that the water it would take to shut down a major international airport, or tie up seven city blocks, would fill one eight-ounce glass. In one glass there is 90×10^{23} molecules of H_2O, or enough atomic energy to send a battleship across the ocean. It is that same swell of power, that same emanation of energy, that is released when even small amounts of pedestrianism are dissolved in the atmosphere of our spirits and dispersed throughout life. Pedestrianism can shut down the church; it can shut down the faith. The church can be so befogged by pedestrian spirits that its mission and mobility come to a screeching halt.

——————————————— 66 ———————————————

Live life as play.
University administrator/researcher/writer/philosopher Plato

——————————————— 99 ———————————————

To get rid of a grown-up faith, we must revel in the fresh awareness of religion's true spiritual giants--its children. Isaac Newton compared himself to a boy collecting shells by the seashore. Contemporary architect/medical foundation trustee Frank Gehry characterizes his own psychological drive for creativity as the desire "to make mud pies that can be shown to mommy. The creative spirit flows from my child-like sense of the world, my sense of play and wonder."[23] A neothanic spirituality abounds in flow activities. It retreats to the renewing, cleansing tub of a childlike faith that splashes away at our sobriety, soaks away at our jadedness, and washes away our encrusted cynicism and pessimism. How to sail away into regions where the concrete ends may be one of the things we learn at our children's knees.

> For the children, they mark,
> and the children, they know
> The place where the sidewalk ends.[24]

One of the biggest indicators of New Light leadership may be whether or not the pastor has children flocking around him or her on Sunday morning.

Neothanic leaders nurture souls big with wonder. They help the church become a house of wonder-full flow experiences. In the autobiography Charles Darwin wrote for his children, he lamented his life's loss of wonder in the scientific scrutiny of nature's wonders. The wonder-full term "natural philosopher" gradually gave way in the modern era to the relatively recently coined "scientist." A small-group exercise measures the degree to which the scientific mind, which "grows **from**" wonder, has "grown **out of**" wonder.[25] Try drawing up one's own personal nominations for the Seven Wonders of the World. If you were putting together a guidebook of the world's greatest wonders, as was drawn up two centuries before Christ for the ancient world (Babylon's hanging gardens, Egypt's pyramids, Olympia's statue of Zeus, Ephesus's temple of Diana, Rhodes's Colossus, Alexandria's Pharos, Halicarnassus's Mausoleum), what wondrous things or events would you select? What takes your breath away today?

— 66 —

To know how to wonder and question
is the first step of the mind toward discovery.

Physicist/immunologist/painter Louis Pasteur[f]

— 99 —

The times I have done this with groups, the selections have ended up being a list of "wonders" that drive out wonder, a variant version of the seven "wonders" of modern science, the seven "wonders" of transportation, the seven "wonders" of communication, the seven "wonders" of medicine, even the seven "wonders" of American engineering (which include the city of Chicago's sewage disposal system). One is ready for threshold experiences when there appear on one's list things that are truly breathtakingly wonder-full, such the wonder of who you are (Augustine said, "Man himself is a greater wonder than any wonder done through his instrumentality"),[26] human consciousness (Pierre Teilhard de Chardin accorded the awe-inspiring phenomenon of consciousness the deepest religious significance), a tree (World War I casualty/poet Joyce Kilmer's first pick), the big voice of a little cricket, West Virginia, unselfishness, and God's continuing love. In the words of the gospel song,

> There's the wonder of sunset at evening
> The wonder as sunrise I see
> But the wonder of wonders that thrills my soul
> Is the wonder that God loves me.

Postmoderns must relearn to take that childlike step that gets us off the "brute-facts" concrete, abandons the modern compulsion to make sense of everything, and enter into neothanic, threshold experiences where eagles soar with angels, where unicorns laugh with leprechauns, where dolphins dance with mermaids, where "the Lord is in this place; and I did not know it" (Gen. 28:16 RSV). New Lights most often learn theology as anecdote and adventure.

Threshold Experiences

A threshold experience is that step, that sight, beyond which chronology fades and synchrony enters, where life begins to take on new colors, words mean different things, and emotions speak different messages. Historian/adventure novelist/explorer Stewart Edward White in *The Unobstructed Universe* (1940) uses the simple illustration of an electric fan to help define the nature of threshold experiences. When the fan is not on, one cannot see what lies behind its thick metal blades. But when the fan is turned on high speed, one can see through the blades clearly. Increased frequencies step up sight and lead one to higher and higher levels of insight.[27]

❝

It is not foolhardy to believe that the eye is made for seeing.

French biologist/metaphysician Lucien Cuénot

❞

As Christians, our seeing is so lazy, so fuzzy, our hearing so dull, so undisciplined, that we take in only a fraction more of the world than others who neither hear nor see. An enfolding and upholding universe of color and sound, motion and taste, is all around us but invisible to us. By far the largest bands on the electromagnetic spectrum are radiations the human eye cannot see: Ultraviolet rays, infrared rays, x-rays, gamma rays, cosmic rays, and rays human instruments cannot yet measure. Our bodies are riddled every day with heat waves, television waves, microwaves, short and long radio waves, yet our awareness of these forces bombarding us is virtually nonexistent. Deep sea shrimp in the Atlantic were thought to be blind because there was nothing to see at such blackened depths. Then a couple of years ago scientists discovered that the shrimp possess eyes located on their backs behind their shells. Scientists are totally mystified by what these shrimp may be seeing at such pitch dark depths.[28]

The space-time dimension is in a higher frequency than the single dimensions of energy, matter, or space. Threshold experiences help raise the vibrations of the mindbody to frequencies that can receive the energy that is available to everyone--threshold experiences like prayer and meditation, both of which have now received "scientific" standing as natural healing agents and cures. A Harvard University study reported on in the *Journal of Personality and Social Psychology* (1989)[29] even goes so far as to claim that meditation can prolong life as well as lower blood pressure and diminish mental malfunctions. Sometimes taking these threshold experiences may be completely voluntary. A few years ago, when I was busy about many things but truly experiencing hardly anything, a friend wrote to entice me off the concrete. "I do admire your creativity, Len, but I still believe you should spend more time enjoying God's."

At other times, threshold experiences knock us off the concrete involuntarily, but whether we clamber back on again is up to us. Early in his life plant manager/psychologist/Brandeis University professor Abraham Maslow was carried off the concrete by a severe heart attack. Out of this threshold experience Maslow, the erstwhile atheist, lived what he called a "post-mortem life"--a life more attuned to cosmic powers wherein can be found the ground of creativity and love. Earlier in his life he wrote:

for such a person, any sunset may be as beautiful as the first one, any flower may be of breath-taking loveliness, even after he has seen a million flowers. The thousandth baby he sees is just as miraculous a product as the first one he saw. He remains as convinced of his luck in marriage thirty years after his marriage and is as surprised by his wife's beauty when she is sixty as he was forty years before. For such people, even the casual workaday, moment-to-moment business of living can be thrilling, exciting, and ecstatic.[30]

The first of the four threshold experiences where the concrete ends is the Mysterium: the magical realms of mystery.

1. The First Threshold of Mystery

All truth ends in mystery. The Enlightenment, which emphasized more the mastery than the mystery of nature, never realized that God leaves more fingerprints than blueprints. God has a particular liking for the magical and mystical. Magic, once a friend of faith, then a rival church, became an antichurch in the modern world. In its degraded modernistic sense, magic means deceptive, neopagan sleight-of-hand ritual. But magic, in its deepest, truest sense, means the presence of the infinite in the finite, the eternal in the mortal, the wondrous in the common. Magical elements play an integrated part in even the most technological life. The law of the waves and wind tips us off to the fabulous working of God's magic: You can't see where they come from or where they go. As one rabbi has observed, "If there is not more than one explanation to an event, then it is not of God." God works mysteriously, anonymously, unpredictably, magically. In fact, Flannery O'Connor's definition of fiction may be one of the best definitions of a quantum spirituality raised to the fourth power: "Mystery that is lived . . . [the] ultimate mystery as we find it embodied in the concrete world of sense experience."[31]

Social anthropologist/theologian John S. Dunne calls mystery "not unintelligibility but inexhaustible intelligibility."[32] The awesomeness and availability of mystery exist everywhere as sacramental and incarnational presences. Like one of those beautiful summer evenings that all have seen but so few have felt, mystery is not something that exists to be analyzed, naturalized, and de-mystified but something that exists to be lived and experienced. Tripping over this first threshold experience of mystery, Soren Kierkegaard wrote that "all of existence intimidates me, from the tiniest fly to the enigmas of the incarnation; as a whole it is unexplicable, my own self most of all."[33]

------------------------------ 66 ------------------------------

They did not let the mystery shine.

Historian/theologian Wilhelm Pauck[8]

------------------------------ 99 ------------------------------

All creation is mangered in mystery. Life is wrapped in what surveyor/ U.S. Consul/novelist Nathaniel Hawthorne termed "mysterious hiero-glyphics," hieroglyphics of holiness that invite our involvement in the mysteries of creation. The Puritans believed that God created the world and gave us the senses to perceive it in order that these mysterious, sensuous experiences might lead us to God. When God is at work, sensational, even strange things will happen. Sensational, even strange things happened at evangelical campmeetings, where the sensual and spiritual blended into one, because once a year these evangelicals let their faith roam freely throughout the space-time dimension. They let themselves get lost--"lost in wonder, love, and praise," as a Charles Wesley hymn puts it. New Light leadership must be prepared to offer postmodern society a faith that can integrate body and soul, psyche and soma, a faith that finds sensuality in spirituality, spirituality in sensuality. There are 1.7 billion Christians in the world today, all of them spirit Christians, only some of them body Christians.[34]

Part of our inability to get lost in wonder is because we rarely unbend. Moderns resist being open to something as accessible and unforeseeable as a sunrise surprise--we keep right on walking as if nothing happened, even after one of God's ambushes. Jesus' first disciples were also guilty of hamstringing the Holy Spirit's working in life. They saw themselves as God's gatekeepers, and tried to confine the Spirit's work to conventional channels. They stopped a man who was "not one of us" from driving out devils in Jesus' name. But Jesus rebuked their presumption and told them, "Do not stop him" (Mark 9:38-39 NIV). There will be surprises in the kingdom of God. "God has many whom the church does not," Augustine wrote, "and the church has many whom God does not." Or in words John Wesley put in a sermon, "Men may differ from us in their opinions as well as their experiences, and nevertheless be partakers with us of the same precious faith. 'Tis possible they may not have a **distinct apprehension** of the very blessing which they enjoy."[35] God has more allies than we think, more servants than we can identify. No doubt, as someone has suggested, the first two questions when we get to heaven will be: "What are you doing here?" and "Where's so-and-so?"

Carl Jung had carved over the doorway of his villa in Küsnacht, Switzerland, the Delphic oracle's motto: *"Vocatus adque, non vocatus, Deus aderit"* (Called or not called, God will be present). In a letter dated 19 November 1960, Jung explained why this inscription meant so much to him, both personally and professionally, that he embossed it on his bookplate and engraved it over his doorway (it was also etched into the family gravestone):

> I have put the inscription there to remind my patients and myself: *Timor dei initium sapientiae* [The fear of the Lord is the beginning of wisdom]. Here another not less important road begins, not the approach to "Christianity," but to God himself and this seems to be the ultimate question.[36]

Scripture is more than God's history, or the church's story, or the clergy's doctrines, or an individual's principles to live by. It is a journey into the holy. It is the opening of a transcendent consciousness that leaks fresh outpourings of the divine.

2. The Second Threshold of Angelic Thinking

If postmoderns are to stray from the concrete, take off their shoes and socks, and wade with their bare feet into the sea of mystery, chaos, instability, disequilibrium, and diversity, then New Light leadership must facilitate a second threshold experience into the imaginary realms of the fourth dimension. Renaissance philosopher/Neoplatonist Marsilio Ficino called it the "Angelic Mind,"[37] the ability to think spiritually as well as scientifically--in images and likenesses, in myths and metaphors, in poetic and artistic forms. Biologist/geneticist Barbara McClintock calls it "a feeling for the organism," an openness to letting the organism "come to you" and hearing "what [it] has to say to you."[38] Indeed, sometimes the only way to think scientifically is to think organismically, nonlinearly, intuitively, imagistically, and artistically. One day Albert Einstein received a letter requesting a rephrasing of the theory of relativity in simple terms explainable to the letterwriter's grandchildren. Einstein wrote back his conviction

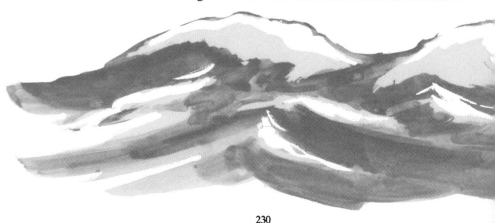

that reason, no matter how simplified, simply will not do. Only something as "straight from the heart" as music would suffice.

Dear Sir, I am sorry that I cannot comply with your request. The theory of relativity cannot be reduced to simple terms. We find it to be true, the further that we look. I hate to disappoint you, but, if you would be willing to come by Princeton some afternoon, I will try to play it for you on my violin.

John Wesley and Jonathan Edwards's spirits may not be too disturbed if we use here their concept of spiritual senses, which they believed exist alongside the more developed physical senses. The spiritual sense is "to the spiritual world, what [physical] sense is with regard to the natural. It is the spiritual sensation of every soul that is born of God."[39] Angelic thinking and spiritual sensing are even the secrets of good science, as atomic physicist/philosopher/humanitarian/churchman Arthur Compton unwittingly intimated in 1927 when he accepted the Nobel Prize in physics: "Every discovery I ever made, I gambled that the truth was there, and then I acted on it with faith until I could prove it true."

―――――――――――――― 66 ――――――――――――――

Water is the commonest symbol for the unconscious. . . .
The unconscious is commonly regarded
as a sort of incapsulated fragment of our most personal
and intimate life . . . and whoever looks into the mirror
of the water will see first of all his own face.

Mystic/mythologist/analytic psychologist Carl Gustav Jung[h]

―――――――――――――― 99 ――――――――――――――

The space-time continuum is where things that are unseen encroach upon things that are seen, where the eternal (no beginning and no end), the perpetual (a beginning but no end), and the temporal (a beginning and an end) are most interrelated, where the spiritual senses are to be trusted over the physical senses.

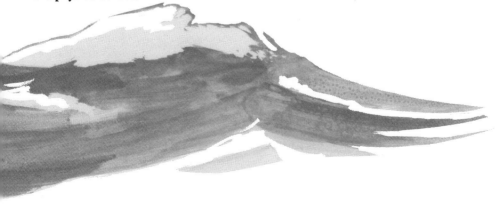

3. The Third Threshold of Psychic Awareness

The third threshold can be a quite forbidding, even spooky place. The psychic realm encompasses the Twilight Zone of theology and the Bermuda Triangle of spirituality. It is the place that can look less adventurous than ludicrous--the lotusland of lunatics.

Even the most educated souls, especially those not biblically masted and without a hand on' history, can easily lose their bearings, get lost, be lured into the shoals or off the deep end by the sibilant sounds of the underworld, never to be heard from again. Every one of us pays more attention to experiences that conform to our beliefs than those that do not. New Light travelers in the fourth dimension would do well to master the four tests of "trustworthiness" detailed by education professor Yvonna A. Lincoln and educational researcher/professor Egon G. Guba in their marvelous book, *Naturalistic Inquiry* (1985): "transferability," "dependability," "credibility," and "confirmability."[40] They provide a good beginning base from which to distinguish between an authentic and a fraudulent spirituality, "a point about which, above many others, the Protestant world is in the dark, and needs instruction," pioneer systematic theologian/ Congregationalist Samuel Hopkins observed over two hundred years ago in the first biography of Jonathan Edwards, a theologian who became more and more preoccupied with this problem of faith's pitfalls.[41]

As Edwards realized, navigation in the fourth dimension's hypersensate zones requires constant vigilance. The sailor is ever voyaging on the edge. The fourth dimension can be the sea from which "no traveler returns." Just because the psychic or paranormal is nonphysical does not mean that it is spiritual. Much of the desire to travel in faith's fourth dimension can be egoistic and self-serving. For this reason Wesley refused to see trances, healings, miracles, and other extraordinary signs as necessary indications of the Holy Spirit at work. Only when the paranormal and spiritual combine in ways that foster ethical and philosophical development "of the highest order," as metaphysician/author David Spangler puts it, will the differences be illuminated between "psychism and mysticism, information and insight, knowledge and wisdom, and self-development and service."[42]

Humans need sleep not primarily because of the need to rest but because of the need to dream. We need to enter other dimensions, to inhabit mythical worlds, to undergo the twitch and twinge of twilight thinking, to tap the invisible energies of the unconscious. God has provided us with third ears (Theodor Reik), inner eyes (William Johnston), sixth senses (Laurie Nadel), and eighth days (Thornton Wilder).[43]

One of the top ten ironies in all of history, the "Linnaeus of dreams"/ Canadian psychologist Harry T. Hunt points out, is the way René Descartes's famous three dreams led him to dismiss dreaming as inferior to reflective, rational consciousness: "The same state that led the meditative traditions to the existential bases of human reality was used by Descartes to justify the Western flight from subjectivity."[44] Because psychologists and others have given scientific credibility to dreams, about which there has been an avalanche of literature since the 1960s, we do not send to the funny-farm dream adventurers like film critic/foreign correspondent/novelist Graham Greene, who attach metaphysical importance to these thoughts of the soul, to which they trace the genesis of some of their creativity (e.g., Greene's *It's a Battlefield* [1934] and *The Honorary Consul* [1973]). Even the church has shown some willingness in recent years to learn from the two Josephs of the Bible, sometimes turning its Sunday schools into sleep labs.

The Bermuda Triangle of Spirituality

But for the most part, Christians keep in good repair prejudices against what may be God's other sign languages of the fourth dimension. Also known as a "Fourth Psychology," transpersonal, transhuman, transcendent states of consciousness include most predominantly extrasensory perception (ESP), the mind's ability to acquire nonsensate information) and psychokinesis (PK), the mind's ability to alter matter.[45] But there are also the familiar out-of-body experiences (OBEs),[46] near death experiences (NDEs), altered states of consciousness ASCs), and precognitive remote perception (PRP), not to mention remote viewing (a variant version of ESP and for some a more precise name than ESP), precognition (time-displaced future information), retrocognition (knowledge of the past through no known means), telepathy (ESP of someone else's thoughts), clairvoyance (ESP of events or objects), and other paranormal, or what are preferably called "anomalous" or "psi," phenomena.

A majority of the population profess one or more psychical experiences.[47] Indeed, sociologist/priest/novelist Andrew Greeley observes that "what was paranormal is now normal."[48] Yet the church, fearing the stamp of lunacy, remains antagonistic or indifferent to even broaching a subject about which everyone seems to know something. In fact, the percentage of Americans who express confidence in paranormal experiences is steadily climbing (from 58 to 67 percent since 1973), while the percentage of Americans who express confidence in organized religion is dramatically plummeting (from 67 to 57 percent in one year, 1985 to 1986). One time Jesuit/theologian/teacher John J. Heaney defines "parapsychology" as "the attempt to apply scientific method and/or critical investigation to phenomena which are 'paranormal.' Paranormal here means whatever is outside the normal paradigms of science and critical reasoning."[49] Unfortunately, "so much nonsense goes on" in the name of the paranormal, Huston Smith has written, "that it takes a bit of courage to say, as did both anthropologist/museum curator Margaret Mead and ecological communications theorist Gregory Bateson, that something does go on."[50]

The names of pioneering figures in psychical research, like Brenda J. Dunne, Elmer E. Green, William McDougall, Raymond Moody, Karlis Osis, K. Ramakrishna Rao, Louisa B. Rhine, Joseph Banks Rhine, and Charles Richet are not exactly household words. The names of the hundred or so scientists currently conducting research in parapsychology, or transpersonal psychology, or the "consciousness disciplines," never appear in the church's continuing education brochures. Dreams are about as far as the church is willing to go into this twilight world of "angelic thinking" and "spiritual senses."

We have only gone this far into the supranormal because science has given us permission, and because the subconscious unlocks more doors to the conscious. The English dream theorist/psychologist/painter/photographer Liam Hudson presents waking thought as more dreamlike than we ever imagined, and sleeping thought as more cognitive and purposive.[51] As Ramakrishna Rao has written, "Religious institutions have taken little notice of the pertinence of psychic phenomena to their world view."[52] Theologians have been much more receptive to the claims of anthropologists (such as Marshall Sahlins) that cultures may have their own logic than they are to the possibility that faith may have its own anomalous logic--logic that loves enemies, that turns cheeks, that walks the second mile, that runs without getting weary, that walks confidently in darkness, that believes improbables are not impossibles.

―――――― **"** ――――――

Between the dreaming and the real there is no line.

Kunduli inscription

―――――― **"** ――――――

It would be as wrong to see psi phenomena vindicating religion (as some early parapsychologists were wont to do) as it would be to see science fiction vanquishing religious faith (as some early scientists were wont to do). What psychic interactions between human consciousness and physical environment substantiate, as Austrian/American physicist Wolfgang Pauli perceived, are the traceable connections that exist between ourselves and others or objects, and the underlying holism of the uni-verse. Transcendent states of consciousness, even those that extend identity beyond the limits of ego and personality, are not those that are most "outside" the community, but those most "inside," most connecting of the self to the cosmos. Most importantly, the anomalous experiences of life force us to make room for God's acting in unique and different ways that may not submit to logical and evidentiary verification. American physicist John Wheeler says about parapsychology, "Where there is smoke there is smoke." When Isaiah saw smoke in the temple, he discovered God (Isa.6:4-5).

Librarian/poet Archibald MacLeish warns all would-be travelers into the unknown: "Once the maps have all been made, a man were better dead than find new continents." Christians are like everyone else--more inclined to clutch old maps than to sail on toward new continents. New Light leadership must be open to a sea change in thinking--to threshold experiences that contradict Western ways of reasoning, to new ranges of reality that call us to nonscientific forms of angelical thinking. Postmoderns already have generous appetites for learning from sources at which most scholars turn up their noses. Religion is far more spacious than historians, or theologians, want to believe. New Light leadership must bring the gospel to bear even on every new cultural disrelish, even on every bad taste howled down by the establishment.

Coincidence, or Connection?

The medieval preoccupation with the problems of duration and time is widely unfamiliar. It is still with us, however, in an arena of study called "proxemics," a field that literally brings new life to John Wesley's belief that "there is no such thing as chance" and to Thomas Merton's claim that "there are no such things as coincidences, only connections." It is also still with us in the biological discovery of the interplay of chance and teleological necessity one finds in the works of Ilya Prigogine and Nobel laureate/ physical chemist/recording musician Manfred Eigen, or in the links between knot theory and quantum physics that demonstrate how "everything seems to be connected to everything else," as one mathematician puts it. Chance now tips us off and tucks us into God's creative presence, and sometimes absence.

———————————— 66 ————————————

When I pray, coincidences start to happen.
When I don't pray, they don't happen.

Theologian/social reformer/ecumenist/archbishop William Temple

———————————— 99 ————————————

My examples here may be eccentric. But consider 8 August 1974. It was the night President Richard Nixon announced to the American people his resignation. The television programs preempted by his announcement were "The Taste of Ashes" (NBC), "The Lost Man" (CBS), and "The Nature of Evil" (ABC).

Coincidence, or connection?

Five of the world's top scientists came from the same town in the same generation--Budapest, Hungary: aeronautical engineer/aerospace scientist Theodore Von Kármán (b.1881); an original atom splitter/nuclear physicist

Leo Szilard (b.1898); pioneer mathematical physicist/1963 Nobel laureate Eugene Paul Wigner (b.1902); mathematician/computer scientist/quantum theorist John von Neumann (b.1903); and the father of the hydrogen bomb/physicist Edward Teller (b.1908).

Coincidence, or connection?

The only thing that enters this planet from the outside, besides meteorite dust, is light. Light is our only energy, our only information. Leadership toward the light is the heart of what it means to be New Light. In one medieval manuscript, *Ring of Fire*, the Trinity is defined as a community of light: God is Sun, Jesus is Light, and the Holy Spirit is Warmth. A surprisingly central feature of all the world's religions is the language of light in communicating the divine and symbolizing the union of the human with the divine: Muhammed's light-filled cave, Moses' burning bush, Paul's blinding light, Fox's "inner light," Krishna's Lord of Light, Böhme's light-filled cobbler shop, Plotinus' fire experiences, Bodhisattvas with the flow of Kundalini's fire erupting from their fontanelles, and so on.[53] Light is the common thread that ties together near-death experiences as they occur in various cultures.

Coincidence, or connection?

For Eastern traditions more accustomed to relational "field thinking" than cause-and-effect linear thinking, it is not coincidence but connection

that things happen in threes. Just as things grow in clusters, they come in clumps. In China, for example, the question is often asked, "What likes to happen together?" It is not superstitious nonsense to them that accidents and tragedies as well as good things occur in groups, but a reflection of the way things like to happen in bunches, the way every part is a microcosm of the whole. A quantum world scrambles linear-time sequences and law systems, revealing God constantly at work bringing new life into being, within a law-chance dialectic (i.e., chance operating within certain lawlike parameters).

———————————— **66** ————————————

Science is a sense of curiosity about life,
Religion is a sense of reverence for life,
Literature is a sense of wonder at life,
Art is a taste for life.
Philosophy an attitude toward life--
Based on a comprehension of the universe
As far as we happen to know it.

Chinese philologist/indexing system inventor/university dean Lin Yu-tang

———————————— **99** ————————————

For people who think more in terms of gestalt than geometry, it is not coincidence but connection that Alfred Wallace and Charles Darwin both uncovered evolution within a year of each other. Evolution was, literally, an idea whose time had come, when time is understood as an outward

expression of the inner system's holistic interactions. Even evolution's idea of natural selection is not a purely random process, as population genetic theory makes clear.[54]

For people who understand the Gaia hypothesis,[55] which posits that the earth behaves like a living system and, indeed, that living things regulate earth's environments, it is not craziness to suggest, as some electrical engineers have argued, that scientists who like their equipment get better results than those who don't.[56] It is rather a reflection of how much better things work out in life when there is a greater sense of cooperation than of confrontation--when food, plants, animals, and machines are seen as part of us, and we of them.

Cultural anthropologists William Condon and Edward T. Hall, two pioneering proxemic researchers, have demonstrated that much of human behavior is influenced not primarily by subjective states of mind, individual moods, and isolated thinking but by an ocean of "rhythms" that engulf and englobe us together. "Entrainment" is the term they use to describe the process whereby two or more people become geared to the rhythms of each other and the universe.[57] In Eastern philosophy this is called the "Tao" experience.[58] In Jungian psychology the metaphor is the collective unconscious rather than "rhythm web," and such meaningful coincidences are called "synchronicity."[59]

One evening Carl Jung returned to his hotel room after delivering a lecture. He could not get to sleep for a long time.

At about two o'clock--I must have just fallen asleep--I awoke with a start, and had the feeling that someone had come into the room; I even had the impression that the door had been hastily opened. I instantly turned on the light, but there was nothing. Someone might have mistaken the door, I thought, and I looked into the corridor. But it was still as death. "Odd," I thought, "someone did come into the room!" Then I tried to recall exactly what had happened, and it occurred to me that I had been awakened by a feeling of dull pain, as though something had struck my forehead and then the back of my skull. The following day I received a telegram saying that my patient had committed suicide. He had shot himself. Later, I learned that the bullet had come to rest in the back wall of the skull.[60]

Who among us has not experienced at least once in our lifetimes a similar psi experience of synchronicity, albeit perhaps not as dramatic--whether it be of the co-incidence of thought or feeling and outer event (which Jung illustrated by his famous stories about the scarab beetle and the fox), the co-incidence of a dream or vision with a simultaneous event taking place at a distance, as in Jung's hotel story, or a premonitory feeling or image of something that later takes place, as in the synchronistic event of the mandala and yellow castle that had such a significant impact on Jung's life.[61]

All of us have had eerie experiences such as knowing beforehand what someone else was going to say or do next, feeling pain that was simultaneously present in someone else's body, thinking of someone only to have the phone ring and it be the person on the phone, not being able to get someone out of our mind only to discover that the person was in special need precisely during those moments our spirit was burdened about him or her. The Puritans designated these experiences "special providences," by which they meant the spiritual manifestations and stupendous coincidences that come to those who pray.

———————————————— 66 ————————————————

Denn da wo die Begriffe fehlen
Stellt ein Wort zur rechten Zeit sich ein.
When the mind is at sea
A new word provides a raft.

Naturalist/poet Johann Wolfgang von Goethe[i]

———————————————— 99 ————————————————

Worship is more than a synchronistic event that calls a community together, brings up new energies of healing and harmony by connecting individuals to God and one another, reaches deep within the realm of unconscious intention, and "re-souls" the body. But it should be at least that. Prayer is more than a form of synchronicity that transcends the space-time continuum, a tuning in to the rhythms of God, and a getting in touch with the "rhythm web" that ties us together. But it is at least that. Intercessory prayer is more than a form of synchronous thought transference, an energy flow of healing, comforting power. But it is at least that.

The 70ish Doonesbury advice to "Go with the flow" has received its share of pulpit rage. But might not "Go with the flow" be a powerful spiritual maxim based on trust in God's knowing what is best for us? If "winging it" is defined as living "on a wing and a prayer," "going with the flow" may be the best advice New Light leaders can offer--provided the flow comes from synchronicity in the Spirit and not in the self or culture, as occurs in so many of the occult--New Age alternatives to Jewish-Christian faith.

New Light leadership helps a community uncover and trust the meaning and language of this fourth dimension for their everyday lives. It revs up the spiritual frequencies so that the doors of perception open to admit messages from the fourth dimension that cannot be greeted in rational ways. It teaches people to live intuitively, to pay attention to dreams and "meaningful coincidences," to take what clinical professor/founder of Psychiatrists for ERA Jean Bolen calls an "Agatha Christie approach" to life's "fluke events."[62] It shows how synchronicity wants to operate continually to bring flickers of the sacred into our experience, to take the daily out of our existence, to give us signs that God is involved in human life.

Most importantly, a postmodern apologetic must incarnate the witness that the kingdom of God is not just coming. It is not simply everywhere. The kingdom of God is "at hand" as a basis for practical, day-to-day living. It is in fulfilling our role as cocreators with God in building up *basileia* that *Theos* shines with the most mysterious brilliance. For example, New Light leaders will offer personal testimony into how "chance" may sometimes be God working incognito. As librarian/Nobel laureate/novelist Anatole France puts it, "Chance is the pseudonym God uses when he does not want to sign his name." At the precise moment the universe threatens to be a chaos, it appears as a cosmos--or as someone has put the two together, a "chaosmos."

― **66** ―

When sorrows come, they come not as single spies,
But in battalions . . .

Actor/dramatist/poet William Shakespeare[j]

― **99** ―

At one time John Wesley was traveling in Ireland. His carriage became stuck in the mud, and his harness broke. While he and his companion were laboring to extricate it, a poor man passed by in great distress. Wesley called to him and asked the reason for his troubled spirit. He said that he had been unable to pay his rent of twenty shillings, and his family was being evicted. "Is that all you need?" asked Wesley, handing him the money. "Here, go and be happy." Then turning to his colaborer, Wesley said pleasingly, "You see now why our carriage stopped here in the mud?" When someone objected to John Wesley that too much importance was being attached to psychical phenomena, ecstatic experiences, and the ethereal, he replied, "Perhaps the danger is that we pay too little attention to them." By not venturing off the concrete, our energies are enfeebled, our communities stunted in their service, our witness without the divine difference. The anthem of praise that plays when the stops are pulled wide open and the soul resonates with the divine is music of unsurpassing beauty.

God has a special way of playing tricks on the "laws" of nature and society. Things take place that we simply cannot explain. As Job put it when he eventually discovered this, "I know that you can do all things. . . . Surely I spoke of things I did not understand, things too wonderful for me to know" (42:2-3 NIV). After being raised from the dead, Lazarus didn't talk (John 11:44). Miracles do happen. Indeed, the burden of proof is not on those who believe in miracles but on those who do not. Let them explain how seeds grow, what brightens the eye of a child, why one person should be in love with another, where the first two hydrogen atoms came from, what makes a yawn contagious, or what constitutes a good loaf of bread.

4. The Fourth Threshold of Miracles and Prodigies

There are two kinds of Christians, those who know nothing of miracles and those who know of nothing else. Moderns are to be counted almost exclusively among the former, postmoderns increasingly among the latter. Indeed, miracles are no longer an apologetic handicap to the postmodern mind. To live life on acceptable terms with the miraculous--to be neither among those who know nothing of miracles nor among those who know of nothing else--is the last threshold experience required of a faith raised to the fourth power. The Apostle Paul called this fourth threshold the "third-heaven" experience (2 Cor. 12:2).

"You do not have, because you do not ask" (Jam. 4:2). The biggest blockage to coming to terms with miracles is the dominance of mistaken understandings of what miracles are. When Walt Whitman wrote, in a line practical theologian/Riverside Church minister Harry Emerson Fosdick loved to quote, "Why, who makes much of a miracle? As to me I know of nothing else but miracles," he was expressing a view that ends up, as Whitman admitted, not making much of miracles. When everything is a miracle, or in the words physicist Henry Margenau chose to title the sequel to his influential *The Nature of Physical Reality* (1950), the "miracle of existence,"[63] then miracles can easily be explained away, and nothing is a miracle. A similar thing happens when we allow Belgian Jesuit/theologian Louis Monden to redefine "miracle" as "prodigy" in his sophisticated treatment of *Signs and Wonders* (1966), with two distinguishing types of prodigies a **minor** prodigy and a **major** prodigy.[64]

———————————— 66 ————————————

Ask, and you will receive; seek, and you will find; knock, and the door will be opened.

Master preacher/molder of lives Jesus the Christ[k]

Ask me when thou wilt, and you shall have it.

Master playwright/molder of language William Shakespeare[l]

———————————— 99 ————————————

When Fyodor Dostoyevsky wrote, "Children, do not seek miracles, for miracles kill faith," this self-proclaimed "frightful hunter after miracles" was not denying the miraculous. "Much is inexplicable in this world without miracles."[65] Rather, Dostoyevsky was pointing to the miracles sought by people who believe that if you are close to God, you are far from trouble. Religion of this variety majors in pretty smiles, blue skies, with no hint of Gethsemane or Golgotha.

Miracles are mistakenly identified with violations of nature's laws. John Wesley had a sister, Patty, who was married to an oily smooth operator named Westley Hall, and suffered all her life with him. She once said, "Evil was not kept from me, but evil has been kept from hurting me." Peter Hodgins, son of pastor Kenneth and Barbara Hodgins of Jamestown, New York, died at six after a long bout with bone cancer. Every day he lived with the cancer a miracle took place. No matter how painful or uncomfortable the day had been, Peter's evening prayers always included these words: "Lord, camp you angels around our house, and on our lawn, and on everything that is ours, in Jesus's name, Amen."[66]

The Apostle Paul said the same thing about himself:
Harassed on all sides, but not hemmed in;
Plunged in doubt, but not in despair;
Persecuted, but not forsaken;
Struck down, but not destroyed.
As dying, but still living on;
As punished, but not put to death;
As sorrowful, yet always having cause for joy;
As poor, yet making many rich;
As having nothing, yet possessing everything.[67]

The miracle Patty, Peter, Paul, and others discovered in life was not the physical miracle that God cured the hurt, the "thorn-in-the-flesh," or the cancer, but the moral miracle that there is no pit so deep that God cannot pull you out of it. There is no loneliness so isolating that God cannot reach you. There is no rejection so brutal that God cannot bring you back. There is no valley so low that God cannot walk you through it. That is the true moral miracle.

The hocus-pocus, holy-show healing of "faith healers" has given physical miracles a bad press. While the church shuffles its feet and turns red at the mention of miracles, the Institute of Noetic Sciences is systematically collecting and cataloging miracle cures or what some would prefer to call "anomalous cures." But the life of a faith at the center of which is the resurrection of Jesus Christ cannot be scrubbed free of all physical miracles. In the debate over whether Jesus rose from the dead, staged in 1985 between the neo-Humean Antony Flew and the evangelical Gary Habermas, the classical positions on miracles were articulated quite vividly.[68] Scottish historian/philosopher David Hume argued in 1825 that "no testimony is sufficient to establish a miracle, unless the testimony be of such a kind that its falsehood would be more miraculous than the fact which it endeavors to establish." With Hume, Flew insisted that the resurrection must consist in a violation of the laws of nature for it to be miraculous. Habermas, on the other hand, contended that since God is the one who created the laws of nature, God can suspend them. What is more, the Humean definition of a miracle is self-contradictory in that evidence supporting the miraculous would be counted as evidence against it.[69]

The problem with the classical presentation of the argumentation is that, from Flew's side, science knew nothing of the "laws of nature" until the

Enlightenment's gift to us of a view of reality based on the scientific method and its belief in the primacy of deductive logic, hard physical evidence, and dispassionate observation of "nature's laws." After three centuries of modern science talking about the "laws of nature," one of the preeminent physicists of our time, John Archibald Wheeler, concluded that in nature "there is no law except the law that there is no law." The biblical understanding of miracle, therefore, must have been something quite different than breaking "nature's laws."

The problem with the debate from Habermas's side is that to argue with Augustine that a miracle is "whatever appears that is difficult or unusual above the hope and power of them who wonder," or most famously, "God does not act contrary to nature but only contrary to the order of nature known to us,"[70] is to remove the miraculous from everyday experience and to reduce God to working through the abnormal powers of created nature.

————————————— 66 —————————————

True religion is to be grounded transparently
in the power that constitutes one.
Existentialist/personalist/theologian Soren Kierkegaard

————————————— 99 —————————————

A miracle is not the abrogation of the "laws" of this world. A miracle is the introduction, or more precisely, the seepage and interpenetration, of the patterns and processes, the mysteries and magic, of other worlds into this one. Or in the words of Lutheran pastor/biblical scholar/religion department chair Darrell Jodock, "A miracle is a creative synchronization of the divine and the human--or the divine and the natural--wherein the presence of God is experienced and the consequences of God's presence are in some way evident."[71] There are overlappings and openings to dimensions of reality that lie beyond even our four-dimensional world. We can no more pin nature down than we can predict God's infinite and awesome creativity.

A faith that trusts a multidimensional universe will know two kinds of healing: natural healing and miraculous healing. Natural healing is expressed in two primary forms: self-healing and medical healing. Miraculous healing finds expression in spiritual or faith healing and psychic healing. A faith for the fourth dimension will witness to a God who always heals.

God Always Heals

A new mythology of medicine is in the making, a new model of health and healing that frees us up to reject the materialist determinism of physiochemical functioning and recognize instead the fundamental importance of spiritual forces. Sometimes called "energy medicine," other times "eternity medicine," it is best designated, according to physician/internist/

North Texas State University psychology professor/Isthmus Institute president Larry Dossey, "hermeneutic medicine."[72] A "medicine of meaning" is based on the belief that the body began in a natural state of wellness and wholeness. We are to find, follow, and facilitate our bodies' unique natural processes of health and harmony. In self-healing the body naturally wants to heal itself, and each of us has healing powers we know not of. Self-healing occurs when the body restores itself to a balance. Disease is largely caused by diets, beliefs, and lifestyles that are out of harmony with the rhythms of the body and the will of God.

—————————————— 66 ——————————————

Theology and medicine lost the intimate connection they originally had, and always should have-- for saving the person is healing him.

Cultural and political theorist/art critic/theologian Paul Tillich[m]

—————————————— 99 ——————————————

Medical healing occurs when the introduction of medicine, whether chemical or electrical, cooperates with the body's natural healing and the spiritual power that heals called love. John Wesley's *Primitive Physic* (1747), one of history's first books of home remedies and natural therapeutics, instructed people in how they might find healing through natural and medical means. For this reason the founder of the Wesleyan tradition is important in the history of medicine (the prominent Philadelphia physician/signer of the Declaration of Independence, Benjamin Rush, said upon

Wesley's death, "I admire and honor that great man above any man that has lived since the time of the Apostles"). Wesley opened some of the first people's health clinics in history. He advocated the deprofessionalization of medicine two centuries before philosopher/critic/one-time catholic priest Ivan Illich. He pioneered in holistic health concepts that connected physical well-being and lifestyles. He proposed a form of "energy medicine" long before it was popular to see the body as an energy unit as well as a chemical one. New Lights will exert leadership in both forms of natural healing. They will not abandon natural and medical healing to either "health food" or "health care" professionals.

Spiritual or faith healing and psychic healing are distinct forms of miraculous healing, although they often overlap. Miraculous healing results from the focused and unexpected introduction into this world of divine powers and presences. It is miracle healing that presents the theological challenge, as John Polkinghorne elaborates it, of a unified understanding of "divine action and purpose, which goes beyond the experience of everyday but which forms with it a coherent whole."[73] Surgeon Charles Mayo, who together with his younger brother William, turned their father's tiny Rochester, Minnesota, clinic into the world famous Mayo Clinic, estimated that the "spiritual and psychological factor in disease varies from 65 percent to 75 percent." Another study estimates that 50 percent to 80 percent of all diseases have their origins in malfunctioning mental and spiritual states.[74] Some healing is in our hands. Some healing is out of our hands. But healing belongs in the church.

Spiritual healing is an activity of the Christian community--a community of love where people do not have to be perfect, where people can be themselves, where suffering is sometimes not so much taken away as shared. The healing force concentrated by the power of the risen Christ, the healing presence generated by the prayers of the faithful, is at the very heart of spiritual healing. In contrast to the religious Barnums and Baileys of the healing circus, no matter how much of the healing touch one possesses, the focus and glory belongs to the community, the body of Christ, not to the healer. Peter and John prayed and worked together to heal the crippled man (Acts 3:1-4). Aeneas and Dorcas were healed at Lydda when others in the house joined Peter in praying (Acts 9:33-42). Barnabas was with Paul when the crippled man at Lystra was healed (Acts 14:8-11). In the words of Rural dean/stewardship advisor/vicar/provost/museum trustee Philip Pare, whereas in the Gospels healings are done "where the Godhead was shining through Jesus in his one Person," today "it takes a number of Christians working together to bring the same kind of love and strength to bear on a sick person as Jesus the Christ could do."[75]

❝

I have no doubt whatever that most people live,
whether physically, intellectually or morally,
in a very restricted circle of their potential being.
They make use of a very small portion
of their possible consciousness . . . much like a man
who out of his whole bodily organism, should get into a habit
of using and moving only his little finger. . . .
We all have reservoirs of life to draw upon,
of which we do not dream.

First distinguished American psychologist/philosopher William James

❞

The test of spiritual healing, however, is not physical miracles so much as faith. After all, what takes more faith? To be blind and accept it with love, grace, dignity, and beauty, or to be healed and regain one's eyesight? Who is more "ill"--a person healthy of body, but with a mind racked with undiagnosable pathologies or a person fatally diseased but with a mind and spirit healthy in the highest sense? Spiritual healing can involve stimulating the body's own resources of natural healing, activating psychosomatic processes, or attuning one's being to receive God's healing power and energy. Its techniques have ranged from the visit to a moldering bone housed at some church shine, to anointing with oil or "fasting spittle" (the saliva in the mouth before the fast was broken was considered by Wesley a powerful cure of many diseases), to the laying on of hands. Not to be excluded from spiritual healing are other members of the community, including plants and animals. Wesley once cured lameness in his horse by prayer.

Psychic healing is the transfer of some kind of healing energy from the healer to the healed. It is a human power more than a spiritual power, by which is meant it transcends particularized spiritualities. It has no definite philosophical or theological content. It should not be confused, although it often is, with either spiritual healing or miraculous healing.

Rainbows and Squash Seeds

A rainbow is the biblical symbol for God's presence. It is emblematic of all true miracles: the product of sun and cloud. Even the simple miracle of walking on grass has its cloudy side: "Every time I walk on the grass," scientist Barbara McClintock confessed, "I feel sorry because I know the grass is screaming at me."[76] The greatest miracles of all--things like friendship, hope, love, walking where the concrete ends--are all products of sun and cloud.

The whole of nature, as Spinoza observed, is a kind of miracle. At Amherst College, researchers experimented with a squash seed that had been planted in rich, fertile soil. Eventually the seed produced a squash the size of a soccer ball. Then the researchers placed a steel band around the squash. Attached to the steel band was a device for measuring lifting power. The purpose of the experiment was to determine the lifting power of the squash. As the squash continued to grow and stretch the steel band, it reached a lifting power of five hundred pounds. Within two months, the lifting power went up to fifteen hundred pounds. A month later it was two thousand pounds. It was not until the lifting power had reached an unbelievable five thousand pounds that the squash's rind broke. When they opened the squash, they discovered that it had built up a whole network of tough fibers to fight against the pressure that was binding its growth. When they traced the roots supporting the squash, they discovered that the roots had reached out some eighty thousand feet in every direction, searching for more and more nourishment to strengthen the fibers.[77]

---------------------------------- 66 ----------------------------------

Nature is full of infinite possibilities
that have never been realized.

Architect/engineer/mathematician/musician/painter/scientist/sculptor Leonardo da Vinci

---------------------------------- 99 ----------------------------------

Miracles of life do not merely happen when there is no sickness or despair or death. Life's real miracles take place when we engage the lifting power of God's universe to turn back the powers of entropy. When we receive into our spirits the "uncreated energies" of the spheres, the celestial powers of the earth, we can be swept into where the concrete ends, singing as we go these words from Charles Wesley:

Faith, mighty faith, the promise sees,
And looks to that alone;
Laughs at impossibilities,
And cries, it shall be done!

One cannot set limits on what God can do. Those who circumscribe too narrowly the boundaries of the possible always get burned. It is dangerous to confuse impasses with impossibilities. When faith is functioning synergistically, all four dimensions working holographically, the Christian life becomes a clairvoyance--a literally unbelievable adventure. With the safety net of a tightly knit community underneath, a quantum spirituality lures the dancer back onto the high-wire of *theos*.

A balance that does not tremble cannot weigh.
A [person] who does not tremble cannot live.

Biochemist/fictionist Erwin Chargaff[P]

Where the concrete ends is where spiritual shivers begin . . . until time becomes Eternity.

THE THIRD
TESTAMENT

The gospel is a story that is only partially completed. Openness to the mysterious surprises of the Spirit working through *Logos, Pathos, Ethos,* and *Theos* must affect our understanding of truth if we are to walk where the concrete ends. Old things need to be said in new ways. New things can only be said in new ways. When they get corseted into old concepts, they get distorted and damaged.

Recent theories of supergravity have postulated that at the moment of creation there were as many as thirty-seven dimensions to reality, with an eleven-dimensional space-time structure of reality still with us. God is not bounded by our four-dimensional space-time continuum while being present in it. Indeed, systematic theologian/chess player/skier/gardener Hans Schwarz has shown how God, dimensionally higher than we are, embraces "all our available possibilities in space and time plus possibilities which are not available to us in our present dimension."[1]

Postmodernity is a time of coming to terms with the plurality of the self as well as the multidimensional nature of the universe. Postmodern thinkers reject the Romantic quest for a unitary self-identity in the same way postmodern egos can be divided and integrated at the same time. Every human being is a complex of multiple personality patterns. Gone are the days when psychologists or neurologists looked at each person as one single self that continues as the same self to death. A single human organism is now seen more like a "household of partially skilled individuals linked by an improvised and varying fabric of cooperation than it is like an orchestra under a single maestro."[2] New Lights are a multidimensional people developing inward and outward at the same time.

The modern era pressured the human organism to fix on one single, identifiable, permanent, and predictable personality structure. Those who persisted in nurturing a personality complex were labeled, sometimes playfully, sometimes clinically, "split" personalities. Some personalities did indeed shatter into shards of selves and become pathologically MPDs (multiple personality disorders), as Scottish storyteller/novelist Robert Louis Stevenson dramatized in his *Strange Case of Dr. Jekyll and Mr. Hyde* (1886).[3] Modernity's obsession with centralization, its constant carping for the "real you" to please stand up, made difficult the emergence of whole personalities able to cope creatively ("when in Rome," as Paul put it) with a complex array of internal and external styles, situations, and selves.

——————————————— 66 ———————————————

By the action of the Godhead--the three persons in One-- all the persons in us are centered in the One.
Church of the Saviour team member/Sarah's Circle housing program founder Elizabeth O'Connor[a]

——————————————— 99 ———————————————

Minister/retreat leader Elizabeth O'Connor and social critic/theologian James Ogilvy were two of the earliest authors who dared to advise Christians to give up their power struggles for unitary selves and to develop decentralized selves for a decentralized world. O'Connor's first words in her book *Our Many Selves* (1971) seemed to many a breath of fresh air, as she gave personal testimony of how she came to "experience [herself] as more than one."[4] It is this postmodern sense of "many selves" that is driving many women writers like Susan Sontag, Fay Weldon, Emma Tennant, and Valerie Martin to re-imagine and re-draw the originally very male story of Jekyll and Hyde.[5]

Each one of us is a rainbow of personalities. We are all of us prisms of God's light, refracting the multidirectional rays of the divine. All living organisms give off an aura of light, an energy field that, if not a second body, is at least a second dimension of the body. There is no aspect of reality that is not multidimensional.

Clio and Time Arrows

The exiled composer/international conductor Igor Stravinsky shuddered whenever he came into contact with what he called "that little bastard myth progress." Postmoderns have largely repudiated the doctrine of progress, a materialist product of modernist, Euro-American culture that sees the locomotive of history always chugging along on an upward slope following a definite, determined course.[6] Historians have demonstrated again and again that the pre-1750, morally neutral definition of "progress" as a course in time or going forward in space more accurately describes the historical journey. "Gains" can take place without much "progress." History does not necessarily have directionality. Humanity does not naturally become more mature, more reflective, more just. Our hope rests in God, not in some historical process or doctrine of progress.

But postmoderns would be mistaken if all ameliorist attitudes toward history, all notions of theological progressivism, were thrown out with the linearity metaphor of directionality. In the helical historical model outlined by Irish literary revivalist/dramatist/poet W.B. Yeats, even our "returns to Eden" can be at a higher level of consciousness than before. In a world of

increasing levels of complexities and reflexivities (i.e., increasing consciousness, freedom, communication, and meaning) progress is more than a
human invention. It seems to be a divine intention. Our problem is that we
have yet to factor the plight of Planet Earth into definitions of progress.

"Enlightenment bashing" has become in academic circles a minor
league sport. A sickbed view of the Enlightenment legacy is commonplace
in the views of Alaisdair MacIntyre, Isaiah Berlin, Christopher Lasch,
Edward K. Erickson, Jr., and Alexander Solzhenitsyn. Bashers and bard-
olaters alike decry the Cartesian-Newtonian bequest to us of a dualism upon
which our whole civilization has been built, a dualism that divides humans
from nature, that separates the knower from the known. Solzhenitsyn calls
it "the calamity of an autonomous, irreligious consciousness."

But autonomous humanity may have had to come before interdependent humanity. All that Descartes did was to put Newtonian laws of motion
into an acceptable philosophical form for his day. The modern world, like
the premodern one before it and the postmodern one after it, represents a
stage in history's halting advance of human consciousness.[7] Modernity has
a noble heritage and is parent to many insights and movements that we
ignore or belittle at our peril.

―――――――――――――――― **"** ――――――――――――――――

To be postmodern we need to develop the practices
and nurture the consciousness
that simultaneously inhabits premodern, modern,
and postmodern realms of actual and potential being.

International lawyer/Princeton professor Richard A. Falk[b]

―――――――――――――――― **"** ――――――――――――――――

Clio (the muse of history) may be aging, but with age can come higher
knowledge and greater wisdom and coherence. Without passing through
the stage of thinking of nature as a mechanism with interchangeable parts,
we never would be passing through the current stage of thinking of nature
as an organism of an implicate order.[8] In a stunning reversal of the classical
concept of entropy, first introduced by mathematical physicist/thermody-
namics pioneer Rudolf Julius Emanuel Clausius in 1865, the Prigoginian
"Brussels School" subverts understanding of the second law of thermodynamics that has the universe running down and losing energy. If there is a
directionality, or as Eddington likes to call it, an "arrow" in time, that arrow
is both reversible and irreversible; it can go either forward or backward in
time, upward or downward in slope. Entropy has, Ilya Prigogine says, "both
positive and negative powers. The positive powers are used to compensate
the negative powers in such a way that the total remains positive."[9] Entropy
is a process that can produce life from death, order from chaos, dissipative
structures from nonequilibrium conditions. The dream of the human spirit

has been to transcend the restrictions of energy, matter, space, and time. But there is no escape. In fact, far from the gospel being kept in pristine, watertight containers, the gospel is so structured that it interacts with inevitable but creative complicity in the confines of history. Kierkegaard provides one of the most powerful arguments for denying "apostolic" status more direct knowledge of God than contemporary status. He rightly insists that our task is no different than that of the first generation of Christians, except (and here he would disagree) we have the advantage of facing in the right historical direction on certain issues. The apostolic church now embraces twenty centuries, not merely the first. We are heirs of every century.

In theological terms, the Holy Spirit does enlarge our understanding of truth over the course of time. God did not stop talking when the canon closed. It is we who set the date of God's withdrawal from history at the closing of the canon, not God. The church's altered perceptions of issues of race and gender provide graphic illustrations of how the Spirit continues to work through history to expand human perception of truth and recall the church to neglected truth. It is for this reason that conservatives who resist the continual "re-rooting" (Filipino José M. de Mesa's term)[10] of the gospel from one cultural and historical milieu to another do not fare that well with Clio. History is prone to side with progressives.

Quantum spirituality is always in flux, always aware of its own incompleteness. The quantum paradigm replaced the classical paradigm of science less than seventy years ago, at the precise moment physics was deemed a closed (and thus dead) subject. Already it is fraying around the edges. Paul Dirac actually claimed at one point that the laws of nature changed over time, that the force of gravity diminished with time.[11] For a New Light apologetic there can be no final statement of theology anymore than there can be any final "laws of nature." All life is change, Anglican priest/Catholic convert John Henry, Cardinal Newman often observed, "and to be perfect is to have changed often."[12] No less than our ancestors, we must not foreclose our minds against the truths of God, even if they are new. It is for this reason that traditionality cannot be equated with orthodoxy. Each generation must enter into and contribute to the words non-conformist/pastor John Robinson spoke to the Pilgrims as they left for the New World in 1620: "God hath yet more light to break forth from his Holy Word." The New Light movement is perhaps better called a "More Light" movement.

It is hard for the church, willing and eager to serve as God's resident know-it-all, to understand that it does not possess all the truth, all the light, all at once. Truth is not apparent *obique, semper, et ab omnibus*--everywhere, at every time, and by every one. Fifty years from now, the United Methodist *Book of Resolutions*, an Answer Book if ever there was one, will read very differently, even self-contradictorily. The church has a sordid record of denouncing or denigrating thinkers and ideas that it will later vindicate and embrace. Comparative literature professor/day laborer/jazz musician Milan Kundera says that it is dangerous to give answers to everything, for it is a form of totalitarianism. Where does it say the church has to have an opinion on everything? Where is the authorization for the church to preach beyond the limits of its experience, much less its revelation? Saul Bellow moved to Chicago from New York, he said, because he was tired of intellectuals who had to have an opinion on everything. Sometimes the church must move ahead under the banner of ignorance, "We don't know," and humility, "This has not yet been revealed," and have the nerve to admit it. There is an important place in the life of a New Light church for a holy irrelevance and searching endurance about certain things.

―――――――――――――― 66 ――――――――――――――

Man has no individuality. He has no single, big I. Man is divided into a multiplicity of small I's.
Russian mystic/precursor of the New Religions movement Georges Gurdjieff

―――――――――――――― 99 ――――――――――――――

A biblical scholar of the First Testament, Harrell F. Beck, and a biblical scholar of the Second Testament, Fred Craddock, stand as two of the great preachers of this century. Beck confessed to being tempted some Sunday mornings to stand in the pulpit and rip the back cover off the Bible, as a way of showing that God's Spirit is still speaking and moving in our midst. The Reformers liked to call God the *Deus Loquens*--the speaking God. Or as a historian colleague puns the Reformers, God is the "Loquacious Deus." At different points in history, God speaks louder and more loquaciously through certain passages of Scripture than others.[13]

Anglican bishop/classic homiletician Lancelot Andrewes spoke in the sixteenth century of "one canon, two testaments, three creeds [the Apostles', Nicene, and Athanasian], four [ecumenical] councils, five centuries, along with the Fathers of that period." According to millennial mathematics, the symbolism of "two testaments" indicates that the number two is an unfinished integer. In the mystical symbolism of celestial calculus, two represents an entity awaiting completion. Three is the number of completion, even perfection.[14]

It Takes Three

Religion thinks in threes. It takes three to comprise the deity. It takes three heavens to comprise heaven--Paul talks about someone (presumably himself) being "caught up to the third heaven" (2 Cor. 12:1-4). It takes three to get to heaven--two or more people, plus God ("where two or three are gathered in my name, there am I in the midst," Matt.18:20). It takes three to get married--a man and a woman, plus God. It takes three to complete the "incarnations" of God, according to the theology of Augustine of Hippo --in the words of Scripture, in the humanity of Jesus, in the action of the sacrament.[15] It takes "three eyes" to see God, according to thirteenth-century Franciscan philosopher/theologian/cardinal/saint Bonaventure's rules of acquisition of knowledge--the eye of flesh (by which we perceive the external world), the eye of reason (by which we attain the knowledge of the internal world of philosophy and mind) and the eye of contemplation (by which we attain knowledge of the transcendent world).[16]

Philosophers thinks in threes. It takes three to form time--past, present, future--and if social critic/fictionist/dramatist/biographer J.B. Priestley is correct, it takes three times to form Time--Time 1 (chronological time), Time 2 (intermediate or pliant time), Time 3 (our true time-home in the future).[17] It takes three "subuniverses" to form the universe in the thought of philosopher/lecturer Karl Popper--World 1 (the physical world), World 2 (the mental world), World 3 (the cultural world).[18] It takes three great "systems" to hold together human society in the thought of economist/educator/pacifist/poet Kenneth E. Boulding--the "threat system," the "exchange system," and the "integrative system." It takes three realms to describe being in traditional philosophy, according to Ken Wilber--the gross (flesh and material), the subtle (mental and animic) and the causal (transcendent and contemplative).[19]

Historians think in threes. It takes three historical ages to complete history, according to Italian mystic/Cistercian abbot Joachim of Fiore (Age of the Father, Age of the Son, Age of the Spirit) and Italian philosopher/ legal theorist Giambattista Vico (the divine, the heroic, and the human). It takes three scales of time to encompass history in the historiography of French economist/historian Ferdinand Braudel--"geographical time" (in which events occur over the course of aeons), "social time" (shorter spans of time for measuring economies, states, and civilizations), and "individual time" (the shortest span of all, the history of human events). It takes three discontinuous stages of human history (hunting/gathering or agriculture/ scientific-industrial) for historian/anthropologist/philosopher Ernest Gellner to explore the three basic types of human activity--production, coercion, cognition.[20]

Scientists thinks in threes. It took three books for Newton to present his *Principia* to the Royal Society of London on 28 April 1686. It takes three levels of consciousness, according to rocket technologist/mathematician/ musician Freeman J. Dyson, to accommodate the increasing diversity and knowledge of the world--the first level of consciousness present in each particle as it makes "quantum choices," the second level of consciousness present in human creation, the third level of consciousness present in God.[21] It takes three distinct "arrows of time" to conceive of time, according to Harvard cosmogenesist/astrophysicist David Layzer--one based on Big Bang expansion, one based on entropy, one based on biological and historical evolution. It looks like it may even take triplets of subprotonic particles (quarks) to constitute the fundamental matter of the universe.

In the divine mathematics of science, religion, philosophy, history, in fact everything, $1+1=3$. In the trigonometry of the trinity, we multiply by dividing: The more we give the more we have. Presbyterian minister/ theologian Letty Russell suspects that "God is not good at math." Perhaps God is part of the new math. Perhaps Jesus taught the higher math of the *tertium quid* (the third way).[22]

Seminary Apostles

Just because Jesus is the same yesterday, today, and forever does not mean he does the same thing in the same way yesterday, today, and forever. Each of us is comprised of sixty trillion cells. Physiologically speaking there is constant movement and re-formation, with 98 percent of the 10^{28} atoms of the human body replaced annually. Each part of the body--bone, blood, brain--has a different rate of re-formation. But every five years there is an entirely new body, all our atoms having been replaced. In a theological sense our present body is the same as it was five years ago. But in a physiological sense, our present body didn't exist at all five years ago. Energymatter is dispersed through space-time in ways we have yet to comprehend.[23]

66

The first creature of God in the works of the days,
was the light of sense; the last, the light of reason;
and his Sabbath work ever since
is the illumination of his Spirit.

Statesman/diplomat/lawyer/intellectual reformer/scientist Francis Bacon

99

A Wallace Stevens poem, "St. Armorer's Church from the Outside," has this phrase that strikes at the heart of the relationship of change to permanence: "a new account of everything old."[24] God the Creator worked through men and women of old to produce the First Testament. God the Redeemer worked through men and women of the first century to produce the Second Testament ("Of old it was said to you . . . but I say . . ." [Matt. 5:21-22]. But we no longer have Jesus in the flesh. We now have Jesus in the Spirit. God the Spirit and Sustainer wants to work through New Lights of the twenty-first century to produce the Third Testament[25]--our "new account of everything old."

New Lights' mission in life, if they choose to accept it, is to continue the work of Scripture. Where I work is called a seminary. Not until recently did I look "seminary" up in the library's trusty *Oxford English Dictionary*. The first entry reads, "A piece of ground in which plants are sown (or raised from cuttings) to be afterwards transplanted: a seedplot or seedbed." The second entry reads, "A place where animals are bred." Moving right along without comment to the third entry: "A place of origin and early development, a place or thing in which something (e.g., an art or science, a virtue or vice) is developed or cultivated, or from which it is propagated abundantly."

Paul is known as the "seminary apostle" because he sowed the seed of the gospel among the Gentiles. A seminarian is anyone who sows seed or is sown seed. And if you are both seed sower and sown seed, you will always be a seminarian whether you ever step foot inside what the church calls a seminary or not. Seeds are pellets of energy and protein. From one little seed emerges something as perfect as an orchid, as vast as a sequoia, as persistent as a dandelion, as patient as a desert wildflower, as gentle as a blade of grass, as all-embracing as a weeping willow, as joyful as a daisy, as prickly as a thistle. The church needs more seeds, more women and men with what Thoreau called "the seed of life in them."

New Light leaders will see the potential for churches to become seminaries, schools of the Spirit where members do not receive maps so much as navigational skills--the texts and traditions of the faith. The challenge of the church in the twenty-first century is to become for its people a "seminary," a seedbed in which the texts and traditions of the faith re-create themselves in and through the body until its molecular imagination is awakened by a living God.[26]

Every believer, every body of Christ is called to become the Third Testament. Philosophical theologian/science watcher Philip Hefner captures wonderfully our simultaneous status as dependent creatures and free agents in his recommendation that human beings be thought of as "created co-creators."[27] God has chosen to work in partnership with us in the ongoing drama of creation. That is why Jesus talked about the "seminary power" of the gospel in John 14:12 (NRSV): "Very truly, I tell you, the one who believes in me will also do the works that I do and, in fact, will do greater works than these, because I am going to the Father." We are called to participate in God's nature (cf. 2 Peter 1:4).

——————————————— **66** ———————————————

Every creature is a word of God and a book about God.
Dominican theologian/Rhineland mystic Meister Eckhart[c]

——————————————— **99** ———————————————

The root and seminary power of the gospel are as much ours as they were Luke's, who began the book of Acts professing to continue the works of Jesus, or as they were Peter's, who told Aeneas to get up and start life over again because "Jesus Christ cures you!" (Acts 9:34 REB). The same cosmic dynamics and primordial energies that created fire, land, wind, and sea are at work today and continue to evolve, if only we develop the sensitivities to tap into them.

To truly exist, argues Roman Catholic philosopher/Yale professor Louis Dupré in *The Other Dimension* (1972), is to "participate in an act of divine communication."[28] History has not yet heard the last from Jesus' life, for it has not yet heard and seen how Jesus' life will be lived in you. Sunday schools have taught this to the church's children in song:

> You are writing a gospel,
> A chapter each day,
> By deeds that you do,
> > By words that you say.
> God reads what you write
> > Whether faithless or true,
> Say! What is the "gospel
> According to you?"

The Gospel of John's mysteriousness about the "much else that Jesus did" (21:25a NEB) and the "many other signs that Jesus performed in the presence of his disciples, which are not recorded in this book" (20:30 NEB) are more than annoying teases. Similarly, John's claim that if all that Jesus did were "written about in detail, I doubt there would be room enough in the entire world to hold books to record them" (21:25b NAB) is more than hypothetical hyperbole. They are challenges for the continual creation of Third Testaments that can summon up the numinous for every generation. The Word of God is not to be exclusively identified with the words of the Bible.

New, Not Novel

The idea of "newness" is so central to Paul that his theology has been called "a dramatic study in newness."[29] The same might be said of Jesus, if not of the entire gospel itself. When Jesus said, "I have yet many things to say to you, but you cannot bear them now" (John 16:12 RSV), he was making reference to more than odd goings on in the "new self" (Eph. 4:24 RSV) and the "new creation" (Gal. 6:15 RSV). John Calvin argues in his *Institutes of the Christian Religion* (1536) that God speaks to us of things "according to our capacity for understanding them, not according to what they are." At the seminary where I used to teach, there are these words carved on the library wall: "All history is an inarticulate Bible." This does not mean that the Spirit works unfoldments of new revelations that are not found in the Bible. "Behold, I make all things new" (Rev. 21:5 RSV), God said, not **novel**. "It overthrows all," is how colonial governor/Boston Puritan John Winthrop responded to the revelations of seventeenth-century feminist/colonist Anne Hutchinson, which left the church and the tradition far behind.[30] This is my major critique of theologian/ecologist Thomas Berry, who denies that there is any definitive form of Christianity, only "an identifiable Christian process." This is also a major critique of the New Age movement, which would have saved itself innumerable embarrassments if it had been less "New Age" and more "New Ageless." The Spirit works new enlargements of truths that the Bible already teaches. "New occasions teach new duties" is how diplomat/essayist/poet James Russell Lowell expressed the continuing radicality of the radical transformation in realities and relationships wrought by the gospel. New Light leaders open doors rather than close them.

―――――――――――――― 66 ――――――――――――――

We are on the threshold of a new age.
The Bible does not necessarily spell out what we can expect
to find when we cross the threshold, but it does reveal
the basic dynamism of human existence under God,
a dynamism of awareness and response,
in which lies "salvation."
Artist/birdwatcher/contemplative/social activist Thomas Merton[d]

―――――――――――――― 99 ――――――――――――――

One of the greatest theologians America has produced, Congregationalist minister/University of California organizer Horace Bushnell, argued that Christianity is "a complete organization, a work done that wants nothing added to finish it." Yet it was still, using Jesus' metaphor, "a complete mustard seed only; which, though it is complete as a seed, so that no additions can be made to it, has yet, nevertheless, much to do in the way of growth." New Light leaders will want to examine from a safe distance Bushnell's attack on a closed canon as "a naked and violent assumption, supported by no word of scripture, and justified by no inference from the complete organization of the gospel." The trilemma of a theology of revelation, a psychology of inspiration, and a sociology of knowledge may be the metaphysical equivalent of computing *pi* (the ratio of a circle's circumference to its diameter) to billions of digits on the world's largest and fastest computer. It is the ultimate computer stress test--"a cardiogram for a computer." I am personally one of those Bushnell would castigate for being "sure that other books of scripture may not some time be necessary."[31] I am not ready to bid farewell, as some earth-centered theologians seem to be, to the traditionalist symbols and old formulations of the Christian tradition. God has not continued giving tablets of stone from every mountaintop because God has given us something better--the living cornerstone of Jesus Christ, on which every generation can build its dwelling place.

But the church would do well to listen to Bushnell's warning about resisting the ongoing creativity of God: "We do not even know that a new dispensation, or many such, may not be required to unfold this seed, and make it the full-grown tree."[32] Indeed, according to professor Gary M.

Burge's marvelous study of the Holy Spirit in the Johannine tradition, the scriptures give revelation activity a "control"--the Spirit's "recalling" activity ("He will remind you of everything," John 14:26 NIV) checks the Spirit's "revelatory" function ("He will guide you into all truth," John 16:13 NKJV).[33] British/evangelical/biblical scholar James D. G. Dunn argues that there is a "sense in which the New Testament's relativizing of the Old becomes a paradigm for the way in which new revelation might relativize the authority of the New Testament." The challenge is for Christians to "save ourselves from the old mistake of erecting what has been the word of God to us into a restrictive and stultifying dogma for others."[34]

"

The rise and fall of images of the future precede or accompany the rise and fall of cultures.

Historian/futurist Fred Polak[e]

"

Something can be all new, yet nothing of the old be lost. The Christian tradition of old-new thoughts mandates a strict diet of "re-" words, preferring instead the prefix "in-" á la "inscendence" (Thomas Berry's version of "transcendence") and "involution" (a substitute for revolution first encountered in Teilhard de Chardin's diary dated 12 November 1919). The Third Testament is thus no simple extrapolation of the First and Second Testaments into the future, but a divine inbreaking into the historical moment through which Alpha beginnings and Omega endings converge. The Third Testament is everything new about the old, old story. Or in Teilhard's more mystical phrasings, a "descendent divine involution" combining with the "ascendent cosmic evolution."[35]

"In the Fullness of Time"

The message of Jesus is so profound that the world is still deciphering it thousands of years later. God's purposes are veiled and understood only "in the fullness of time." Truth often unfolds as slowly as a symphony. A note struck early on might be picked up much later and developed fully even later than that. The music of truth may take centuries to play itself out. Not all of God's communications are released overnight. Indeed, many of them may be in the process of being created as we go along.

The Bible begins with the book of Genesis and Abraham's affirmation, even from his exile among the persecuting Philistines, in "the God of time past and time to come," the literal translation of the Hebrew *El Onam* in Genesis 21:33-4 (NEB): "There [Abraham] invoked the Lord, [the God of time past and time to come], by name, and he lived as an alien in the country of the Philistines for many a year." The Bible ends with the book of

259

Revelation and John's affirmation, even from his exile on the slave-camp island of Patmos, of God's "everlasting birth" and our ability to live in two worlds at once, the alien culture of Patmos or Philistia, and the new heaven and the new earth of the *basileia* of God spoken of in Revelation 21:5-7 (NEB):

> Then he who sat on the throne said, "Behold! I am making all things new!" (And he said to me, "Write this down; for these words are trustworthy and true. Indeed they are already fulfilled.") "I am the Alpha and the Omega, the beginning and the end. A draught from the water-springs of life will be my free gift to the thirsty. All this is the victor[s'] heritage; and I will be [their] God and [they] shall be my [children]."

While a good portion of the book of Revelation is mostly beyond comprehension (John Wesley confessed, "How little do we know of this deep book. At least, how little do I know")[36], it still is one of the Bible's most precious gifts to us. For it stands as a "drawbridge" (skier/cook/naturalist/anthropologist/novelist Laurens Van der Post's metaphor) let down to the future, a promise that God will lead us safely over history's moat of misery and uncertainty. Though we cannot see what is on the other side of this drawbridge, we can travel into that future confident that God is always there to be found, that the road to the end of time will be open to new spiritual dimensions and fresh revelations. Jesus as the "human face of God" means nothing less than God's assurance that we can build our lives knowing that the universe in front of us has a face and a heart.

"Crooked Lines"

Theologian Paul Tillich made a Portuguese saying his own to illustrate the directive activity of the divine: "God writes straight with crooked lines." With the crooked lines of our lives God is wanting to write "a new account of everything old," a Third Testament. This book has been breathed forth with the prayer that the crooked lines and cracks of New Light ministries, whatever they may be, will become openings through which God's light can shine. New Light leadership is nothing more or less than a living testament to the beauty, truth, and goodness of an all-mighty and all-loving God.

The power of New Lights is not in their numbers. When John Wesley died, he left behind only three hundred itinerants, one thousand local preachers, and eighty thousand members of societies. New Light power is in the multidimensional faith of their Third Testament. The Third Testament calls us to imitate and participate in God's creativity--to abandon our unbelief and doubts, to expel feelings of weakness and impotence, to relinquish our immobilizing obsession with crookedness and brokenness, and to send a letter to postmodern culture, like steamboat pilot/journalist/humorist/novelist Mark Twain sent to printer/carpenter/editor/poet Walt

Whitman in 1889 on his seventieth birthday, that opens the future to hope: "FOR THE GREATEST IS YET TO COME."[37]

──────────────── **"** ────────────────

Glad Amen . . .
When the chorus of I am's
surrender to the solo--
He is.

Poet/playwright Alma Loftness[f]

──────────────── **"** ────────────────

Quantum spirituality is nothing more than **your** "new account of everything old"--your part of the "I Am" that we are.

POSTFACE

Do Bears Always Face the Front of Their Tracks?

The popularity of popular culturalist/moralist/Unitarian minister Robert Fulghum's *All I Really Need to Know I Learned in Kindergarten* (1986)[1] is one of the marvels of the publishing world. These fourteen common-sense lessons learned in the sandbox of life have tremendous cultural appeal. In fact, "common sense" are the first two words of eighty-two book titles currently in print. Little wonder, then, that Fulghum's wash-behind-the-ears wisdom is one of Christian bookstores' best sellers. It was the number one purchase at a pastor's school where I spoke as late as 1990.

I am sorry to disagree. But contemporary "common-sense" approaches to life, whether in the areas of natural resource management, or economic development, or ethical decision making, now get us into trouble. Common sense is no longer sound theology. Common sense is no longer Christian sense. Indeed, when applied to the structures of the postmodern world, common sense is nonsense.

The quantum mind doesn't try to make sense of things like the modern mind did. Quantum physics doesn't profess to make sense. Indeed, it is most often counter sense. Many of the lessons my kindergarten teacher taught me are wrong for the postmodern era in which we are living.

Watching Tails or Facing Toes

One of the most fascinating books to come out on educational theory in recent years was educational psychologist/suspense novelist/wilderness lover Guy R. Lefrançois's *Psychology for Teaching: A Bear Always Faces the Front* (1972).[2] He uses the interesting discovery that a bear always faces the front of its tracks, and advocates a teaching style that is as sensible as bear behavior. The second edition introduced Bear II, who took note of certain realities, namely, that "only the more stupid bears did not occasionally look backward." Hence the second edition was subtitled *A Bear ~~Always~~ Usually Faces the Front* (1975). Bear III was an "older and much wiser" bear who had been "approached from the rear on so many occasions" that the subtitle of the third edition was *A Bear ~~Always Usually~~ Sometimes Faces the Front* (1979). Bear IV, that "much older, battle scarred" bear who has come under attack from every economic and social angle imaginable, has been forced into watching its backtail almost constantly. Bear IV only rarely faces the front, hence the subtitle *A Bear ~~Always Usually Sometimes~~ Rarely Faces the*

Front (1982). The fifth edition bear is so spooked and chastened by the changing conditions of contemporary life that the subtitle is *A Bear ~~Always Usually Sometimes Rarely~~ Never Faces the Front* (1985). Thankfully, Bear VI has found a new way of moving into the future, a "second naïveté,"[3] if you will, that learns from the experiences of Bears I to V. In a return that is not a return, the sixth edition is subtitled *A Bear ~~Always Usually Sometimes Rarely Never~~ Always Faces the Front* (1988).

The same realities ambushing that bear and preventing common-sense locomotion are ambushing postmoderns. No longer can we trust our "original sense" or "natural sensation." These were the words Scottish universities of the eighteenth century used to popularize "common-sense realism," the philosophy and psychology that came to dominate the American phase of the Enlightenment era. No longer can we take things at "face value." Common sense is no longer a reliable guide to draw all creation to its Creator, as the Deists believed. Nor does it serve as "a natural inclination that persons have to excellence and order" or "a natural sensation of a certain fitness or agreeableness," as Jonathan Edwards phrased his two definitions of this empirical, inductive method of arriving at egalitarian, "self-evident" truth.

————————————————— **"** —————————————————

How quaint the ways of paradox--
At common sense she gaily mocks.

Comic opera duo--librettist/lawyer Sir William Gilbert
and composer/choirmaster Sir Arthur Sullivan[a]

————————————————— **"** —————————————————

Even those who are working the hardest to preserve the canons of logic have had to introduce the theoretical concept of "fuzziness" to accommodate the postmodern chords of transition, interrelatedness, complexity, felt relations, subtlety, paradox, vagueness, and uncertainty. As developed in the mid-sixties by Russian-born/Berkeley computer science professor Lofti Zadeh, "fuzzy logic" has already sired neural network computer chips that learn from experience to control "fuzzy" air conditioners, "fuzzy" cameras, "fuzzy" subways, and "fuzzy" shower stalls, to name only a few.

In brief, fuzziness is a mathematical system of description and explanation designed to alter traditional "yes-no" set theory to integrate the "almost/about" imprecisions, the contradictory/grayish realities of quantum observables, first portrayed in the thought experiment known as Schrödinger's Cat. In terms of conceptual clarity, which is how moderns defined "fuzzy," real fuzz covered the modern picture of the world, which was a "pure abstraction" from the concrete world and thus a gross distortion of reality and truth. *Fuzzy Systems* (1981), *Fuzzy Set Theory* (1985), *Fuzzy Reasoning and Its Applications* (1981), and the Laboratory for International

Fuzzy Engineering Research, are but a few of the titles and projects underway (mostly in Japan) studying this new brand of "logic" and invention.[4] The future bodes appliances rated not on horsepower and size but on fuzziness standards such as smartness and service.

The New Sensibility

Calls for a "fuzzy theology" and "fuzzy spirituality" would receive a prickly reception in our decidedly nonfuzzy churches, which resist measuring themselves in terms of wisdom and service in favor of growth and size. Yet it is hard to evade the conclusion that postmoderns are not trying to "make" and "make sense" of things as the modern world tried to do. Instead, there has emerged a "New Sensibility" (Susan Sontag) about life that is not based exclusively on rational credibility but also on imagination, analogy, and intuition.

French philosopher/religionist Blaise Pascal's *Pensées*, first published in 1670, represents the often fragmentary notes of Pascal's major work, *An Apology for the Christian Religion*, which was left unfinished at his death. In it Pascal maintained that there are two kinds of intelligence. One is more logical and sequential (some would say today "left-brained") and the other more intuitive and random (i.e., "right-brained").[5] Similarly, Pascal's contemporary/Dutch philosopher Benedict Spinoza argued that there were three kinds of knowledge. *Imaginatio* consisted of sense, cognition, or unscientific knowledge. *Ratio* was common empirical cognition or more scientific knowledge. The third type of knowledge, *intuitio*, represented for Spinoza "the highest endeavor of the mind and the highest virtue." *Intuitio* proceeds, Spinoza believed, "from an adequate idea of the absolute essence of certain attributes of God to an adequate knowledge of the essence of things."[6] Two hundred years later (1890), American philosopher/psychologist William James published *Principles of Psychology*, a two volume description of nineteenth-century psychological thought noted both for its literary style and its scientific accuracy. In it James distinguished between two modes of intellect: one analytical and the other intuitive.[7]

One of the distinguishing features of the modern era was its preference for the mathematical mind over the intuitive mind. But the logical/mathematical/analytic mind was understood to have a "common" component, a rational "sense" accessible to everyone. This democratic logic, this simplification of reason, this intuition of logic was known as "common sense."

It was the Enlightenment that elevated common sense to iconic status, until it became often spelled as one word. In fact, it was less reason and logic and more common sense and reasonableness that governed the Enlightenment sensibility. Philosophers and writers, especially those working in the first half of the eighteenth century, demonstrated high levels of distrust for the release of reason unrestrained by common sense. As a *homo modems*

John Wesley boasted that in writing their hymns, Methodists "talk common sense, whether they understand it or not, both in verse and prose, and use no word but in a fixed and determinate sense."[8]

It took Anglo-American pamphleteer/political scientist Thomas Paine's *Common Sense* (1776), however, to permanently fix the category in the modern mind. Four hundred thousand copies (one hundred thousand in the first three months) of this pamphlet were sold to a national population of three million, equal to gross sales of twenty-four million today. Ironically, when Paine died in New York on 8 June 1809, no one paid much attention. A Quaker watchmaker, an old Frenchwoman alleged (falsely) to be his mistress, her two little boys, and two black pallbearers were the only people to attend the graveside service. A New York newspaper supplied this epitaph: "Paine had lived long [he was 72], done some good, and much harm."

Leave Common Sense at the Door

Paine will continue to do much harm if postmoderns fail to realize that the collapse of Enlightenment categories includes the category of common sense. Nelson Goodman, one of the world's greatest living philosophers, built an entire philosophy of "constructivism" on the premise that "contrary to common sense there is no unique 'real world' that preexists and is independent of human mental activity and human symbolic language."[9] More common, however, is the attempt by the "ordinary language" school of philosophy founder/ethicist G.E. Moore to challenge Cartesian dualism and the atomistic self by a strategy that Moore defined in an essay entitled "The Defense of Common Sense."[10] Some physical scientists have even begun complicating everyone's confusion further by labeling common-sense views as "intuitions" to accommodate the postmodern distrust of common sense. The battle to vindicate common sense stands to become even more of a preoccupation among contemporary philosophers, whether popular like Fulghum or highbrow like Alan Bloom. Why?

———————————— 66 ————————————

If it will be, it's up to me.

Old folk saying often quoted by Dan Rather

———————————— 99 ————————————

Postmoderns are not trying to "make sense" of things as the modern world tried to do. Their every move is not rationally established. Instead, a new sensibility about life has emerged that is based not on common sense, but on the counter sense of intuition. "Leave your common sense at the door!" is what pioneer Catholic ecumenist/theologian Gustave Weigel used to tell his students on the first day of class. This is not just Ivy League ivory-towerism. This is quantum wisdom. For street sense is not common sense any longer. In terms of street sense, common sense is nonsense, or worse. It can get you killed.

As with Bear VI, who seems to end where he begins, but really doesn't, postmoderns will still live by a wisdom that is common-sensed and rational, but one that is radically different than the one built on the orthodox, cognitive, scientific foundations of Humean sense experience and Cartesian dualism. Some of modernity's most brilliant minds, such as the great philosopher Ludwig Wittgenstein, captured modernity's iconography of common sense. In one of his lectures, he spontaneously launched into a discussion of the nature of philosophy: "Philosophy can be said to consist of three activities. To see the common sense answer, to get yourself so deeply into the problem that the common sense answer is unbearable, and to get from that situation back to the common sense answer." Philosopher/mathematician/poetry lover Alfred North Whitehead, whose rationalistic side has been appealed to by process theologians far more than his own appeals to experience ("causal efficacy") would allow, was a prophet of postmodernism in so many ways. Yet he wrote how "you may polish up common sense, you may contradict it in detail, you may surprise it. But ultimately your whole task is to satisfy it."[11]

Philosopher/mathematician Murray Code is right about a mechanistic, monodimensional science and common sense growing up together. To be sure, as physicist/historical fictionist Robert Scott Root-Bernstein argues, intuition has always played a major role in what he calls "discovering," the exercise of the free scientific spirit.[12] But Humean empiricism and its handmaiden, scientism, joined to form the worldviews out of which emerges Fulghum's kindergarten wisdom of common sense. Code is wrong in suggesting, however, that the "fundamental guidelines" are still being provided by common sense in postmodern culture. Albert Einstein was the last of the great determinists. His common-sense approach to truth is gone forever. Science has now spawned a new field called "antisense" replete with "antisense drugs," "antisense therapy," "antisense technology," "antisense companies," and a peer-reviewed scientific journal *Antisense Research and Development.*

"Fundamental guidelines" in postmodern culture are being provided not by common sense or the intuitions of logic but by the sense of the common, or what might best be termed "the logics of intuition." Spanish existentialist/poet/playwright/novelist/university rector/political exile Miguel de Unamuno describes the "common sense" view anymore as similar to the comment of the "artillery sergeant who said that a cannon was made by taking a hole and enclosing it in steel."[13] Common sense is one of those intoxicating verbages that skew our judgment, slur our speech, and slow our speed. In short, common-sense statements are bright and beautiful declarations that are powerful, dangerous intoxicants to quantum faith in a postmodern world.

To demonstrate how wrong common-sense wisdom can be, this postface presents ten things my kindergarten teacher taught me wrong, ten common-sense precepts that fail the tests of the new sensibility being taught in our postmodern philosophical cradle. Each is concluded by a postmodern schema about the same subjects that spells not the abandonment of "good sense" but the initiation of a more realistic, more postmodern sense of the common.

66

Every age poses new challenges and new temptations
for the people of God on their pilgrimage,
and our own is no exception.

Bishop of Rome/skier/poet/pope John Paul II[b]

99

In the Chinese language, "opportunity" and "danger" are combined to make the symbol for "crisis." Before the church celebrates the challenges of postmodernity, it had best be careful about where the "pomo" world is leading us. The almost unparalleled blend of peril and promise in postmodern sensibilities is suggested below, using the phrases sometimes found in ancient maps "There be Treasures" and "Here be Monsters." Particular attention is focused on the barmy religiosity of the New Age movement.

Protocol #1

You Can Only Do One Thing at a Time. When my eleven-year-old son comes in from outside, the first thing he often does is go to his room, turn on the stereo or television, and get out his work. As a good parent, the first thing I do is yell up to his room, "Justin, turn off that TV and do your work! You can't concentrate with all that stuff going on. When you finish your assignments, **then** you can turn on the TV."

Telling Justin he can do only one thing at a time is like telling organic farmer/seminary graduate David Vetter to grow only one crop at a time. Or telling organist/choirmaster Frederick Swann not to do two things at once: only read the score, or play one keyboard, or kick the pedal keys, or direct the choir, not all together at the same time. Or telling the polymathic Martin E. Marty he can only write one book at a time. Or telling the master preacher William Hinson he can't write twelve sermons at once.

The truth is that you can never do **only** one thing, as ecologists have been warning us for decades. Eighty percent of kids today learn **less** without any audio/visual stimulation. Perception is wider than conception. Knowing is broader than the narrowing of focused minds in their squeezing concentrations. "One-track" minds are always needed and useful. But their glorification has distorted our experience of the world and betrayed us into believing that the world is much more isolated and autonomous than it really is. Robert Pittman, the president of Quantum Media and cofounder of MTV, says:

We now have a generation of people--the TV babies--who can absorb enormous amounts of information and do multiple activities at the same time. . . . My parents are used to finishing one train of thought before starting another. I can carry on two conversations while I'm reading my mail, and still manage to keep an eye on the TV I've got on in the background.[14]

It is not just our kids who are seeing double. Big screen televisions now advertise "split screens" that enable viewers to watch multiple programs at once. Bars use as customer-bait multiple television sets, which allows patrons to watch all the major stations simultaneously. CNN constantly flashes stock reports at the bottom of the screen during its newscasts. The burgeoning mobile books industry, brought to us by audio firms like Caravan of Dreams and Books of the Road, reflect more than modernism's waste-not, want-not appeal of efficiency. Commuters and travelers and joggers consume books while doing something else because "full attention" is now defined less in terms of object than of subject, less segmentally and sequentially (What can I do next?), and more incrementally and exponentially (What else can I do?).

Postmodern society is a multiple-vision, multioption society where the more options we exercise, the more human we become. Choice is no longer a choice. It is now a necessity, a virtue. In the words of Os Guinness, the successor to Francis Schaeffer in the world of evangelicalism, "Choice is not just a state of affairs, it is a state of mind. Choice has become a value in itself, even a priority."[15] In over half of all American homes, there are more than twenty television channels from which to choose. Revlon now makes 158 shades of lipstick; Crest offers thirty-six sizes and flavors of toothpaste. Less than twenty years ago, the average supermarket carried nine thousand items. It now carries twenty-four thousand.

People resent it when you don't give them choices. They stay away from places (especially churches) that don't give them choices. They even read books that give them choices. When I was growing up, I cut my historical teeth on the "You Were There" Adventure Series, which took me back in time to some momentous historical period. My son's favorite books are the Choose Your Own Adventure Series, where the reader chooses what characters to follow, which figures win, who loses, and how the ending turns out. There are now even competing versions of audio books, something inconceivable in printed books--that is, there are at least three different abridgements of journalist/social commentator/artist/window shopper Tom Wolfe's *The Bonfire of the Vanities* (1988) alone.

Because postmoderns love contradicting themselves, in postmodern culture many things can happen at the same time. Ratings for the Cosby show rise with racial tensions. The economic trend in the 1990s is toward "brull" markets--neither bull nor bear but a bit of both. A new psychological syndrome has emerged called "mixed bipolar," in which people are both manic and depressed at the same time. A restaurant near United Seminary is named El Greco's Pizza Villa. Its advertised specialties are tacos and "Peta Submarines." Pittsburgh Pirates' Neal Heaton calls the new pitch that won for him all sorts of games in 1990 the "screw-knuckle-change" ball. It used to be someone was either (M) married or (S) single. Now people want to be both, and there are plenty of options whereby postmoderns can pursue both. In fact, John Naisbitt quips that during the 1970s and 1980s about the only people who **wanted** to be married were Roman Catholic priests. Postmodern life is a chaos of contradictions.

Scottish playwright/novelist/painter Alasdair Gray has a character McMenamy (in *Unlikely Stories, Mostly*, 1983) who observed that his grandmother "knitting as she rocked, rocking as she knitted, comprised two sources of energy."[16] Postmoderns believe in knitting and rocking, working and playing at the same time. We do postmoderns no favors by insisting on their "undivided attention," or by judging them impolite when they read, sign letters, or knit when attending our meetings.

The first new sensibility for postmodern culture is a deconstructionist reversal: **Do many things at once.**

 There be Treasures #1

1. Bifocalism of styles and selfhoods, or what systems philosopher/ concert pianist Ervin Laszlo calls "biperspectivism,"[17] is the ideal state of integrated, interactive unity sought by the human organism. The modern world's obsession with cyclopean certainty, and cyclopean selves, may be over.

2. Postmoderns will learn the art of "thriving on chaos" (Tom Peters). Without pre-creational chaos and havoc there is no genesis.

3. The postmodern world, in the words of Harvard educator/comparative religionist Diana Eck, is "where East is no longer East, West no longer West, where the twain have met, and where the outcome of that meeting [will be] of the utmost consequence for the future of humankind."[18]

4. Tolerance and shelter will be given to many forms of life--social and

individual, biological and ideological.

Here be Monsters #1

1.   Postmodernism's catalogue-shopping consciousness can easily turn postmoderns into religious consumers, picking and choosing and browsing about for the belief brands that "best work" for them, out of which they construct, piece by piece, their own autoreligion. Denominations will be increasingly under pressure to cater to this "religion á la carte" and self-salvation by offering particular items of faith that may be inimical to their heritage.[19]

2.   As Christians become multiply resourceful, scissors-and-pasting (with the latter in the shortest supply) religious insight and inspiration from a dizzying array of sources, the greater will be the temptation of syncretism and the danger of trivializing spirituality in some theological collage. The New Age movement in particular shops around in all the world religions in self-service fashion, picking and mixing in ways that often abuse the autonomy and identity of the religious tradition. "A sort of intellectual Velcro dragged over history," to use the unforgettable metaphor of B.J. Williams, "it has picked up odd bits of philosophical lint from unlikely and often contradictory sources."[20]

3.   The "merchandising" of the gospel ministry and message, which popular English Baptist preacher/Colportage Association leader Charles H. Spurgeon was one of the first to denounce, produces religious Barnums and Baileys at best, Elmer Gantrys and Jim Bakkers at worst--though the worst in self-advertising antics and large-scale religious fraud is no doubt yet to come.

4.   When moral values become something chosen by us, not revealed by God, humans become the measure of everything in existence, even what is good and evil.

5.   Jerusalem, the place where East and West meet symbolically, will be even more of a place of contention than in the past.

Protocol #2

There Is a Right Way and a Wrong Way to Do Everything. Or as my father's version of this common-sense adage went, "Leonard, there is one way to do it--and it's my way as long as you're living in my house."

There is no one way of doing things, or "one best way" of doing anything. Modernism yielded to the prejudice of rationalism that truth always leads to a "yes" or a "no," to a rigid structure of values, and to a "right" way or a "wrong" way of thinking and acting. In a trinitarian model of theology, however, there are many best ways to do the will of God. Presbyterian clergyman/Billy Graham Evangelistic Association executive Leighton Ford, at the 1989 Lausanne II Congress on World Evangelization in Manila, expressed this new sensibility beautifully. He told the delegates:

There are many valid styles of worship based on the word of God. In Lausanne we are bound to none and we exclude none. Freedom in the Spirit means that we should be free, but not forced. You may want to try some expressions of worship that are new to you, and you many find them helpful. But do not feel forced, whether to hug, to hold hands, to clap. Only feel your heart lifted to praise our great God. At Lausanne [I], I was impressed that some raised their hands in worship, some didn't--and no one felt they had to do it or couldn't do it![21]

The Bible's many-mansioned God delights in diversity. Premoderns lived in black and white, moderns in smudged gray; postmoderns live in a crayon box. The higher the level of living system in an evolutionary cosmos, the greater the variety and novelty. Modernizers created a spiritual self obsessed with being "best" and proving they were "right" because that was the prime way modern selves could feel "best" and "all-right." The postmodern self finds its security and "all-rightness" in other experiences than in always needing to be "right" and "best." Contemporary polysymbolism is inclusivistic, syncretistic, eclectic, and niched according to taste and interest. In polycentric preaching, for example, openness and paradox abound.[22]

Example One: Marketing researcher/social analyst George Barna has isolated a "multiple church" megatrend especially among both single and married young adults. Findings come from syndicated reports conducted by the Barna Research Group and published under the title *America 2000: What the Trends Mean for Christianity* (1989).[23] The traditional concept of having a "church home" is being replaced by one in which several churches are chosen on an "as-needed" basis in order to satisfy a wide range of life needs. One can interpret the phenomenon as a consequence of the "lack of felt commitment to any single congregation, the low premium placed upon loyalty in the Baby Boomer mind, the heightened selfishness of perspective; and the inability of most churches to develop a ministry which addresses a wide enough range of needs, or does so with quality." But the fact is that the "multiple church trend" is no longer limited to "snow-bird" retired members with winter homes in the South. Three to seven million Americans, church management consultant/church growth researcher Lyle Schaller reveals, have been attending two churches every week in order to have their religious needs met. Increasingly, they are opting for "one-stop shopping" at a megachurch (now numbering in the thousands and growing), which Schaller calls "one of the four or five most-significant developments in contemporary American church history."[24] The same phenomenon is manifesting itself in the arena of politics, with the collapse of the two-party system. Truth transcends any single political ideology; it transcends any single denominational tradition. The ecclesiastics as well as the politics of the future will be multiple choices.

Example Two: In my seminary days, German theologian Joachim Jeremias was the biblical scholar famous for the rationalistic prejudice that the parables of Jesus were intended to have one meaning, and only one meaning. Now we know how wrong he was. Biblical scholars are now examining again, to cite one example, fourteenth-century theologian/second (St. Jerome was first) greatest early biblical scholar/Franciscan Nicolas of Lyra's elaboration of a fourfold dimensionality to every biblical passage: the literal (*litera*), the ethical (*moralis*), the historical (*allegoria*), and the mystical (*anagogia*). The Bible itself has many levels of meaning. Every text is multilayered and multileveled. Nothing should ever be read or understood at a single level. Every text, every tradition, every idea, every person can be seen in multiple variations and in endlessly changing ways, simultaneously.

Rigid norms and "right opinions" are as much a thing of the past as monolithic modes of production. Postmoderns respond less to commanding principles and combative directives than to compelling visions and collective ventures. The boxing match approach to truth, whereby one perspective has to defeat the other and win the day, has given way to leadership which is democratic-participative over hierarchic-authoritative; it elicits belonging over bending. John Wesley himself anticipated this in his famous declaration that he was sick and tired of "right opinion." "Persons may be quite right in their opinions and yet have no religion at all. And on the other hand persons may be truly religious who hold many wrong opinions."[25] People are looking to find their own unique path in the world, each in his or her own way. "Condemn no man for not thinking as you think," Wesley admonished; "let every one enjoy the full and free liberty of thinking for himself."[26] Postmoderns can take opposite paths, make contrasting choices, and still be "right."

Postmodern authority must win respect rather than require or demand it. Authoritarian stances of "We know the best way!" or "We have the Truth!" or "The Bible says it: That settles it!" or "Why? I said so!" no longer suffice. Indeed, they are resented. In their *Handbook of Human Resources Communications* (1988), Myron Emanuel and Arthur M. York demonstrate how appeals to timeless laws and abstract principles no longer work even in the workplace. "Communication," they say, "has replaced authority as a way to manage."[27] Instead of rational argumentation over what is "truth" and "falsehood," authoritarian directives over what is "right" and "wrong," ethical guidelines over what is "success" and "failure," storytelling is the postmodern means of governance--whether personal or national life. Storytellers now make our best politicians. Since the intent is now to persuade and not to dominate, there must be larger roles in religion's rhetoric for wit, elegance, and charm.

On top of the "multiple church" megatrend there has emerged the complicating phenomenon of serial adhesion, moving effortlessly from one set of religious commitments to another, or stacking adhesion, stockpiling commitments on top of one another. Allegiances prove shallow, individually tailored, and suited to choice and style, as the movement of a high school classmate from Jesus Freak to Jehovah's Witness to New Ageism symbolizes. The church already is facing Baby-Boomer believers holding crystals while they pray to Jesus, chanting mantras during their meditation moments, listening to gospel rock music, and buying books like *What Sign Is Your Pet?* (1989).[28]

---- **"** ----

People who don't know anything think everything is possible.

Nobel laureate/economist Wassily Leontieff[c]

---- **"** ----

This is where the distinction between "inclusivistic" versus "eclectic" or "pluralistic" becomes crucial. Inclusivism allows many possible ways of following Christ without relativizing Jesus Christ as one among many possibilities. For the Christian, Jesus Christ is not one choice among many. He is not one good teacher among many good teachers. He is not simply, as one ecumenical litany tried to put it, "a way, a truth, a life," as opposed to "The Way, The Truth, The Life." His gospel is not one among the list of 150 different ways of salvation listed in historian/cultural critic Theodore Roszak's *Unfinished Animal* (1975). "Salvation is found in no one else," Peter said, "for there is no other name under heaven . . . by which we must be saved" (Acts 4:12 RSV). But the fact that God's revelation in Jesus Christ is absolute does not justify absolutizing our understanding of that revelation. Christ is not some property that belongs to one group alone.

There is no precise formula for living the Christian life. But while there is more than one way of being a true believer, there is still one way, and that way is Christ. Like the mathematical model of the Möbius Strip, there is only one side. But that one side is the "inside" and "outside" of the strip. Once again, theologian/evangelism professor William J. Abraham says it best: "It is perfectly consistent to hold both that Jesus is the exclusive path to God and that people may genuinely encounter God outside the Christian church without explicitly knowing about Jesus of Nazareth."[29]

New sensibility number two for postmodern culture is, **There are**

many best ways to do God's will.

There be Treasures #2

1.   Postmodernism may achieve something the modern world never could pull off: Clarity between the normative and relative components of life, cooperation between what are theological absolutes and what are relative truths or *adiaphora* ("things indifferent to salvation").
2.   Reconciling people is a more scriptural approach than always winning people over to one's side.
3.   The definition of power as working in synergy with rather than in supremacy over or competitively against others will inaugurate a host of more creative, more rational, and more fulfilling hierarchical arrangements.
4.   An absolute faith stance can be shown to be compatible with the notion that truth is relative.[30] In Philosophy of Religion Society founder Joseph Runzo's words, "To believe that your faith is best, you need not believe that only the beliefs inherent in your faith can be right."[31]
5.   Renewed commitment to the democratic ideal of freedom of expression.

Here be Monsters #2

1.   Everyone must be free to make up his or her own mind. Christians must keep an open mind. But as government official/satirist/poet C.H. Sisson once said, "Minds must actually be filled with something."[32] The future bodes fewer strongly etched doctrinal positions through which to rally Christian communities.
2.   Openness is one thing. Relativistic rot that retains nothing is quite another.[33] Relativism has proven to be the longest nail in liberalism's coffin. There are some absolute truths in the world. Life is not simply an essay exam. There are some true or false answers. If there were no such thing as truth, the notion that there is no such thing as truth could not be true.
3.   The greatest challenges to the church in the future may come precisely here--adherence to Christian faith increasingly means adding it on to one's religious life, like taking on another activity in an already crowded schedule, not turning from one commitment to another. Postmoderns can collect beliefs like moderns collected coins and stamps.
4.   Both/and can be too easy an alternative to either/or. The notion that your truth is as good as my truth encourages postmoderns to spin from

within a self-god rather than a transcendent God. Sometimes God calls all lovers of paradox to choose which side we are on--or in the words of Soren Kierkegaard's book, *Either/Or* (1843)--life or death?[34]

5.   A principle danger in both inclusivism and pluralism is the emergence of tribalism and the violence of nasty nationalisms and denomi-nationalisms.

Protocol #3

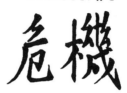

You Can't Do Everything. Social theorist/philosopher/college president Isaiah Berlin speaks of the character distinction between a fox of many interests as opposed to a hedgehog who works away at a single idea.[35] Modernity was the era of the hedgehog. Specialization was the **order** of the day, literally. Individuals were educated to burrow away their lives in a single hole. Institutions were instructed to choose carefully their priorities, or "ruts," since they would spend the foreseeable future routed in them. "You can't do everything" (*non omnia possumus omnes* is the Latin expression), modernizers warned, as moderns learned to specialize, or to "know more and more about less and less until finally you know everything about nothing," as one postmodernist critic put it.

The despecialization, decentralization of postmodernism is best symbolized in the shopping mall phenomenon, where the marketing principle of "niche or be niched" brings together the best of the country store and boutique shop under one roof to sell just about everything. The mentality behind the mallification of America was expressed perfectly in the late nineteenth century by feminist/college president/social reformer Frances Willard, who chose as the motto for the Women's Christian Temperance Union "Do Everything!" As long as "everything" is "niched," as long as one doesn't go off "half-niched," one can indeed just about "do everything" and appreciate everything. Irish wit/poet/dramatist Oscar Wilde's principle, that the only person who could appreciate all works of art was the auctioneer, is now the exception rather than the rule.[36]

"Do I contradict myself?" carpenter/newspaper editor/humanitarian/ poet Walt Whitman asked rhetorically. "Very well then . . . I contradict myself,/I am large. . . . I contain multitudes."[37] A similar exchange occurs in Lewis Carroll's *Alice's Adventures in Wonderland* (1865). "Who are you?" asks the caterpillar. . . . "I-I hardly know, Sir, just at present," Alice replies rather shyly, "at least I knew who I was when I got up this morning, but I think I must have been changed several times since then." Postmodern culture is a culture of multitudes--multimedia productions; multichannel cable system; multitalented people with multiple competencies and multiple interests.

───────────── **"** ─────────────

In the world of today you have got to be everything
or you are going to be nothing.

English biologist/educator/painter C.H. Waddington[d]

───────────── **"** ─────────────

Musical "fusion" and "worldbeat music" as well as the programming punched in on our car radios reflect postmoderns' inclination toward multiple music forms--one button for classic, another for country, another for rock, another for jazz, another for space music, another for southern gospel. Noam Chomsky, called by some the "Galileo of the science of the mind," writes a book a year in linguistics and a book a year in political theory. Judith Weir, the postmodern opera composer, introduced her *A Night at the Chinese Opera* (1988) to a cacophony of queries: Is this opera? Is this drama? Is this comedy? Is this tragedy? Is this musical theater? Weir's postmodern answer: It is all of the above. It is everything. Playwright/producer/director/actor Charles Ludlam calls his Evergreen Theater "very classical, and yet modern at the same time." *Foucault's Pendulum*, the 1989 novel by Italian medievalist/semiotician Umberto Eco, is mystifying reviewers looking for a single, overall assessment because it is many books in one: a realist novel of the Second World War, a novelistic commentary on Italy's revolutionary left, a historical assessment of Western mysticism, a detective story, a primer on esoterica, and a comic satire of the Milan publishing world.

New sensibility number three for postmodern culture is: **Be everything**.

 There be Treasures #3

1.   The attitudes postmoderns cultivate are expansive and holistic, not cramping and specializing.

2.   For the first time in history, we may be able to see both the forest and the trees.

3.   "You can have it all--but not at once."[38] Or in the 1969 words of the biologist C.H. Waddington, "The acute problems of the world can be solved only by **whole** men, not by people who refuse to be . . . anything more than a technologist, or a pure scientist, or an artist."[39]

4.   Postmoderns enjoy a fuller appreciation of the expansiveness of grace,

as presented in John 10:10 (NRSV): "I have come that [you] may have life, and have it more abundantly."

Here be Monsters #3

1.   "Don't-tell-me-you-can't-do-it" sensibilities may ignore the fact that there are some things we legitimately cannot do, and some things morally we should not do. In the Apostle Paul's words, "'We are free to do anything,' you say. Yes, but not everything is good for us . . . not everything builds up the community" (1 Cor. 10:23 REB).

2.   Postmodern society is creating a new social creature--overstimulated, instantly gratified, self-absorbed, almost totally enamored with personal liberation and without much social or political consciousness except for the environment.

3.   Issues of pain, suffering, and evil are conspicuous in their absence from New Ageism, which blurs the doctrines of creation and fall.[40] Sin is more than an addiction or a disease; and redemption is more than therapy or healing.

4.   Judith Weir's postmodern protestation against accusations of borrowing--"I cannot do quotes"--is as bogus as planter/soldier/statesman George Washington's bourgeois "I cannot tell a lie."

5.   How postmoderns love the hymn "Lord We Are Able." The New Age movement tells postmodern culture that all people have within them what it takes to get them through life--their mind power, their higher consciousness, their "getting in touch with themselves" is going to do it for them. "Wrong!", to quote country-western singer/guitarist/composer Waylon Jennings. It is Christ's power, the Christ consciousness, our getting in touch with who Christ is, that is going to do it for us.

6. A reduced appreciation of the cost of discipleship as presented in Luke 9:23: "Take up your cross daily, and follow me."[41]

Protocol #4

You Can Do Anything You Put Your Mind to Do. Or in its more "Sesame Street" version: "You can do anything you **want** to do."

The new sensibility is coming to terms with what it means to live within limits while simultaneously stretching limits. It follows Carlyle Marney's suspicion, articulated just before his death, that Christopher Columbus was actually wrong: The earth has limits beyond which one cannot go. It is indeed possible to sail so far that one can topple over the edge of the universe. There is a place for the restraining rigidity of right angles and straight lines.

As Adam and Eve were the first to find out, life has its limitations. There are no unlimited choices. We cannot do anything we want to do. Some things are even forbidden some of us for biological, psychological, and immunological reasons (i.e., alcohol, barbiturates, crustaceans) that are not forbidden all of us.

Postmodernism is coming to these conclusions partly because the modernist preoccupation with the problem of relating historical truth to religious faith is ending. Just as the modern mind looked to history as the social category of meaning, an arena where humans are the chief actors, the postmodern mind looks to nature, less as the social category for meaning than for experience, an arena where humans are more guests than hosts. Furthermore, in an era of technological horizons that seem rounded, even unbounded, postmodern wisdom feels the need to come to terms with where and when to draw the line.[42]

66

The man who lets himself do everything that is allowed will very soon become slack and do what is not allowed.
Third-century Greek theologian/near saint Clement of Alexandria
and fifth-century North African theologian/saint Augustine of Hippo[e]

99

A prying reporter once asked theatrical performer/triple Academy Award winner Katharine Hepburn why she never married and had children. She replied, "You can't have it all." Either I don't have the talents to do anything I put my mind to do, or I don't have the time to do anything I want to do. English professor/atmospheric, imagistic poet Robert Pinsky, in a long poem entitled *An Explanation of America* (1979), gives the name "grace unrealized" to this fourth sensibility:

A boundary is a limit. How can I
Describe for you the boundaries of this place
Where we were born: where Possibility spreads
And multiplies and exhausts itself in growing
And opens yawning to swallow itself again?
What pictures are there for that limitless grace
Unrealized, those horizons ever dissolving?[43]

In a world of incomprehensively complex and "spreading" possibilities, one can do many more things than the fixated modern mind ever imagined or the truncated modern world ever created. But one cannot do everything. The world is much more complex, diverse, and richer than any one individual. The historical moment is one of "grace unrealized" and receding horizons. Larger meanings must be found on smaller scales. Push the life experience to its limit. But know your limits.

New sensibility number four for postmodern culture is, **Accept constraints. Live within limits**.

 There be Treasures #4

1. Postmodernity may be a time when there will be a sense of "enoughness",[44] when the ecocidal waste and wantonness of modernity will come to an end.
2. The creation of a synergy culture and a moral guidance system that knows how to "do more with less."
3. The reorientation of technology away from the Machine and its "hypertrophy of the intellect" (Susan Sontag) and toward the Garden and its organic vision.

❝

More! More! is the cry of a mistaken soul,
less than all cannot satisfy man.

Mystical poet/myth-maker/artist/engraver William Blake

❞

Here be Monsters #4

1. If postmodernism can be criticized for trying to do too much, it can also be criticized for not trying at all. There are a lot of narcissistic no-hopers out there.
2. Playing the game of "Spirit, Spirit, Who's Got the Spirit?" (or "Guru, Guru, Who's Got the Guru?") is a pandemic postmodern sport.
3. The "fascination" of the New Age movement "with primitivism and the rites and rituals of vanished civilizations" is "paradoxically more oriented to celebrating the past than the future," metaphysician/retreat leader David Spangler points out.[45]
4. In the same way romantics attempted the substitution of religion with art in the modern era, postmoderns would elevate nature to the status of God in their ethics and ecology.

Protocol #5

If At First You Don't Succeed, Try, Try, Again. Or in the southern version I learned in the Virginia mountains: "If at first you don't secede, try, try, again."

This was one of the worst things my kindergarten teacher taught me. "Keep knocking yourself out, Leonard!" "Keep beating yourself to a pulp." "Keep knocking your head against a brick wall." Our continued reliance on a "hit-em-again-harder-harder" mentality represents another try at rattling those moldering bones of modernism.

It is not true that if you try and try and try, you can open any door. Many times it is only when you stop trying that you can begin to succeed. The postmodern sensibility is to look for another door when the one you're banging on doesn't open, or slams in your face. Jesus called this the sacrament of failure: Shake the dust off your feet and go elsewhere. Even God did not get it right the first time: "Then the Lord God said, it is not good that the man should be alone" (Gen. 2:18 RSV). In other words, the work of creation involves learning from experience, indeed, creating as creation goes. The translator Charles B. Williams takes Paul's phrase "struck down, but not destroyed" (2 Cor. 4:9 NRSV) and turns it into "always getting a knockdown, but never a knockout."

"

We were deliberately designed to learn only by trial and error.
We're brought up, unfortunately,
to think that nobody should make mistakes.
Most children get de-geniused
by the love and fear of their parents--
that they might make a mistake.
But all my advances were made by mistakes.
You uncover what is when you get rid of what isn't.

Designer/engineer/architect R. Buckminster Fuller[f]

"

The new sensibility lets go of the negative experiences of the past. It is not afraid to penetrate the power centers of society--film, television, medicine, music, education, economics. There is no sin in trying and failing. Failure to move forward is now worse than making a mistake. We can be encouraged to fail, knowing that we don't have to repeat failures and that failures can be made into mistakes. Or in the words attributed to juggler/ "world's greatest comedian"/screenwriter W.C. Fields, "If at first you don't succeed, try again. Then quit. No use being a damn fool about it."

New sensibility number five for postmodern culture is, **If at first you don't succeed, try something else**.

 ## There be Treasures #5

1.   The church can be more flexible, faster on its feet, and able to change directions quicker than ever before.
2.   An end to the incapacitating consequences of having to stand in place, of being bound to a single post.
3.   Failures plant seeds for greater harvests.
4.   Moving targets prove the most difficult to hit.
5.   The postmodern sensibility leaves people with tasks, not just thoughts.[46]

Here be Monsters #5

1.   Lack of endurance, impatience with doctrinal formulation and structural institutionalization, and the missed opportunities that come to those without staying power are disabling dangers when it's not a sprint we're in but a long-distance run.
2.   The coloring of the postmodern mind excludes cautionary yellow. The bourgeois virtues of moderation, strategic thinking, discipline, and caution must not be thrown to the wind.
3.   Postmoderns have already demonstrated many times over the trouble they have recognizing the difference between cuckoos and nightingales. "Easybelievism" makes the need for discernment training absolutely imperative.
4.   "Wanting to be rich without working, smart without studying, and holy without giving up any vices" is how one New Age critic characterizes the reigning mentality.[47]

66

The earth is a communion of subjects
not a collection of objects.

Ecologist/theologian Thomas Berry

99

Protocol #6

You Can't Be Two Places at Once. If we had a dollar for every time we've been told "You can't be two places at once," we'd all be living in Hawaii. This is the most awful rubbish, and so obviously an obsolete idea that it scarcely seems worthy of a response. But it is one of the most entrenched of the modernist pieties, as generations of postmoderns are being admonished and taught how to stand in place rather than spread themselves out.

―――――――――― 66 ――――――――――

The glory of the local church is that it is not local.

Seminary president/Baptist theologian Albert W. Beaven

―――――――――― 99 ――――――――――

In an electronic culture, we can be many places at once. "Fast intercommunication between points," the "brain and Buddha of American Zen"/ philosopher Alan Watts predicted, "is making all points the same point."[48] The operative adverb for the transportation age, according to journalist/ ethicist Rushworth M. Kidder, was "where." The operative adverb for the onrushing communications era will be "what." In Kidder's words, "What you know how to do will matter greatly. Where you choose to do it will be relatively insignificant."[49] Distances are no longer geographical. Distance is now mainly a state of mind.

The French deconstructionist philosopher Jacques Derrida, the English Anglican theologian John Bowker, the American Calvinist theologian Nicholas Wolterstorff, the Belgian chemist Ilya Prigogine, all have global faculty appointments at cross-continental institutions.[50] President George Bush governed the nation during the 1990 Iraqi crisis from Kennebunkport, Maine. While millions across America were with actor/singer Willie Nelson on television, he and members of his family spent a quiet evening with some "outlaw preachers" at his mountaintop lodge outside of Austin. Television and other communication technologies enable postmoderns to vault over all boundaries and be present at multiple sites simultaneously. More and more Americans are bicoastal and bicontinental in their residences, their jobs, even their marriages. The events around the world are eloquent testimony to the fact that in a small global village within a galactic Great Wall, Iron/ Bamboo Curtains and concrete walls (Berlin, China) come tumbling down.

New sensibility number six for postmodern culture is: **You can be**

many places at the same time.

There be Treasures #6

1. A sense of "homeland," a sense of place and a sense of being "in-place," will replace the modern era's infatuation with uprootedness. Postmoderns will put down roots and value new visions of homesteading and homemaking, with home sometimes an experience as well as a place.
2. Physical space will be becoming less and less of a barrier to ministry. The church's reach can now be extended to every corner of the globe. The whole universe is becoming the habitat for ministry.
3. The dynamic principle of evolution is the completion of space-time binding.

Here be Monsters #6

1. Homogenizing, centralizing forces will increase.
2. The appeal of technologized, centralized suprasystems (especially governmental) will become dangerously irresistible, making postmodernism a potentially reactionary force in social and cultural life.
3. "The tragic quest for meaning and justification, for transcendence," Gerald Graff has observed about postmodernism, "gives way to glorification of **energy**, conceived as pure immanence and process."[51]

Protocol #7

Learn to Do It Yourself. The admonition to "learn to do it yourself" or "figure things out for yourself" partly explains the continuing lure of the circuit rider romance, the Lone Ranger figure who rides off solo to work God's miracles. Forget that it was supply lines staffed by local pastors, class leaders, lay preachers, ministers' wives, and laity that kept early circuit riders going.

"Learn to do it yourself" has encouraged beneficial self-reliance and self-help at the same time it has fostered an unseemly kind of spiritual privateering and do-it-yourself individualism. The predominant modernist disposition toward the church was to see it as a person's private chapel. Membership in the church brought with it the right to have one's own private chaplain, and pastors were expected to be available at a need's notice.

―――――――――――――― 66 ――――――――――――――

IMU URI

Personalized license plate

―――――――――――――― 99 ――――――――――――――

Do-it-yourself options have limited relevance to a postmodern environment. Postrationalist sensibilities are collaborative and participatory. As Alfred North Whitehead expressed the new relational sensibility in *The Concept of Nature* (1920), all of nature is relatedness. For life lived close to nature's bosom, nothing is more fundamental, or real, than relation. Each action breathes life into, or chokes, the cosmos itself. Southern gothic school novelist/pianist Carson McCullers talked about "the we of me." No entity in existence can be itself without another. Each person amplifies the inner fire by joining with others. No nation in the world today has a "national" economy--all economies are interdependent. No nation in the world today has a "national" environment--all ecologies are interrelated. Relationalism must begin to manifest itself in the church's life through networking, roundtabling, electronic bulletin boards, and the like.

―――――――――――――― 66 ――――――――――――――

The old gods are dead or dying
and people everywhere are searching, asking:
What is the new mythology to be,
the mythology of this unified earth as one harmonious being?

Mythologist/metaphysician Joseph C. Campbell[8]

―――――――――――――― 99 ――――――――――――――

New sensibility number seven for postmodern culture is, **Make the net work.**

 There be Treasures #7

1. A tiny piece of the history of the universe hangs in the balance of each decision we make.
2. Strong in naturalist narrative, postmodern theology demonstrates a vital appreciation for the interconnectedness of every part of the universe, and the enfoldment of the whole universe in each part. Tears are not just drops in a vast ocean; tears are the ocean itself.

3. The cult of the "autonomous individual" may be coming to a close.

Here be Monsters #7

1. Letting go can be another way of possessing twice.
2. At bottom, and bottom is a long way down but it can be reached, there lurks New Ageism's "Know not that ye are gods?" mentality.
3. At the same time we dance with the person/century who brought us, there is a need for a kind of "dancing distance" (sociologist/educator Philip Rieff)[52] with life. Dance too close, and one loses one's head. Dance too far, and one loses the rhythm first, and then one's partner.
4. New Age politics have a spiritual dimension, but it is a romantic, tell-me-why-the-ivy-twines spirituality that conflates Christ and the cosmos and is without the Hardyesque notion of the dark forces and violence of nature. Baalim were heathen nature gods supposed to dwell in trees, in springs, in mountain tops, in rocks. The Jews were strictly forbidden to worship them. Just as the premodern Hebrews rejected the nature god of the animists; just as the moderns Wesley and Edwards rejected the generic god of the deists and the social god dividing the world into snobs and yobs: So are postmoderns to set their faith in the God defined by the biblical narratives.

Protocol #8

There are Simple, Easy Answers to Every Problem. Like "Just Say No." Like the "simple arithmetic" that led British Nobel laureate/chemist Sir Robert Robinson to claim in a letter to the London Times in 1971 that adding leaded compounds to the oceans would pose no problems for oceanic plankton.

The problem with simple, easy answers in a postmodern era is that they are simple, easy, and wrong. Rather, there are complex, difficult, tricky responses to every challenge. A quantum economy of space and time does not yield a life of reduced complexity. Welder/farmhand/biologist/Land Institute director Wes Jackson quotes Paul Hawken, James Ogilvy, and Peter Schwartz's *Seven Tomorrows* (1982) in which optimism and pessimism are seen as opposite sides of "the same surrender to simplicity." Relieved of the burden of complex options with complicated consequences, both optimists and pessimists carry on without caring about the consequences of their actions."[53]

———————————————— 66 ————————————————

The flaw lies in the simplistic way scientists are trained.
Missing in the constant attempts
to study smaller and smaller components of reality
is any real concern in the scientific community
*with the **integration** of all the knowledge*
that is being produced. . . No Nobel prizes are given
for understanding how the earth is being transformed,
for knowing what the sum total of modern science means
for society.
Psychologist/Institute president Robert Ornstein and biologist/ecologist Paul Ehrlich[h]

———————————————— 99 ————————————————

The postmodern sensibility is not to seek simplifying or centralizing processes. It is rather to find ways of living with imperfections and complexities, and with making complex things clearer. The latter is accomplished increasingly through design and graphic components, now more content than packaging. The former is accomplished less through listening to the regular, linear beats of the heart than listening to the irregular, nonlinear, complex impulses of the brain--a nonlinear offshoot of a nonlinear evolution on a nonlinear Earth in which nonlinear changes take place all the time.

———————————————— 66 ————————————————

There is no permanent solution
to any important problem in human life.
Government research consultant/economist/political biographer Edward Shils[i]

———————————————— 99 ————————————————

Every simplification gives rise to at least two new complexifications. "The idea of simplicity is falling apart," the "poet of thermodynamics" Ilya Prigogine says; "any direction you go in there's complexity." Newtonian physics tried to break down complex things into simple things, to shrink knowledge into certitudes and platitudes. Quantum physics tries to break into the world of universality, nonrationality, integration, and complexity. No computer in the world, for example, is large or complex enough to identify all the interactions that take place in one single cell. Discernment of the Spirit is oriented less to finding simplicities and solving problems than to removing the fear and faithlessness that prevents us from moving forward into strange new worlds.

The postmodern sensibility also thinks less in terms of problems that we solve than of complex intellectual viruses that we "get over" (John Dewey) and "outgrow" (Carl Jung)[54] or mysteries that transcend "solutions."

Theopoeticist/religion professor David L. Miller's marvelous *Hells and Holy Ghosts* (1989) uses French philosopher Gabriel Marcel's "two-roses" distinction--"one that appears in a seed catalog and one that is written about in a poem"--as the defining difference between a problem (the presence of the former) and a mystery (the presence of the latter). In the words of Marcel:

> A problem is something which I meet, which I find complete before me, but which I can therefore lay siege to and reduce. But a mystery is something in which I myself am involved, and it can therefore only be thought of as "a sphere where the distinction between what is in me and what is before me loses its meaning and its initial validity."[55]

---------------------------------- 66 ----------------------------------

I am convinced that the nations and people
who master the new sciences of complexity
will become the economic, cultural, and political superpowers
of the next century.

Quantum physicist/communicator of scientific ideas to non-scientists Heinz Pagels[j]

---------------------------------- 99 ----------------------------------

When one wants to understand the origins and future evolutions of life, the global environment, or brains, one studies complexity, not simplicity.[56] The category of beauty has largely replaced simplicity among many physicists. Simplicity may be more beautiful than complexity, but the First Commandment's injunction to "tend and till the garden" commits the human species both to preserving the richness and variety of life and to increasing, in science fictionist/humanist Ursula LeGuin's words, "the intensity and complexity of the field of intelligent life."[57] It is our bounden duty, philosopher of science/fictionist/poet Frederick Turner writes, to increase the organized complexity of the world through good technology. "To serve God is to increase the scope, power, beauty, and depth of technology," a process he calls "natural technology."

> It is not our job to leave nature alone or to coexist peacefully with it; we are it, we are its future, its promise, its purpose. We must actively continue its project. But if we are to do so we desperately need more knowledge and research.[58]

The postmodern sensibility is to seek the simplicity on the "other side" of complexity without stripping truth of its variousness and contrariness. On this side of complexity, simplicity is simple-mindedness. There is no more pathetic scene than an adult Christian praying a child's prayer like the elementary "Now I lay me down to sleep." There is no more beautiful scene than an adult Christian praying a child's prayer like the elemental "Now I lay me down to sleep."

There is such a thing as one complexity too many. Beyond a certain threshold of complexity one reaches the "entropy barrier" (Prigogine), after which there is no return to the previous state, before which there is unpredictable change. This inability to "fix" the future or limit the range of creative possibilities is called the "new uncertainty principle."

New sensibility number eight for postmodern culture is, **There are complex, hard responses to life's challenges.**

 ## There be Treasures #8

1.   Learning to handle complexity frees us to live more intuitively, more insightfully, more inspirationally--the only dynamics that enable us to create, change, and connect with complex systems.
2.   Accepting decay and chaos means embracing life.
3.   The development of a theology of technology that can distinguish between "good" and "bad" technology and the emergence of an environmental ethic that does not draw unnecessary distinctions between the human and the natural.

Here be Monsters #8

1.   The tendency to forget that the same groups whom Jesus charged with loving darkness rather than light are still with us.
2.   Going through life "blissed out," without antecedence or consequence, leads to the Yuppie creed:
>   Consider all,
>   Commit to little,
>   Keep moving.
3.   Postmodernism commits acts of diagnosis easier than acts of prognosis.
4.   Postmoderns have the tendency to come down hard with two feet firmly planted on both sides of an issue. They dislike having to put all their eggs in one basket. They like to sit on fences.
5.   Skepticism towards simplicities can make life complicated instead of complex, generating unreal solutions that then function as simplicities--witness magic crystals, extraterrestrials, and the like.
6.   There are yet insufficient checks to the tendency of postmodernism's ironist perspective to become merely a winking, witty, whimsical neutrality.

> *Complementary doesn't mean contradictory,*
> *unbelievable doesn't mean irrational,*
> *unknown doesn't mean unknowable,*
> *and to say that language is inaccurate*
> *doesn't mean that it is altogether inadequate.*
>
> Mathematician/quantum theorist/computer culturalist Allen Emerson[k]

Protocol #9

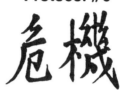

You Don't Know Everything. How many times have moderns heard this line, not just from our kindergarten teachers, but all the way up the educational staircase. The world of modernity cautioned against moving until everything that could be known was gathered and analyzed and corroborated "beyond a shadow of doubt" or less impossibly "beyond a reasonable doubt." This bred an academic indecisiveness, a "you-don't-know-everything" sensibility that made movement difficult without the "absolute proof" of science.[59]

The truth is that you can know too much: "always learning but never able to acknowledge the truth" (2 Tim. 3:7 NIV). The more moderns knew, the more reasons there were for knowledge not to lead to acknowledgment. It became virtually impossible for moderns to agree on any move, for if someone insisted on a particular course of action, others would protest the suppression of incompatible evidence, of which modernity was accumulating plenty. All the while moderns did know on many issues everything essential for action.

> *We do not know one millionth of one percent about anything.*
>
> Newsboy/telegraph operator/inventor Thomas Alva Edison

Or, in the words of philosopher/prime minister/scholar of ancient writings Confucius, to a student admiring him for knowing so many things: "I know only one thing. But that permeates everything." Postmodernism is not the defense of ignorance. Ignorance is never bliss. The familiar adage

"Ignorance is bliss" is a misquote. Eighteenth-century poet/professor of modern history Thomas Gray, in the final line of his poem "On a Distant Prospect of Eaton College" (1742), actually said "Where ignorance is bliss/ 'tis folly to be wise." The problem postmoderns have is not wanting to know what they already know. We already know, but don't want to get wise about the fact that Americans are 5 percent of the world's population consuming 20 percent of the world's energy, 40 percent of the world's resources. To really **know** this would force us off the fence.

Sherlock Holmes, the greatest practitioner of common sense pieties who ever lived in literature, made it a maxim that "it is a capital mistake to theorize before one has data." This is but the obverse side of the scientific method, which if philosopher/logician of science Karl Popper is correct, consists primarily in the falsification of hypotheses. Despite the vast quantity of data moderns managed to accumulate, because the burden of proof demanded by science required **all** the facts to be **in**, the verdict still had to be **out**. As long as "the experts disagree," moderns were careful not to draw conclusions.

And the experts? They were always wanting to know more, never eager to move until more was known, never wanting to "rush off" to a conclusion on acid rain, on asbestos, on tobacco, on ozone layers, on AIDS viruses. Forgotten was the fact that not deciding was a decision for stasis over dynamism, and while the experts were debating and "perfecting," the problems kept mounting. Or in the words of the psalmist, "While I mused, the fire burned" (Ps. 39:3 NRSV). Geophysicist/government agency staff member S. Fred Singer offered some advice in April 1989 as Congress began revising the Clean Air Act. In spite of all the evidence accumulated by the $500 million National Acid Precipitation Assessment Program (NAPAP) proving that sulfur- and nitrogen-based air pollutants emitted during fossil fuel combustion are largely responsible for most of the acidification of lakes and streams in the eastern states, scientists still can't come to a conclusion. Since it is still a mystery how sulfates react with other chemicals (even though acid rain was first diagnosed in England in 1872), Singer held out for empirical certainty: "Look at the science before you leap. Let's not have environmental laws that are not backed by facts."[60] It is now nearly too late. And the "facts" are still not all **in**.

Modernity's conceit was scientistic orthodoxy, or what Huston Smith calls the modern West's "Promethean epistemology": The refusal to recognize beliefs as legitimate until they pass certain scientific tests.[61] Philosopher/mathematician/politician/Nobel laureate Bertrand Russell's concluding chapter to *History of Western Philosophy* (1945) argues that outside science there is no knowledge or true knowing. Scientistic orthodoxy gave us a "two realms"[62] quantitative epistemology which told us that scientific rationality could know everything, while faith, feeling, meaning, and purpose had little to say: "**You** don't know everything." Moderns came to see their intuitions and indeed themselves in an inferior and demeaning relation to science, which billed itself as a "neutral observer." What did dialectical materialism do, after all, but claim that it explained everything? Moderns sitting on the fence of indecision were really stuck on a fence of fear.

The equation of science with knowledge has reached the limits of its use and has begun to be a real hindrance.[63] Postmodern scientists like physicist/ Nobel laureate Eugene Wigner now admit that scientists don't know everything, that indeed "it would not be good if we knew everything."[64] Or, as another physicist/Nobel laureate, Richard Feynman, put it shortly before his death, "A great deal more truth can be known than can be proved."[65] They dispute the dichotomy of a know-it-all science and a know-nothing religion. Some things are unsuited to "scientific" testing. Besides, we will never have all the facts, and there is no such thing as a "neutral observer" or "the naked eye." Decisions must be made without knowing everything that would help to make the decision and without bracketing one's beliefs. The longer we wait, the more facts we will have, but the more facts also will change. In other words, you can know too much. On many issues we already know everything we need to know to be "actants" (Gerhard Lohfink's wonderful word) of God's purposes, especially in the most critical arena of ecotheology--the theological deliberations on economics and ecology.

New sensibility number nine for postmodern culture is: **Keep learning what you already know.**

 There be Treasures #9

1.   Spiraling toward truth and the future, the postmodern era may make radical strides in preserving this planet and protecting all life forms from inner and outer assaults. This would effect the realization of Wittgenstein's claim that the purpose of philosophy is to liberate flies.
2.   Postmoderns are poised for the development of a value-laden scientific vocabulary that puts God central to any pursuit of wisdom.
3.   "Whatever you do see that you do it."

Here be Monsters #9

1.   Postmodernism's dance around the "hermeneutical circle" can often lead to a theological fugue involving flight from real insights about God; that is, postmodernism can become too much of an intimist activity, the scholastic quibbling of hermetic hermeneutics.
2.   Postmodernists can be too fast on their feet, putting trend

before truth, the torch of truth abandoned by the wayside as expressed in the title of the memoirs of Aidan Crawley: *Leap Before You Look* (1989).

3. More and more people live entirely by their own light. **Discerning** God's will must take place before **doing** God's will.

4. We must never abandon "education for **surprise**" (Huston Smith) and its fundamental tenet: When compared with what we do not know, what we do know is nothing.[66]

5. The half-hatched metaphysics of the New Age movement is the postmodern version of gnosticism. As with Adam and Eve, postmoderns are lured from paradise by the temptation of secret, greater knowledge.

Protocol #10

The Truth Lies Somewhere in the Middle. This is one of the most difficult things to get right. The truth lies now in the extremes, both held together simultaneously. Ever since Danish physicist Niels Bohr's enunciation of the complementarity principle, the union of logically contradictory opposites (such as "wave" [world of connection] and "particle" [world of disconnection] to describe light) has stood at the heart of the comprehension of truth. Oppositions are no longer antagonisms but electrifying outlets. The limitation of language to evoke satisfactorily the soul's encounter with God drives one to extremes. The postmodern sensibility is not the reconciliation of opposites, but the extension of extremes.

———————————— 66 ————————————

Those who try to exclude the moral quality from social science as a whole lose the scientific quality also.
German political theorist/educator Wolf-Dieter Narr[1]

———————————— 99 ————————————

Funny and serious at the same time, postmoderns are in love with oxymorons--built in contradictions in terms. We already know many of them: "down escalator," "long shorts," "fresh frozen," "jumbo shrimp," "pretty ugly," "frugal gourmet." Some are getting less contradictory (like "Roman Catholic" or "modern myth" or "virgin birth"); some are getting more so (like "Postal Service," "Reagan's memoirs," "inactive Christian," "House Ethics," "TV News," "holy war," "authentic reproductions," "institutional integrity," "fast foods," "express lane," "scientific creationism," perhaps even "United Methodist"). An advertisement for Santa Fe, New Mexico,

293

touted the city as a center for "charged relaxation." New Jersey Ginsberg and Wong restaurants feature appetizers of "Mrs. Ginsberg's Chicken Soup" and "Mr. Wong's Wonton Soup." Macheezmo Mouse franchise restaurants specialize in a "Fresh-Fit-Fast" Mexican-style menu. A commercial for coffee promises to "Lift You Up and Calm You Down" at the same time. Postmodern novelist/liturgical art collector Kurt Vonnegut calls himself a "God-fearing agnostic." Evidence abounds that baby-boomers and baby-busters want to be lavish and thrifty at the same time. Timothy Mo's novel *Sour Sweet* (1982), Monica Furlong's biography of Alan Watts *Genuine Fake* (1986), and Angela Carter's short story about "atrocious gentleness," from the *Best Short Stories 1989* collection,[67] encapsulate the May/December--dragon/maiden--beauty/beast sensibilities of postmodernism.

The movement from premodern (medieval) to modern to postmodern replaced dichotomies first with dialectics and now with interactions. Hostility to the triumphalist teleologies and doctrinal/moralistic/experiential chains of modernity has generated an understanding of truth that lies now less in dogmatism than in discussion, in the dialogue of the voices, in the ordered disorder of sound. Dow Edgerton uses the Hebrew Scriptures to show how this never-ending binding and freeing works: If it is halakah, a matter of law, there will be a ruling, but all the dissenting voices remain. They remain because without them the ruling could never have been tested and refined. They remain because they are themselves authoritative.

Edgerton goes on to tell the famous story of a dispute between the houses of Hillel and Shammai, the two schools of Pharisaism operative in Palestine at the time Rabbi Jesus was preaching. Shammai was dedicated to the letter of the law. Hillel emphasized the spirit of the law. "After they could reach no agreement, at last a voice came from heaven saying, 'the law is according to Hillel, but both of them are the words of the living God.'"[68] The authority of truth proceeds from the process of dialogue itself: "What Shammai binds, Hillel looses." There are no losers. Oxymorons, polarities, and oppositions cannot be exorcised out of a religion that revels in logical illogicalities such as "having nothing . . . but possessing all things"; "sorrowful . . . always rejoicing"; "poor . . . but rich in faith and heirs of the Kingdom."[69]

The bitter-sweet bind of postmodern culture is, **The truth lies in the extremes being held together.**

 There be Treasures #10

1. Unitary thinking, the highest level of understanding reality, opens us up to a wider sensory realm and mystical dimension of the divine; it also heals

the divisions that separate us from one another and life's highest values.
2. Wholeness unites, not eliminates, opposites, bringing them into dynamic balance--the coming together of earth and water, air and fire, through the merger of the Antaean sensibility (Antaeus the hugger of the ground, from which came his strength) with the Herculean sensibility (Hercules the master of air and fire, who defeated Antaeus by lifting him off the ground.)[70]
3. The discovery of the euphoric state of wholeness will prove to be the highest form of ecstasis.

Here be Monsters #10

1. New Ageism is marked by the normality of the bizarre; hence its restless search for the extremes of experience. New Agers are often little more than thrill consumers, looking for new "peak experiences" through religious ecstasies, sexual experimentation, athletic highs, travel adventures, etc.
2. Two souls, as chicken farmer/naturalist/poet Robert Frost once remarked, can be too widely met.
3. Postmoderns can suffer severe confusion of identities, like the little boy who said to the girl, "Are you the opposite sex, or am I?" Or more diabolically, as historian/New Age unmasker Douglas R. Groothius points out, mass murderer/cult leader Charles Manson's followers knew him as both Satan and Christ.
4. Sometimes you really can't have it both ways. Some contradictions can be resolved only through penitence and prayer.

66

The real issue for me is creating an environment that is both present and absent. When you are not working, the office has to disappear. When you are in the office, the home has to be absent.

Prominent architect/Cooper Union distinguished professor Peter Eisenman[m]

99

The Sense of the Common

It is time to rescue sense from a common reputation, as the modernist era defined "common." In the early church, another name for Holy Spirit was the "Common Sense." But the "Common Sense" meant something very different from what the Enlightenment meant by "common sense." The "Common Sense" meant rather the "Sense of the Common." The postmodern sense of the common rejects tests on intuitive grounds first, **then** on rational, empirical grounds.

The common sense, or the intuition of logic, is being squeezed for room in contemporary philosophy by the sense of the common, or the logics of intuition. The distinguished educator/philosopher Daniel C. Dennett names "intuition pumps" as the "real legacy of the history of philosophy."[71] For the common sense to be the common good in the postmodern era, it must come to respect the authority of intuitive modes of knowing. The mature Aristotle, who rejected intuition, must revert to the ways of the early Aristotle, who appealed to intuition.

Ever since scientific developments gathered force in Western Europe in the seventeenth and eighteenth centuries, moderns governed their destiny by the rational application of objectivist, positivist, and reductionist assumptions. A few, like German literary revivalist/Lutheran theologian/historian Johann Gottfried von Herder in his *Die Älteste Urkunde des Menschengeschlechts* (1774-1776) argued that lying at the bases of all knowledge is "the philosophy of intuition." But for the most part, only those deemed fools or "antiintellectuals" or superstitious religionists bent on fanaticism would direct their lives by other than logic. Humans were not given their full emotional or intuitional space by canonical modernism.

Postmodern destinies, in contrast, are governed by intimations, by intuitional guidance, by inner promptings. Novelist/essayist John Updike offers the word "intuition" as his best definition of spirituality.[72] The think tank Cato Institute promotes its new line of books under the heading "Un-Common Policy Sense." Mazda advertises its cars on the basis of their "emotional ergonomic design," an engineering based not primarily on scientific aeronautical principles but on how it feels to drive the vehicle. Toyota promises to light your fire through the experience of driving its new MR2--"The passion is back." Buick markets its Reatta Roadster by toasting, "Here's to going with your gut. Listening to your heart. Letting your passion rule. **Because common sense, after all, is common.**" America's most beloved politician, Bob Kerrey, nicknamed "Senator Perfect," admits he listens to an inner voice and sees himself as a visionary.[73] The journal *Monk*, a travel magazine that actually travels, boasts an editorial direction that is arrived at by "intuition" and the vicissitudes of the motor home. Americans flock to a movie (*Field of Dreams*, 1989) about a farmer who acts on the voices of his soul rather than following the dictates of reason and common sense. Philosopher Andy Clark boxes the ears of science for its reliance on the "folk psychology" of common sense.[74]

Modernity dismissed "intuition" as something only women took seriously, enthroning reason and logic and common sense so firmly that "antiintellectual" or "irrational" became one of the most deadly epithets one could hurl at anyone. To become unreasonable and illogical was to become a traitor to the Enlightenment tradition. Postmodernity, on the other hand, thrives on intuitional experience, elevating its attributes to the status of a true leader: Someone "gifted more than ordinary people with a mystical quality--intuition--which gives him 'inner conviction' and enables him to make difficult decisions in a manner denied to the common person."[75] It is through creative intuition that postmoderns continue the work of divine creation.

Structuralist/anthropologist Claude Levi-Strauss calls our day "the final collapse of rationalism." But "rationalism" (or what psychologist/ theologian/brain researcher James Ashbrook calls "reflective conscious- ness") captured some key insights we abandon at our peril. Postmodernity needs to be careful lest logic and reason become its treason. Logic can be too infrequent a quest in precincts patrolled by postmodern orthodoxy. For Jacques Derrida, for example, conventional standards of rationality mean nothing. Indeed, it is precisely the canons of logic and the category of common sense that Derrida is bent on attacking. Derrida deems all writing (even his writings) as meaningless. There can be no Derridean position or thesis because Derrida tears to shreds the very notion of "sense." All literature is thus literally "nonsensical."

It would be especially grievous to condemn intellectualism as anal- analytic, enthroning intuition and perception so firmly that "antiintuitional" becomes the new brickbat to drive people into the outer darkness. Any New Light apologetic must employ all three (not two) modes of knowing: the empirical mode, the rational mode, and the intuitive mode.[76] It must retain its strong commitment to rational discourse and robust common sense while being open to the sense of the common and all that lies beyond reason's reach.[77] The rational/nonattached and the intuitive/participatory are not antinomies but aspects of each other, in the same way straight sides are aspects of sliced circles.[78] An adequate spirituality for the postmodern era has components that are both linear and field, both rational and intuitive, both five senses and "sixth sense.".

But the church has a long way to go before it needs to worry about a dogmatic intuitionism prejudiced against the critical and conceptual. The "nonrational" is still too often seen as the "irrational." Right now the church needs to hear the words of postmodernist prophets like the philosopher/ mathematician/diplomat/Nobel laureate Henri Bergson, who argued for the wisdom of intuition as a balance to keep the five senses in order and harmony.

Science and metaphysics therefore come together in intuition. A truly intuitive philosophy would realize the much-desired union of science and metaphysics. While it would make of metaphysics a positive science--that is, a progressive and indefinitely perfectible one--it would at the same time lead the positive sciences, properly so called, to become conscious of their true scope, often far greater than they imagine. It would put more science into metaphysics, and more metaphysics into science. It would result in restoring the

continuity between the intuitions which the various sciences have obtained here and there in the course of their history, and which they have obtained only by strokes of genius.[79]
Similar words can be found throughout the writings of the greatest New Light prophets for the postmodern era, ecologist/forester/zoologist Aldo Leopold, whose life exemplified a spirituality that "breathed from one's heels."[80]

The Kiss of God

This book is nothing more than an attempt to let this one word breathe--spirituality. The life of the word "spiritual" has trouble staying within calling distance of the meaning of the word "spiritual." With roots in the Latin *spiritus*, the Hebrew *ruach* and the Greek *pneuma*, "spiritual" fundamentally means "aliveness." Genesis 2:7 first presents the concept. Life is very rare. In this cosmos, life is not common. The human species, the first Adam, is designed and created to be God's gardener for earth, the garden planet of the Milky Way Galaxy: "Then the Lord God formed man from the dust of the ground, and breathed into his nostrils the breath of life; and the man became a living being" (NRSV). The Latin word *spirare* means "breathing." Far from our coming into the world, we come out of the world, as God forms the human species out of the dust of the earth and "breathes" into Adam's nostrils the "breath of life." The gift of life was the first kiss of God.

———————————— 66 ————————————

Dum Spiro Spero.
As long as I breathe, I hope.

Old Latin saying

———————————— 99 ————————————

Spirituality refers first of all to the universal gift of aliveness that exists within all religions and outside of religions. It breathes out the air that "in-spires." Those who have been in-spired with aliveness by the kiss of God will "con-spire" to kiss others into coming alive to the spiritual dimensions of existence. "In-spire" means to breathe in. "Con-spire" means to breathe together. "Conspiracy" enters by the same door as "spirituality." A world gagging on smog and smut needs a breath of fresh air. The New Light movement begins as a fresh air conspiracy of "aliveness."

But it is more than that. Spiritual consciousness can be something greater than aesthetics or aliveness. The Bible tells us that the human species has been twice kissed by the divine. If the first kiss brought us breath and birth, the second kiss brought us rebirth and a second breath. John 20 recounts Jesus' post-resurrection appearances, first, as a gardener to Mary, then, as the Second Adam to his disciples: "Jesus said to them again, 'Peace be with you. As the Father has sent me, so I send you.' When he had said this, he breathed on them and said to them, 'Receive the Holy Spirit'" (John 20:21-22 NRSV). The Second Testament refers to God "breathing" on the human species when the Holy Spirit was breathed into the disciples.

The first kiss of God quickened us to come alive. Adam was God's first kiss. The second kiss of God quickens us to come alive in Christ and be "born of the Spirit" (John 3:8 RSV). Jesus is God's second kiss (or in the words of Bernard of Clairvaux, "Jesus is God's kiss"). The Spirit is the breath of God in the body of the church. In his classic sermon "The New Birth," John Wesley likened the life of faith to "a kind of spiritual respiration" of breathing in the means of grace and breathing out good works.[81] For too long the church has warned its members, "Don't breathe in," highlighting the dangers of aliveness. Furthermore, for too long those in the church who have "breathed in" spiritual aliveness have not breathed out the activism and engagement that aliveness requires. Their hyperventilations on the Holy Spirit have sickened those considering receiving God's second kiss. A postmodern spirituality has outbreaths to go with every inbreath.

────────────────── 66 ──────────────────

On the seventh day [God] rested and drew breath.
First Testament recorder of oral tradition[n]

────────────────── 99 ──────────────────

Sevening

The literal translation of aerobics is "with air." These ten deep breathing exercises sample some of the aerobic principles able to improve the physical fitness of postmoderns.

1. Get in touch with your lungs by closing your eyes. Visualize in your mind a tennis court. The total surface area of your lungs is roughly the size of a tennis court, providing enough space for some three hundred billion capillaries. If stretched from end to end, these capillaries would reach from New York to Florida.

2. Take the breath of life. You are that one breath away from eternity. Every twenty-four hours you are 23,240 one-breaths away from eternity. God is constantly pouring out puffs of life into you, life that is that fragile.

3. Listen to yourself breathe the breath of life. Every twenty-four hours you breathe in some twenty million particles of foreign matter, if you live in an urban area. Our ancestors also breathed in polluted air, although they did not have to contend with ozone levels that cause breathing difficulties, chest tightness or pain, and inflammation of the lungs even in otherwise healthy persons. Carbon deposits from inhaling wood smoke in unventilated dwellings are commonly found in the lungs of preserved mummies. To help rid the lungs of foreign matter is why God made us with

so many capillaries.

    4.   Breathe in a large amount of oxygen and hold it. Thirty-five percent of the oxygen molecules we inhale in one breath comes from the rain forests, which we are chopping down at a rate of twenty-five million hectares a year. Every minute, four football fields of forests disappear from the face of the earth. Every minute, two hundred football fields of arable land disappear under concrete. Breathe out a prayer of repentance.

―――――――――――― 66 ――――――――――――

Every year,
the average automobile (traveling 10,000 miles) emits
about six-hundred-and-fifty pounds of carbon monoxide,
over one hundred pounds of hydrocarbons,
fifty pounds of nitrogen oxides,
and twelve pounds of particles into the air.

―――――――――――― 99 ――――――――――――

    5.   Take a deep breath of life holding someone's hand. Nothing is more personal and private than breathing. Yet nothing connects us more to one another and the earth than breathing. Each breath we take contains approximately a quadrillion (10^{15}) atoms breathed by the rest of humanity within the past few weeks.

    6.   Take another deep breath while holding a pet or plant. The connectedness of our breathing encompasses not simply the human order but all creatures that breathe, including persons, plants, and animals.

    7.   Stand in front of a picture of a family member who has died. Recall joyful memories of them and laugh. With the breath you took for that laugh, your loved one literally became a part of you. In every breath there are more than a million atoms breathed personally at one time or another by every breathing earthling that has ever lived.

    8.   Hold your Bible and breathe meditatively. The breathtaking, nay, breathgiving truth of aliveness is more than Methuselean in its span: Part of your body right now was once actually, literally part of the body of Abraham, Sarah, Noah, Esther, David, Abigail, Moses, Ruth, Matthew, Mary, Lı ke, Martha, John, Priscilla, Paul . . . and Jesus.

    9.   Keep breathing quietly while holding your Bible. You have within you not just the powers of goodness resident in the great spiritual leaders like Moses, Jesus, Muhammed, Lao Tzu. You also have within you the forces of evil and destruction. The youthful comrade and confidant of Joan of Arc was Gilles de Rais, a marshall of France and one of the wealthiest men in Europe, who was condemned to the stake in 1440 for the crimes of witchcraft, heresy, sodomy, and the sexual abuse and murder of over 140 children. Resident in each breath you take is the body of angels like Joan of Arc and devils like Gilles de Rais, Genghis Khan, Judas Iscariot, Herod,

Hitler, Stalin and all the other destructive spirits throughout history.

10. Gather a group together for a Navajo breathing ceremony. Stand in a circle, everyone facing the center of the circle. If there are any present in special need of prayer, ask them to "center" the circle. Place your hands in the center of the backs of those standing on either side of you and observe silence. Get in touch with one anothers' breathing patterns. Now breathe together as a circle, bending the knees slightly as you inhale, straightening up as you exhale. Keep doing this until the circle becomes one breath.

Breathe on Me, Breath of God

These latter days of the twentieth century are filled with background noises and subliminal forces that speak in shouted whispers, "Don't breathe in." A spirituality for the twenty-first century begins with an experience of aliveness and deep breathings of life. After all, . . .

Jesus took a deep breath . . . when he chose Simon the Zealot as a disciple . . .

. . . and **political** barriers were blown away.

Jesus took a deep breath . . . when he dined with Zacchaeus the despised publican . . .

. . . and **class** barriers were blown away.

Jesus took a deep breath . . . when he conversed with a woman of Samaria . . .

. . . and **sexual** barriers were blown away.

Jesus took a deep breath . . . when he celebrated a Roman centurion's faith . . .

. . . and **racial** barriers were blown away.

Jesus took a deep breath . . . when he allowed a woman who was a sinner to touch him . . .

. . . and **ideological** barriers were blown away.

Jesus took a deep breath . . . when he praised a poor widow who offered her mite . . .

. . . and **economic** barriers were blown away.

Jesus took a deep breath . . . when he heeded the appeal of a Syrophoenician woman . . .

. . . and **national** barriers were blown away.

Jesus took a deep breath . . . when he washed his disciples' feet . . .

. . . and **social** barriers were blown away.

Jesus took a deep breath . . . when he rebuked the disciples for criticizing a follower who was an outside to the group . . .

. . . and **denominational** barriers were blown away.

Jesus took a deep breath . . . when he chastised the adults for not suffering the children to come unto him . . .

. . . and **ageist** barriers were blown away.

Jesus took a deep breath . . . when he told Lazarus to come forth . . .
. . . and **physical** barriers were blown away.
Jesus, God's breath made flesh, took deep breaths . . .
Will we?
Will we be God's breath made flesh?

———————————————— ❝ ————————————————

Let everything that breathes praise the Lord.

Hebrew psalmist[o]

———————————————— ❞ ————————————————

Endnotes

PREFACE
Does God Have a Big Toe?
(pages 1 - 13)

a.   Demetrius R. Dumm, "Luke 24:44-49 and Hospitality," in *Sin, Salvation, and the Spirit: Commemorating the Fiftieth Year of The Liturgical Press*, ed. Daniel Durken (Collegeville, Minn.: Liturgical Press, 1979), 236.

b.   Gerhard Casper, "A Golden Age of Education," *University of Chicago Record* 25 (8 August 1990): 2.

c.   Jacques Derrida, *L'Écriture et la Différence* (Paris: Seuil, 1966), 111; *Writing and Difference* (Chicago: University of Chicago Press, 1978), 74.

d.   These are words Sir Isaac Newton uttered shortly before his death. See Sir David Brewster, *Memoirs of the Life, Writings, and Discoveries of Sir Isaac Newton* (Edinburgh: T. Constable, 1855), 2:407.

e.   Mary Midgley, *Wisdom, Information, and Wonder: What is Knowledge For?* (New York: Routledge, 1989), 49-50.

f.   This is the question that led to the Tower of Babel according to Marc Gellman in his *Does God Have a Big Toe?: Stories About Stories in the Bible*, paintings by Oscar de Mejo (New York: Harper and Row, 1989), 43.

g.   As quoted in Robert D. Young, *Religious Imagination: God's Gift to Prophets and Preachers* (Philadelphia: Westminster Press, 1979), 129.

h.   Edwards's last words are recorded in Iain H. Murray, *Jonathan Edwards: A New Biography* (Edinburgh: Banner of Truth Trust, 1987), 441; Wesley's words, spoken a few hours before his death, are recorded in Luke Tyerman, *The Life and Times of the Rev. John Wesley, M.A., Founder of the Methodists* (New York: Harper, 1872), 654. His final words before death were "I'll praise, I'll praise" and "Farewell" (655).

1.   In the words of Jesus' prayer for his disciples:
I will remain in the world no longer, but they are still in the world. . . . I am coming to you now, but I say these things while I am still in the world, so that they may have the full measure of my joy within them. I have given them your word and the world has hated them, for they are not of the world any more than I am of the world. My prayer is not that you take them out of the world but that you protect them from the evil one. (John 17:11,13-15 NIV)

2.   It is ironic that H. Richard Niebuhr's preferred attribute of "Christ the Transformer of Culture," which is presented last after "Christ Against Culture," "The Christ of Culture," "Christ Above Culture" and "Christ and Culture in Paradox," is built on the conversionist motif in the Fourth Gospel but never uses the Johannine terminology itself. See Niebuhr's *Christ and Culture* (New York: Harper, 1951).

3.   The incompleteness of Niebuhr's fivefold typology of the relationship between Christian faith and human culture is becoming more and more obvious to contemporary scholars. The wildly popular *Resident Aliens: Life in the Christian Colony* (Nashville: Abingdon Press, 1989) by Stanley Hauerwas and William H. Willimon pointedly leaves Niebuhr in the wings, asking John Howard Yoder to dance instead. In Yoder's threefold typology (the activist, the conversionist, and the confessing church) Hauerwas and Willimon find the basis for building a confessing church posture toward the culture, which they term a "counter cultural colony" of "resident aliens." For a critique of this sectarian alternative proposed by Hauerwas and Willimon, see Anthony B. Robinson, "The Church as Counter-cultural Enclave," *Christian Century*, 8-15 August 1990, 739-41.

4.   I have been greatly influenced by the theological method of David Tracy, which he calls the "mutually critical correlational method." See his *Plurality and Ambiguity: Hermeneutics, Religion, Hope* (San Francisco: Harper and Row, 1987). I have also been stirred by the

call of David Buttrick for "apologetic strategies" that fit "between the times" and that risk "cultural dalliance." See his "Preaching to the 'Faith' of America," in *Communications and Change in American Religious History*, ed. Leonard I. Sweet (forthcoming).

5.   Jeffrey S. Wicken, "Theology and Science in the Evolving Cosmos: A Need for Dialogue," *Zygon* 23 (March 1988): 45.

6.   The quote arises from a conversation with David Bohm and Rupert Sheldrake, "Matter as a Meaning Field," in Renée Weber's *Dialogues with Scientists and Sages: The Search for Unity* (New York: Routledge and Kegan Paul, 1986), 113.

7.   Heinz R. Pagels, *The Cosmic Code: Quantum Physics as the Language of Nature* (New York: Simon and Schuster, 1982), 160-76.

8.   Allan Megill, *Prophets of Extremity: Nietzsche, Heidegger, Foucault, Derrida* (Berkeley: University of California Press, 1985), 291.

9.   Richard E. Brantley, "Charles Wesley's Experiential Art," *Eighteenth-Century Life* 11 (May 1987): 1-11. See also Brantley's award-winning *Locke, Wesley, and the Method of English Romanticism* (Gainesville: University Presses of Florida, 1984). His *Coordinates of Anglo-American Romanticism* is due out shortly.

10.   Maureen O'Hara, one of the most relentless critics of "pseudoscience" and "mythmongering," defines practioners of "recombinant information" as those who would "strip knowledge of both its context and concreteness, turning it into 'data' or bits of information that can be recombined without regard to any disciplinary integrity, rules of evidence, attention to questions of logical coherence, validity, or counter-evidence." See her "Science, Pseudoscience, and Mythmongering," in *Not Necessarily the New Age: Critical Essays*, ed. Robert Basil (Buffalo, N.Y.: Prometheus Books, 1988), 145-64, esp. 155.

11.   Wolfhart Pannenberg, "Spirit and Mind," *Mind in Nature: Nobel Conference XVII*, ed. Richard Q. Elvee (San Francisco: Harper and Row, 1982), 150; See also Kevin J. Sharpe's chapter entitled "Mysticism in Physics," in *Religion and Nature--With Charles Birch and Others*, ed. Sharpe and John M. Ker (Auckland, New Zealand: University of Auckland Chaplaincy, 1982), 48.

12.   The whole history of science has been a direct search for God; deliberate and
     conscious, until well into the eighteenth century, and since then unconscious, for
     the most part, because so much had been discovered about God by then that
     scientists began to think fit to change the name of the subject of their search. . . .
     Copernicus, Kepler, Galileo, Newton, Leibnitz and the rest did not merely believe
     in God in an orthodox sort of way, they believed that their work told humanity
     more about God than had been known before. (John Langdon-Davies, *Man and
     the Universe* [London: Harper, 1930], 10-11)
An excellent interdisciplinary study of the relationships between theology and the physical sciences is *Portraits of Creation: Biblical and Scientific Perspectives on the World's Formation*, by Howard J. Van Till et al. (Grand Rapids: Eerdmans, 1990).

13.   Rustum Roy, *Experimenting with Truth: The Fusion of Religion with Technology Needed for Humanity's Survival* (New York: Pergamon Press, 1981), 69.

14.   See the subtitle of the superb volume edited by Ted Peters, *Cosmos as Creation: Theology and Science in Consonance* (Nashville: Abingdon, 1989). Sir Arthur Stanley Eddington, commenting on the collapse of the determinism and materialism of the Newtonian world-view, stated that
     Religion first became possible for a reasonable scientific man about the year 1927.
     . . . If our expectation should prove well founded that 1927 has been the final
     overthrow of strict causality by Heisenberg, Bohr, Born and others, the year will
     certainly rank as one of the greatest epochs in the development of scientific
     philosophy. (Eddington, *The Nature of the Physical World* [Cambridge: Cambridge
     University Press, 1928; repr. Ann Arbor: University of Michigan Press, 1958], 350)
I was drawn to this quote by Erwin N. Hiebert in "Modern Physics and Christian Faith," *God and Nature: Historical Essays on the Encounter Between Christianity and Science*, ed. David C. Lindberg and Ronald L. Numbers (Berkeley: University of California Press, 1986), 432.

15.   Freeman J. Dyson began a recent paper entitled "Time without End: Physics and

Biology in an Open Universe" with this bold declaration: "I hope . . . to hasten the arrival of the day when eschatology, the study of the end of the universe, will be a respectable scientific discipline and not merely a branch of theology." As quoted in Robert John Russell's "Cosmology, Creation, and Contingency," in *Cosmos as Creation*, ed. T. Peters, 202; Russell quotes from Dyson's article as found in *Review of Modern Physics* 51 (1979): 447-48.

16.   John Steward Collis, *Living with a Stranger* (New York: George Braziller, 1979), 177.

17.   See Ilya Prigogine and Isabelle Stengers, *Order Out of Chaos: Man's New Dialogue with Nature* (Boulder, Colo.: New Science Library, 1984), 47.

18.   As quoted in Renée Weber, "Truth and Beauty," *Chrysalis* 4 (Spring 1989): 101.

19.   Menachem Kellner believes this is a false reading of Maimonides. He presents an alternative interpretation of the parable of the palace in *Maimonides on Human Perfection* (Atlanta: Scholars Press, 1990).

20.   A provocative portrayal of separationist and interactionist positions, with particular attention to the emergence in the last ten years of a "new interactionism" is William A. Rottschaefer's "The New Interactionism Between Science and Religion," *Religious Studies Review* 14 (July 1988): 218-24.

21.   See Huston Smith's *Beyond the Post-Modern Mind* (New York: Crossroad, 1982), 70-71. Psychologist/medical school professor Frances E. Vaughan makes a similar case to Smith's. See her remarks at a Swedenborgian conference on "Science and Spirituality," in Louis B. King, "The New Philosophy: Panel Discussion Highlights," *Chrysalis* 4 (Spring 1989): 73-74. I would further argue with Smith over whether theological and spiritual values have not already insinuated themselves into the core of scientific discourse, as apologist/philosopher James P. Moreland argues in *Christianity and the Nature of Science: A Philosophical Investigation* (Grand Rapids: Baker Book House, 1989).

22.   Maureen O'Hara also marshals powerful arguments against a synthesis of science and religion, insisting instead on the autonomy of local knowledge: "Different realms of reality require different methods of enquiry, different modes of thinking--different paradigms." Perhaps reflecting on philosopher/educator/logician Willard van Orman Quine's position that physics is 99 percent speculation and 1 percent observation, O'Hara is convinced that physics is the **least** likely source of contemporary knowledge and insight into the human predicament. See "Reflections in Sheldrake, Wilber, and 'New Science,'" *Journal of Humanistic Psychology* 24 (Spring 1987): 119; see also "Of Myths and Monkeys: A Critical Look at a Theory of Critical Mass," *Journal of Humanistic Psychology* 25 (Winter 1988): 73. From another angle, reviewer Edward Norman laments the "internal secularization" that comes as an "unhappy consequence" of the "vulgar scramble" to mix Christian truth and science. See his comments in "The Church's Many Foundations," *TLS: The Times Literary Supplement*, 21-27 September 1990, 1003.

23.   David Ray Griffin's, review of *Mind in Nature: Nobel Conference XVII*, *Zygon* 19 (March 1984): 108. See also Prigogine and Stengers's comment that "classical science, the mythical science of a simple, passive world, belongs to the past, killed not by philosophical criticism or empiricist resignation but by the internal development of science itself" (*Order Out of Chaos*, 55).

24.   See Max L. Stackhouse, "Politics and Religion" in *Encyclopedia of Religion*, ed. Mircea Eliade (New York: Macmillan, 1987), 11:408-23, esp. 413.

25.   See Rosabeth Moss Kanter, *When Giants Learn to Dance: Mastering the Challenge of Strategy, Management, and Careers in the 1990s.* (New York: Simon and Schuster, 1989).

26.   Jonathan Edwards, "The Justice of God in the Damnation of Sinners," in *The Works of President Edwards* (London: 1817; repr. New York: Burt Franklin, 1968), 6:361-98.

27.   Bernard J.F. Lonergan, *Insight: A Study of Human Understanding* (New York: Philosophical Library, 1957). See also Robert Sessions Woodworth's comment of sixty years ago on the methods of sound and vision engineers: "They have to depend on the method of impression, because they are not concerned simply with the physics of light or sound, but with the effects produced upon the human being who sees or hears." See his *Contemporary Schools of Psychology* (New York: Ronald Press, 1931), 22.

28. The difficulty of keeping boundaries erect in postmodern scholarship is wonderfully captured in anthropologist Loring M. Danforth's model study of *Firewalking and Religious Healing: The Anastenaria of Greece and the American Firewalking Movement* (Princeton: Princeton University Press, 1989), esp. chapter 9, "Contemporary Anthropology in a Postmodern World," (289-305), where he explores the "blurred boundaries" of self and other.

29. See Thomas F. Torrance's concluding chapter "The University Within a Christian Culture," in *The Christian Frame of Mind* (Edinburgh: Handsel Press, 1985), 49-62.

30. See the explication by Edward P.J. Corbett, *Classical Rhetoric for the Modern Student*, 2nd ed. (New York: Oxford University Press, 1971).

31. For a more poetic way of expressing this truth which judges "the problems, if we describe them accurately, are all private and small," see Wendell Berry, "The Futility of Global Thinking," *Harper's Magazine*, September 1989, 16-22, esp. 17.

32. John Briggs and F. David Peat, *Turbulent Mirror: An Illustrated Guide to Chaos Theory and the Science of Wholeness* (New York: Harper and Row, 1989), 131.

33. Alfred North Whitehead, *Religion in the Making*, Lowell Institute Lectures (New York: Macmillan, 1926).

34. As quoted in Bernard Bergonzi, T.S. *Eliot* (New York: Macmillan, 1972), 162.

35. See "Theological Guidelines: Sources and Criteria," *The Book of Discipline of the United Methodist Church, 1988* (Nashville: United Methodist Publishing House, 1988), 80-89; see also the earlier formulation in *The Book of Discipline of the United Methodist Church, 1972* (Nashville: United Methodist Publishing House, 1972), 75-79. The best study of this theological method is Donald A.D. Thorsen's *The Wesleyan Quadrilateral: Scripture, Tradition, Reason, and Experience as a Model of Evangelical Theology* (Grand Rapids: Francis Asbury Press, 1990).

36. Stephen Hawking, *A Brief History of Time* (New York: Bantam Books, 1988). For the role of non rational elements in mathematics, believed by Hawking to be the highest form of rationality, see *The Collected Works of Kurt Gödel*, ed. Solomon Feferman et al. (New York: Oxford University Press, 1986-date). Hawking does not represent New Light thinking for several reasons. First, he is an unrepentant modernist, an absolutist, and an advocate for the positivistic wing of science. Second, he despises mysticism or any movement of science into "meaning." Third, he is trying to prove or disprove God's existence, a rather arrogant pursuit in itself, solely by equation and evidence.

37. This is the analogy of Heinz R. Pagels who was executive director of the New York Academy of Sciences until his tragic death in a mountaineering accident. See his *Perfect Symmetry: The Search for the Beginning of Time* (New York: Simon and Schuster, 1985), 264. An excellent introduction to the phenomenon is Dennis Flanagan's chapter "Physics Seeks Its Holy Grail" in *Flanagan's Version: A Spectator's Guide to Science on the Eve of the 21st Century* (New York: Alfred A. Knopf, 1988), 30-61. For discussions of GUTs, see *Perfect Symmetry*, 267-84, and Michael Disney, *The Hidden Universe* (New York: Macmillan, 1985), 240-41. A dissenter to this attempt at unification is mathematician/physicist/astronomer/biologist Freeman J. Dyson. His 1985 Gifford lectures, *Infinite in All Directions* (New York: Harper and Row, 1988), celebrate the diversity underlying the structure of the universe over the great unifying physical theories of Newton, Maxwell, Einstein or Hawking.

38. In two earlier publications I made tentative probings into this quadrilateral. See "Can a Mainstream Change Its Course?" in *Liberal Protestantism: Realities and Possibilities*, ed. Robert S. Michaelson and Wade Clark Roof (New York: Pilgrim Press, 1986), 235-62; see also my "The Four Fundamentalisms of Oldline Protestantism," *Christian Century*, 13 March 1985, 266-70.

39. Some reviewers have gone now to recommending certain books be read from back to front. See Robert Royal's comments about Robert J. Lifton and Eric Markusen's *The Genocidal Mentality: Nazi Holocaust and Nuclear Threat* (New York: Basic Books, 1990) as found in *First Things*, January 1991, 55.

40. "I have taken as my patron saint St. Thomas of Didymus, who always insisted on an examination with his own hands," are the words of François de Voltaire, the personifier

of the Enlightenment whose thoughts were greatly influenced by Isaac Newton.

41. See "Thomas Merton's View of Monasticism," [delivered in Calcutta, October 1968], in *The Asian Journal of Thomas Merton*, ed. Naomi Burton, Patrick Hart, and James Laughlin (New York: New Directions, 1973), 308.

FIRST COMMANDMENT
(pages 15 - 55)

a. God's plea and Jeremiah's complaint as found in Jeremiah 2:7-8 and 12:4 (RSV).

b. "Making the Spiritual Connection," *Lear's* 2 (December 1989): 75.

c. Eugene Wigner, "Remarks on the Mind-Body Question," in *Symmetries and Reflections: Scientific Essays of Eugene P. Wigner* (Bloomington: Indiana University Press, 1967), 72.

d. Private correspondence with the author.

e. William Blake to Thomas Butts, 22 November 1802, in *The Letters of William Blake*, ed. Geoffrey Keynes, 3rd ed. (Oxford: Clarendon Press, 1980), 46.

f. Alexander Pope's proposed epitaph for Sir Isaac Newton, who died in 1717.

g. J.C. Squire, "Answer to 378," as quoted in *The Oxford Dictionary of Quotations*, 3rd ed. (New York: Oxford University Press, 1980), 517.

h. This self-referential paradox and iterative weapon was used by Captain Kirk to burn out alien mainframe semiconductors.

i. Alan Durning, "How Much is 'Enough'?" *World-Watch* 3 (November/December 1990): 15.

j. W.H. Auden, "Elegy for J.F.K.," in *Collected Poems*, ed. Edward Mendelson (New York: Random House, 1976), 567. Copyright by Edward Mendelson, William Meredith and Monroe K. Spears, executors of the Estate of W.H. Auden. Used by permission.

k. Jean-Paul Sartre, *Nausea*, translated by Lloyd Alexander (New York: New Directions, 1964), 39.

l. William H. Calvin, "Simulations of Reality: Deciding What to Do Next," in *Speculations*, ed. John Brockman, The Reality Club, vol. 1 (New York.: Prentice-Hall, 1990), 115.

m. *Pascal's Pensées*, with an English translation, brief notes and introduction by H.F. Stewart (New York: Modern Library, 1947), 114-15.

n. As quoted in Ralph Metzner, *Opening to Inner Light: The Transformations of Human Nature and Consciousness* (Los Angeles: Jeremy P. Tarcher, 1986), 75.

o. David, on human wickedness and divine guidance (Ps.36:9 NRSV); James, writing to the twelve tribes in the Dispersion (James 1:17 NRSV).

p. Erwin Chargaff, *Heraclitean Fire: Sketches From a Life Before Nature* (New York: Rockefeller University Press, 1978), 7.

q. As quoted in Metzner, *Opening to Inner Light*, 181.

r. Nelson Manfred Blake, "How to Learn History from Sinclair Lewis and Other Uncommon Sources," in *American Character and Culture in a Changing World: Some Twentieth-century Perspectives*, ed, John A. Hague (DeLand, Fla.: Everett Edwards Press, 1964), 47.

s. Soren Kierkegaard, as quoted in Martin E. Marty's *Context*, 15 October 1990, 3.

t. Judith Wechsler, ed., *On Aesthetics in Science* (Cambridge, Mass.: MIT Press, 1978), 1.

u. Arthur Rimbaud, "Bad Blood," in *Une Saison en Enfer and Le Bateau Ivre. A Season in Hell and The Drunken Boat*, trans. Louise Varése (Norfolk, Conn.: New Directions, 1945), 10-11.

v. As quoted in Thomas Ryan, *Wellness, Spirituality, and Sports* (New York: Paulist Press, 1986), 196.

w. Lawrence Ferlinghetti's poem "Olbers' Paradox," in his *Endless Life: Selected*

Poems (New York: New Directions Publishing Corp., 1981), 146. Copyright 1976 by Lawrence Ferlinghetti. Reprinted by permission of New Directions Publishing Corp.

1.　Paul Ehrlich, *The Machinery of Nature* (New York: Simon and Schuster, 1987); P. Ehrlich and Anne H. Ehrlich, *Extinction: The Causes and Consequences of the Disappearance of Species* (New York: Random House, 1981); P. Ehrlich and A.H. Ehrlich, **Earth** (New York: Franklin Watts, 1987); P. Ehrlich and Jonathan Roughgarden, *The Science of Ecology* (New York, Macmillan, 1987); Robert E. Ornstein and P. Ehrlich, *New World, New Mind: Changing the Way We Think to Save Our Future* (London: Methuen, 1989).

2.　See P. and A.H. Ehrlich, *Extinction*. For an excellent critique of the "modern" way of thinking and its role in engendering the environmental crisis, see Douglas C. Bowman, *Beyond the Modern Mind: The Spiritual and Ethical Challenge of the Environmental Crisis* (New York: Pilgrim Press, 1990). A survey of resources and studies for explaining the connection between ecology and theology can be found in my "State of the Ark" issue of *Bibelot* (vol.4, no.4-6 [1989]).

3.　As quoted in I. Wickelgren, "Plants Poised at Extinction's Edge," *Science News* 134 (10 December 1988): 372.

4.　Wes Jackson, *Altars of Unhewn Stone: Science and the Earth* (San Francisco: North Point Press, 1987), 31. Jackson calls "tend the garden" our "true first commandment." See also John Shelby Spong, *The Living Commandments* (New York: Seabury Press, 1977), 19-26, where the way Jewish law is broken down into 613 separate injunctions is discussed.

5.　Henry Wadsworth Longfellow, "Paul Revere's Ride," in his *Tales of a Wayside Inn* (1863).

6.　Lynn Francis, "The Empire State Building: The Construction and Aging of a Metaphor," *Journal of American Culture* 10 (Summer 1987): 83-90.

7.　See Frank Gehry, "Of Detritus and Denial," *New Perspectives Quarterly* 5 (Winter 1988-89): 59. "That's how it feels when people try to cover-up the crap of the cultures, when they try to avoid reality," is Gehry's more graphic way of putting it.

8.　Eric J. Hobsbawm, "The Missing History--A Symposium," *TLS: The Times Literary Supplement*, 23-29 June 1989, 690.

9.　I am indebted to my wonderful colleague Neal Fisher, President of Garrett-Evangelical Theological Seminary, for knowledge of this Chinese greeting.

10.　This analogy is the basis for the title of George Barna's book *The Frog and the Kettle: What the Christian Community Needs to Know About Life in the Year 2000* (Ventura, Calif.: Regal Books, 1990).

11.　This is the thesis of Ornstein and P. Ehrlich in their book *New World, New Mind*, the best treatment available of "the human mental system failing to comprehend the modern world."

12.　John Snow, *The Impossible Vocation: Ministry in the Mean Time* (Cambridge, Mass.: Cowley Publications, 1988).

13.　Roy A. Sorensen, *Blindspots* (Oxford: Clarendon Press, 1988), 1.

14.　Henryk Skolimowski, "Reverential Thinking," in *Through the '80s: Thinking Globally, Acting Locally*, ed. Frank Feather (Washington: World Future Society, 1980), 271-74.

15.　Arthur Koestler, *The Roots of Coincidence* (New York: Random House, 1972), 138-39.

16.　*National and International Religion Report*, 4 June 1990, 6.

17.　See Jerold J. Kreisman and Hal Straus, *I Hate You--Don't Leave Me: Understanding the Borderline Personality* (Los Angeles: The Body Press, 1989): "The price tag of social change has come in the form of stress and stress-related disorders, such as heart attacks, strokes, and hypertensions. We must now confront the possibility that mental illness has become part of the psychological price" (66).

18.　Jacob Needleman, *A Sense of the Cosmos: The Encounter of Modern Science and Ancient Truth* (Garden City, N.Y.: Doubleday, 1975: "Without active attention, is it ever possible for man to see the inner aspects of reality? Is it because of passive attention that he is beguiled by appearances, both with regard to the nature of the universe and the teachings which are offered to him?" (158).

19. James Clifford, *The Predicament of Culture: Twentieth-Century Ethnography, Literature, and Art* (Cambridge, Mass.: Harvard University Press, 1988), 9.

20. Pierre Teilhard de Chardin, *The Phenomenon of Man* (New York: Harper, 1959), 212.

21. Allan Megill, *Prophets of Extremity: Nietzsche, Heidegger, Foucault, Derrida* (Berkeley: University of California Press, 1985), 348.

22. The comparison with America's public school system is irresistible. Despite $300 billion spent on them annually, our antiquated public educational system fails to turn out enough people with the skills or knowledge to compete in today's world. No wonder 700,000 kids drop out of high school annually (that's one out of four teenagers in America who leave high school before receiving a diploma), or that our thirteen year olds trail most of their counterparts around the world in math and science.

23. For a fuller discussion of his "Uncertainty Principle", also known as the "Principle of Indeterminacy," see Werner Heisenberg, *Physics and Philosophy: The Revolution in Modern Science* (New York: Harper and Row, 1958).

24. Werner Heisenberg, *The Physicist's Conception of Nature* (New York: Harcourt, Brace, 1958). See also Charles W. Misner, Kip Thorne, and John Archibald Wheeler, *Gravitation* (San Francisco: W.H. Freeman 1973).

25. Jerome Bruner argues the case for our living amid a "cultural revolution" in *Actual Minds, Possible Worlds* (Cambridge, Mass: Harvard University Press, 1986): "We are living through a cultural revolution that shapes our image of the future in a way that nobody, however titanic, could have foreseen a half-century ago. It is a revolution whose shape we cannot sense, although we already sense its depth." (148).

26. Francis Fukuyama, "The End of History?" *National Interest* 3 (Summer 1989): 3-18. For a technologist's response to Fukuyama, see civil engineer Samuel C. Florman's "The End of History," *Technology Review* 93 (April 1990): 70.

27. George F. Will, "Europe's Second Reformation," *Newsweek*, 20 November 1989, 90.

28. Michael H. Hart, *The One Hundred: A Ranking of the Most Influential Persons in History* (Secaucus, N.J.: Citadel Press, 1987, c1978), 33-51. Hart ranks Muhammad first, Isaac Newton second, and Jesus Christ third.

29. See Hans Dieter Betz's "Cosmogony and Ethics in the Sermon on the Mount," in *Cosmogony and Ethical Order: New Studies in Comparative Ethics*, ed. Robin W. Lovin and Frank E. Reynolds (Chicago: University of Chicago Press, 1985), 158-76.

30. The best brief account of these shifts is in Peter Hodgson's *Revisioning the Church: Ecclesial Freedom in the New Paradigm* (Philadelphia: Fortress Press, 1988). Robert Wuthnow explores deftly the social and cultural changes of the Reformation and the Enlightenment in his magisterial *Communities of Discourse: Ideology and Social Structure in the Reformation, the Enlightenment, and European Socialism* (Cambridge, Mass.: Harvard University Press, 1989).

31. Frederick Ferré, *Shaping the Future: Resources for the Post-Modern World* (New York: Harper and Row, 1976), 1. See also Ervin Laszlo, "The Obsolescence of Modernism," in *Through the '80s*, ed. F. Feather, 279-84.

32. See my *When the Cat's Away . . . . : Paradigms Lost, Paradigms Regained* (Grand Rapids, Mich.: Eerdmans, forthcoming).

33. For Max Stackhouse's dissent from the convention that modern democracy emerges out of the French Enlightenment and Revolution, see his *Creeds, Society, and Human Rights: A Study in Three Cultures* (Grand Rapids, Mich.: Eerdmans, 1984).

34. David Tracy, "God, Dialogue and Solidarity: A Theologian's Refrain," *Christian Century*, 10 October 1990, 904. An excellent discussion of the prefix "post" can be found in constructive theologian/feminist critic Catherine Keller's "Toward a Postpatriarchal Postmodernity," in *Spirituality and Society: Postmodern Visions*, ed. David Ray Griffin (Albany: State University of New York Press, 1988):

The prefix **post** generates the dialectical tension of a double negative. Somehow out of the energy of critique and consciousness, the vision for the new is to emerge. ... With this desire comes a protectiveness, a sense that the new, like a seedling, is delicate and capable of being destroyed. ... This is evident even in the caution the term **postmodern** signals--as though to name too positively the difference coming about might be to foist upon it the same old presuppositions, to crush it inadvertently without still controlling modernity. (64-65)

35. The Möbius Strip, named for German mathematician/theoretical astronomer August F. Möbius, is a two-dimensional object (e.g, a paper strip) that, when twisted one-half turn and its ends held together, traces through three dimensions.

36. For a contrasting listing that inspired this one, see Hodgson, *Revisioning the Church*, 17. Donald W. Shriver, Jr., is the author of the warning against standing still, which leads him to revise Luther's famous "Here I stand" with "This way we walk." See his "Response to the Future of Mission in a Pluralistic World," *Theological Education* 27 (Autumn 1990), 51.

37. Alvin Toffler distinguishes the collapsing "Second Wave" industrial society or Machine Age with the emerging "Third Wave" society in the second volume of his trilogy that began with *Future Shock* (New York: Random House, 1970), continued with *The Third Wave* (New York: William Marrow, 1980), and is now complete in *Powershift* (New York: Bantam Books, 1990).

38. David B. Barrett, "Three Waves of Renewal," *International Bulletin of Missionary Research* 12 (July 1988): 119. See also C. Peter Wagner, *The Third Wave of the Holy Spirit: Encountering the Power of Signs and Wonders Today* (Ann Arbor: Servant Publishing, 1988).

39. The best short description of this process can be found in Toffler's "Science and Change," the Foreword to Ilya Prigogine and Isabelle Stengers's *Order Out of Chaos: Man's New Dialogue with Nature* (Boulder, Colo.: New Science Library, 1984), xiv-xvi. "Such physical or chemical structures are termed 'dissipative,' Toffler writes, "because compared with the simpler structures they replace, they require more energy to sustain them" (xv).

40. "To serve the present age/My calling to fulfill" are Charles Wesley's words from the second stanza of the hymn "A Charge to Keep I Have."

41. Rowan Williams, *The Truce of God* (New York: Pilgrim Press, 1983), 20-21.

42. Williams, *The Truce of God*, 24.

43. Williams, *The Truce of God*, 17.

44. Williams, *The Truce of God*, 24.

45. For the thesis that postmodernism is best interpreted through paradox, see Linda Hutcheon, *A Poetics of Postmodernism: History, Theory, Fiction* (New York: Routledge, 1988). See also her *The Politics of Postmodernism* (New York: Routledge, 1989). In *Paradoxicon* (Garden City N.Y.: Doubleday, 1983), Nicholas Falletta creatively explores the nature of privatized reasoning.

46. Edmund B. Keller, *Some Paradoxes of Paul* (New York: Philosophical Library, 1974), 8.

47. *Sebastian Franck: 280 Paradoxes or Wondrous Sayings*, trans. and introd. by E.J. Furcha (Lewiston, N.Y.: Edwin Mellen Press, 1986).

48. See R.M. Sainsbury, *Paradoxes* (New York: Cambridge University Press, 1988); see also Sorensen, *Blindspots*.

49. This is the theme of Marvin C. Shaw's *The Paradox of Intention: Reaching the Goal by Giving Up the Attempt to Reach It* (Atlanta: Scholars Press, 1988).

50. Gerald Graff, "The Myth of the Postmodernist Breakthrough," *TriQuarterly* 26 (1973): 384.

51. See Jackson, *Altars of Unhewn Stone*, esp. 11-16.

52. Conrad Cherry, "Boundaries and Frontiers for the Study of Religion: The Heritage of the Age of the University," *Journal for the American Academy of Religion* 57 (Winter 1989): 807-27, esp. 817.

53. Gibson Winter, *Community and Spiritual Transformation: Religion and Politics in a Communal Age* (New York: Crossroad, 1989), 95.

54. Miles Davis, *Miles: The Autobiography* (New York: Simon and Schuster, 1989), 411.

55. *The Unchurched American--10 Years Later* (Princeton, N.J.: Princeton Religious Research Center, 1988).

56. Russell Chandler, *Understanding the New Age* (Dallas: Word Publishing, 1989). The best interpreter of New Age thought is Catherine Albanese. See her "Religion and the American Experience: A Century After," *Church History* 57 (1988): 337-51; see also her *Nature Religion in America: From the Algonkian Indians to the New Age* (Chicago: University of Chicago Press, 1990), 153-98.

57. See "Have Modern Doctors Lost Their Souls?" The *Door* Interview with Richard Selzer, *Wittenberg Door*, Summer 1989, 27.

58. Robert Basil in his "Introduction" to *Not Necessarily the New Age*, ed. R. Basil (Buffalo: Prometheus Books, 1988), 10.

59. Peter Mullen, *The New Babel* (London: SPCK, 1987), 71.

60. See Aidan Kavanagh, *On Liturgical Theology: The Hale Memorial Lectures of Seabury-Western Theological Seminary, 1981* (New York: Pueblo Publishing Company, 1984).

61. See Gabriel Josipovici, *The Book of God: A Response to the Bible* (New Haven: Yale University Press, 1988).

62. See Huston Smith's introduction ("Does Spirit Matter?" in *Spirit Matters: The Worldwide Impact of Religion on Contemporary Politics*, ed. Richard L. Rubenstein, (New York: Paragon House, 1987), x.

63. Marianne Wiggins, *John Dollar: A Novel* (New York: Harper and Row, 1989), 210.

64. Thomas Berry's chapter entitled "The New Story," in *The Dream of the Earth* (San Francisco: Sierra Club Books, 1988), 123-37; Prigogine and Stengers, *Order Out of Chaos*, 36. Calls for "a new story" are coming from everywhere. See, as an example, Sean McDonagh's chapter entitled "The New Story," in *To Care for the Earth: A Call to a New Theology* (Santa Fe: Bear and Company, 1986), 77-103; Thomas E. Boomershine, *Story Journey: An Invitation to the Gospel of Storytelling* (Nashville: Abingdon Press, 1988); and Frederick Turner, "Natural Technology," *Chronicles* 14 (August 1990): 27.

65. Rosabeth Moss Kanter, *When Giants Learn to Dance: Mastering the Challenge of Strategy, Management, and Careers in the 1990s* (New York: Simon and Schuster, 1989), 175-76, 201-25.

66. Robert Wuthnow, *Communities of Discourse*, 3.

67. See Dean Charles K. Piehl's insightful review of *Communities of Discourse, Christian Century*, 10 October 1990, 912.

68. Mark Noll, "The Evangelical Enlightenment (1776-1865-1914) and the Task of Theological Education," in *Communications and Change in American Religious History*, ed. Leonard I. Sweet (forthcoming).

69. See William G. McLoughlin, *Revivals, Awakenings, and Reform: An Essay on Religion and Social Change in America, 1697-1977* (Chicago: University of Chicago Press, 1978).

70. Ornstein and P. Ehrlich, *New World, New Mind*, 10, 133.

71. Jonathan Edwards, "True Grace Distinguished from the Experience of Devils," in *The Works of President Edwards* (London: 1847; repr. New York: Burt Franklin, 1968), 8:124-25.

72. Edwards, "The True Excellency of a Gospel Minister," in *The Works of President Edwards* (1968) 10:496-512; see also his "Farewell Sermon," in *The Works of President Edwards: With a Memoir of his Life* (New York: S. Converse, 1829), 1:626-51, esp. 634.

73. Without faith, hope, and love being grounded in Jesus Christ, the light of theology becomes no different than the light of ecology.

74. John Archibald Wheeler, "Bohm, Einstein, and the Strange Lesson of the Quantum," in *Mind in Nature: Nobel Conference XVII*, ed. Richard Q. Elvee (San Francisco: Harper and Row, 1982), 4.

75. Dalai Lama and David Bohm, "Subtle Matter, Dense Matter," in *Dialogues with Scientists and Sages: The Search for Unity*, by Renée Weber (London: Routledge and Kegan Paul, 1986), 267.

76.   For light as the metaphor of consciousness, see Ernst Cassirer, *The Philosophy of Symbolic Forms*, trans. Ralph Manheim (New Haven: Yale University Press, 1955), 2:96-99.

77.   Ron Loewinsohn, "Jonathan Edwards' Opticks: Images and Metaphors of Light in Some of His Major Works," *Early American Literature* 8 (1973): 23.

78.   David Bohm, "The Implicate Order and the Super-implicate Order," in R. Weber, *Dialogues with Scientists and Sages*, 44.

79.   Edwin Scott Gaustad, *The Great Awakening in New England* (New York: Harper, 1957), 81. The best study of Jonathan Edwards's grasp of Enlightenment thought and his critique of these principles for the Christian faith and for American society is Robert W. Jenson's *America's Theologian: A Recommendation of Jonathan Edwards* (Oxford: Oxford University Press, 1988).

80.   The "new dark age" is used by Charles Colson in the subtitle of his book *Against the Night: Living in the New Dark Age* (Ann Arbor, Mich.: Servant Publications, 1989).

81.   The "missing mass" mystery is the subject of Welsh astronomer/space shuttle scientist Michael Disney's *The Hidden Universe* (New York: Macmillan, 1984), 3.

82.   Bruner, *Actual Minds, Possible Worlds*, 44.

83.   *Areopagitica: A Speech of Mr. John Milton for the Liberty of Unlicenc'd Printing To the Parliament of England* (London, 1644; rep. London: Percy Lund, Humphries, 1928), 29.

84.   Transcript of Public Affairs Television special *Facing Evil*, with Bill Moyers; executive producer, Joan Konner (New York: Journal Graphics, 1988), 3.

85.   Quoted in Benjamin Franklin, *Representative Selections*, with introduction, bibliography, and notes by Chester E. Jorgenson and Frank Luther Mott, rev. ed. (New York: Hill and Wang, 1962), cxxvii.

86.   I am grateful to David Spangler for his help in formulating this "new cell" understanding of New Light leadership.

87.   New Lights are always waiting and watching for "more lights." Max L. Stackhouse, *Apologia: Contextualization, Globalization and Mission in Theological Education* (Grand Rapids, Mich: Eerdmans, 1988), 214-15.

88.   Kenneth Clark, *What is a Masterpiece?* (London: Thames and Hudson, 1979), 9.

89.   See J.G. Taylor, ed., *Tributes to Paul Dirac* (Briston: Adam Hilger, 1987), 20, 45; see also Paul Davies, *God and the New Physics* (New York: Simon and Schuster, 1983), 220-21.

90.   Pierre Delattre, "Beauty and the Esthetics of Survival," *Utne Reader* 34 (July-August 1989): 64-67, esp. 70.

91.   In his introduction to *Jewish Way of Life and Thought* (New York: Ktav, 1981), Abraham Karp quotes Oliver Wendell Holmes II, to the effect that "Life is painting a picture, not doing a sum" (xxi).

92.   This is the argument of Douglas John Hall in his superb *Thinking the Faith: Christian Theology in a North American Context* (Minneapolis: Augsburg, 1989), 316-23.

93.   Clark, *What is a Masterpiece*, 11.

94.   Suzanne W. Morse, "The Role of Colleges and Universities in Developing a New Kind of Public Leader," *National Civic Review* 78 (November/December 1989): 439-55.

95.   Clark, *What is a Masterpiece*, 10-11.

96.   Clark, *What is a Masterpiece*, 12; see also 16, 20.

97.   See my "From Catacomb to Basilica: The Dilemma of Oldline Protestantism," *Christian Century*, 2 November 1988, 981-84.

98.   Clark, *What is a Masterpiece*, 39.

99.   Quoted in Russell Stannard, *Science and the Renewal of Belief* (London: SCM Press, 1982), 195.

100. Colin Wilson, *The Outsider* (Los Angeles: Jeremy P. Tarcher, 1956), 15.

101. James D.G. Dunn, *The Living Word* (Philadelphia: Fortress Press, 1987), 61.

102. This is the argument of consciousness historian/literature professor Fredric Jameson's, "Postmodernism and Consumer Society," in *The Anti-Aesthetic: Essays on Postmodern Culture*, ed. Hal Foster (Seattle: Bay Press, 1983), 111-25.

103. *Memoirs of Rev. Charles G. Finney*, written by himself (New York: Fleming H.

Revell, 1876), 7.

104. Clark, *What is a Masterpiece*, 43, 44.

105. Novelist/critic/English professor David Lodge says this of slang: "Slang is the poetry of ordinary speech in a precise linguistic sense; it draws attention to itself qua language, by deviating from accepted linguistic norms, substituting figurative expressions for literal ones, and thus 'defamiliarizes' the concept it signifies." See his "Where It's At: California Language," in *The State of the Language*, ed. Leonard Michaels and Christopher Ricks (Berkeley: University of California Press, 1980), 506.

106. The full Aristotle quote, as reproduced by Anthony Hecht, in "Master of Metaphor: Richard Wilbur's *New and Collected Poems*," *New Republic*, 16 May 1988, is as follows:

It is a great thing, indeed, to make a proper use of these poetical forms, as also of compound and strange words. But the greatest thing by far is to be a master of metaphor. It is one thing that cannot be learnt from others; and it is also a sign of genius, since a good metaphor implies an intuitive perception of the similarity in dissimilars. (23)

107. "Pathographies" is Joyce Carol Oates's term for biographies specializing in "dysfunction" and "disaster."

108. John W. Gardner, *On Leadership* (New York: Free Press, 1990), 159.

109. See Jane Wegscheider Hyman, *The Light Book: How Natural and Artificial Light Affect Our Health, Mood, and Behavior* (Los Angeles: Jeremy P. Tarcher, 1990).

INTERMEZZO I
(pages 56 - 58)

1. Susan Page, "All About Pigeons," *Atlantic*, November 1974, 5.

2. B.J. Frost, "The Optokinetic Basis of Head-bobbing in the Pigeon," *Journal of Experimental Biology* 74 (1978): 187-95.

LOGOS
(pages 59 - 96)

a.   As quoted in Ralph Metzner, *Opening to Inner Light: The Transformation of Human Nature and Consciousness* (Los Angeles: Jeremy P. Tarcher, 1986), 59.

b.   Charles A. Lindbergh, *Autobiography of Values* (New York: Harcourt Brace Jovanovich, 1977), 393.

c.   As quoted in Hugo Rahner *Man at Play* (New York: Herder and Herder, 1967), 23.

d.   As quoted by Orthodox Syrian Church Metropolitan/World Council of Churches' president Paulos Mar Gregorios, "Six Bible Studies," in *The New Faith-Science Debate: Probing Cosmology, Technology, and Theology*, ed. John M. Mangum (Minnesota: Fortress Press, 1989), 119.

e.   As quoted in *Sri Aurobindo, or The Adventure of Consciousness*, by Satprem, trans. from the French by Tehmi (San Francisco: Harper and Row, 1968), 301.

f.   Simone Weil, *First and Last Notebooks*, trans. Richard Rees (London: Oxford University Press, 1970), 280.

g.   Jesus, on the cause of division and discord, Luke 12:49 (NEB).

h.   "Roan Stallion," in *The Selected Poetry of Robinson Jeffers* (New York: Random House, 1938), 149. Reprinted with permission from the publisher.

i.   Mary Wollstonecraft, from her *A Vindication of the Right of Woman* (1792), as quoted in David Bromwich, "Passion the Mother of Reason," *TLS: The Times Literary Supplement*, 19-22 January 1990, 52.

j.   This Goethe quote is from his masterpiece *Faust* (1808-1839).

k.   "Sailing to Byzantium," *The Collected Works of W.B. Yeats* (New York: Macmillan, 1956), 191. Reprinted with permission of Macmillan Publishing Company. Copyright 1934 by Macmillan Publishing Company, renewed 1962 by Bertha Georgie Yeats.

l.   George Eliot, "Making Life Worthwhile," *Masterpieces of Religious Verse*, ed. James Dalton Morrison (New York: Harper, 1948), 361.

m.   This quote is Tom Wolfe's description of astronaut John Glenn's strange response during America's first orbital flight in February 1962, as presented in *The Right Stuff* (New York: Farrar, Straus, Giroux, 1980), 322-23.

n.   David W. Tracy, "God, Dialogue and Solidarity: A Theologian's Refrain," *Christian Century*, 10 October 1990, 904.

o.   Christian Zervos, "Conversation with Picasso," in *The Creative Process: A Symposium*, ed. Brewster Ghiselin (New York: New American Library, 1952), 56.

p.   Langdon Winner, *The Whale and the Reactor: A Search for Limits in an Age of High Technology* (Chicago: University of Chicago Press, 1986), 167.

q.   Alan Watts, *The Book: On the Taboo Against Knowing Who You Are* (New York: Collier Books, 1967), 9.

r.   Carlo Carretto, *Letters From the Desert* (Maryknoll, N.Y.: Orbis Books, 1972), 19.

s.   This couplet was composed by Luther to critique those who could or would not sing their Creator's praise. As quoted in Walter R. Wietzke, *The Primacy of the Spoken Word: Redemptive Proclamation in a Complex World* (Minneapolis: Augsburg, 1988), 159.

t.   "Fragments," aphorisms left unpublished at the time of his death, in *The Poems of Coventry Patmore*, ed. Frederick Page (New York: Oxford University Press, 1949), 486.

u.   Quoted in Wilfrid Mellers, *Bach and the Dance of God* (New York: Oxford University Press, 1981), 209.

v.   Alfred R. Orage, *On Love: Freely Adapted From the Tibetan* (Edmonds, Wash.: Holmes Publishing Group, 1989).

1.   For the interchangeability of spirit and mind, see Wolfhart Pannenberg, "Spirit and Mind," in *Mind in Nature: Nobel Conference XVII*, ed. Richard Q. Elvee (San Francisco: Harper and Row, 1982), 134-48.

2.   Quoted in Renée Weber, *Dialogues With Scientists and Sages: The Search for Unity* (London: Routledge and Kegan Paul, 1986), 231; see also Arthur Koestler, *The Roots of Coincidence* (New York: Random House, 1972), 59.

3.   This is argued forcefully in Michael Lockwood, *Mind, Brain, and the Quantum: The Compound 'I'* (New York: Blackwell, 1989).

4.   "The primacy of spiritual energy" is the first principle of a postmodern spirituality, according to social analyst/institute director Joe Holland: "The foundation of all social energies--economic, political, and cultural--is spiritual." See his "A Postmodern Vision of Spirituality and Society," in *Spirituality and Society: Postmodern Visions*, ed. David Ray Griffin (Albany: State University of New York Press, 1988), 49.

5.   This is only one of many brilliant insights that can be found in Erich Auerbach's *Mimesis: The Representation of Reality in Western Literature* (Princeton, N.J.: Princeton University Press, 1953).

6.   The best development of these "two modes of thought," which are presented as two ways of knowing, **both** means of cognitive functioning and constructing reality, is by Jerome Bruner in his book *Actual Minds, Possible Worlds* (Cambridge, Mass.: Harvard University Press, 1986). I shall be returning to this provocative study again and again throughout the book.

7.   David Boucher, *The Social and Political Thought of R.G. Collingwood* (New York: Cambridge University Press, 1989), 119.

8.   A fascinating if difficult study of the mathematical character of the word *logos* is mathematician/minister/philosopher Granville C. Henry, Jr.'s, *Logos: Mathematics and Christian Theology* (Lewisburg: Bucknell University Press, 1976).

9.   Sophiology was introduced into Russian religious thought via philosophical attempts to clarify the relationship between God and the world much earlier than it entered

America via feminist theology. Compare the chapter, "Religion and Philosophy: Vladimir Solovyev," in *Philosophy in Russia: From Herzen to Lenin and Berdyaev*, by Frederick C. Copleston (Notre Dame: University of Notre Dame, 1986), 201-40, with Susan Cady's *Sophia: The Future of Feminist Spirituality* (San Francisco: Harper and Row, 1986).

10.   I owe this observation to Susan Griffin, *Woman and Nature: The Roaring Inside Her* (New York: Harper and Row, 1987), xi.

11.   Quoted in Renée Weber, *Dialogues with Scientists and Sages*, 229.

12.   H.H. Price, *Thinking and Experience* (Cambridge, Mass.: Harvard University Press, 1953). For a flow of energy as the causal connection between the physical and the mental, see W.D. Hart, *The Engines of the Soul* (New York: Cambridge University Press, 1988).

13.   The best discussion of *Logos* doctrines is "Creator Spirit," chapter 9 of George S. Hendry's *Theology of Nature* (Philadelphia: Westminster Press, 1980), 163-74. The quotes are taken from 168 and 171.

14.   See English poet Christina Rossetti's "Who has Seen the Wind," which includes these lines: "But when the trees bow down their heads/The wind is passing by," (*The Complete Poems of Christina Rossetti*, ed. R.W. Crump [Baton Rouge: Louisiana State University Press, 1986], 2:42).

15.   For the problems raised by the marriage of evolutionary theory and philosophical reductionism, also known as the neo-Darwinian synthesis, see the collection of essays edited by David J. Depew and Bruce W. Weber entitled *Evolution at the Crossroads: The New Biology and the New Philosophy of Science* (Cambridge, Mass: MIT Press, 1985). The ways in which the values of eugenics adopted by the Nazi movement were shared by the international scientific community, including the United States, is explored by Robert Proctor, *Racial Hygiene: Medicine Under the Nazis* (Cambridge: Harvard University Press, 1988).

16.   See Mark Twain's "He was a good man in the **worst** sense of the term" or Henry David Thoreau's "If I knew for a certainty that a man was coming to my house with the conscious design of doing me good, I should run for my life." The greasiness of that word "good" is fingered by Thoreau: "The greater part of what my neighbors call good, I believe in my soul to be bad, and if I repent of anything, it is very likely to be my good behavior. What demon possessed me that I behaved so well?"

17.   *The Journal of the Rev. John Wesley*, ed. Nehemiah Curnock (London: Epworth Press, 1909, repr. 1938), 1:423.

18.   *The Journal of . . . John Wesley*, 1:472-76. The scripture passages are quoted from this text. Curnock tentatively identifies the lay person at Aldersgate as William Holland, a successful London painter.

19.   Jonathan Edwards, "The Pure in Heart Blessed," in *The Works of President Edwards* (Edinburgh: 1847; repr. New York: Burt Franklin, 1968), 10:363. Edwards credits the Cambridge Platonists for this phrase.

20.   John Stuart Mill, *Autobiography* (New York: Henry Holt, 1874), 137.

21.   David Bohm, "Creativity: The Signature of Nature," in R. Weber, *Dialogues with Scientists and Sages*, 99.

22.   It is faith that motivates us, according to G.C. Henry, Jr., to "use *logos*, reason, in its general character to secure a knowledge that *Logos*, word of God, exists in a particular way, which in itself **cannot be known** by rational categories." See *Logos: Mathematics and Christian Theology*, 111.

23.   William James, *The Varieties of Religious Experience: A Study in Human Nature* (New York: Longmans, Green, 1919), 508.

24.   For Wesley's vision of Christianity as *orthokardia* (right heart), see the illuminating study by Gregory S. Clapper, *John Wesley on Religious Affection: His Views on Experience and Emotion and Their Role in the Christian Life and Theology* (Metuchen, N.J.: Scarecrow Press, 1989), 154-56, 171-73. For a rationality of emotions, see Ronald De Sousa, "The Rationality of Emotions," in *Explaining Emotions*, ed. Amelie O. Rorty (Berkeley: University of California Press, 1980), 128-36.

25.   Jonathan Edwards, *Freedom of the Will*, ed. Paul Ramsey (New Haven: Yale

University Press, 1957), 133.

26.   See Sharon D. Welch's, chapter entitled "The Transformation of the Modern Episteme," in her *Communities of Resistance and Solidarity: A Feminist Theology of Liberation* (Maryknoll, N.Y.: Orbis, 1985), 9-14.

27.   James H. Forest, *Making Friends of Enemies: Reflections on the Teachings of Jesus* (New York: Crossroads, 1988), 27.

28.   The best definition of a "structure of experience" I have been able to find is this one from Bernard Meland's *Realities of Faith: The Revolution in Cultural Forms* (New York: Oxford University Press, 1962): A structure of experience is when we know we are "aware of [ourselves] existing in, participating in, and belonging to a cluster of interrelated events which make up [our lives] and the lives about [us], and which, at the level of creation itself, gathers in all lives that have ever existed" (193).

29.   Galway Kinnell, "The Gallows," in his *The Avenue Bearing the Initial of Christ into the New World* (Boston: Houghton Mifflin, 1974), 19.

30.   Research psychologist Mihaly Csikszentmihalyi is chairman of the Department of Behavioral Sciences at the University of Chicago. See his *Beyond Boredom and Anxiety: The Experience of Play in Work and Games* (San Francisco: Jossey-Bass, c1977), 36, 22.

31.   See Csikszentmihalyi, *Beyond Boredom and Anxiety*, especially his chapter on "Effects of Flow Deprivation," 161-78.

32.   See Murray Code's explication of Whitehead's ontological principle in *Order and Organism: Steps to a Whiteheadian Philosophy of Mathematics and the Natural Sciences* (Albany: State University of New York Press, 1985).

33.   Csikszentmihalyi specializes in the study of "flow states." See his marvelous work *Flow: The Psychology of Optimal Experiences* (New York: Harper and Row, 1990). A fine definition of "flowing" can be found in Hans Lenk, "Sport Between Zen and the Self," in *Sport*, Concilium 205, ed. Gregory Baum and John Coleman (Edinburgh: T. & T. Clark, 1989), 119-30. Psychologist Abraham Maslow defined a peak experience as "a moment when a person's powers are at their height and he becomes a spontaneous, coordinated, efficient organism functioning with a great flow of power that is so peculiarly effortless that it may become like play." Quoted in Thomas Ryan, *Wellness, Spirituality, and Sports* (New York: Paulist Press, 1986). 135.

34.   Alan W. Watts, *The Wisdom of Insecurity* (New York: Pantheon Press, 1951), 9, as quoted in Marvin C. Shaw's *The Paradox of Intention: Reaching the Goal by Giving Up the Attempt to Reach It* (Atlanta, Ga.: Scholars Press, 1988), 5. A systematic and illuminating exposition of Watts's thought can be found in Michael Brannigan's *Everywhere and Nowhere: The Path of Alan Watts* (New York: Peter Lang, 1988).

35.   For an experiment that demonstrates how touch therapy can change hemoglobin content in the blood, see Dolores Kreiger, *The Therapeutic Touch: How to Use Your Hands to Help or to Heal* (Englewood Cliffs, N.J.: Prentice-Hall, 1979), 92; see also, Patricia Heidt and Marianne Borelli, *Therapeutic Touch: A Book of Readings* (New York: Springer, 1980).

36.   Peter Mullen, *The New Babel* (London: SPCK, 1987), 98.

37.   The best treatments of aesthetic forms are Hans Urs von Balthasar's multi-volume *The Glory of the Lord: A Theological Aesthetics* (New York: Crossroad Publications, 1982-date); Frank Burch Brown's, *Religious Aesthetics: A Theological Study of Making and Meaning* (Princeton, N.J.: Princeton University Press, 1989); James Alfred Martin, Jr.'s, *Beauty and Holiness: The Dialogue between Aesthetics and Religion* (Princeton, N.J.: Princeton University Press, 1990). For Robert J. Sternberg, see his *The Triangle of Love: Intimacy, Passion, Commitment* (New York: Basic Books, 1988).

38.   George Gallup, Jr., and Jim Castelli *The People's Religion: American Faith in the 90s* (New York: Macmillan, 1989).

39.   Peter L. Berger, *The Sacred Canopy: Elements of a Sociological Theory of Religion* (Garden City, N.Y.: Doubleday, 1967).

40.   Joseph Campbell, *The Power of Myth* (New York: Doubleday, 1988), 3. I want to thank Parker Palmer for first steering me in Campbell's direction.

41.   Robert Bellah, *Habits of the Heart: Individualism and Commitment in American*

Life (Berkeley: University of California Press, 1985).

42.	This quote is Baudrillard's response to an East Village correspondent reporting to the Swiss art journal *Parkett*. See his *America*, trans. by Chris Turner (New York: Verso, 1989). Also see Mark Poster's provocative introduction to his edition of Baudrillard's *Selected Writings*, trans. by Jacques Mourrain (Stanford, Calif.: Stanford University Press, 1988), 1-9. The best single treatment of Baudrillard is Douglas Kellner's *Jean Baudrillard: From Marxism to Postmodernism and Beyond* (Stanford, Calif.: Stanford University Press, (1989).

43.	Saul Bellow, *Mr. Sammler's Planet* (Greenwich, Conn.: Fawcett Publications, Inc. 1969).

44.	Koestler, *The Roots of Coincidence*. For the joining of mysticism and the new physics, see Michael Talbot, *Mysticism and the New Physics* (New York: Bantam Books, 1980); see also John A. Schumacher and Robert M. Anderson, "In Defense of Mystical Science," *Philosophy East and West* 29 (January 1979): 73-90; Martin Lebowitz, "Physics and Mysticism: The Twain Meet" [review of *The Tao of Physics*, by Fritjof Capra], *Virginia Quarterly Review* 52 (Autumn 1976): 734-36. The best critical review of the bibliography in this area can be found in the "Notes" of Kevin J. Sharpe's "Mysticism in Physics," in *Religion and Nature*, ed. Sharpe and John M. Ker (Auckland: The University of Auckland Chaplaincy, 1982), 49-52.

45.	Quoted in Ignacio Larrañaga, *Sensing Your Hidden Presence: Toward Intimacy with God* (Garden City, N.Y.: Image Books, 1987), 11.

46.	This I learned from Josiah Royce, *The World and the Individual: First Series: The Four Historical Concepts of Being* (New York: Dover Publications, 1959): "Mysticism defines Real Being as wholly within Immediate Feeling" (86).

47.	The first person I heard use this phrase was Anglican Bishop of Edinburgh Richard Holloway who wrote of "peeping Tom religion" in his book *New Vision of Glory* (New York: Seabury Press, 1974).

48.	For the Enlightenment's encouragement of "spectatoring," see David Marshall, *The Surprising Effects of Sympathy: Marivaux, Diderot, Rousseau and Mary Shelley* (Chicago: University of Chicago Press, 1988).

49.	Robert S. Root-Bernstein's "Ends & Means" column entitled "Sensual Education," *The Sciences* 30 (September/October 1990): 12-14.

50.	*The Complete Poems of Emily Dickinson*, ed. Thomas H. Johnson (Boston: Little, Brown, 1960), 39-40.

51.	Abner Shimony, "Controllable and Uncontrollable Non-locality," in *Foundations of Quantum Mechanics in the Light of New Technology*, ed. S. Kamefuchi et al. (Tokyo: Physical Society of Japan, 1984), 225-30. These are the proceedings of the first International Symposium of Quantum Mechanics in the Light of New Technology.

52.	Henry P. Stapp, "Quantum Nonlocality and the Description of Nature," in *Physical Consequences of Quantum Theory: Reflections on Bell's Theorem*, ed. James T. Cushing and Ernan McMullen (Notre Dame, Ind.: University of Notre Dame Press, 1989), 159.

53.	The best book to bring Bohr's "Complimentarity Principle" to bear on the spiritual journey is John L. Hitchcock's *Atoms, Snowflakes and God: The Convergence of Science and Religion* (Wheaton, Ill.: Theosophical Publishing House, 1986).

54.	Henryk Skolimowski's important work in a participatory methodology is discussed by Willis W. Harmon in "The Need for a Restructuring of Science," *ReVision* 11 (Fall 1988): 15-16.

55.	Brian Swimme, *The Universe Is a Green Dragon: A Cosmic Creation Story* (Santa Fe: Bear and Company, 1984).

56.	Peter Berger, *The Heretical Imperative: Contemporary Possibilities of Religious Affirmation* (Garden City, N.Y.: Anchor Press, 1979), 52.

57.	T.S. Eliot, *Four Quartets*, "Little Gidding," V, in *The Complete Poems and Plays, 1909-1950* (New York: Harcourt, Brace, 1958), 145.

58.	For an account of Pascal's 1654 "Night in November," see Blaise Pascal, *Thoughts, An Apology for Christianity*, ed. by Thomas S. Kepler (New York: World Publishing Company, 1955), 8-10.

59.   Nick Herbert lists eight distinct varieties of quantum realities. See his *Quantum Reality: Beyond the New Physics* (Garden City, N.Y.: Anchor Press, 1985), 156-97.

60.   From Hymn no. 490 in *A Collection of Hymns for the Use of the People Called Methodists*, repr. in *The Works of John Wesley* (Oxford: Clarendon Press, 1983), 7:678.

61.   Catherina Halkes, "Feminism and Spirituality." *Spirituality Today* 40 (Fall 1988): 234-35.

62.   "Prophets Who Cannot Sing," *The Poems of Coventry Patmore*, ed., Frederick Page (New York: Oxford University Press, 1949), 437.

63.   Henrik Ibsen, "Caesar's Apostasy," in *Emperor and Galilean: A World-Historical Drama*, vol. 5 of *The Collected Works of Henrik Ibsen* (New York: Charles Scribner's Sons, 1911), 212.

64.   See Eduard Schillebeeckx, *Jesus: An Experiment in Christology* (New York: Seabury Press, 1979), 160. For this view Schillebeeckx draws on Étienne Trocmé's, *Jesus as Seen by His Contemporaries* (Philadelphia: Westminster Press, 1973), 90-91.

65.   Ilya Prigogine, "The Reenchantment of Nature," in R. Weber, *Dialogues with Scientists and Sages*, 193. One of the best studies on Christian worship is *Dance as Religious Studies*, ed. Doug Adams and Diane Apostolos-Cappadona (New York: Crossroad, 1990).

66.   The quote is from Francis Baur, *Life in Abundance: A Contemporary Spirituality* (New York: Paulist Press, 1983), 256. Baur continues: "This is perhaps the gentlest and truest of images for spirituality that we will ever discover." See also T. Ryan, *Fasting Rediscovered: A Guide to Health and Wholeness for Your Body-Spirit* (New York, Paulist Press, 1981); T. Ryan, *Wellness, Spirituality, and Sports*; and T. Ryan, "Towards a Spirituality for Sports," in *Sport*, 111.

67.   The popular song "The Lost Chord," with words by Adelaide Procter and music by Sir Arthur Sullivan, was the sole outward expression of Sullivan's grief over the death of his brother Frederick.

68.   Wilfrid Mellers, *Bach and the Dance of God* (New York: Oxford University Press, 1981), 193, 242, 275.

69.   Stanzas 3, 7, 8, and 11 of the hymn "Methodist," in *A General Selection of the Newest and Most Admired Hymns and Spiritual Songs, Now in Use*, comp. Stith Mead (Richmond: Printed by Seaton Grantland, 1807), 151-53. See also Winthrop S. Hudson, "Shouting Methodists," *Encounter* 29 (1968): 73.

70.   As quoted in William T. Ellis, *"Billy" Sunday: The Man and His Message, With His Own Words Which Have Won Thousands for Christ* (Philadelphia: Winston, 1914), 261, 78.

71.   See Richard Cartwright Austin, *Baptized into Wilderness: A Christian Perspective on John Muir* (Atlanta: John Knox Press, 1987); see also Esther Lanigan Stineman, *Mary Austin: Song of a Maverick* (New Haven: Yale University Press, 1989).

72.   Lynn White, "Historical Roots of our Ecological Crisis," *Science* 155 (10 March 1967): 1206-7.

73.   John B. Cobb, Jr., *Is It Too Late? A Theology of Ecology* (Beverly Hills, Calif.: Bruce, 1972), 48-53. René Dubos, in his *A God Within* (New York: Charles Scribner's Sons, 1972), 168, backs away from Francis of Assisi as the patron saint of conservation, proposing instead Benedict of Nursia. So to does Robertson Davies in his *The Rebel Angels* (New York: Viking Press, 1982):

> People have tried to assure me that St. Francis was rich in humor, but I don't believe it. He was merry, perhaps, but that is something else. And there have been moments when I have wondered if St. Francis were not just the tiniest bit off his nut. Didn't eat enough, which is not necessarily a path to holiness. How many visions of Eternity have been born of low blood-sugar? (As quoted in W. Cary McMullen, "Villainy, Humor, and Heresy," *Theology Today* 46 [October 1989]: 286).

74.   Quoted in Peter Singer, *Animal Liberation: A New Ethic for the Treatment of Animals* (New York: New York Review, 1975), 215. Saint Francis also ate flesh foods.

75.   David Tracy is one of the few if not the only theologian to argue that Francis was "a Christian of such excess and challenge to ordinary, even good, Christian ways of understanding all of God's creation as beloved that we still cannot see him clearly." See his

"God, Dialogue and Solidarity: A Theologian's Refrain," *Christian Century*, 10 October 1990, 904. The best starting point for understanding Francis's views of the natural world is Roger D. Sorrell, *St. Francis of Assisi and Nature: Tradition and Innovation in Western Christian Attitudes Toward the Environment* (New York: Oxford University Press, 1988).

76.   Marion Hatchett, in his *Commentary on the American Prayer Book* (New York: Seabury Press, 1980), states that "the prayer attributed to St. Francis is by an unknown author" and "cannot be traced back earlier than the present century" (568). See also Simon Tugwell, *Ways of Imperfection: An Exploration of Christian Spirituality* (Springfield, Ill.: Templegate Publishers, 1985), 125.

77.   "There may be a road to truth which has nothing to do with experience," Ilya Prigogine admits for the sake of argument. "But I have nothing to say about that. It's not my domain and therefore I cannot address such questions." See Prigogine, "The Reenchantment of Nature," 186.

78.   With the words and music composed in 1953 by Artie Glenn, "Crying in the Chapel" became a million-seller for Elvis Presley in 1965. Copyright: Valley Publishers, Inc. New York, N.Y. 10019.

79.   X.J. Kennedy, *Cross Ties: Selected Poems* (Athens: University of Georgia Press, 1985), 159. Reprinted by permission of the publisher.

80.   This is Brad Edmondson's phrase as found in *Whole Earth Review*, Spring 1987.

81.   Carl Jung to William G. W----, 30 January 1961, as reprinted in *Re-Vision* 10 (Fall 1987): 21.

82.   See Ronald K. Siegel's chapter, "The Fourth Drive: Motivation for Intoxication," in his *Intoxication: Life in Pursuit of Artificial Paradise* (New York: E.P. Dutton, 1989), 207-27, esp. 207. For Siegel the human body is designed "to respond to chemical intoxicants in much the same way it responds to rewards of food, drink, and sex" (10), which are for him the other three drives. See also Arianna Stassinopoulous Huffington's essay "The Fourth Instinct," *Lear's* 2 (December 1989): 76-79.

83.   Thomas Merton, *Conjectures of a Guilty Bystander* (Garden City, N.Y.: Doubleday, 1966), 260. See also the excellent article by Belden C. Lane, "Merton as Zen Clown," *Theology Today* 46 (October 1989): 256-68.

84.   *New York* magazine, as quoted in Laurence Shames's "What a Long Strange (Shopping) Trip It's Been: Looking Back at the 1980s," *Utne Reader* 35 (September/October 1989): 66.

85.   John P. Robinson, "When the Going Gets Tough," *American Demographics*, February 1989, 50.

86.   "But I struck one chord of music, Like the sound of a great amen" are lines from Sullivan and Procter's "The Lost Chord." The song concludes: "It may be that only in heav'n I shall hear that grand amen."

PATHOS
(pages 101 - 163)

a.   Thomas Ryan, *Wellness, Spirituality, and Sports* (New York: Paulist Press, 1986), 188.

b.   Mary Austin, *Land of Little Rain* (Boston: Houghton Mifflin, 1903), 6.

c.   This poem was the frontispiece to Alice Corbin Henderson, *Red Earth: Poems of New Mexico* (Chicago: Ralph Fletcher Seymour, 1920), 3. Alice Corbin was the wife of the Southwest artist William Penhallow Henderson.

d.   As quoted in Robert D. Young, *Religious Imagination: God's Gift to Prophets and Preachers* (Philadelphia: Westminster Press, 1979), 128.

e.   Dorothy Sayers, *The Whimsical Christian: 18 Essays* (New York: Macmillan, 1978), 48.

f.   Victor J. Papanek and James Hennessey, *How Things Don't Work* (New York: Pantheon Books, 1977), 27.

g.   "A Prayer for Old Age," *The Collected Poems of W.B. Yeats* (New York: Macmillan, 1956), 281. Reprinted with permission of Macmillan Publishing Company. Copyright 1934 by Macmillan Publishing Company, renewed 1962 by Bertha Georgie Yeats.

h.   These words are printed on the title page of many of the editions of E.M. Forster's *Howards End* (e.g., New York: Vintage Books, 1954). See also chapter 6 ("Only connect....") of Edmund R. Leach's B.B.C. 1967 Reith Lectures, *A Runaway World?* (New York: Oxford University Press, 1968), 77-92.

i.   "Windsor Forest" [1713], *The Complete Poetical Works of Pope* (Boston: Houghton Mifflin, 1903), 28.

j.   Quoted in David M. Guss, ed., *The Language of the Birds: Tales, Texts, and Poems of Interspecies Communication* (San Francisco: North Point Press, 1985), ix.

k.   From the letter "without father, without mother, without genealogy," Heb. 11:16 (NRSV)

l.   As quoted by David Bohm, "The Implicate Order and the Super-implicate Order," in Renée Weber, *Dialogues with Scientists and Sages: The Search for Unity* (London: Routledge and Kegan Paul, 1986), 30.

m.   William Cowper as quoted in Richard Gregory, *Discovery, or the Spirit and the Service of Science* (London: Macmillan, 1916), 56.

n.   A psalm for David when he was in the Wilderness of Judah, Psalm 63:1 (NJB).

o.   Arne Næss, *Ecology, Society, and Lifestyle: Ecosophy* (Cambridge: Cambridge University Press, 1989), 175; quoting statistics from Paul R. and Anne Ehrlich, *Population, Resources, Environment: Issues in Human Ecology* (San Francisco: W.H. Freeman, 1970), 180.

p.   Aldo Leopold, "The Land Ethic," in *A Sand Country Almanac and Sketches Here and There* (New York: Oxford University Press, 1949), 216.

q.   E.P. Sanders, *Jewish Law from Jesus to the Mishnah: Five Studies* (Philadelphia: Trinity Press International, 1990), 323.

r.   Frederick Turner, "Natural Technology," *Chronicles* [Rockford, Ill.] 14 (August 1990): 30.

s.   See Jean Renoir, *Renoir on Renoir: Interviews, Essays, and Remarks* (London: Cambridge University Press, 1989), 114. Two of his greatest masterpieces are "Grand Illusion" (1937) and "Rules of the Game" (1939).

t.   Pharisees' judgment on Jesus, Matt.12:25 (NKJV) and God's judgment on Israel, Hos. 10:2 (Douay)

u.   C.S. Lewis to T.S. Eliot, 25 May 1962, declining his invitation to comment on the *New English Bible*. See *Letters of C.S. Lewis*, ed., with a Memoir by W.H. Lewis (London: Geoffrey Bles, 1966), 304.

v.   As quoted by Stephanie Mills in "Salons and Beyond," *Utne Reader*, March/April, 1991, 77.

w.   Matt. 18:10 (RSV) I am indebted to William Kincaid, a lay leader from First United Methodist Church, Ann Arbor, Michigan, for this insight.

x.   A reminder of faith in the olden days, Heb. 11:27 (NJB).

y.   See England's Royal Military Academy mathematics professor Joseph Sylvester's, "Algebraical Researches Containing a Disquisition on Newton's Rule for the Discovery of Imaginary Roots," *Philosophical Transactions of the Royal Society of London* 154 (1864): 613n.

z.   Quoted in Dolores LaChapelle, *Earth Wisdom* (Los Angeles: Guild of Tutors Press, 1978), 9.

aa.   Alexander Pope, *An Essay on Criticism* (1711), as quoted in *Words About Music: An Anthology*, sel. and ed. John Amis and Michael Rose (London: Faber, 1989), 355.

bb.   Carnegie said this to answer a question on why he refused to give money for church construction but donated seven million dollars for church organs. Quoted in Burton J. Hendrick, *The Life of Andrew Carnegie* (Garden City, N.Y.: Doubleday, 1932), 2:261.

cc.   William Shakespeare, *The Merchant of Venice* (1596-1597), act V, scene 1, line 83.

dd.   Jacket notes to Bob Dylan's *Bringing It all Back Home* (New York: Columbia Records, 1965).

ee.   Lewis Thomas, *The Lives of a Cell: Notes of a Biology Watcher* (New York: Viking

Press, 1974), 20-22.

1.   This phrase is from Charles Wesley's Christmas hymn "Hark! the Herald Angels Sing."

2.   Belden C. Lane, *Landscapes of the Sacred: Geography and Narrative in American Spirituality* (New York: Paulist Press, 1988), vii.

3.   For the cutting down of Longfellow's chestnut-tree, see "Home and Foreign Gossip," *Harper's Weekly*, 13 May 1876, 387. The "old mills" serve as a reflection of Colonial refinement. First built to provide the basics of food and shelter for a village (sawmills, gristmills, fullingmills), they were later used to provide the cultural refinements of life that a more developed society could afford (papermills, spicemills, hatters' establishments). "Like old clothes or left-over rituals, they were nicer when 'done over.'" See Marion Nicholl Rawson, *Little Old Mills* (New York: E. P. Dutton, 1935), 326.

4.   See David R. Williams, *Wilderness Lost: The Religious Origin of the American Mind* (Selinsgrove: Susquehanna University Press, 1987).

5.   Mary Austin, *The Land of Little Rain* (Boston: Houghton Mifflin, 1903), 16. See also the review article "Mary Austin, 'The Land of Little Rain,'" *Atlantic Monthly* 91 (January 1903): 99.

6.   Jean Baudrillard, *America* (London: Verso, 1988), 5.

7.   Page Stegner, *Outposts of Eden: A Curmudgeon at Large in the American West* (San Francisco: Sierra Book Club, 1989), 51.

8.   Paul Gruchow, *The Necessity of Empty Places* (New York: St. Martin's Press, 1989).

9.   There are any number of excellent accounts of Christians making desert pilgrimages. One of my favorites is by lawyer/hiker David Douglas, *Wilderness Sojourn: Notes in the Desert Silence* (San Francisco: Harper and Row, 1987), who presents the desert as, in his words, "a house of prayer."

10.   Ephraim Radner, "From 'Liberation' to 'Exile': A New Image for Church Mission," *Christian Century*, 18 October 1989, 933.

11.   Belden C. Lane, "Fierce Landscapes and the Indifference of God," *Christian Century*, 11 October 1989, 910.

12.   Austin, *The Land of Little Rain*, 21.

13.   Three desert dwellers in particular--June and Taylor McConnell and Kirstin Hardenbrook--helped me understand more fully the spirituality of the desert.

14.   Donald B. Rogers, "Coyotes and Sheep: What the Exile Teaches the Church about Ecological Education," *Journal of Theology* 94 (1990): 7-19.

15.   Rabbi/theologian/storyteller Lawrence Kushner makes an intriguing contrast between the Jewish and Christian traditions precisely at this point in *The River of Light: Spirituality, Judaism, and the Evolution of Consciousness* (San Francisco: Harper and Row, 1981).

> For Christianity, the central problem is how God could have become person. How spirit could transform itself into matter. Word become flesh. Consciousness become protoplasm. The direction is from the top down. For Judaism, on the other hand, the problem is how humanity could possibly attain to God's word and intention. How matter could raise itself to spirit. How simple desert souls could hear the word. Human substance attain consciousness. The intention is "to permeate matter and raise it to spirit." The direction is from the bottom up. Perhaps the two traditions, one moving down, the other moving up, are destined to meet in the divinity of humanity. (82)

16.   Theologian/theosophist/biblical scholar/natural scientist/pietist Friedrich Oetinger was one of eighteenth-century Württemberg's leading ecclesiastical figures. Jürgen Moltmann uses Oetinger's dictum as a chapter title in the second volume of his five-volume work on "mission and theology." See *God in Creation: A New Theology of Creation and the Spirit of God* (San Francisco: Harper and Row, 1985), 245.

17.   This is why my discomfort with editor/speechwriter/conservationist/social visionist George Gilder's phrase "the overthrow of matter" to describe the quantum vision. See

part one, "The Overthrow of Matter," of his *Microcosm: The Quantum Revolution in Economics and Technology* (New York: Simon and Schuster, 1989), 15-57.

18.   See, for example, Richard Sennett, *The Fall of Public Man* (New York: Alfred A. Knopf, 1977).

19.   Psychoanalyst/educational theorist/institute director Francis A.J. Ianni contends that the much publicized "adolescent problems" are less caused by a rebelliousness toward adult society than by the "fragmentation of the adolescent experience" due to the loss of traditional communities. See his *The Search for Structure: A Report on American Youth Today* (New York: Free Press, 1989), 169.

20.   For a sensitive probing of the postmodern quest for community pitched to a more popular audience, see *Common Cause Magazine* editor Deborah Baldwin's "Creating Community," *Common Cause Magazine* 6 (July/August 1990): 15-19, 39.

21.   See Peter Steinhart, "Personal Boundaries," *Audubon* 88 (March 1986): 10.

22.   As quoted in Douglas G. Flemons, *Completing Distinctions* (Boston: Shambhala, 1990).

23.   In the words of Biblical theologian J. Christiaan Beker, Paul's "emphasis is on communal life-style, not on individual existence. . . . The 'works of the flesh' (Gal. 5:19) and 'the fruit of the Spirit' (Gal. 5:22) are predominantly social vices and virtues that are primarily addressed to the community as a whole and must guard its inner cohesion." See his *Paul the Apostle* (Philadelphia: Fortress Press, 1980), 306.

24.   Vincent P. Branick, *The House Church in the Writings of Paul* (Wilmington, Del.: Michael Glazier, 1989), 76.

25.   See Adam Blatner and Allee Blatner, *The Art of Play: An Adult's Guide to Reclaiming Imagination and Spontaneity* (New York: Human Sciences Press, 1988), 163.

26.   See also these words of conservationist John Muir: "When we try to pick out anything by itself, we find it hitched to everything else in the universe. . . . The whole wilderness is unity and interrelation is alive and familiar." As quoted in Thomas Ryan, *Wellness, Spirituality, and Sports* (New York: Paulist Press, 1986), 189-90.

27.   Anna F. Lemkow, *The Wholeness Principle: Dynamics of Unity Within Science, Religion and Society* (Wheaton, Ill.: Theosophical Publishing House, 1990).

28.   See Peter Russell's *The Awakening Earth: Our Next Evolutionary Leap* (London: Routledge and Kegan Paul, 1982), 170-71.

29.   Andrew Sullivan, "Washington Diarist" column "Not Everybody Does It," *New Republic*, 31 August 1987, 43.

30.   "Of the Church," in *The Works of John Wesley* (Nashville: Abingdon Press, 1986), 3:46.

31.   Leander E. Keck, *Paul and His Letters* (Philadelphia: Fortress, 1979), 60.

32.   See Patrick J. Brennan, *Re-Imagining the Parish: Base Communities, Adulthood, and Family Consciousness* (New York: Crossroad, 1990), for some good suggestions on how to restore congregational life to the people.

33.   Robert J. Banks, *Paul's Idea of Community: The Early House Churches in Their Historical Settings* (Grand Rapids, Mich.: Eerdmans, 1980), 52-70.

34.   Keck, *Paul and His Letters*, 64.

35.   Dietrich Bonhoeffer, *The Communion of Saints: A Dogmatic Inquiry into the Sociology of the Church* (New York: Harper and Row, 1963), 160.

36.   Peter B. Hinchliff, *Holiness and Politics* (Grand Rapids: Eerdmans, 1983), 121.

37.   Georges Florovsky, *The Byzantine Fathers of the Fifth Century*, ed. Richard S. Haugh (Vaduz: Büchervertriebsanstalt, 1987), 56. Florovsky is quoting from 2 Clement 14:2.

38.   Beker, "The Church as the Dawning of the New Age," chapter 14 of his *Paul the Apostle*, 303-27.

39.   Beker, *Paul the Apostle*, 313, 318-19.

40.   "The Reformation of Manners," *The Works of John Wesley* (1985), 2:302.

41.   Robin Scroggs, *Paul for a New Day* (Philadelphia: Fortress Press, 1977), 39.

42.   David Kolb, *Postmodern Sophistications: Philosophy, Architecture, and Tradition* (Chicago: University of Chicago Press, 1990), 6.

43.   For Gibson Winter's social analysis of the search for community in a high-tech world, see his *Community and Spiritual Transformation: Religion and Politics in a Communal Age* (New York: Crossroad, 1989).

44.   Mark R. Schwehn, "Religion and the Life of Learning," *First Things*, August/ September 1990, 34, 36.

45.   Bernard Loomer, "S-I-Z-E is the Measure," in *Religious Experience and Process Theology: The Pastoral Implications of a Major Modern Movement*, ed. Harry James Cargas and Bernard Lee (New York: Paulist Press, 1976), 73-74. Originally published as "S-I-Z-E," *Criterion* 13 (Spring 1974): 7.

46.   Ralph Martin, comp., *The Spirit and the Church: A Personal and Documentary Record of the Charismatic Renewal, and the Ways It Is Bursting to Life in the Catholic Church* (New York: Paulist Press, 1976), 179. The use of cell and nerve cell theories, metaphysician/ philosopher/author Charles Hartshorne argues, "have yet to be adequately assimilated by speculative philosophy." Alfred North Whitehead comes the closest in his example of how "a tree is a democracy. . . . There is no dominant monad or individual . . . in trees, but we know in ourselves such a dominant individual." See Hartshorne, "A Metaphysics of Universal Freedom," in *Faith and Creativity: Essays in Honor of Eugene H. Peters*, ed. George Nordgulen and George W. Shields (St. Louis, Mo.: CBP Press, 1987), 36-37.

47.   Robert Bellah et al., *Habits of the Heart: Individualism and Commitment in American Life* (Berkeley: University of California Press, 1985), 221.

48.   Lionel Trilling, *Sincerity and Authenticity* (Cambridge, Mass.: Harvard University Press, 1972).

49.   John Bowlby, *Attachment and Loss*, 3 vols. (New York: Basic Books, 1969-1980).

50.   The best introduction to Vygotsky's thought is "The Inspiration of Vygotsky," chapter 5 of Jerome Bruner, *Actual Minds, Possible Worlds* (Cambridge, Mass: Harvard University Press, 1986), 70-78; see also 132-32, 142-43.

51.   The trend for more economic activity to consist in processing information than in processing materials has been a long history. An "information sector" in American society began well over a century ago, growing from less than 1 percent of the work force in 1830 to 4 percent by the end of the century. In 1930 fully 25 percent of the American work force was handling information for a living. By 1960, 42 percent of the work force was part of the "information sector," 35 percent was part of the manufacturing sector, 6 percent part of the agricultural sector, and 17 percent in the services sector. See James R. Beniger's excellent *The Control Revolution: Technological and Economic Origins of the Information Society* (Cambridge, Mass.: Harvard University Press, 1986).

52.   This is the estimate of Susan Engeleiter, who oversees the Small Business Administration for George Bush, as reported in *Research Recommendations*, 27 August 1990, 6.

53.   See the excerpt from Alvin Toffler's *Powershift: Knowledge, Wealth and Violence at the Edge of the 21st Century*, in *Newsweek*, 15 October 1990, 87.

54.   This is the argument of Nicholas Maxwell, *From Knowledge to Wisdom: A Revolution in the Aims and Methods of Science* (New York: Basil Blackwell, 1984) and Mary Midgley, *Wisdom, Information, and Wonder: What is Knowledge For?* (New York: Routledge, 1989).

55.   See Midgley, *Wisdom, Information, and Wonder*.

56.   Simone de Beauvoir, *Les Belles Images* (New York: G.P. Putnam's Sons, 1968), 105-6.

57.   Gregory Bateson, *Steps to an Ecology of the Mind: Collected Essays in Anthropology, Psychiatry, Evolution, and Epistemology* (San Francisco: Chandler, 1972), 135, 469, 487-88.

58.   The best discussion of Edward Fredkin's work is in Robert Wright, *Three Scientists and Their Gods: Looking for Meaning in an Age of Information* (New York: Times Books, 1988), 1-80.

59.   Jim L. Waits, "Toward a Knowledgeable Ministry," *ATS Notes*, November 1990, 2. See also William Hasker, *God, Time, and Knowledge* (Ithaca, N.Y.: Cornell University

Press, 1989).

60.   John Bowker, *Licensed Insanities: Religions and Belief in God in the Contemporary World* (London: Darton, Longman and Todd, 1987), 114.

61.   Compare John W. Gardner's eight characteristics as outlined in "Building Community," *Kettering Review*, Fall 1989, 73-81.

62.   See Russian/zoologist/geographer Peter Kropotkin, *Mutual Aid: A Factor of Evolution* (New York: Knopf, 1917), where he writes:

> Of the followers of Darwin, the first, as far as I know, who understood the full purport of Mutual Aid **as a law of Nature and the chief factor of evolution**, was a well-known Russian zoologist, the late Dean of the St. Petersburg University, Professor [Karl] Kessler. He developed his ideas in an address which he delivered in January 1880, a few months before his death, at a congress of Russian naturalists; but like so many good things published in the Russian tongue only, that remarkable address remains almost entirely unknown. (14-15)

63.   Alfie Kohn, *No Contest: The Case Against Competition* (Boston: Houghton Mifflin, 1986).

64.   The best presentation of the nature of synergies is Rosabeth Moss Kanter, *When Giants Learn to Dance: Mastering the Challenge of Strategy, Management, and Careers in the 1990s* (New York: Simon and Schuster, 1989), 57-116.

65.   Sallie McFague develops "the world as God's body" as a primary metaphor for God's relationship to creation in *Models of God: Theology for an Ecological, Nuclear Age* (Philadelphia: Fortress Press, 1987).

66.   See Matthew Fox, *The Cosmic Christ: The Coming of the Cosmic Christ: The Healing of Mother Earth and the Birth of a Global Renaissance* (San Francisco: Harper and Row, 1988).

67.   Books on creation spirituality include Matthew Fox, *Original Blessing: A Primer in Creation Spirituality Presented in Four Parts, Twenty-six Themes, and Two Questions* (Santa Fe, N.M.: Bear and Company, 1983); Fox, *Creation Spirituality: Liberating Gifts for the Peoples of the Earth* (San Francisco: HarperSanFrancisco, 1990); Ron Miller and Jim Kenney, *Fireball and the Lotus: Emerging Spirituality from Ancient Roots*, Santa Fe, N.M.: Bear and Company, 1987). See also other volumes in the Creation Spirituality Series published by Bear and Company; issues of *Creation: A Magazine of Earthly Spirituality for an Evolving Planet*, published by Friends of Creation Spirituality; and other resources available from Friends of Creation Spirituality, P.O. Box 19216, Oakland, CA 94619.

68.   The quote is taken from "Miscellanies," No. 108, Yale Collection of Edwards Manuscripts (Yale University).

69.   See physicist/environmentalist Adam Trombly's, "This is Our Body," *Design Spirit* 1 (Summer 1989): 3-5.

70.   Arthur Peacocke, *God and the New Biology* (San Francisco: Harper and Row, 1987), 104.

71.   F.L. Cross and E.A. Livingstone, eds., *The Oxford Dictionary of the Christian Church*, 2nd ed. (London: Oxford University Press, 1974), 1027.

72.   See Thomas Berry, *Dream of the Earth* (San Francisco: Sierra Club Books, 1988), 287-88.

73.   Erich Jantsch, *The Self-Organizing Universe: Scientific and Human Implications of the Emerging Paradigm of Evolution* (Oxford: Pergamon Press, 1980), 150.

74.   Rupert Sheldrake, *A New Science of Life: The Hypothesis of Formative Causation* (Los Angeles: Jeremy P. Tarcher, 1981) and *The Presence of the Past: Morphic Resonance and the Habits of Nature* (New York: Times Books, 1988).

75.   Gil Bailie was first quoted to me by McGregor Smith, director of the Environmental Ethics Institute, Miami-Dade Community College, Miami, Florida.

76.   Cryptons are being touted as a new kind of particle that could account for some of the dark matter of the universe, which exerts a gravitational force but gives off no detectable radiation. See I. Peterson, "Steps to a Grand Unified Superstring Theory," *Science News* 138 (13 October 1990), 230.

77. Aldo Leopold, "Wildlife in American Culture," *A Sand Country Almanac*, 177-79.
78. David C. Steinmetz, *Memory and Mission: Theological Reflections on the Christian Past* (Nashville: Abingdon Press, 1988), 72; this chapter was originally published as "The Protestant Minister and the Teaching Office of the Church, *Theological Education* 19 (Spring 1983): 45-59.
79. Steinmetz, *Memory and Mission*, 77.
80. John Calvin, *Institutes of the Christian Religion*, ed. John T. McNeill (Philadelphia: Westminster Press, 1955). "For, where they are called to office, it is at the same time enjoined upon them not to bring anything of themselves, but to speak from the Lord's mouth" (2:1150-51).
81. Edmund R. Leach, *A Runaway World?* The BBC Reith Lectures, 1967 (New York: Oxford University Press, 1968), 43-45.
82. Noel Leo Erskine, *Decolonizing Theology: A Caribbean Perspective* (Maryknoll, N.Y.: Orbis Books, 1981).
83. Comparative religion professor Diana L. Eck singles out the Southern Baptists as the first U.S. denomination to propose any such document. See her "Response of the Church to New Religious Movements: A Report from North America," in *New Religious Movements and the Churches*, ed. Allan R. Brockway and J. Paul Rajashekar (Geneva: WCC Publications, 1987), 147-48. The revised Southern Baptist guidelines, *Factors in Effective Interfaith Witness* (Atlanta: Home Mission Board, 1987) reflect a dramatically more conservative denominational position than Eck portrays in her article.
84. John R. Landgraf, *Creative Singlehood and Pastoral Care* (Philadelphia: Fortress Press, 1962), 52. For the further development of Landgraf's creative ideas see his *Singling: New Way to Live the Single Life* (Louisville: Westminster Press, 1990).
85. Frederick Turner goes too far in asserting that the human mission in the universe is to help God grow from a "fetus" to a "fully developed being" through technology. See his "Natural Technology," *Chronicles* [Rockford, Ill.] 14 (August 1990): 30.
86. Langdon Winner, *The Whale and the Reactor: A Search for Limits in An Age of High Technology* (Chicago: University of Chicago Press, 1986), 10. Historian Daniel Grossman, whose writings first put me in touch with Winner, also cites David Noble's list of three criteria for judging technologies: First, do they "degrade people and diminish their freedom and control without any apparent economic or other compensating benefit"; second, do they "pose serious social problems" while possessing ambiguous "technical and economic viability"; and third, do they offer what are "clearly viable in the narrow technical or economic sense but are nonetheless destructive for society as a whole." As quoted in Grossman's "Neo-Luddites: Don't Just Say Yes to Technology," *Utne Reader*, March/April, 1990, 49.
87. George Barna, *Marketing the Church* (Colorado Springs: NavPress, 1988), 113-15.
88. See the work of California-based futurologist/science fictionist Robert Anton Wilson and his quarterly newsletter *Trajectories*.
89. Ecunet, sponsored by the National Council of Churches, links computer networks from several different denominations--such as Presbynet, a pioneering attempt by the Presbyterian Church (USA) to link electronically church leaders, staff, and lay people for the purpose of sharing messages, articles, information, and ideas. Another such computer network linking denominations is NWI (Network World Information). See "Computer Networks for Churches," *The Futurist*, September/October, 1990, 50.
90. Robert Wright, *Three Scientists and Their Gods: Looking for Meaning in an Age of Information* (New York: Times Books, 1988), 222. The best elaboration of this position is F. Turner's "Natural Technology," 27-31.
91. See Jantsch, *The Self Organizing Universe*, 273.
92. *Dionysius the Pseudo-Areopagite: The Ecclesiastical Hierarchy,* trans. and annotated by Thomas L. Campbell (Washington D.C.: Catholic University of America Press, 1955), 19-20.
93. *Dionysius the Pseudo-Areopagite*, 29.
94. Biblical Scholar/Jesuit Joseph A. Fitzmyer believes that Acts 2:42 is a fundamental definition of what the Bible means by *koinonia*. See his "Jewish Christianity in Acts in Light

of the Qumran Scrolls," in *Studies in Luke-Acts: Essays Presented in Honor of Paul Schubert, Buckingham Professor of New Testament Criticism and Interpretation at Yale University*, ed. Leander E. Keck and J. Louis Martyn (Nashville: Abingdon Press, 1966), 241.

95.   *Drawing the Line: The Political Essays of Paul Goodman* (New York: Free Life, 1977), 185.

96.   Stephano Sabetti, *The Wholeness Principle* (Sherman Oaks, Calif.: Life Energy Media, 1986).

97.   For Alfie Kohn's contention that "excellence and victory are conceptually distinct," see his *No Contest*.

98.   Thomas J. Peters, *Thriving on Chaos: Handbook for a Management Revolution* (New York: Knopf, 1987); Rosabeth Moss Kanter, *When Giants Learn to Dance*.

99.   This is a paraphrase of Prov. 29:18: "Where there is no vision, the people perish."

100.   Anthropologist/lecturer Edith L.B. Turner, "Encounter with Neurobiology: The Response of Ritual Studies," *Zygon* 21 (1986): 219-32.

101.   George Plimpton, *The X-Factor* (Knoxville, Tenn.: Whittle Direct Books, 1990), 10. Plimpton traces the lineage of what he calls the "'X' Factor" to New York City's Marble Collegiate Church pastor/*The Power of Positive Thinking* author Norman Vincent Peale's "The Plus Factor" and Georgia Tech's athletic director Homer Rice's "Inner Power Success Force" (16).

102.   Ignatius of Antioch, *The Epistles to the Ephesians*, 13, in *The Epistles of St. Clement of Rome and St. Ignatius of Antioch*, newly trans. and annotated by James A. Kleist (Westminster, Md.: Newman Bookshop, 1946), 65.

103.   See Günther Bornkamm's *Paul, Paulus*, trans. D.M.G. Stalker (New York: Harper and Row, 1971): "*Ecclesia* is in fact the church assembled for worship" (186).

104.   Kirkpatrick Sale, *Human-Scale* (New York: Perigee Books, 1982, ᶜ1980) 68, 82-96.

105.   "Hottest Product is Brand X," *Fortune*, 25 September 1989, 128.

106.   Barna, *Marketing the Church*, 113.

107.   David Kelsey, "The Bible and Christian Theology," *Journal of the American Academy of Religion* 48 (1980): 393.

108.   For a fuller commentary and explication of Kelsey's views, see pastor/religion professor Darrell Jodock's excellent *The Church's Bible: Its Contemporary Authority* (Minneapolis: Fortress Press, 1989), especially chapters 4 ("The Bible in Postmodern Culture," 71-88) and 7 ("Recontextualizing the Bible," 129-43). Jodock elaborates two "interlocking features" to biblical authority--"the Bible mediates the presence of God and . . . the Bible provides the language of faith"--while insisting on the communal and contextual way in which "an authority relationship develops as the Bible is used in the community of faith" (125, 129).

109.   Gabriel Josipovici, *The Book of God: A Response to the Bible* (New Haven: Yale University Press, 1988).

110.   See especially the final chapter ("The Role of the Reader: Actualizing of Biblical Discourse") of Edgar V. McKnight's *Post-Modern Use of the Bible: The Emergence of Reader-Oriented Criticism* (Nashville: Abingdon, 1988), 219-72.

111.   Josipovici, *The Book of God*. See also Carlos Mesters, *Defenseless Flower: A New Reading of the Bible*, trans. from the Portuguese by Francis McDonagh (Maryknoll, N.Y.: Orbis Books, 1989).

112.   Jerome Bruner, *Process of Education* (Cambridge, Mass.: Harvard University Press, 1961), 33.

113.   For the reasons why biblical scholars, with the exception of those studying the parables, have exhibited little interest in imagery, see the chapter on "The Use of Imagery in the Old Testament" in Kirsten Nielsen's 1985 Danish doctoral thesis *There Is Hope for a Tree: The Tree as Metaphor in Isaiah* (Sheffield, Eng.: JSOT Press, 1989), 25-67.

114.   Dean Keith Simonton, *Scientific Genius: A Psychology of Science* (New York: Cambridge University Press, 1988), esp. 29, 30, 35.

115.   See Sociologist Philip Selznick, "The Demands of the Community," *Center Magazine*, January/February 1987, 33-54.

116.   See Joseph Campbell's *The Inner Reaches of Outer Space: Metaphor as Myth and as*

Religion (New York: Alfred Van Der Marsh, 1986).

117. James F. Cobble, Jr., *The Church and the Powers: A Theology of Church Structure* (Peabody, Mass.: Hendrickson, 1988), 44.

118. Most of my statistics for the first two come from the massive compilation of research found in Kirkpatrick Sale's *Human Scale,* 181-89.

119. See John Keegan's *The Face of Battle* (New York: Viking Press, 1976), 52-53.

120. Former Dean of the Ecumenical Continuing Education Center (Yale University) Parker Rossman, "Computers and Religious Research," *National Forum of the Phi Kappa Phi Journal* 63:2 (Spring 1983): 24.

121. See Rustum Roy, *Experimenting with Truth* (New York: Pergamon Press, 1981), 69.

122. I originally got the idea for this metaphor from Marie-Louise Von Franz, *On Divination and Synchronicity: The Psychology of Meaningful Chance* (Toronto: Inner City Books, 1980), 43.

123. "That emotional experience out of which Art is made" is how Mallory described mountain climbing, as quoted in *Beyond Boredom and Anxiety: The Experience of Play in Work and Games,* by Mihaly Csikszentmihalyi (San Francisco: Jossey-Bass, 1977, ᶜ1975)), 90. For a superb theological treatment of the role of the mountain in ordering freedom, see Kosuki Koyama's *Mount Fuji and Mount Sinai: A Critique of Idols* (Maryknoll, N.Y.: Orbis Books, 1985, ᶜ1984). Muir is quoted in Richard Cartwright Austin's *Baptized into Wilderness: A Christian Perspective on John Muir* (Atlanta: John Knox Press, 1987), 15-16.

124. Parker J. Palmer, "On Staying at the Table: A Spirituality of Community," *Call to Growth/Ministry* 13:1 (Fall,1987), 33-39.

125. See Parker J. Palmer, "The Monastic Way to Church Renewal," *Weavings* 1:1 (September/October, 1986): 17.

126. William H. Willimon, *What's Right with the Church* (San Francisco: Harper and Row, 1985), 25.

127. For a helpful critique of the way the concept of "critical mass" has been adulterated and pejorated, specifically in the pseudoscientific "Hundredth Monkey Phenomenon," see Maureen O'Hara, "Of Myths and Monkeys: A Critical Look at a Theory of Critical Mass," *Journal of Humanistic Psychology* 25 (Winter 1985): 61-78.

128. Mary Tew Douglas, *Purity and Danger: An Analysis of Concepts of Pollution and Taboo* (London: Routledge and Kegan Paul, 1966), 35.

129. Edmund Leach, *Culture and Communication: The Logic by Which Symbols Are Connected: An Introduction to the Use of Structuralist Analysis in Social Anthropology* (New York: Cambridge University Press, 1976), 62.

130. John W. Connor, "Misperception, Folk Belief, and the Occult: A Cognitive Guide to Understanding," *Skeptical Inquirer* 8 (Summer 1984): 344-54.

131. Maureen O'Hara, "Science, Pseudoscience, and Mythmongering," in *Not Necessarily the New Age,* ed. Robert Basil (Buffalo, N.Y.: Prometheus Books, 1988), 152.

132. Christopher Lasch, "Soul of a New Age," *Omni* 10 (October 1987): 81-82. I was first tipped off to this article by O'Hara's "Science, Pseudoscience, and Mythmongering," 149.

133. For the entrenched attachment of "illicit" religion throughout American religious history, see Jon Butler's *Awash in a Sea of Faith: Christianizing the American People* (Cambridge, Mass.: Harvard University Press, 1990).

134. The best epidemiological studies to date exploring the connections between music and science are in Robert Scott Root-Bernstein, *Discovering* (Cambridge, Mass.: Harvard University Press, 1989), especially his "Artistic Proclivities Among Emminent Scientists and Inventors" (318-27) and Jamie C. Kassler, "Music as Model in Early Science," *History of Science* 20 (1982): 103-39. See also Kassler, "Man--A Musical Instrument: Models of the Brain and Mental Functioning Before the Computer," *History of Science* 22 (1984): 59-92; Root-Bernstein, "Harmony and Beauty in Biomedical Research." *Journal of Molecular and Cellular Cardiology* 19 (1987): 1-9; Willard Marmelzat, *Musical Sons of Aesculapius* (New York: Froeben Press, 1946); George Gamow, *Thirty Years That Shook Science* (New York: Doubleday, 1966), 80-83. Root-Bernstein explores the way "music has long exerted unusual power over the scientific temperament" in his "Sensual Education," *The Sciences* 30

(September/October 1990): 12-14. It is Root-Bernstein's conviction that "only a sensual imagination can vivify the sterile, motionless symbols and words through which scientists are forced to convey the shadows of their understanding" (13).

135. Max Weber liked to talk of the world as an "enchanted garden."

136. Marshall and Eric McLuhan, *Laws of Media: The New Science* (Toronto: University of Toronto Press, 1988), 39-66.

137. Music critic Simon Frith has written a provocative essay, "The Industrialization of Music," in which he argues that the modern entertainment business is responsible for transforming "music-as-expression" into "music-as-commodity." See *Music for Pleasure: Essays in the Sociology of Pop* (New York: Routledge, 1988), 11-23.

138. Martin E. Marty, "Melodic Ammunition," *Christian Century*, 25 July-1 August 1990, 719.

139. Thomas J. O'Grady, Jr., Whitesell Company, 1 Executive Campus, Route 70, Cherry Hill, NJ 08002.

140. According to the Barna Research Group, when stacked up against both secular and Christian magazines, *The Singing News* came in third behind *Readers Digest* and *Guideposts* but ahead of *Better Homes and Garden, Family Circle, National Geographic, McCall's*, etc.

141. See *Dayton Daily News*, 6 April 1990, 1A.

142. See letter from Edwards to Sir William Pepperell, Governor of Massachusetts, 28 November, 1751, in *The Life of President Edwards*, by S.E. Dwight (New York: G. and C. and H. Carvill, 1830), 478.

143. George Steiner is quoted in David Martin, *The Breaking of the Image: A Sociology of Christian Theory and Practice* (New York: St. Martin's Press, 1980), 133. Martin himself is quite critical of the way "the record begins to take over from the book, the concert audience--or the rock festival--replaces the congregation, and the quest for ecstasy displaces concern for dogmatic assent" (140). See also Steiner's "The Politics of Music," *TLS: The Times Literary Supplement*, 6 May 1977, 557.

144. Quoted in John Amis and Michael Rose, *Words about Music: An Anthology* (London: Faber, 1989), 1.

145. Richard Wagner to Hans Von Bulow 26 October 1854, in *Selected Letters of Richard Wagner*, trans. and ed. Stewart Spencer and Barry Millington (New York: W.W. Norton, 1988), 322.

146. One of the few pastors to have addressed this issue in sermonic form is John M. Buchanan in his pioneering "Trumpet, Timbrel, and Loud Clashing Cymbals," delivered to Chicago's Fourth Presbyterian Church on 14 October 1990.

147. See Ivan Amato's "Muscle Melodies and Brain Refrains," *Science News* 135 (1 April 1989): 202-3.

148. For Arthur R. Peacocke, see his *God and the New Biology* (San Francisco: Harper and Row, 1986), 97-98; see also his *Creation and the World of Science* (Oxford: Clarendon Press, 1979), 105-6. For Peter F. Drucker, see his "The Coming of the New Organization," *Harvard Business Review* 66 (January-February 1988): 47-50.

149. See the provocative passage by Elias Canetti on "The Orchestral Conductor" as the embodiment of social power in *The Music Lovers' Literary Companion*, ed. Dannie Abse and Joan Abse (London: Robson, 1988), 163-65.

150. These are the descriptive words of war correspondent/*Daily Telegraph* music critic/editor Richard Capell.

151. David M. Cummings and Dennis K. McIntire, eds., *International Who's Who in Music and Musicians' Directory* (Cambridge, Eng.: Melrose Press, 1975), 525.

152. This was the fourth of the "Ten Golden Rules" Strauss wrote for the album of a young conductor in 1922. For the complete list see Amis and Rose, *Words About Music*, 119.

153. See Sigmund Kvaloy, "Complexity and Time: Breaking the Pyramid's Reign," in *Sacred Land Sacred Sex--Rapture of the Deep: Concerning Deep Ecology and Celebrating Life*, by Dolores LaChapelle (Silverton Colo.: Finn Hill Arts, 1988), 319-28.

154. This is the phrase of music critic/publisher Samuel Lipman in "Does the Piano

Have a Future?" *Commentary* 88 (December 1989): 53.

155. Andre Carothers, "Can Rock 'n' Roll Save the World?" *Greenpeace*, November/ December 1989, 6-11.

156. See Becky Loop's "Still Rockin'," letter to the editor, *Greenpeace*, July/August 1990, 27.

157. Greil Marcus, *Lipstick Traces: A Secret History of the Twentieth Century* (Cambridge, Mass.: Harvard University Press, 1989) and Tipper Gore, *Raising PG Kids in an X-Rated Society* (Nashville: Abingdon, 1987).

158. Martha Winburn England, "Enthusiasm Without Mysticism," in *Hymns Unbidden: Donne, Herbert, Blake, Emily Dickinson and the Hymnographers* (New York: New York Public Library, 1966), 96; also quoted in Richard E. Brantley's, "Charles Wesley's Experimental Art," *Eighteenth Century Life*, 11 (May 1987): 8.

159. Norman J. Kansfield, "'Study the Most Approved Authors': The Role of the Seminary Library in Nineteenth-century Protestant Ministerial Education," Ph.D. diss., University of Chicago, 1981, 35-36. See also the *Minutes of Several Conversations Between the Rev. Thomas Coke, the Rev. Francis Asbury and Others... Composing a Form of Discipline for the Ministers, Preachers and Other Members of the Methodist Episcopal Church in America* (Philadelphia: Charles Cist, 1785), where the method of study is discussed.

> We advise you, 1. As often as possible to rise at four. 2. From four to five in the morning, and from five to six in the Evening, to meditate pray, and read partly the Scripture with Mr. Wesley's Notes, partly the closely practical Parts of what he has published. 3. From six in the Morning till twelve (allowing an Hour for Breakfast) to read in Order, with much Prayer, **the Christian Library** and other pious Books. (16)

The *Doctrines and Discipline of the Methodist Episcopal Church*, 1787, contains this dialog:

> Read the **most useful** books, and that regularly and constantly. Steadily spend all the morning in this employ, or at least five hours in four and twenty.
> "But I have no **taste** for reading." Then contract a taste for it by use.
> "But I have no books." We desire the Assistants will take care that all the large societies provide Mr. **Wesley's** works for the use of the preachers. (15)

160. Quoted by Thomas Ryan, *Wellness, Spirituality, and Sports* (New York: Paulist Press, 1986), 190.

161. The beginning story of music's changing role in a culture of consumption from a culture of production is marvelously told by Craig H. Roell, *The Piano in America, 1890-1940* (Chapel Hill: University of North Carolina Press, 1989).

162. See Esther M. Adams, contribution to "Personal Glimpses," in *Reader's Digest*, April 1976, 126.

163. Jean Renoir captures the filmmaker's collaborate creativity in these words: "It's difficult to be sincere when you're all alone. Some people manage to do it, and they are gifted writers. I'm much less gifted, and I can only really find my own experiences when I'm in contact with others." See the collection of interviews Renoir gave to the editors of the French journal *Cahiers du Cinema*, and talks delivered on French Television between 1954 and 1962, entitled *Renoir on Renoir: Interviews, Essays, and Remarks* (New York: Cambridge University Press, 1989). See also his autobiography *My Life and My Films* (New York: Atheneum, 1974).

INTERMEZZO III
(pages 164 - 166)

1.   This interpretation of the Lukean passage is derived from folksinger/pastor/ theologian Buell H. Kazee, who has greatly influenced my thinking about a variety of topics. See his *Faith is the Victory: The Secret of Dynamic Living* (Grand Rapids, Mich.: Tyndale House, 1983).

ETHOS
(pages 167 - 213)

a.   Vítor Westhelle, "The Challenge of Theology to Science and the Church," in *The New Faith-Science Debate: Probing Cosmology, Technology, and Theology,* ed. John M. Mangum (Minneapolis: Fortress Press, 1989), 25.

b.   Brian Pippard, "God and the Physical Scientist," *TLS: The Times Literary Supplement,* 23 May 1986, 556.

c.   As quoted and translated by Westhelle, "The Challenge of Theology to Science and the Church," 24.

d.   Jan Morris, *Hong Kong: Xianggang* (New York: Random House, 1988), 67.

e.   Roland Barthes, who died in 1980 from injuries received when he was struck by an automobile while crossing a Paris street, is quoted in Alan Durning, "How Much is 'Enough'?" *World-Watch* 3 (November/December 1990): 15.

f.   "Fragments" (aphorisms left unpublished at the time of his death), in *The Poems of Coventry Patmore,* ed. Frederick Page (New York: Oxford University Press, 1949), 479.

g.   Charles Birch and John B. Cobb, Jr., *The Liberation of Life: From the Cell to the Community* (New York: Cambridge University Press, 1981), 184.

h.   As quoted in Robert D. Young, *Religious Imagination: God's Gift to Prophets and Preachers* (Philadelphia: Westminster Press, 1979), 193.

i.   Walter B. Cannon, *The Wisdom of the Body,* rev. ed. (New York: W.W. Norton, 1939), 20.

j.   *Pascal's Pensées,* with an English translation, brief notes and introduction by H.F. Stewart (New York: The Modern Library, 1947), 342-43.

k.   Tertullian, a well educated convert to Christianity, often held views in conflict with the main stream Christianity of his day. He defended and joined the Montanists and later founded what became know as the Tertullianists. The quote is from *De Praescriptione Haereticorum, "Omnes ecclesiae una; probant unitatem ecclesiarum communicatio pacis et appellatio fraternitatis et contesseratio hospitalitatis"* (20).

l.   D.T. Niles, *This Jesus . . . Whereof We Are Witnesses* (Philadelphia: Westminster Press, 1965), 50.

m.   Hall W. Trovillon, *Faces and Places Remembered,* (Herrin, Ill.: Trovillon Printing Press, 1956), 56.

n.   Edmund Spenser, as quoted in Wilfrid Mellers, *Bach and the Dance of God* (New York: Oxford University Press, 1981), 18.

o.   "Fragments," *The Poems of Coventry Patmore,* 479.

p.   Sallie McFague, *Metaphorical Theology: Models of God in Religious Language* (Philadelphia: Fortress Press, 1982), 181.

q.   From the parable of the Great Dinner, Luke 14:12-14 (RSV).

1.   See Clive James's essay, "Three Staggering Questions," in his *From the Land of Shadows* (London: Jonathan Cape, 1982), 208.

2.   See Edward Hall, *The Hidden Dimension* (Garden City, N.Y.: Doubleday, 1966).

3.   Richard Feather Anderson, "The W.I.S.E. Approach," *Design Spirit* 1 (Summer 1989): 10-13. See also Patrick F. Sheeran, "The Ideology of Earth Mysteries," *Journal of Popular Culture* 23 (Spring 1990): 67-73.

4.   Historian James Nelson has reminded me that the missional understanding of the church was fairly commonplace among the German Pietists, and the term "our" parish was found in contemporary Moravian documents. The private nature of the writing in which Wesley "coined" the expression suggests that the term did not originate with Wesley.

5.   Stanley G. Browne, "Leprosy in the Bible," in *Medicine and the Bible,* ed. Bernard Palmer (Exeter: Published for the Christian Medical Fellowship by the Paternoster Press, 1986), 101-124.

6.   See, for example, Gustavo Gutiérrez's *The Power of the Poor in History,* trans. from

the Spanish by Robert R. Barr (Maryknoll, N.Y.: Orbis Books, 1983), 92.

7.　Dorothy Wilson, *Twelve Who Cared: My Adventures with Christian Courage* (Chappaqua, N.Y.: Christian Herald Books, 1977), 122.

8.　"WOG" is also a British slang acronym for "Westernized Oriental Gentleman".

9.　Richard Palmer, "The Church, Leprosy and Plague in Medieval and Early Modern Europe," in *The Church and Healing*, ed., W.J. Sheils (Oxford: Basil Blackwell, 1982), 81.

10.　Jonathan Edwards, "To the Rev. William McCulloch of Cambuslang, Scotland," 12 May 1743, as cited in Edwards, *The Great Awakening*, ed. C.C. Goen (New Haven: Yale University Press, 1972), 541.

11.　This is a variation of the phrase "It's OK. You're safe. We'll take care of you. We are Christians here," suggested by L. Gregory Jones, "Eucharistic Hospitality: Welcoming the Stranger into the Household of God," *Reformed Journal*, March 1989, 12-17, especially 12. Another writer on "hospitality" I have profited from is John Koenig, *New Testament Hospitality: Partnership with Strangers as Promise and Mission* (Philadelphia: Westminster Press, 1985).

12.　Wayne A. Meeks, *The First Urban Christians: The Social World of the Apostle Paul* (New Haven: Yale University Press, 1983), 109.

13.　See Jane Jacobs, *The Death and Life of Great American Cities* (New York: Random House, 1961).

14.　The latest statistics available from the Chicago Presbytery office show a total of 9,107 members in the city's forty-two Presbyterian churches.

15.　Ervin E. Hastey, "Reaching the Cities First: A Biblical Model of World Evangelization" in *An Urban World*, ed. Larry L. Rose and C. Kirk Hadaway (Nashville: Broadman Press, 1984), 147-65.

16.　For the New Jerusalem as the eschatological form of the Garden, see Gary Waldecker's "The City--The Eschatological Garden," *Urban Mission*, March 1988, 18-26.

17.　See Robert K. Jewett's marvelous commentary on Hebrews entitled *A Letter to Pilgrim People* (New York: Pilgrim Press, 1981).

18.　The "Four Spiritual Laws" have found widespread acceptance in the full spectrum of the Christian tradition. See, as an example, *Evangelizing Youth*, ed. Glenn C. Smith (Wheaton, Ill.: Tyndale House, 1983), 90. These laws are as follows: Law One: "God loves you, and offers a wonderful plan for your life"; Law Two: "Man is sinful and separated from God. Therefore, he cannot know and experience God's love and plan for his life"; Law Three: "Jesus Christ is God's only provision for man's sin. Through Him you can know and experience God's love and plan for your life"; Law Four: "We must individually receive Jesus Christ as Savior and Lord; then we can know and experience God's love and plan for our lives."

19.　Quoted in Joanna Rogers Macy, *Despair and Personal Power in the Nuclear Age* (Philadelphia: New Society Publishers, 1983), 25. The brilliant use of thermodynamics and information theory to forge a new evolutionary synthesis can be found in Jeffrey S. Wicken's *Evolution, Thermodynamics, and Information: Extending the Darwinian Program* (New York: Oxford University Press, 1987). Wicken is insistent that the concept of "entropy" be restricted to thermodynamic organisms, and that applied mathematician/educator Claude E. Shannon's "loose language" associating entropy with "disorder" and "disorganization" has done a disservice to the scientific community (21-25). Wicken would replace "complexity" for "entropy" in information theory. For opposition to biologists using information theory, see also Rupert Sheldrake, *A New Science of Life: The Hypothesis of Formative Causation* (Los Angeles: Jeremy P. Tarcher, 1981), 57.

20.　Erich Jantsch, *The Self-Organizing Universe: Scientific and Human Implications of the Emerging Paradigm of Evolution* (Oxford: Pergamon Press, 1980), 303.

21.　There are three general types of systems, each one conventionally defined in terms of its energy exchange. First, in isolated systems there is no exchange at all with the environment. In closed systems, exchanges of energy but not of matter occur with the environment. In open systems, both matter and energy exchanges can take place. My view of systems theory is an amalgam of general systems theory especially as reflected in the work of

331

Gregory Bateson, Ilya Prigogine (physics), Humberto R. Maturana (biology), and the appropriation of these theories to family systems by Bradford Keeney and Karl Thomm.

22. Jantsch, *The Self-Organizing Universe*, 26.

23. I found this example in Frank Gehry, "Of Detritus and Denial," *New Perspectives Quarterly* 5 (Winter 1988-1989): 57.

24. No post-modern writer does this better than Isaac Bashevis Singer. See the excellent study by Grace Farrell Lee, *From Exile to Redemption: The Fiction of Isaac Bashevis Singer* (Carbondale, Ill.: Southern Illinois University Press, 1987).

25. Elizabeth Barrett Browning, "Casa Guidi Windows," pt. 1, line 416 (1851), in *The Poetical Works of Elizabeth Barrett Browning*, Cambridge ed. (Boston: Houghton Mifflin, 1974), 230.

26. J. David Bolter, *Turing's Man: Western Culture in the Computer Age* (Chapel Hill: University of North Carolina Press, 1984).

27. Michael W. Kammen, *Selvages and Biases: The Fabric of History in American Culture* (Ithaca: Cornell University Press, 1987), 55.

28. Allan Megill, *Prophets of Extremity: Nietzsche, Heidegger, Foucault, Derrida* (Berkeley: University of California Press, 1985), 316. Thomas Pynchon's *Gravity's Rainbow* (New York: Viking Press, 1973) makes explicit the manipulating/massaging/masturbating use of condition: "yes and now what if we--all right, say we **are** supposed to be the Kabbalists out there, say that's our real Destiny, to be the scholar-magicians of the Zone, with somewhere in it a Text, to be picked to pieces, annotated, explicated, and masturbated till it's all squeezed limp of its last drop" (520).

29. See Ralph Waldo Emerson's essay on "Self-Reliance," in his *Essays*, 1st ser. (Boston: Houghton, Mifflin, 1903), 43-90.

30. George A. Miller, "What Is Information Measurement," *American Psychologist* 8 (1953): 3.

31. *Jonathan Edwards: Representative Selections*, with introduction, bibliography, and notes, rev. ed., by Clarence H. Faust and Thomas H. Johnson (New York: Hill and Wang, 1962), 38.

32. Larry Dossey, *Space, Time and Medicine* (Boulder: Shambhala, 1982), 75.

33. Carmen R. Berry, *When Helping You is Hurting Me: Escaping the Messiah Trap* (San Francisco: Harper and Row, 1988).

34. Jantsch, *The Self-Organizing Universe*, 6.

35. Robert E. Ornstein and Paul Ehrlich, *New World, New Mind: Changing the Way we Think to Save Our Future* (London: Methuen, 1989), 17.

36. James M. Yates, "Systems Theory and Natural Systems," unpublished manuscript (1990), 52.

37. Dick Teresi, "The Lone Ranger of Quantum Mechanics," *New York Times Book Review*, 7 January 1990, 15.

38. Tom W. Boyd, "Clowns, Innocent Outsiders in the Sanctuary: A Phenomenology of Social Folly," *Journal of Popular Culture* 22 (Winter 1988): 103.

39. John Hopkins, *Talking to A Stranger: Four Television Plays* (Baltimore: Penguin Books, 1967). Parker J. Palmer, *The Company of Strangers: Christians and the Renewal of American Public Life* (New York: Crossroad, ᶜ1981).

40. Douglas R. Hofstadter, *Gödel, Escher, Bach: An Eternal Golden Braid* (New York: Basic Books, 1979).

41. John Stewart Collis, *Living With A Stranger: A Discourse on the Human Body* (New York: Braziller, 1979); G. Wilson Knight, *Symbol of Man: On Body-Soul for Stage and Studio* (Washington D.C.: University Press of America, 1981), 40.

42. Patrick Keifert in "Guess Who's Coming to Worship? Worship and Evangelism," *Word and World* 9 (Winter 1989) accents worship as public space and a public act.

The first reason the stranger belongs in public worship follows from what a public is. According to social psychologist Richard Sennett, "the interaction of strangers through a common set of actions constitutes a public." Where there is no space for strangers, there is no public. It follows that if worship is to be public, then strangers

are characteristic of, not incidental to it. (47)
43.   Keifert, "Guess Who's Coming to Worship?" 48.
44.   Richard J. Mouw, "The Call to Holy Worldliness," *Reformed Journal*, January, 1989, 13.
45.   Irma Joyce, *Never Talk to Strangers* (New York: Golden Books, 1967).
46.   J.R.R. Tolkien, *The Lord of the Rings* (Boston: Houghton Mifflin, 1954-1956.
47.   Albert Camus, *The Stranger* (New York: Knopf, 1946).
48.   Mark Twain, *The Mysterious Stranger and Other Stories* (New York: Harper, 1916).
49.   Michael Ignatieff, *The Needs of Strangers* (New York: Viking Press, 1985, c1984).
50.   See Henri J.M. Nouwen, "From Hostility to Hospitality," in *Reaching Out: The Three Movements of the Spiritual Life* (Garden City, N.Y.: Doubleday, 1975), 43-78.
51.   See Abraham J. Malherbe, "The Inhospitality of Diotrephes," in *God's Christ and His People: Studies in Honour of Nils Alstrup Dahl*, ed. Jacob Jervell and Wayne A. Meeks (Oslo: Universitetförlaget, 1977), 222-32, for the portrayal of Diotrephes as one individual's attempt at founding an independent local community; see also Pheme Perkins, "Koinonia in 1 John 1:3-7: The Social Contest of Division in the Johannine Letters," *Catholic Biblical Quarterly* 45 (January 1983): 631-41.
52.   Josephus, *Antiquitates Judaicae*, 1.11.1.
53.   John Feinberg, *Harm to Others Law*, vol.1 of *The Moral Limits of the Criminal Law* (New York: Oxford University Press, 1984), 185-86.
54.   Thomas Ryan, "Towards A Spirituality for Sports," in *Sport*, ed. Gregory Baum and John Coleman, Concilium: Religion in the Eighties (Edinburgh: T. & T. Clark, 1989), 111.
55.   See Peter Kerr, "Playing Away," *Theology* 88 (1985): 374-81.
56.   William J. Abraham, *The Logic of Evangelism* (Grand Rapids: Eerdmans, 1989), 200.
57.   The best illustration of the latter is, from one end of the theological spectrum, the work of Harvey Cox (see my "Theology á la Mode," *Reformed Journal* 34 [October 1984]: 17-22) and from the other end, Fred Brown, *Secular Evangelism* (London: SCM, 1977). The best treatment of Brown, a British Salvation Army major who risked his career to write *Secular Evangelism*, is in W.J. Abraham, *The Logic of Evangelism*, 191-200.
58.   For rabbi Lawrence Kushner's suggestion of a developmental sequence to the names of God, see *The River of Light: Spirituality, Judaism, and the Evolution of Consciousness* (San Francisco: Harper and Row, 1981), 118-19, 140-42.
59.   K.H. Ting, *No Longer Strangers: Selected Writings*, ed. with an introd. by Raymond L. Whitehead (Maryknoll, N.Y.: Orbis Books, 1989), 96.
60.   This is the thesis of Harry R. Boer in *Pentecost and Missions* (Grand Rapids, Mich.: Eerdmans, 1961).
61.   The phrase "gossiping the gospel" is that of Michael Green in *Evangelism in the Early Church* (Grand Rapids: Eerdmans, 1970), 173. It is echoed by J.I. Packer, in his introduction ("On Being Serious about the Holy Spirit") to David F. Wells's *God the Evangelist: How the Holy Spirit Works to Bring Men and Women to Faith*, (Grand Rapids: Eerdmans, 1987), xiv.
62.   See Betty O'Brien, "Choices: Holy Hardware or *Bibelot*," *Bibelot* 3 (Spring Runoff, 1988): 4.
63.   See Episcopal Chaplain to the University of Chicago Sam Portano's wonderful article on Miss Manners "Before Truth The Right Fork: A Theological Reflection on Ministry and Manners," *Criterion*, 26 (Autumn 1987), 13-19. See also Pamela Payne Allen, "Feasting on Herbs in the Midst of Love: A Conversation with Jeff Smith," *Christian Century*, 2 December 1987, 1087-90.
64.   See John Koenig, *New Testament Hospitality: Partnership With Strangers As Promise and Mission* (Philadelphia: Fortress Press, 1985).
65.   I have reservations about the phrase "hospitality," and "hospitality evangelism." "Hospitality" summons images of plates piled high with fried chicken ("southern hospitality") or entertainment of guests at tea parties, cocktail hours, etc. Robert E. Meagher, in "Strangers at the Gate," *Parabola*, 26 (1977) says that

Hospitality has become a harmless urbane quality in the order of observances represented by general civility, politeness, and table manners. It is on the verge of being regarded as a matter of personality, which means that it stands not far removed from the peculiar oblivion spread ever wider by our obsession with the particular and private. If we manage, across some period of time, not to be rude to our friends within our own house, and even a bit unsparing, then we are deemed hospitable--should we happen to have among our friends anyone given to archaisms. We forget that proper hospitality has to do with unrecognizable strangers rather than with kith and kin. (10-11)

66.   Bernard P. Prusak, "Hospitality Extended or Denied: *Koinonia* Incarnate from Jesus to Augustine," in *The Church as Communion*, ed. James H. Provost (Washington, D.C.: Canon Law Society of America, 1984), 89-126, 89.

67.   The eschatological dimensions of evangelization are developed more fully in J.C. Hoekendijk's *The Church Inside Out* (Philadelphia: Westminster Press, 1966).

68.   George Barna, *Marketing the Church*, (Colorado Springs: NavPress, 1988), 111. See also the works of Lyle E. Schaller, Charles Arn, and Win Arn. The Arns's research on how Americans come to join a church revealed that

1 to 2 percent recognized personal need (crisis, etc.)

2 to 3 percent were walk-ins

5 to 6 percent were attracted by pastoral leadership

1 to 2 percent responded to a visitation

4 to 5 percent were first involved in Sunday School (or other small church group)

½ of 1 percent came through evangelistic crusades (including radio and television ministries)

75 to 90 percent came because a friend or relative invited them

See the Arns's *The Master's Plan for Making Disciples: How Every Christian Can Be an Effective Witness Through an Enabling Church* (Pasadena, Calif.: Church Growth, 1982), 43. Special thanks to Church Growth staff member Barbara Arn for elaborating on these statistics.

69.   See Chan-Hie Kim, "The Papyrus Invitation," *Journal of Biblical Literature* 94 (1975): 391-402, exp. 391.

70.   Kim, "The Papyrus Invitation," 393.

71.   Kim, "The Papyrus Invitation," 397.

72.   Gaylord Noyce, "Mandate for the Mainline," *Christian Century*, 8 November 1989, 1017.

73.   Murray Code, *Order and Organism: Steps Toward a Whiteheadian Philosophy of Mathematics and the Natural Sciences* (Toronto: University of Toronto Press, 1985), 61.

74.   William Law, *Fire From a Flint: Daily Readings with William Law*, ed. Robert Llewelyn and Edward Moss (London: Darton, Longman and Todd, 1986), 60.

75.   Nouwen, **Reaching Out**, 51.

76.   Nikos Nissiotis, "The Gospel Message in a Time of Revolution," *One World* (Geneva), September 1975, 16-18, esp. 17.

77.   C. Peter Wagner, *Our Kind of People: The Ethical Dimension of Church Growth in America* (Atlanta: John Knox Press, 1979).

78.   Prusak, "Hospitality Extended or Denied," 98.

79.   Keifert, "Guess Who's Coming to Worship?" 50.

80.   Dell Upton, *Holy Things and Profane: Anglican Parish Churches in Colonial Virginia* (Cambridge, Mass.: MIT Press, 1986), 166.

81.   Sharon H. Ringe, "Hospitality, Justice and Community: Paul's Teaching on the Eucharist in 1 Corinthians 11:17-34," *Prism*: 1 (Fall 1986): 59-68: "The eucharist is an event of hospitality" is how she begins her article. "Sharing in meals was a hallmark of Christian communities."

82.   Arland J. Hultgren, "The Johannine Footwashing (13:1-11) as Symbol of Eschatological Hospitality," *New Testament Studies* 28 (1982): 542.

83.   Upton, *Holy Things and Profane*.

84.   Upton, *Holy Things and Profane*, 165, 166.

85.   Upton, *Holy Things and Profane*, 166, quoting Robert Beverley, *The History and Present State of Virginia* . . . (London: Printed for R. Parker, 1705).
86.   Harold Bloom, *Ruin the Sacred Truths: Poetry and Belief From the Bible to the Present* (Cambridge: Harvard University Press, 1989),
87.   For an alternative viewpoint, see Annie Dillard's *Teaching a Stone to Talk* (Harper and Row, 1982), where she comments:

> I know of one congregation in New York which fired its priest because he insisted on their "passing the peace"–which involves nothing more than shaking hands with your neighbors in the pew. The men and women of this small congregation had limits to their endurance; passing the peace was beyond their limits. They could not endure shaking hands with people to whom they bore lifelong grudges. They fired the priest and found a new one sympathetic to their needs. (23)

88.   See A.S. (Andrew Sullivan's) "Washington Diarist" column, "Not Everybody Does It," *New Republic*, 31 August 1987, 43.
89.   Marcianus Aristides, *Apologia* 15.7-9.
90.   Richard Howard, "Oracles." *No Traveller* (New York: Alfred A. Knopf, 1989), 79. Reprinted with permission of the publisher.

INTERMEZZO IV
(pages 214 - 216)

1.   Samuel Taylor Coleridge, *Biographia Literaria*, ed. J. Shawcross (London: Oxford University Press, 1907), 1:85-86.
2.   The late Roman Catholic theologian Karl Rahner wrote "To keep on, through dull, tedious, everyday existence can often be more difficult than a unique deed whose heroism makes us run the danger of pride and self satisfaction. See his *Meditations on Hope and Love* (New York: Seabury Press, 1977), 23.

THEOS
(pages 217 - 248)

a.   Robert Louis Stevenson, "El Dorado," *Virginibus Puerisque and Other Papers, vol. 6 of The Works of Robert Louis Stevenson*, ed. Charles Curtis Bigelow and Temple Scott (New York: Charles C. Bigelow, 1906), 236.
b.   Muhyiddin Ibn al-'Arabi, *Journey to the Lord of Power: A Sufi Manual on Retreat* (New York: Inner Traditions International, 1981), 27.
c.   An anonymous thirteenth century quotation as translated by Richard C. Dales, "Time and Eternity in the Thirteenth Century," *Journal of the History of Ideas* 49 (1988): 29.
d.   From Richard Wagner's final composition, *Parsifal*, unveiled at the 1882 Bayreuth Festival.
e.   Jürgen Moltmann, *God in Creation: A New Theology of Creation and the Spirit of God* (San Francisco: Harper and Row, 1985), 34.
f.   Quoted in Robert Scott Root-Bernstein, *Discovering* (Cambridge, Mass.: Harvard University Press, 1989), 329.
g.   This was Wilhelm Pauck's deathbed assessment on the decline and fall of liberal Christianity.
h.   Carl Gustav Jung, *The Archtypes and the Collective Unconscious*, 2d ed. (Princeton, N.J.: Princeton University Press, 1968), 18-20.
i.   Quoted and paraphrased by Arthur Koestler, *The Roots of Coincidence* (New York: Random House, 1972), 43.
j.   William Shakespeare, *The Tragedy of Hamlet, Prince of Denmark* (1600-1601), act IV, scene 5, line 78.
k.   Jesus on God's answering of prayer, from the Sermon on the Mount, Matt. 7:7

(NEB).
    l.   William Shakespeare, *King Henry the Fourth*, Part 1 (1598), act II, scene 4, line 69.
    m.   As quoted by chaplain William M. Young in his introduction to Fred C. Lofton, *Help Me, Somebody!* (Elgin, Ill.: Progressive Baptist Publishing House, 1988), 16.
    n.   Erwin Chargaff, *Heraclitean Fire: Sketches From a Life Before Nature* (New York: Rockefeller University Press, 1978), 179.

    1.   Robert Louis Stevenson, *Travels with a Donkey in the Cevennes* (New York: Scribner's Sons, 1926), 63.
    2.   These are William James's words which Robert Frost loved to quote. See William H. Pritchard, *Frost: A Literary Life Reconsidered* (New York: Oxford University Press, 1984), 50. The cosmic dynamics of the "sea," states Brian Swimme, are the powers of "cosmic sensitivity." In his words, "To develop the power of cosmic sensitivity is to understand that to be in reality means dissolving the universe, absorbing it into your new self. To be is to dissolve and draw up, to be dissolved and drawn up." See his *The Universe is a Green Dragon: A Cosmic Creation Story*, (Santa Fe: Bear and Company, 1985), 93. Marilyn Ferguson used the symbol of Aquarius, the waterbearer of the zodiac, as the basis of her book on the consciousness revolution entitled *The Aquarian Conspiracy: Personal and Social Transformation in the 1980s* (Los Angeles: Jeremy P. Tarcher, 1980).
    3.   Wittgenstein's quote is from his *Philosophical Investigations*, trans. C.B.M. Anscombe (New York: Macmillan, 1953), 31, and is quoted in D.Z. Phillips' *Through a Darkening Gloom: Philosophy, Literature and Cultural Change* (Notre Dame: University of Notre Dame Press, 1982), 90.
    4.   J.B. Priestley, *Man and Time* (Garden City, N.Y.: Doubleday, 1964), 62.
    5.   See Paulo Freire's *Pedagogy of the Oppressed* (New York: Herder and Herder, 1970).
    6.   For Popper's four-shelved bookcase, the bottom shelf labeled "Physical Sciences," the second shelf up labeled "Life Sciences," the third shelf labeled "Human Sciences," and the top shelf tagged "Spiritual Sciences," see Karl R. Popper and John C. Eccles, *The Self and Its Brain* (New York: Springer International, 1977); see also Willis W. Harmon, "The Transpersonal Challenge to the Scientific Paradigm: The Need for a Restructuring of Science," *ReVision* 11 (Fall 1988): 16-18.
    7.   John G. Kemeny, *A Philosopher Looks at Science* (Princeton, N.J.: D. Van Nostrand, 1959), 58-59.
    8.   Hermann Minkowski, "Space and Time," in *Problems of Space and Time*, ed. J.J.C. Smart (New York: Macmillan, 1964), 297. Reprinted from *The Principle of Relativity*, by Albert Einstein and others (London: Methuen, 1923).
    9.   See Jill Purce, *The Mystic Spiral: Journey of the Soul* (London: Thames and Hudson, 1974).
    10.   Eugene L. Lowry, *Doing Time In the Pulpit* (Nashville: Abingdon, 1985). David Buttrick, Frederick Buechner, and Fred B. Craddock have made similar arguments using different metaphors.
    11.   J.T. Fraser, *Time: The Familiar Stranger* (Amherst: University of Massachusetts Press, 1987).
    12.   See the chapter on "The Limits of Science" in J.P. Moreland, *Christianity and the Nature of Science: A Philosophical Investigation* (Grand Rapids, Mich.: Baker Book House, 1989), 103-38; also the chapter "The Limits of Science" in Eugene P. Wigner, *Symmetries and Reflections: Scientific Essays* (Bloomington: Indiana University Press, 1967), 211-21.
    13.   For the limitations of science as well as the quote from Jaspers and Wittgenstein, see Huston Smith's *Beyond the Post-Modern Mind* (New York: Crossroad, 1982), 67-68.
    14.   Nicholas Rescher, *The Limits of Science* (Berkeley: University of California Press, 1984), 214, as quoted by J.P. Moreland, *Christianity and the Nature of Science*, 138.
    15.   The next sentence of the quote deserves to be cited as well: "Sound theology, if it ignores biology, can give at most incomplete--and at times faulty--understanding of human nature." See Philip T. Spieth's review of *Evolution: A Theory in Crisis*, by Michael Denton,

Zygon 22 (1987): 257.

16. Albert Einstein, *Out of My Later Years* (New York: Philosophical Library, 1950), 26.

17. Jeffrey S. Wicken, "Theology and Science in the Evolving Cosmos: A Need for Dialogue," *Zygon* 23 (March 1988): 47.

18. Jacob Bronowski, *Science and Human Values* (New York: Harper and Row, 1958), 67-68.

19. Ilya Prigogine and Isabelle Stengers, *Order Out of Chaos: Man's New Dialogue With Nature* (Boulder: New Science Library, 1984), 34.

20. Ursula K. LeGuin, *The Left Hand of Darkness* (New York: Ace Books, 1976, c1969), 220.

21. See Muriel Spark's autobiographical *Loitering With Intent* (New York: Coward McCann and Geoghegan, 1981).

22. Quoted in Ignacio Larrañaga, *Sensing Your Hidden Presence: Toward Intimacy with God* (Garden City, N.Y.: Doubleday, 1987), 275-76.

23. See Frank Gehry, "Of Detritus and Denial," *New Perspectives Quarterly* 5 (Winter 1988-1989): 57.

24. Shel Silverstein, *Where the Sidewalk Ends* (New York: Harper and Row, 1974).

25. This is the marvelous phrasing of philosopher/psychologist/founding dean of the School of Cognitive and Computing Sciences (University of Sussex) Margaret A. Boden in "Wonder and Understanding," *Zygon* 20 (1985): 391-400.

26. "Men go abroad to wonder at the height of mountains, at the huge waves of the sea, at the long courses of the rivers, at the vast compass of the ocean, at the circular motion of the stars; and they pass by themselves without wondering." This quote from St. Augustine appears on the title page of John Stewart Collis's *Living with a Stranger: A Discourse on the Human Body* (New York: George Braziller, 1979).

27. Steward Edward White, *The Unobstructed Universe* (New York: E.P. Dutton, 1940), 60.

28. Richard Monastersky, "Deep-See Shrimp," *Science News* 135 (11 February, 1989): 90-93.

29. See Charles N. Alexander et al, "Transcendental Meditation, Mindfulness, and Longevity: An Experimental Study with the Elderly," *Journal of Personality and Social Psychology* 57 (1989): 650-64.

30. Abraham Maslow, *Motivation and Personality*, 2d ed. (New York: Harper and Row, 1970), 163. In my notes the following post-heart attack quote is attributed to Maslow, but I have been unable to verify it. "Everything gets doubly precious, gets piercingly important. You get stabbed by things, by flowers, by babies and by beautiful things. Just the very act of living, of walking, of breathing and eating and having friends and chatting, everything seems to look more beautiful rather than less."

31. Flannery O'Connor, *Mystery and Manners: Occasional Prose*, sel. and ed. Sally and Robert Fitzgerald (New York: Farrar, Straus, Giroux, 1969), 125.

32. John S. Dunne, *A Search for God in Time and Memory* (London: Macmillan, 1967), 7.

33. Entry for 12 May 1839, *The Diary of Soren Kierkegaard*, ed. Peter P. Rohde (New York: Philosophical Library, 1960), 19.

34. David B. Barrett, *Cosmos, Chaos, and Gospel: A Chronology of World Evangelization from Creation to New Creation* (Birmingham, Ala.: New Hope: 1987), 96.

35. John Wesley, "The Lord Our Righteousness," in *Sermons*, ed. Albert C. Outler, vol. 1 of *The Works of John Wesley* (Nashville: Abingdon Press, 1984), 254.

36. To Eugene Rolfe, 19 November 1960, in C.G. Jung, *Letters*, ed. Gerhard Adler and Aniela Jaffé (Princeton, N.J.: Princeton University Press, 1973-1975): 2:611.

37. Sears Reynolds Jayne, trans. and ed., "Marsilio Ficino's Commentary on Plato's *Symposium,*" *University of Missouri Studies* 19 (1944): 208-11. "The Soul is above the Body, the Angelic Mind above the Soul and God Above the Angelic Mind" (208). See also David L. Miller, "Theologia Imaginalis," in *The Archaeology of the Imagination*, ed. Charles Winquist,

Journal of the American Academy of Religion Thematic Studies 48, no. 2 (Missoula, Mont.: American Academy of Religion, 1981), 7.

38.   For Barbara McClintock's pushing of science beyond conventional ways of knowing, see chapter 12, "A Feeling for the Organism," in *A Feeling for the Organism: The Life and Work of Barbara McClintock* by Evelyn Fox Keller (San Francisco: W.H. Freeman), 197-207. The quotes are taken from p. 198.

39.   John Wesley, *The Appeals to Men of Reason and Religion* (1743), ed. Gerald R. Cragg (Oxford: Oxford University Press, 1975), 46.

40.   For Yvonna A. Lincoln and Egon G. Guba, see *Naturalistic Inquiry* (Beverly Hills, Calif.: Sage Publications, 1985). For the criteria of simplicity, extensibility, multiple corrections, logical fertility, reliability, causality, and elegance, see the chapter "Guiding Principles in the Search for Scientific Theories" in *Einstein's Space and Van Gogh's Sky: Physical Reality and Beyond*, ed. Lawrence LeShan and Henry Margenau (New York: Macmillan, 1982), 72-82.

41.   Samuel Hopkins, *The Life and Character of the Late Reverend Mr. Jonathan Edwards* (Boston, 1765), iii.

42.   Private correspondence between the author and David Spangler.

43.   See, for example, Theodor Reik, *Listening with the Third Ear* (New York: Farrar Strauss, 1948); William Johnston, *Inner Eye of Love: Mysticism and Religion* (New York: Harper and Row, 1978); Laurie Nadel, *Sixth Sense: A Whole Brain Guide to Intuition, Hunches, Gut Feelings, and Their Place in Your Everyday Life* (New York: Prentice Hall, 1990); Thornton Wilder, **The Eight Day** (New York: Carroll and Graf, 1967).

44.   Harry T. Hunt, *Multiplicity of Dreams: Memory, Imagination and Consciousness* (New Haven: Yale University Press, 1989), 135-36.

45.   Herbert Thurston's *The Physical Phenomenon of Mysticism* (London: Burns Oates, 1952) attempts to document the psychokinetic (PK) phenomenon among saints.

46.   For philosopher Michael Grosso's fascinating theory that the body is more precisely seen as being in the soul than the soul in the body, making the "out" in OBE's not the soul's out of the body but the body's getting out of the soul, see his *The Final Choice: Playing the Survival Game* (Walpole, N.H.: Stillpoint Pub., 1985). One of the most balanced assessments of OBEs is world-leading OBE expert Susan Blackmore's essay "Out of the Body?" as found in *Not Necessarily the New Age: Critical Essays*, ed. Robert Basil (Buffalo, N.Y.: Prometheus Books, 1988), 165-84.

47.   Andrew M. Greeley and W.C. McCready, "Are We a Nation of Mystics?" *New York Times Magazine,* 26 January 1975, 12; George Gallup, *Adventures in Immortality: A Look Beyond the Threshold of Death* (New York: McGraw-Hill Book Company, 1982); see also *Venture Inward: The Magazine of the Association for Research and Enlightenment*, July/August 1988.

48.   Andrew M. Greeley, "Mysticism Loves Mainstream," *American Health* (January/ February, 1987), 47. See also public relations director/evangelical Ken Waters, "Confronting the Movement that Seeks to Change the World," *Charisma and Christian Life* 14 (May 1989): 55-61.

49.   John J. Heaney, *The Sacred and the Psychic: Parapsychology and Christian Theology* (New York: Paulist Press, 1984), 5. This is the most balanced and astute book on the parapsychological available today.

50.   H. Smith, *Beyond the Post-Modern Mind*, 74.

51.   Liam Hudson, *Night Life: The Interpretation of Dreams* (New York: St. Martin's Press, 1985).

52.   K. Ramakrishna Rao, "Parapsychology: Implications for Religion and Science," *Perkins Journal* 39 (April 1986): 1.

53.   A helpful survey of the various light metaphors in different religious traditions can be found in Ralph Metzner, *Opening to the Inner Light: The Transformation of Human Nature and Consciousness* (Los Angeles: Jeremy P. Tarcher, 1986).

54.   Ernst Mayr, "Evolution," *Scientific American* 239 (September 1978): 46-55.

55.   James Lovelock, *The Ages of Gaia: A Biography of Our Living Earth* (New York:

Norton, 1988).
56.   Roger Corless, *The Art of Christian Alchemy* (New York: Paulist Press, 1981), 34.
57.   For the problem Christianity has in this area, see John P. Dourley, *The Illness That We Are: A Jungian Critique of Christianity* (Toronto: Inner City Books, 1984).
58.   I am grateful to psychiatrist/Jungian analyst Jean Shinoda Bolen's book *The Tao of Psychology: Synchronicity and the Self* (San Francisco: Harper and Row, 1979) for bringing together for me the concept of Tao and synchronicity.
59.   The publication of Carl G. Jung's definitive statement entitled "Synchronicity: An Acausal Connecting Principle" was itself a symbolic event of the uniting of physics and psychology, timed as it was to be a joint publication in 1952 with physicist Wolfgang Pauli's study of "The Influence of Archetypal Ideas on the Scientific Theories of Kepler." See *The Interpretation of Nature and the Psyche*, trans. R.F.C. Hull and Priscilla Silz (London: Routledge and K. Paul, 1955).
60.   Carl G. Jung, *Memories, Dreams, Reflections* (New York: Pantheon Books, 1961), 137-38.
61.   See Jung, *Memories, Dreams, Reflections*, 195-99.
62.   See the chapter entitled "The Agatha Christie Approach to Synchronicity," in Bolen, *The Tao of Psychology*, 25-36.
63.   Henry Margenau, *The Miracle of Existence* (Woodbridge, Conn.: Ox Bow Press, 1984).
64.   Louis Monden, *Signs and Wonders: A Study of the Miraculous Element in Religion* (New York: Desclee, 1966).
65.   Quoted in R.L. Jackson, *Dostoyevsky's Quest for Form: A Study of His Philosophy of Art* (New Haven: Yale University Press, 1966), 82, 90.
66.   See my "Can a Mainstream Change Its Course?" in *Liberal Protestantism: Realities and Possibilities*, ed. Robert S. Michaelsen and Wade Clark Roof (New York: Pilgrim Press, 1986), 260-61.
67.   See 2 Cor. 4:8-9; 6:9-10.
68.   Gary R. Habermas and Antony G.N. Flew, *Did Jesus Rise from the Dead?* (San Francisco: Harper & Row, 1987).
69.   See K. Ramakrishna Rao, "Hume's Fallacy," *Journal of Parapsychology* 45 (June 1981): 147-52.
70.   This is the point of Colin Brown in *Miracles and the Critical Mind* (Grand Rapids, Mich.: Eerdmans, 1984), 291.
71.   Darrell Jodock, *The Church's Bible: Its Contemporary Authority* (Minneapolis: Fortress Press, 1989), 97. For the argument that miracle involves either the creation or annihilation of mass/energy--"All physical events, including miracles, can be described in terms of a certain amount and ordering of energy," see Robert A.H. Larmer, *Water into Wine? An Investigation of the Concept of Miracle* (Kingston, Ont., Montreal: McGill-Queen's University Press, 1988), 29.
72.   Larry Dossey, "Medicine, Mind, and Meaning," *Chrysalis* 4 (Spring 1989): 1-15. See also his *Space, Time and Medicine* (Boulder, Colo.: Shambola, 1982) and his *Beyond Illness* (Boston: New Science Library, 1984).
73.   John Polkinghorne, *One World: The Interaction of Science and Theology* (Princeton University Press, 1986), 75.
74.   Matthew and Dennis Linn, *Healing of Memories* (New York: Paulist Press, 1974), 434. See also *Psychology Today* 10 (February 1973): 35.
75.   Philip Pare, *God Made the Devil?: A Ministry of Healing* (London: Darton, Longman and Todd, 1985), 19.
76.   Keller, *A Feeling for the Organism*, 200.
77.   A similar illustration is from my notebooks. It is attributed to Annie Dillard, but to date I have been unable to verify it: "One rice plant in only four months can grow 378 miles of roots and fourteen billion root hairs. In one cubic inch of sod the length of these root hairs would total 6,000 miles.

THIRD TESTAMENT
(pages 249 - 261)

a.   Elizabeth O'Connor, *Our Many Selves* (New York: Harper and Row, 1971), 27.

b.   Richard A. Falk, "In Pursuit of the Postmodern," in *Spirituality and Society: Postmodern Visions* (Albany: State University of New York Press, 1988), 97.

c.   Quoted by Matthew Fox, "Creation-centered Spirituality from Hildegard of Bingen to Julian of Norwich: 300 Years of an Ecological Spirituality in the West," in *Cry of the Environment*, ed. Philip N. Joranson and Ken Butigan (Santa Fe: Bear and Company, 1984), 90.

d.   Thomas Merton, *Opening the Bible* (London: George Allen and Unwin, 1972), 84.

e.   Fred Polak, *The Image of the Future* (San Francisco: Jossey-Bass Inc., 1973), 19.

f.   This is a poem I found preserved in my notebooks. It is attributed to Alma Loftness, but efforts to identify it further have to date been unsuccessful.

1.   Hans Schwarz, "God's Place in a Space Age," *Zygon* 21 (September 1986): 365-67.

2.   Adam Morton, "Creators of Ourselves," *TLS: The Times Literary Supplement*, 27 January-2 February 1989, 77.

3.   MPD cases have been popularized in recent years through such books and films as *The Three Faces of Eve* (1956), *Sybil* (1977), *The Minds of Billy Mulligan* (1981), etc.

4.   James Ogilvy, *Many Dimensional Man: Decentralizing Self, Society, and the Sacred* (New York: University Press, 1977); Elizabeth O'Connor, *Our Many Selves* (New York: Harper and Row, 1971), 3.

5.   See Susan Sontag's *I, Etcetera* (New York: Farrar, Strauss, and Giroux, 1978); Fay Weldon's *The Life and Loves of a She-Devil* (New York: Pantheon Books, 1984); Emma Tennant's *Two Women of London: The Strange Case of Ms. Jekyll and Mrs. Hyde* (London: Faber, 1989); Valerie Martin's *Mary Reilly* (New York: Doubleday, 1990).

6.   For but one example, see Kirkpatrick Sale, *Human Scale* (New York: Perigee Books, 1982, ᶜ1980), 64-65. An excellent discussion of the breakdown of the modern mentality as reflected in the loss of confidence in inevitable progress, can be found in Diogenes Allen's "The Fields are White for the Harvest," in *Evangelism in the Reformed Tradition*, ed. Arnold Lovell (Decatur, Ga.: CTS Press, 1990), 12-15.

7.   I am especially indebted to the private correspondence of Wesley A. Hotchkiss to John and Virginia Smith dated 8 May 1990, for this corrective. Hotchkiss chided me for "not getting beyond this" and for not seeing that "our creator had to take us through this Cartesian-Newtonian stage 'before' she could deal us to this new era now emerging." I have also been influenced by theologian Catherine Keller's itemization of modernist contributions "no postmodernism would want to abandon" (namely, its "emphasis upon democratic equality, its liberation from certain forms of political and ecclesial authoritarianism, the potential and sometimes actual benefits to reason and to real people made by scientific empiricism and technological tools") and by Richard A. Falk's arguments in the same volume. See Keller's "Toward a Postpatriarchal Postmodernity" (65) and Falk's "In Pursuit of the Postmodern" (81-98), in *Spirituality and Society: Postmodern Visions*, ed. David Ray Griffin (Albany: State University of New York Press, 1988).

8.   Joseph Needam, *Science and Civilization in China* (Cambridge: Cambridge University Press, 1956), 2:303ff.

9.   Quoted in Ilya Prigogine and Isabelle Stengers, *Order Out of Chaos: Man's New Dialogue with Nature* (Boulder, Colo.: New Science Library, 1984), 148.

10.   Quoted in Joseph Mitsuo Kitagawa, "The Asian Christian Tradition," *Anglican Theological Review* 71 (1989): 424.

11.   Stephen R.L. Clark, "A Matter of Habit?" *TLS: The Times Literary Supplement*, 24-30 June 1988, 702.

12.   Quoted in John J. Pilch's, *Wellness Spirituality* (New York: Crossroad, 1985), 79.

13.   I am heavily dependent here on the insights of David Kelsey, who argues that the

authority of Scripture resides in its ecclesiastical functioning to form new human identities and transform the life of individuals and communities. See his "The Function of Scripture," in *Readings in Christian Theology*, ed. Peter C. Hodgson and Robert H. King (Philadelphia: Fortress Press, 1985), 51; reprinted from his "The Bible and Christian Theology," *Journal of the American Academy of Religion* 48 (September 1980): 393.

14.   Even philosophers such as Karl Popper can't help but think trinitarily. For his distinctions between "World 1, World 2, and World 3," see his "The Place of Mind in Nature," in *Mind in Nature, Nobel Conference XVII*, ed. Richard Q. Elvee (San Francisco: Harper and Row, 1982), 53-57.

15.   T.J. van Bavel, "De la Raison á la Foi: Le Conversion d'Augustin," *Augustiniana* 86 (1986): 5-27.

16.   Ken Wilber, "Eye to Eye: Science and Transpersonal Psychology," in *Beyond Ego: Transpersonal Dimensions in Psychology*, ed. Roger N. Walsh and Frances Vanaton (New York: Jeremy P. Tarcher, 1980), 216-20.

17.   J.B. Priestley, *Man and Time* (New York: Doubleday, 1964), 292-308.

18.   Karl R. Popper, *Objective Knowledge: An Evolutionary Approach* (Oxford: Clarendon Press, 1972).

19.   Ken Wilber, *The Atman Project: A Transpersonal View of Human Development* (Wheaton, Ill.: Philosophical Publishing House, 1980).

20.   Ernest Gellner, *Plough, Sword and Book: The Structure of Human History* (London: Collins Harvill, 1988).

21.   See Freeman Dyson's *Infinite in all Directions* (New York: Harper and Row, 1988).

22.   See Walter Wink's discussion of "Jesus' Third Way" as an alternative to fight or flight in his study of enemies, *Violence and Nonviolence in South Africa: Jesus' Third Way* (Philadelphia: New Society Publishers, 1987), 12-23, as quoted in Richard F. Vieth, *Holy Power, Human Pain* (Bloomington, Ind.: Meyer-Stone Books, 1988), 124.

23.   Guy Murchie, *The Seven Mysteries of Life* (Boston: Houghton Mifflin, 1978), 321. See also Larry Dossey's chapter on "The Biodance," in *Space, Time, and Medicine* (Boston: New Science Library, 1982), 72-81. The skin is regenerated in a month. The liver in five months, the stomach lining in a week.

24.   "St. Armorer's Church from the Outside," in *The Collected Poems of Wallace Stevens* (New York: Knopf, 1985), 529. In addition to being a poet and insurance lawyer, Stevens was a philosopher of aesthetics. I wish to thank Professor Peter Hawkins of Yale Divinity School for first introducing me to this poem.

25.   Radio broadcaster/former British spy/cultural critic Malcolm Muggeridge titled his study of six men of faith who influenced his own search for God *A Third Testament* (Boston: Little, Brown, 1976). Unfortunately, he did nothing more with the metaphor than the title. For the rationale of the new terminology "First" and "Second Testament," see James A. Sanders, "First Testament and Second," *Biblical Theology Bulletin* 17 (April 1987): 47-49.

26.   Carnegie Samuel Calian's instructive study *Where is the Passion for Excellence in the Church? Shaping Discipleship Through Ministry and Theological Education* (Wilton, Conn.: Morehouse Publishing Co., 1989) makes the case for local congregations seeing themselves as seminaries, which Calian argues are built on four cornerstones: study, prayer, discipline, and integration of faith with daily life.

27.   Philip Hefner, "The Evolution of the Created Co-Creator," in *Cosmos as Creation: Theology and Science in Consonance*, ed. Ted Peters (Nashville: Abingdon Press, 1989), 211-34.

28.   Louis Dupré, *The Other Dimension: A Search for the Meaning of Religious Attitudes*, (New York: Doubleday, 1972), 389.

29.   Clark H. Pinnock, "The Structure of Pauline Eschatology," *Evangelical Quarterly* 37 (1965): 13.

30.   Quoted in Charles Francis Adams's *Antinomianism in the Colony of Massachusetts Bay, 1636-1638* (Boston: Prince Society, 1894), 277. The Protestant Reformers feared mysticism for precisely this reason.

31.   Horace Bushnell, *Nature and the Supernatural, as Together Constituting the One*

System of God (New York: Charles Scribner's Sons, 1901), 447.

32. Bushnell, *Nature and the Supernatural*, 447.

33. Gary M. Burge, *The Anointed Community: The Holy Spirit in the Johannine Tradition* (Grand Rapids, Mich.: Eerdmans, 1987), 211-17.

34. James D.G. Dunn, *The Living Word* (Philadelphia: Fortress Press, 1987), 63, 64.

35. As reproduced in Piet Smulders, *The Design of Teilhard de Chardin: An Essay in Theological Reflection*, trans. Arthur Gibson (Westminster, Md.: Newman Press, 1967), 126. Thomas Berry's concept of "inscendence" can be found in his *The Dream of the Earth* (San Francisco: Sierra Book Club, 1988), 207-8.

36. Entry for Monday, 6 December 1762 in *The Journal of the Rev. John Wesley*, ed. Nehemiah Curnock (London: Epworth Press, 1913), 4:540.

37. "Yes, you have indeed seen much--but tarry for a while, for the greatest is yet to come." Mark Twain to Walt Whitman, in Lewis Mumford, *The Golden Day: A Study in American Literature and Culture* (New York: W.W. Norton, 1926), 174.

POSTFACE
(pages 263 - 302)

a. Sir William Gilbert and Sir Arthur Sullivan, *Pirates of Penzance* (1879).

b. The pontiff spoke in front of St. Mary's Cathedral in San Francisco during his ten-day pastoral visit to the United States in September of 1987, and is quoted in *Los Angeles Times* religion editor Russell Chandler's, *Understanding the New Age* (Dallas: Word Publishing Co., 1988), 278.

c. As quoted in *Religion and Nature--With Charles Birch and Others*, ed. Kevin J. Sharpe and John M. Ker (Auckland: University of Auckland Chaplaincy, 1982), 17.

d. As quoted by Robert Scott Root-Bernstein, "Sensual Education," *The Sciences* 30 (September/October 1990): 14.

e. As quoted in Thomas Ryan's *Fasting Rediscovered: A Guide to Health and Wholeness for Your Body-Spirit* (New York: Paulist Press, 1981), 17.

f. As quoted by J. Brien McGarvey, *The 1990 UMRF Jubilee Booklet* (Columbus, Ohio: Center for Town and Rural Ministries [P.O. Box 29044, Columbus, OH 43229]), 1990.

g. Joseph Campbell, *The Inner Reaches of Outer Space: Metaphors as Myth and as Religion* (New York: Alfred van der Marck Editions, 1986), 17.

h. Robert E. Ornstein and Paul Ehrlich, *New World, New Mind: Changing the Way We Think to Save Our Future* (London: Methuen, 1989), 248.

i. As quoted in William E. Johnston, Jr., "The Crisis of the West: Machiavelli, Rousseau, and the Imperative of Salvation," *First Things*, June/July 1990, 42.

j. Heinz R. Pagels, *The Dreams of Reason: The Computer and the Rise of the Sciences of Complexity* (New York: Simon and Schuster, 1988), 15.

k. Allen Emerson, "A Disorienting View of God's Creation: Faith in the Crucible of the New Physics," *Christianity Today*, 1 February 1985, 24.

l. Wolf-Dieter Narr, "Reflections on the Form and Content of Social Science: Toward a Consciously Political and Moral Social Science," in *Social Science as Moral Ingenuity*, ed. Norma Haan et al. (New York: Columbia University Press, 1983), 293.

m. This was Peter Eisenman's response when asked to design his dream home office. Quoted in *Omni*, July 1990, no pagination.

n. Hebrew oral tradition as recorded in the tenth to sixth century B.C. in Exodus 31:17 (NJB).

o. Praise for God's greatness, Psalm 150:6 (RSV).

1. Robert Fulghum, *All I Really Need to Know I Learned in Kindergarten: Uncommon Thoughts on Common Things* (New York: Ivy, 1986; Villard Books, 1988).

2. Guy R. Lefrançois, *Psychology for Teaching: A Bear Always Faces the Front*

(Belmont, Calif.: Wadsworth Publishing Company, 1972).

3.   For the possibility of a second hermeneutical innocence--a "critical" (Barth) or "second" (Ricoeur) naïveté--see Mark I. Wallace, *The Second Naïveté: Barth, Ricoeur, and the New Yale Theology* (Macon, Ga.: Mercer University Press, 1990).

4.   Commenting on why he is a hero in Japan but little known in the United States, Zadeh observes that "In the US, there's a tradition for what is precise, for Cartesian logic. In Japan there is more appreciation of the imprecise, of ambiguity." Quoted in "The Future Looks 'Fuzzy,'" *Newsweek*, 28 May 1990, 47. For a peep show into our technological future, especially the "genius VCR" Sonar TV, see Malcolm Abrams and Harriet Bernstein, *Future Stuff: A Consumer's Guide* (New York: Penguin, 1989).

5.   See *Pascal's Pensées*, introd. by T.S. Eliot (New York: Dutton, 1958), where Pascal writes:

> There are then two kinds of intellect: the one able to penetrate acutely and deeply into the conclusions of given premises, and this is the precise intellect; the other able to comprehend a great number of premises without confusing them, and this is the mathematical intellect. The one has force and exactness, the other comprehension. Now the one quality can exist without the other; the intellect can be strong and narrow and can also be comprehensive and weak. (3)

6.   As quoted in Wilfrid Mellers, *Bach and the Dance of God* (New York: Oxford University Press, 1981), 303-4.

7.   For further discussion of William James's "There are two kinds of knowledge ... **knowledge of acquaintance** and **knowledge-about**," see his *Principles of Psychology* (New York: Henry Holt, 1902), 1:221.

8.   *The Works of John Wesley*, 3rd ed. (London: Wesleyan Book Room, 1872; repr. Grand Rapids, Mich.: Baker Book House, 1978), 14:341.

9.   Nelson Goodman, *Of Mind and Other Matters* (Cambridge: Harvard University Press, 1984).

10.   George Edward Moore, "The Defense of Common Sense," in *Philosophical Papers* (New York: Macmillan, 1959), 32-59.

11.   Quoted by philosopher of mathematics Murray Code in his *Order and Organism: Steps Toward a Whiteheadian Philosophy of Mathematics and the Natural Sciences* (Albany: State University of New York Press, 1985), 1. Code argues that "it is one of the more simplistic and pernicious of modern myths that science is unequivocally superior to common sense." In pleading for the interdependence of the two, Code presents the thesis that "science and common sense grow together in mutual dependence and with reciprocal influence, each, as it were, lifting the other a notch at a time up the metaphysical ladder" (88).

12.   Robert Scott Root-Bernstein, *Discovering* (Cambridge, Mass.: Harvard University Press, 1989).

13.   Miguel de Unamuno, *The Tragic Sense of Life in Men and Nations* (Princeton: Princeton University Press, 1972), 8. Reprinted by permission of the publisher. For the postmodern philosophical task of finding better ways of defining self "than those embedded in contemporary common sense," see Adam Morton, "Creators of Ourselves," *TLS: The Times Literary Supplement*, 22 January-2 February 1989, 77; see also George Gilder in, *Microcosm: The Quantum Revolution in Economics and Technology* (New York: Simon and Schuster, 1989), 19ff. For the new science of "antisense" see Rick Weiss, "Upping the Antisense Ante," *Science News* 139 (16 February 1991): 108-9.

14.   Quoted in Tony Schwartz, "Acceleration Syndrome: Does Everyone Live in the Fast Lane Nowadays?" *Utne Reader* 31 (January/February 1989): 38.

15.   Os Guinness, *The Gravedigger File: Papers on the Subversion of the Modern Church* (Downers Grove, Ill.: InterVarsity Press, 1983), 96.

16.   The words are those of Adam Mars-Jones, "Illuminating Caledonian Virtue," *TLS: The Times Literary Supplement*, 18 March 1983, 258.

17.   Ervin Laszlo, *Introduction to Systems Philosophy: Toward a New Paradigm of Contemporary Thought* (New York: Gordon and Breach, 1972), 152-63.

18.   Diana L. Eck, "Response of the Church to New Religious Movements: A Report

from North America," in *New Religious Movements and the Churches*, ed. Allan R. Brockway and J. Paul Rajashekar (1987), 154.

19.   Dan Ashley, a United Methodist pastor from the North Indiana Conference, tells of asking someone he had just met about his church affiliation. "I am a Christian. I attend whatever church floats my boat," was the reply. In a recent survey conducted by Switzerland's National Program of Research, 85 percent of the Swiss polled held that "there is no need of the church" in order to be a believer. Thirty-three percent of those Christians who believe in resurrection consider it "unproblematically compatible with a belief in reincarnation." See *Religion Watch*, July 1990, 8.

20.   As quoted in James J. Kilpatrick, "Similes, Metaphors and the Happiest Pun of the Year," *Chicago Sun-Times*, 22 July 1990. See also *Parabola* senior editor Philip Zaleski's comments on how New Agers "systematically absorb, digest, and regurgitate in degenerate form genuine traditional teachings, so that a noble imperative such as 'know thyself,' or ideas that quicken--that we possess a divine spark within, . . . turn into shibboleths, utterly lacking the necessary buttresses of systematic thought and sustained practice to lead to genuine self-transformation," See "Easy Answers," *Parabola* 13 (Fall 1988): 87.

21.   Alan Nichols, ed., *The Whole Gospel for the Whole World* (Pasadena: Lausanne Committee for World Evangelism, 1989), 56.

22.   For the contrast between "either/or" versus "both/and" preaching, see Fred B. Craddock, *Preaching* (Nashville: Abingdon Press, 1985), 173-74.

23.   George Barna, *What the Trends Mean for Christianity* (Glendale, Calif.: Barna Research Group, 1989).

24.   Lyle E. Schaller, "Megachurch!" *Christianity Today*, 5 March 1990, 20.

25.   John Wesley, "On the Trinity," in *The Works of John Wesley* (Nashville: Abingdon Press, 1985), 2:374. For Wesley's distinction between "essentials" and "opinions," see theologian John R. Tyson, "Essential Doctrines and Real Religion: Theological Method in Wesley's *Sermons on Several Occasions*," *Wesleyan Theological Journal* 23 (Spring/Fall, 1988): 163-79.

26.   John Wesley, "Advice to the People Called Methodists," in *The Works of John Wesley* (Nashville: Abingdon Press, 1989), 9:130.

27.   Myron Emanuel and Arthur M. York, *Handbook of Human Resources Communications* (Greenvale, N.Y.: Panel Publishers, 1988), xvi.

28.   For the way postmoderns are moving away from exclusivistic "conversionist" models of religious affiliation and toward nonexclusive, adhesionist ones, see Arthur Darby Nock's classic study of *Conversion* (New York: Oxford University Press, 1933), which needs to be read and consulted again for its insight into a time when adhesion was the central religious category.

29.   William J. Abraham, *The Logic of Evangelism* (Grand Rapids, Mich.: Eerdmans, 1989), 219. Abraham ingeniously begins his approach to understanding Christianity's relationship to other religions by looking at early Christians' relationship to Judaism.

30.   An excellent beginning in bringing together absolute faith and "theological relativism" is Joseph Runzo's *Reason, Relativism and God* (London: Macmillan, 1986).

31.   Runzo, *Reason, Relativism and God*, 264.

32.   Out of this background anthropologist Mary Tew Douglas's warning takes on new significance: "One of the gravest problems of our day is the lack of commitment to common symbols." See her *Natural Symbols: Explorations in Cosmology* (New York: Pantheon, 1970), 1.

33.   "Openness is one thing," Maureen O'Hara writes in a variant version, "gullibility and intellectual irresponsibility are quite another." See her "Of Myths and Monkeys: A Critical Look at a Theory of Critical Mass," *Journal of Humanistic Psychology* 25 (Winter 1985): 63.

34.   There is a "plurality of pluralism," ethicist Richard J. Mouw warns us, which a "theology of pluralism" must differentiate if "pluralist sensitivity" is not to slip into an "anything-goes relativism." See "Humility, Hope, and the Divine Slowness," *Christian Century*, 11 April 1990, 364-68, esp. 367.

35.   See Isaiah Berlin, *The Hedgehog and the Fox: An Essay on Tolstoy's View of History* (New York: Simon and Schuster, 1953).

36.   Educator/ecologist/engineer Arthur E. Morgan provides one of the most beautiful analogies for not having to decide between two alternatives in his autobiography. Responding to H.G. Wells's insistence, during a lunch with members of the President's Cabinet, that America has to decide between big business and small business, between individualism and socialism, Morgan interjected his objection:

I countered that we did not intend to make any such decision. I said that America, I hoped, would become like one of our great forests that I visited recently. There were trees one and two centuries old towering a hundred and fifty feet overhead; underneath them was another level of trees--ironwoods, sourwoods, birches--growing half as high, and filling in the interstices where the sunlight was not being used by the larger trees. Then another order of trees--hawthorns, dogwood, and sassafras--filled in the unoccupied places in the more humble positions. Next below were viburnums and laurel, and beneath them blueberry bushes and smaller plants only a few feet high; and still underneath them. . . . Let each respect the effective functions of the other, recognizing that size may not determine enduring qualities." (*The Long Road*, [Yellow Springs, Ohio: Community Services, Inc., 1938], 53-54).

37.   Walt Whitman, "Song of Myself," (1.1315) in *Walt Whitman's Poems*, ed. Gay Wilson Allen and Charles T. Davis (New York: New York University Press, 1955), 126.

38.   Elizabeth Cook McCabe first cooked up this slogan as director of the Boston Advertising Club.

39.   C.H. Waddington's words are quoted by Robert Scott Root-Bernstein, "Sensual Education," *The Sciences* 30 (September/October 1990): 14.

40.   According to Shirley Maclaine's latest book, *Going Within* (New York: Bantam Books, 1989), if people with AIDS just "took responsibility" for their condition, they might come to "understand and even to love [their] decision" (27).

41.   The person who has captured the essence of the axial differences as reflected in Luke 9:23 and John 10:10 is social analyst/theologian/St. Paul School of Theology professor Tex Sample. See chapter 1, "Shifting Values: Self Fulfillment vs. Self-Denial," in his *U.S. Lifestyles and Mainline Churches: A Key to Reaching People in the 90's* (Louisville, Ky.: Westminster/John Knox Press, 1990), 9-21.

42.   An excellent example of this attempt at a critical philosophy of technology is Langdon Winner's *The Whale and the Reactor: A Search for Limits in an Age of High Technology* (Chicago: University of Chicago Press, 1986).

43.   Robert Pinsky, *An Explanation of America* (Princeton: Princeton University Press, 1979), 42. Reprinted with permission of the publisher.

44.   See Bp. John V. Taylor's book *Enough is Enough* (Naperville, Ill.: SCM Press, 1975).

45.   See the dialogue between David Spangler and Ken Wilber, "Critiquing the New Age," *Yoga Journal*, July/August 1988, 49. For David Spangler's explication of the emergence of the New Age see his *Revelation: The Birth of a New Age* (Middletown, Wisc.: Lorian Press, 1976).

46.   This helps explain the rapid acceptance of "Eastern" practices in Western hospitals, health clubs, and corporate training seminars: breathing and yoga exercises, meditation, guided visualization, relaxation exercises, therapeutic touch, stress management techniques, etc.

47.   Daniel Davis, as quoted in Russell Chandler, *Understanding the New Age,* 244.

48.   Alan Watts, *The Book: On the Taboo Against Knowing Who You Are* (New York: Collier Books, 1967), 39.

49.   See Rushworth M. Kidder's "A Look Back, a Look Forward, and a Bow," *Christian Science Monitor,* 11 June 1990, 13. This was his last "Perspectives" as senior columnist before establishing The Institute for Global Ethics, a think-tank dedicated to the study of ethics in a transcultural context.

50.   Jacques Derrida now holds a position at École des Hautes Études en Sciences Sociales and is on the faculty of Yale University and University of California in Irvine; John Bowker is Dean of Chapel, Trinity College, Cambridge, and adjunct professor at the Universities of Pennsylvania and North Carolina State; Nicholas Wolterstorff, who currently holds a professorship at Yale University, until June 1990 held faculty appointments at Calvin College and the Free University of Amsterdam; Ilya Prigogine directs the Solvay International Institute of Physics and Chemistry and teaches at the Free University of Brussels while also heading up the Ilya Prigogine Center for Statistical Mechanics and Thermodynamics at the University of Texas in Austin.

51.   Gerald Graff, "The Myth of the Postmodernist Breakthrough," *TriQuarterly* 26 (1973): 393-94.

52.   Philip Rieff, *Fellow Teachers: Of Culture and Its Second Death* (Chicago: University of Chicago Press, 1973), 5, as cited in Conrad Cherry, "Boundaries and Frontiers for the Study of Religion: The Heritage of the Age of the University," *Journal of the American Academy of Religion* 57 (Winter 1989): 824.

53.   Paul Hawken, James Ogilvy and Peter Schwartz's *Seven Tomorrows* (New York: Bantam Books, 1982) is quoted by Wes Jackson, *Altars of Unhewn Stone: Science and the Earth* (San Francisco: North Point Press, 1987), 83.

54.   For Jung, see his "Commentary," in *The Secret of the Golden Flower: A Chinese Book of Life*, trans. and explained by Richard Wilhelm (New York: Harcourt, Brace, 1938), 77-137.

55.   David L. Miller, *Hells and Holy Ghosts: A Theopoetics of Christian Belief* (Nashville: Abingdon Press, 1989), 189-94, 191. See also Gabriel Marcel, *The Mystery of Being* (Chicago: Henry Regnery, 1950), 1:211, and his "A rose in a poem can be something that is present to us in this [magical] way, but not, in most cases, a rose in a seedman's catalog" (1:208).

56.   An excellent example of the study of complexity is California Institute of Technology postdoctoral fellow Seth Lloyd's "The Calculus of Intricacy: Can the Complexity of a Forest Be Compared with That of Finnegans Wake?" *The Sciences* 30 (September/October 1990): 38-44. For the failure of orthodox neo-Darwinianism to deal adequately with complexity, see philosopher/economist C. Dyke, "Complexity and Closure," in *Evolution at a Crossroads: The New Biology and the New Philosophy of Science*, ed. David J. Depew and Bruce H. Weber (Cambridge, Mass.: The MIT Press, 1985), 97-127,

57.   Ursula LeGuin, *The Left Hand of Darkness*, as quoted in Frederick Turner's "Natural Technology," *Chronicles* [Rockford, Ill.] 14 (August 1990): 30.

58.   Frederick Turner, "Natural Theology," 30-31. This is part of the Tenth Axiom Turner proposes for a natural theology. I am in profound disagreement with some of his other axioms, although I heartily support the general drift of his argument and the eloquence with which it is stated. Here is a sample:

My claims is that nature itself, like ourselves, is fallen, is falling, and has always been falling, outward into the future from the initial explosion of the Big Bang; onward into more and more conscious, beautiful, tragic, complex, and conflicted forms of existence, away from the divine simplicities and stupor of the primal energy-field. (28)

59.   For an apropos parable that ends "verily, it is easier for a camel to pass through the eye of a needle than for a scientific man to pass through a door," see Eddington's article "Defense of Mysticism," in *Quantum Questions: Mystical Writings of the World's Great Physicists*, ed. Ken Wilber (Boulder, Colo.: New Science Library, 1984), 207-8.

60.   Public Agenda Forum Foundation, *The Environment at Risk: Responding to Growing Dangers*, ed. Keith Melville, prepared and published through a joint project of the National Issues Forum and the Public Agenda Forum (Dubuque, Iowa: Kendall/Hunt Publishing Co., 1989), 28.

61.   Huston Smith, *Beyond the Post-Modern Mind* (New York: Crossroad, 1982), 77.

62.   See, for example, the works of Owen Barfield.

63.   This is the argument of Nicholas Maxwell's *From Knowledge to Wisdom: A Revolution in the Aims and Methods of Science* (Oxford: Basil Blackwell, 1984).

64.   Eugene Wigner, "The Limitations of the Validity of Present-Day Physics," *Mind in Nature: New Concepts of Mind in Science and Philosophy; The Nobel Conference XVII,* ed. Richard Q. Elvee (San Francisco: Harper and Row. 1983), 132.

65.   As quoted by physicist John Hitchcock in Carol Skinner Lawson, "The New Medicine: Panel Discussion Highlights," *Chrysalis* 4 (Spring 1989): 16.

66.   H. Smith, *Beyond the Postmodern Mind,* 85.

67.   Timothy Mo, *Sour Sweet* (London: Deutsch, 1982); Angela Carter, "'Tis Pitty She's a Whore," in *Best Short Stories 1989,* ed. Giles Gordon and David Hughes (London: Heinemann, 1989), 33-53.

68.   W. Dow Edgerton, "The Exegesis of Tears," *Theology Today* 46 (April 1989): 25.

69.   See W.H.C. Frend, *Saints and Sinners in the Early Church: Differing and Conflicting Traditions in the First Six Centuries* (London: Darton, Longman and Todd, 1985).

70.   Poet Seamus Heaney develops these two sensibilities in "Hercules and Antaeus," in his *North* (Boston, Mass.: Faber and Faber, 1985), 52-53.

71.   As quoted in the "Mélange" column, *Chronicle of Higher Education,* 19 December 1990, B3.

72.   I cannot resist a fuller quotation of Updike's response to the question of how to define "spirituality":

Myself, I associate spirituality with intuition, which is often labeled 'feminine.' The ability to make one's way among the unseen currents, to arrive at the truth while bypassing induction and deduction, to pluck things out of the air--a gender tilt in this area would help account for the female preponderance of fortune-tellers and churchgoers. A spiritual person of either sex embodies an alternative to the obvious, to bank accounts and syllogisms, to death and taxes. But there is little obvious, obviously, about being human. ("Making the Spiritual Connection," *Lear's,* December 1989, 70)

73.   See Jacob Weisberg's cover story, "Senator Perfect," *New Republic* 18 December 1989, 19.

74.   Andy Clark, *Microcognition: Philosophy, Cognitive Science, and Parallel Distributed Processing* (Cambridge, Mass.: MIT Press, 1989), 36-59.

75.   F.G. Bailey, *Humbuggery and Manipulation: The Art of Leadership* (Ithaca: Cornell University Press, 1988), 91.

76.   For the full explanation of these three kinds of knowledge, see Ken Wilber, *Eye to Eye: The Quest for the New Paradigm* (New York: Anchor Books, 1983).

77.   "There are two equally dangerous extremes"--Pascal has written--"to shut reason out, and to let nothing else in." Quoted in Evelyn Fox Keller, *A Feeling for the Organism: The Life and Work of Barbara McClintock* (San Francisco: W.H. Freeman, 1983), 197.

78.   Hungarian mathematician Miklos Laczkovich has now proved it possible to cut a circle into a finite number of pieces and rearrange them into a square.

79.   Henri Bergson, *An Introduction to Metaphysics,* trans. T.E. Hulme (New York: G.P. Putnam's Sons, 1912), 74-75.

80.   Thomas Merton, *The Way of Chung Tsu* (New York: New Directions Publishing Corporation, 1965), 38.

81.   God is continually breathing, as it were, upon his soul, and his soul is breathing unto God. Grace is descending into his heart, and prayer and praise ascending to heaven. And by this intercourse between God and man, this fellowship with the Father and the Son, as by a kind of spiritual respiration, the life of God in the soul is sustained and the child of God grows up, till he comes to "the full measure of the stature of Christ." (See John Wesley' sermon, "The New Birth," in *Sermons,* ed. Albert C. Outler, vol. 2 of *The Works of John Wesley* [Nashville: Abingdon Press, 1985], 193)
My colleague James Nelson likes to point out to students the mutuality of grace and good works, inhaling and exhaling, by reminding them of what happens when people hold their breath and don't let it out: they turn purple and pass out. Without "spiritual respiration," there is spiritual expiration.

BIBLICAL INDEX

NAME INDEX

Leonard I. Sweet is President of United Theological Seminary in Dayton, Ohio. Part of the first generation to grow up not watching the radio, Sweet's numerous books and articles thicken history and theology with multiple disciplines. The writer and editor of *Bibelot* and co-writer of *Homiletics*, Sweet looks out at a world in which "arts" and "sciences," "politics" and "religion" are not specialist areas of human activity but things that everyone does, thinks, speaks and practices.

WHALEPRINTS ™

Production Notes

Design and Artwork
  Cover design and inside illustrations by Karen Ingle, KLI design, Dayton, Ohio
  Cover illustration by Joe Sample, Springfield, Ohio
  Author photographs by Richard Kallas, Dayton, Ohio

Type
  Display type: Cover is Berkeley Medium Condensed
  Text types: Intermezzos are Helvetica, Body is Times Roman
  Typesetting by Thelma J. Monbarren, United Theological
  Seminary, Dayton, Ohio, with PageMaker

Printing and Binding
  Cover: Printed on Carolina 12 point coated one side
  Endpapers: Printed on 17 pound Gilbert Gilclear
  Text: Printed on acid-free 70 pound Cougar Natural
  Digital Color Separations and Printing by Hammer Graphics, Inc., Piqua, Ohio
  Binding by Dayton Bindery Service, Inc., Dayton, Ohio